Voices of Modernity
Language Ideologies and the Politics of Inequal

Language and Tradition have long been relegated to the sidelines as scholars have considered the role of politics, science, technology and economics in the making of the modern world. This novel reading of over two centuries of philosophy, political theory, anthropology, folklore and history argues that new ways of imagining language and representing women and supposedly premodern people – the poor, laborers, country folk and non-Europeans – made political and scientific revolutions possible. The connections between language ideologies, privileged linguistic codes, and political concepts and practices shape the diverse ways we perceive ourselves and others. Bauman and Briggs demonstrate that contemporary efforts to make schemes of social inequality based on race, gender, class and nationality seem compelling and legitimate rely on deeply rooted ideas about language and tradition. Showing how critics of modernity unwittingly reproduce these foundational fictions, they suggest new strategies for challenging the undemocratic influence of these voices of modernity.

RICHARD BAUMAN is Distinguished Professor of Communication and Culture, Folklore, and Anthropology, and Director of the Folklore Institute at Indiana University, Bloomington. His previous books include *Story, Performances and Event: Contextual Studies of Oral Narrative* (1986) and *Folklore, Cultural Performances and Popular Entertainments: A Communications-centered Handbook* (ed., 1992). He is a former editor of the *Journal of American Folklore* and past President of the Society for Linguistic Anthropology.

CHARLES L. BRIGGS is Professor of Ethnic Studies and Director, Center for Iberian and Latin American Studies, University of California, San Diego. His previous books include *Learning How to Ask: A Sociolinguistic Appraisal of the Role of the Interview in Social Science Research* (CUP, 1986) and *Stories in the Time of Cholera: Racial Profiling During a Medical Nightmare* (2003, with Clara Mantini-Briggs). He is currently completing a book on the global circulation of practices for creating civil society.

Voices of Modernity

Language Ideologies and the Politics of Inequality

Richard Bauman
Charles L. Briggs

CAMBRIDGE
UNIVERSITY PRESS

CAMBRIDGE UNIVERSITY PRESS
Cambridge, New York, Melbourne, Madrid, Cape Town, Singapore, São Paulo

Cambridge University Press
The Edinburgh Building, Cambridge CB2 2RU, UK

Published in the United States of America by Cambridge University Press, New York

www.cambridge.org
Information on this title: www.cambridge.org/9780521810692

First published 2003

A catalogue record for this publication is available from the British Library

ISBN-13 978-0-521-81069-2 hardback
ISBN-10 0-521-81069-8 hardback

ISBN-13 978-0-521-00897-6 paperback
ISBN-10 0-521-00897-2 paperback

Transferred to digital printing 2006

We dedicate this book
in loving memory of
Feliciana Briggs
1978–2002

Contents

Preface

Back some thirteen years and many life changes ago, we had an idea. Both of us had been thinking about questions of performance, how the enactment of discursive, bodily, and material forms in performative settings produces and transforms people and social relations. But we were unsatisfied with the ability of our own work and other frameworks with which we were familiar to capture the richness of events that we witnessed and the broad political, social, and historical questions that they raised. In particular, the way that friends George and Silvianita López, Francisco Pérez, or José Antonio Pérez used performances as political tools in challenging racism and nation-states seemed to be much more sophisticated than any framework we could muster in accounting for it. Sharing discomfort with received categories of language, aesthetics, culture, tradition, and other truths that generally seemed to be held to be self-evident, we had the vague feeling that some sort of magic act had been performed long before our time that transformed certain problematic categories into supposedly universal features of the world around us. While we saw our scholarly work as part of a progressive political project, we were not satisfied with our efforts to tie theorizing and analysis to struggles to challenge social inequality and structures of oppression.

At first we agreed to organize a conference. If only a wide range of scholars from different disciplinary backgrounds could get together for a few days, we hoped, our collective wisdom might help us to sort out the problems and chart more productive ways to forge ahead. After a few conversations, though, we decided that a much more sustained dialogue and a great deal of reading would be required. We made the fateful decision: we decided to write a book. Each of us accuses the other of having broached this suggestion. If we had known then that it would take thirteen years and thousands upon thousands of hours of work to accomplish this goal, we would probably have shared one last beer and another collegial *abrazo* and returned to our individual research projects.

Our initial efforts focused on rethinking theories and analytic frameworks of the twentieth century, particularly those that had come into prominence in the preceding quarter century. We published a few papers, laying out ways of thinking about performance, performativity, text, intertextuality, and similar notions. Although we felt that we had loosened the grip of some of the demons that were haunting us, we concluded that we had failed to escape the fundamental constraints that limited the ways that we could imagine culture, language, community, tradition, temporality, and power. The great magicians seemed to have begun their work long before, particularly in the early modern period. That's when we really got started.

From that point to the present, we have tried to read works that have shaped received notions of language, nature, history, tradition, politics, society, and science. We have read through three hundred years of what is now classified as philosophy, political theory, anthropology, linguistics, folklore, history, literary theory, sociology, and art history. We had encountered some of these texts in the course of our undergraduate and graduate educations, others in research projects and general reading since that time. And others we read for the first time. But even texts that we knew well seemed suddenly to change in character. Works from the seventeenth century that we had previously appreciated for their sense of temporal and cultural remoteness, for their seeming lack of connection with contemporary perspectives, suddenly seemed to be in close dialogue with those demons that haunted us in the late twentieth century. Hobbes, Locke, Herder, and their kin seemed to be sitting in the room with us as we read. And their presence did not always seem like that of a trusted ally.

These were moments of tremendous exhilaration and not a little despair. We had the sense that we had found many of the doors that blocked passageways to new modes of thinking and acts of political resistance. The ghosts that had left us with vague feelings of intellectual and political claustrophobia suddenly had names, voices, political positions, and historical locations. At the same time, we live in a world in which the pressure to turn insight into lectures and publications is constant. And we had very, very little idea how rereading Kant's first and third critiques and exploring the second critique, his anthropology, and other writings would ever find its way into any texts to which we could sign our names.

We found our collective voice when reading John Locke's *Essay Concerning Human Understanding* and his *Two Treatises of Government*. We had, like others, learned to read them separately, as if they were written by two Lockes or were exploring two separate terrains. But then our reading took a subversive turn. What would happen if we read the *Essay* against the *Treatises*, to allow our reading of one text to inform the other? Soon we discovered how deeply the project developed in the second *Treatise*, the famous map of modern politics, depended upon the notions of rational, autonomous, self-aware subjects who could speak with voices that seemed to be divorced from their own social locations, interests, and particular experiences. It also led us to read the first *Treatise* seriously – which happens altogether too seldom these days. We discovered that the first blow struck in Locke's attack on Robert Filmer and his Royalist politics was textual; it embodied what we call Locke's anti-rhetorical rhetoric, his development of a new rhetorical framework for undermining certain types of rhetoric. We then read back into the *Essay* with an eye to how deeply its claims to make language neutral and apolitical formed part of a bold political project. As we read into Locke's writings on money, religion, and education, we learned that Locke had embodied his ideas about the politics of language in attempts to shape which ways of speaking would afford access to power, how privileged discursive practices would be learned, and how one would learn them.

Meanwhile, the other member of the team was tracking down some of Locke's contemporaries in the Royal Society as they journeyed away from scientific experimentation and the Society's quarters in Gresham College into the countryside. Focusing on John Aubrey in particular was initially a side line, an attempt to figure out what the Royal Society crowd was doing when it was not charting modernity in scientific or political terms. Aubrey's inscription of songs, charms, and stories from his nanny and other ignorant country people, as he characterized them, seemed to be entirely divorced from what Robert Boyle was doing, for example, with his air pump and other scientific technologies. But then we began comparing notes. The terms, concepts, and rhetorical strategies that one of us was finding in Hobbes, Locke, Boyle, and other students of the modern seemed to be cropping up, generally in inverted ways, in Aubrey. Then another subversive move took place: we began to read Aubrey and other antiquarians not as pre-Romantics who turned their backs on modern political theory and the tumultuous events of the day but as playing a key role in imagining modernity. A Great Divide could only be projected if *pre*modernity was itself constructed, shaped as a primordial realm that existed apart from modernity; indeed, it was premodern ignorance, magic, superstition, and downright disorder that seemed to make modernity necessary. This part of our reading was triply subversive: we dared to read texts that had been marginalized and largely forgotten alongside canonical works. We read them as part of hegemonic constructions of modernity rather than reflections of premodernity. And we began to read Locke with regard to the role that constructions of day laborers, the illiterate, country people, women, and the residents of Asia and the Americas played in enabling him to define modern linguistic and political practices.

As we looked back at other texts we had examined thus far and continued to read in other times and areas, we discovered that these neglected ties between language and tradition with science, nature, politics, and society – that is with modernity – were hardly limited to early modern England alone. Right up through much of the work from the second half of the twentieth century that had shaped our own thinking, we found that strategies of writing and reading as well as the institutional structures of the academy placed boundaries between what were construed as autonomous epistemological domains. This is not to say that the story kept repeating itself. Rather, we found that the sorts of boundaries that were constructed, how they were maintained, and the sorts of political and social interests that they served changed dramatically over time, although in anything but a linear fashion. We came to see our own epoch, including many of the critical studies of modernity that had seemed most clearly aligned with our own ways of thinking and our political sensibilities, as embodying ever-shifting combinations of different strategies for relating language to science and politics and for positioning notions of tradition (premodernity, the Other, etc.) in relationship to modernity. We did not – nor have we since – gained the impression that we can chart a course for future research and progressive agendas that can simply leave behind these mélanges. But we do feel that we have sorted out some of the most persistent and poorly understand ways that even progressive intellectuals reproduce modern ideologies and practices, thereby helping to keep structures of inequality and domination in place.

This emergent collective voice was developed through constant correspondence and more long-distance telephone calls than our personal and department budgets could comfortably bear. We also found spaces whenever possible – before or after meetings and conferences or visits to each other's home ground – that enabled us to spend a few days engaged in near non-stop debate. We began to plot texts. Some were chapters that we assigned to one author. Others involved the distribution of sections of a single essay or chapter between the two of us. At first, the passage from conversation to text was difficult. Although it seemed as if we had a shared vision when we exchanged *abrazos* upon leaving the conference hotel or airport, the texts that emerged from manila envelopes were, to paraphrase Cher, traveling to the beat of quite different drums. While one of us stayed very close to the texts he was analyzing and often focused on valuable precedents for contemporary theorizing, the other had implications that were more broadly synthetic and deconstructive, moving between authors in locating ideological charters for persistent practices of oppression. We agreed a lot about new analytic frameworks, and we published a couple of papers that suggested how contemporary theories could be rethought. But what to say about the Locke and Aubrey and Kant was a different story.

That we persevered is probably more a tribute to a deep friendship than a sense that realistically we would ever find common ground. Perhaps even more importantly, however, we had the strong sense that we were learning more than at any other period in our lives. Even if no book ever got attached to the project, it was worth it. But after sticking with it for a difficult couple of years, things changed. As before, carefully charting collective textual maps in the form of detailed outlines resulted in drafts that took unanticipated routes; we realized with increasing frequency that we had not followed the course to which we had committed ourselves in the outlines. When each of us read what our collaborator had written during those same months, however, even on a topic that lay at some temporal and topical distance, it seemed as if we had been walking five feet apart the whole time.

It still took many years to reach this moment of sending the final manuscript across the ocean to Cambridge. Beyond commitments to other research projects as well as teaching and administrative obligations – not to mention life's vicissitudes outside the walls of academe – what delayed us in particular was trying to figure out how to locate our voice in relationship to those of others. We were keenly aware that we were trespassing, reading texts that not only belonged to other disciplines but which had been claimed by well-entrenched specialists. In writing about Locke, Herder, and the Grimm Brothers for instance, we were quite cognizant that we would have to respond not only to specialists on each of those writers but to scholars who dedicated much of their scholarly energies to particular texts. Our scholarly instincts told us that we had to master the mountains of biographical, historical, and critical works that had been written about these writers and texts; we also knew that specialists would hold us accountable to them. But we also knew that if we surrendered our readings to their issues and interpretations, our critical edge and the very possibility of analyzing familiar texts from unusual points of departure would vanish. This sense of humility and angst has not gone away over the years. Bitter experience has also taught us that reading texts with long canonical trajectories against the grain and asking critical political questions about them can make people mad, even close colleagues who have agreed with us over the years on a wide range of topics.

As a result, we have completely rewritten most of these chapters several times over. We have also left mountains of text that relate to other authors, periods, and issues to, as Marx once put it, the gnawing criticism of the mice – or perhaps now the virtual prison house of unused computer

files. We decided to focus intensively on texts and authors that we believe
to have played crucial roles in shaping how scholars and others are able
to imagine themselves, their communities and societies, possibilities for
political action, the past and the future. We gained the sense that our subversive readings were less productive when we tried to move too quickly
between authors, texts, periods, and places. Rather than systematically
tracing historical lines of influence or attempting to include all of the authors, places, and periods that contributed – even significantly – to these
debates, we provide extended discussions of a small group of authors
and texts, acknowledging that a wide range of others are equally worthy
of attention. We hope that our readers will agree that this selectivity is
worthwhile even as they tell us of other figures we should have included.

Another problem involved in finding a voice, as M. M. Bahktin showed
us, entails finding an audience (really a range of audiences). As the project
developed, we found it necessary to enter into a dialogue with readers in
a wide range of fields. We thus came to the conclusion that our project
would fail if we addressed it to a narrow range of specialists, because we
would then (in spite of any protestations to the contrary) be reproducing
the same atomistic reading practices that are bounded by epistemologies
and disciplines. We believe that anyone who wishes to think critically
about modernity will find this book challenging and worthwhile. We attempt to reach beyond the ranks of scholars who are already interested
in questions of language and tradition; we believe that many people who
thought that these areas had nothing to do with their work and were best
left to specialists mired in academic backwaters will come to realize that
some of the most persistent obstacles they face are rooted precisely in
the way their conceptions of society, politics, nature, and science contain
problematic unexamined assumptions about language, communication,
texts, and tradition. Our goal is to get theorists and historians of politics,
law, and science, for example, to think seriously about how notions of
language and tradition structure their presuppositions and textual practices. We hope that people who consider themselves to be discourse an-
alysts – but who adopt highly contrastive critical *versus* empirical views
of discourse – will find that they have more common ground than they
imagined. We hope to foster a dialogue that crosses both disciplines and
the boundaries of the academy itself. We hope to have launched such
an effort here, to have challenged the problematic constructions of language and tradition – and thus of science, nature, society, and politics –
that emerged from hegemonic modern texts and that hold relations of
social inequality in place. But this project involves a much broader range
of experiences and perspectives than can be offered by two persistent
interlocutors.

When you work this long and hard on a project, the number of debts you accumulate is staggering. Bauman was a Fellow at the Center for Advanced Study in the Behavioral Sciences in Stanford, California, in 1992–93 (with the support of funds from the Andrew W. Mellon Foundation), just as the project was seriously getting underway. Briggs spent the 2001–2 academic year there, and the Center provided him with a delightful setting in which to revise several chapters. Both authors received fellowships from the National Endowment for the Humanities in 1989–90. Bauman was a Guggenheim Fellow in 1990; Briggs was a Fellow at the Woodrow Wilson International Center for Scholars in Washington, DC in 1997–98. Without the time for reading, reflection, conversation, and writing afforded by these institutions, we would have been unlikely to have completed the book. We thank the administrations and staffs as well as other fellows for their kindness and stimulation. Indiana University, the University of California, San Diego, and Vassar College provided travel and other types of support. Our thinking was stimulated by seminars and working groups sponsored by the Center for Psychosocial Studies (later the Center for Transcultural Studies) in Chicago and the School of American Research in Santa Fe, New Mexico. We thank the *American Anthropologist, American Quarterly,* the *Journal of American Folklore, Pragmatics,* and *Western Folklore* for permission to reprint passages that have been adapted from articles that appeared in these journals and in *Regimes of Language,* a volume edited by Paul V. Kroskrity that was published by the School of American Research Press. Thanks too to the American Philosophical Society for permission to quote from the Boas correspondence and to Robert Cox for his generous guidance through the Boas collection.

Conversations with colleagues have informed our thinking and writing in countless ways. While a mere list certainly does not do justice to their contributions, we would at least like to name some of the people who have engaged with us on these issues over the years: Roger Abrahams, Asif Agha, Judith Berman, Iain Boal, Vincent Crapanzano, Steve Epstein, Joe Errington, Don Foster, Sue Gal, Akhil Gupta, Ramón Gutiérrez, Ian Hacking, Richard Handler, Bill Hanks, Karsten Harries, Galit Hasan-Rokem, Michael Herzfeld, Jane Hill, Judy Irvine, Ira Jacknis, Martha Kaplan, John Kelly, Barbara Kirshenblatt-Gimblett, Ben Lee, Michael Murray, John Nichols, Robert Norton, Alfonso Ortiz, Hector Romero, Yolanda Salas, Bambi Schieffelin, Dan Segal, Steve Shapin, Amy Shuman, Denise Silva, Michael Silverstein, George Stocking, Beverly Stoeltje, Greg Urban, Jackie Urla, Lisa Valentine, and Kit Woolard. We have presented papers that emanate from the project at a wide range of academic and cultural institutions in the United States and abroad, and we would like to thank audiences there for questions and comments that contributed to the development of our work. Special thanks are due to James Clifford for challenging us to be explicit about the stakes of our argument. For the following individuals, who read all or part of various drafts, we have only the deepest of gratitude: Ruth Finnegan, Jane Hill, Dell Hymes, Ira Jacknis, George Lipsitz, Michael Silverstein, and Barbara Tomlinson. We thank Helen Barton, Judith Irvine, Jessica Kuper, and Bambi Schieffelin for their editorial support and their patience.

This work has gone on so long and taken so many of our waking hours that it is woven into the fabric of our family lives. The forbearance of Beverly Stoeltje and of Clara Mantini-Briggs, Feliciana Briggs, Gabriel Fries-Briggs, and Jessie Fries-Kraemer are inexpressible. We hope that now that all is said and done, they, too, will think that it was all worthwhile. Or at least most of it. We lovingly dedicate this work to Feliciana, a bright and shining spirit, who died, tragically, as the book was in production. May its publication help us celebrate her love of languages, her gift as a writer, and the beauty that she brought into the lives of those who knew her.

1   Introduction

One can see how a conception of the state–society relation, born within the parochial history of Western Europe but made universal by the global sway of capital, dogs the contemporary history of the world.

Chatterjee 1993: 238

The project of provincializing "Europe" therefore cannot be a project of "cultural relativism." It cannot originate from the stance that the reason/science/universals which help define Europe as the modern are simply "culture-specific" and therefore only belong to the European cultures. For the point is not that Enlightenment rationalism is always unreasonable in itself but rather a matter of documenting how – through what historical process – its "reason," which was not always self-evident to everyone, has been made to look "obvious" far beyond the ground where it originated.

Chakrabarty 1992: 23

In the summer of 1643, fearing for his son's safety in the face of the Civil War violence then swirling around Oxford, John Aubrey's father summoned him home from his beloved university to the family estate at Broadchalke, in the south of Wiltshire. Young John languished in rustic isolation for three long years; he describes his sojourn in the country as "a most sad life to me... not to have the benefitt of an ingeniose Conversation." For Aubrey, whose company was widely valued in his later life for his skill and grace as a conversationalist, it was a special hardship to have "none but Servants and rustiques" – he terms the local inhabitants "Indigenae, or Aborigines" – with whom to converse (Aubrey 1847 [1969]: 11). "*Odi prophanum vulgus et arceo*" (I hate and shun the common herd), he writes, lamenting his lack of refined interlocutors. Finally, in the spring of 1646 and "with much adoe," he received his father's leave to depart for London to read law at the Middle Temple, and at last, in November, he was able to return to Oxford and, to his "great joy," to the "learned conversation" of the fellows (Aubrey 2000: 11–12). For the remainder of his adult life, Aubrey pursued the pleasures of sociability with the most distinguished minds of his day. He was one of the original members of the Royal Society, to which he was elected in 1662, and his learned friends and interlocutors included such luminaries as Thomas Hobbes, Robert Boyle, William Petty, John Locke, and Robert Hooke, with whom he enjoyed an especially close relationship. Aubrey was an early devotee of the Oxford and London coffeehouses and the opportunities for male sociability they provided, extolling "the extreme advantage of coffee-houses in the great Citie, before which men knew not how to be acquainted other than with their own Relations or Societies" (quoted in Tylden-Wright 1991: 202).

In Aubrey's learned conversations with his fellow Royal Society members and coffeehouse companions, we may identify in concrete, experiential terms what has been conceived in more abstract and general terms as the discursive construction of modernity. The Royal Society was Britain's preeminent scientific society, an institutional nexus for the cultivation and dissemination of a scientific ideology based on the rational, empirical pursuit of knowledge and the conviction that reason and science will yield universal laws and secure the progress of humankind, now freed from the shackles of traditional authority, blind faith, and superstition. And the coffeehouse looms large – notwithstanding the challenge of other contenders – in foundation narratives of the bourgeois public sphere and related social and political formations widely accepted as diagnostic of modernity. In drawing the contrast, then, between the vulgar conversation of "rustiques" and the "ingeniose conversation" of learned men, Aubrey is contributing to the construction of a particularly modernist opposition between the provincial (he uses the term; see, e.g., Aubrey 1898, II: 326) and the universal, in discourse-centered terms.

There is in addition a temporal, as well as a social and a spatial, dimension to this opposition. Aubrey came to see the temporal juncture that marked the contrastive periods of provincial and learned discourse in his own life, that is, the Civil Wars, as marking also a more epochal watershed between the "old ignorant times" and the "modern" present that is at the center of his antiquarian vision. We discuss this vision more fully later in the book, but it is worth noting here the periodizing leitmotif that runs through Aubrey's writings, locating the full currency of the customs and beliefs to which he devoted his antiquarian researches not only among "Countrey-people" but in the period "when I was a Boy, before the Civill warres" (Aubrey 1972a: 203, 241). Thus, what emerges in Aubrey's autobiographical and antiquarian constructions is not only a personal, but a more general pair of associational complexes that resonate strongly through the social thought of the past 300 years: rural (or aboriginal), lower class, ignorant, old-fashioned, indigenous – in a word, *provincial* – versus urban, elite, learned, cosmopolitan, that is to say, *modern*.

It is just these associational complexes that represent the critical focus of recent works by Dipesh Chakrabarty and Partha Chatterjee from which we have drawn our epigraphs. As Chakrabarty and Chatterjee suggest, Western domination did not rely solely on military might and the imposition of particular forms of capitalism but on the promulgation of certain crucial epistemological and ideological orientations as well. In an argument recently extended by Chakrabarty (2000), they suggest that both colonialism and contemporary inequalities between "First" and "Third Worlds" resulted from a process of "deprovincializing Europe." As part of the process of constructing modernity, European elites produced ideologies and practices and then elevated them to the status of universals that could be used in comprehending and dominating the rest of the world. These schemas "liberally" provided all peoples everywhere the right to cultivate their inherent capacities for rationality, individual autonomy, and the ability to dominate nature in producing wealth. European elites thus provided both the model for assessments as to how a given individual or population measured up to these ideals and accorded themselves the right to occupy the role of assessors for the entire world.

Chakrabarty and Chatterjee thus provide us with a useful point of departure for tracking how particular practices came to be seen, in spite of their heterogeneity and contradictions, as a single modernity that could be applied to the entire world in a temporally and spatially defined teleology. At the same time, however, they do not enable us to comprehend the particular logic that was used in making the cosmopolitan leap from historically and socially specific provincialities to a supposedly universal schema. Scholars have long argued that the emergence of modern science in seventeenth-century Europe played a key role in this process. Historical narratives have widely suggested that modern science transformed European society by increasing acceptance of a secular, naturalistic worldview that posited a universe governed by natural laws. Practitioners in science studies have recently presented much more complex and interesting ways of telling the story. Shapin and Schaffer (1985) suggest that the "mechanical philosophy" of seventeenth-century England was hardly as bounded, autonomous, and transparent as received interpretations would suggest. Rather, it revolved around complex and expensive technologies, as quintessentially exemplified by Boyle's air pump, needed for experimentation. The monumental jump in scale from a host of questions as to whether the air was really removed when the pump was in operation, whether the machine leaked, and who could witness its operation, to decontextualized, abstract principles that defined basic properties of all nature were mediated by a host of discursive, social, and political-economic "provincialities," to invoke Chakrabarty and Chatterjee's notion. In order for the discourse of leading scientists to become a model for transparency and order for speech and civil society (see Shapin 1994), it took a lot of social work to construct a scientific realm and project it as authoritative and disinterested.

Bruno Latour (1993) draws on work in science studies in presenting an interpretation of the underpinnings, power, and contradictions of modernity. He argues that it was not scientific thinking *per se* that fueled modernity but rather the construction of cultural domains of "society" and "science" as separate and autonomous. On the one hand, science was deemed to be not a social product but to be derived from a sphere of nature that existed apart from humans; Enlightenment thinkers viewed society, on the other hand, as constructed by humans. The ideological, social, and political wellspring of modernity, according to Latour, involved two contradictory way of relating these two entities. The two realms were constantly linked through processes of mediation and the production of hybrids, forms that linked social characteristics to scientific or technological elements. While the air pump provides a salient seventeenth-century example, nuclear warheads, cellular telephones, and amniocentesis exemplify the way that scientific and technological "advances" in the twentieth century become imbued with powerful social meanings. While this hybridization process invests both social and scientific forms with political-economic and social power, the work of "purification" seeks to erase awareness of these connections in order to maintain the illusion of the autonomy of these realms. At the same time that purification has, in his estimation, been a constitutive preoccupation for societies that claim to be modern, Latour ironically argues, as the title of his book suggests, that *We Have Never Been Modern*; if communities must rigorously separate society from science and nature to truly be modern, the proliferation of hybrids excludes everyone from fully deserving this designation.

In our view, Latour's characterization of modernity has a number of things to recommend it. It neatly captures the way that science, society, and modernity are always precarious works in progress, powerful notions that must be constantly (re)constructed, imbued with authority, and naturalized. It is thus necessary to break constantly with the premodern past and devise reformist schemes for modernizing societies and technologies, because hybrids keep modernity from ever achieving the order and rationality that it is supposed to embody. Latour stresses the constructed and artificial character of these entities, their reliance on socially and historically situated and materially interested practices, and he thus challenges his readers to be wary of assumptions regarding definitions, boundaries, and effects of social categories. At the same time, however, Latour argues that we must see science and society as more than "just" social constructions, that we cannot lose sight of the ways that they get materially embodied or their physical and other effects on human bodies. Latour thus helps us imagine ways of seeing epistemologies, social relations, technologies, and material entities as simultaneously constructed, real, consequential, *and* dependent on situated and interested practices.

Latour does not devote a conspicuous amount of attention to rigorous definitions of purity, hybridity, or mediation, and to the extent that we employ these notions in the pages that follow, our own scholarly (modernist? purifying?) impulses require us to specify at least a bit more closely what we take them to mean.[1] When applied to epistemological constructions or to cultural forms more generally, of course, hybridity is a metaphor, which carries with it from taxonomic biology the notion that the hybrid "offspring" is a heterogeneous mixture of relevant constituent elements contributed by the homogeneous (pure) "parent" forms. To be sure, classificatory purity is itself an epistemological construction, and every "pure" form can also be conceived as hybrid by some measure or other. But that is just the point: it is not the ontological status of supposedly "pure" forms that interests us here, but rather the epistemological *work* of purification, and the concomitant vulnerability of pure, bounded constructions to hybridizing relationships. Mediation is a structural relationship, the synthetic bringing together of two elements (terms, categories, etc.) in such a way as to create a symbolic or conventional relationship between them that is irreducible to two independent dyads. A hybrid is thus a mediating form, but we use the term mediation to foreground the role of mediating terms in bringing "pure" elements – the categorical products of purifying practices – into relational conjunction.

Terminology aside, however, we do have one larger objection to Latour's formulation: he left out two of the key constructs that make modernity work and make it precarious! We can refer to them in shorthand as language and tradition, even though adopting these modern designations might draw the reader into the sorts of modern categories (and thus oversimplifications and subordinations) that we scrutinize in this book.

Making language in the seventeenth century

Let us take John Locke as a point of departure. Locke would seem to fit Latour's narrative perfectly. The second of his *Two Treatises of Government* (1960 [1690]) is credited with constructing the notions of civil society,

[1] We are indebted here to Stross (1999) on the metaphor of hybridity and Parmentier (1985) on mediation.

individual rights, and government that have shaped modern societies up to the present. His "social contract" theory provides a classic example of the notion that society is a product of human action. He was a member of the Royal Society, thus collaborating with leading figures in establishing the authority of mechanical philosophy. At the same time, he separated his reflections on the social realm from experimentation, asserting that his own role was that of "an under-labourer in clearing the ground a little, and removing some of the rubbish that lies in the way to knowledge" (1959 [1690] I: 14) in comparison with the efforts of such "master-builders" in "the commonwealth of learning" as Boyle, Huygens, and Newton. So far so good for Latour. But when we come to the last sentence of Locke's similarly famous *Essay Concerning Human Understanding*, we reach a stumbling block:

> For a man can employ his thoughts about nothing, but either, the contemplation of *things* themselves, for the discovery of truth; or about the things in his own power, which are his own *actions*, for the attainment of his own ends; or the *signs* the mind makes use of both in the one and the other, and the right ordering of them, for its clearer information. All which three, viz. *things*, as they are in themselves knowable; *actions* as they depend on us, in order to happiness; and the right use of *signs* in order to knowledge, being *toto coelo* different, they seemed to me to be the three great provinces of the intellectual world, wholly separate and distinct one from another. (1959 [1690]: IV. xxi. 4; emphasis in the original)[2]

The first two of these "great provinces" of modern knowledge correspond to autonomous realms that we would now label natural or scientific and social. But Locke does not simply place language as an epiphenomenal part of the realm of society, as Latour seems to do, but rather accords it a separate province; the *Essay* is devoted precisely to mapping this sphere and defending its borders aggressively against both nature and society. Are the Locke of the *Essay* and the Locke of the second *Treatise* the same person? Locke tried to shape how these works would be read by relegating them to separate provinces, and, with few exceptions, critics have followed his instructions to the letter, seeing them as unrelated bodies of theory. So the work of purification, to return to Latour's lexicon, would seem to be just as engaged in keeping language walled off from science and society as it was invested in keeping the latter two domains separate. Locke warned that the stakes were high. Unless language was rescued from the false conceptions of its nature that had been commonly accepted, even by scientists, then words would continue to be confused with things and

---

[2] We will cite the *Essay* by placing the book number in upper-case Roman numerals, followed by the chapter number in small Roman numerals, followed by the section number in Arabic numerals. All emphasis is in the original.

would be used in shifting, imprecise ways. Language would accordingly fail to provide a solid base for mechanical philosophy, thereby making scientific progress and communication between practitioners impossible.

On the language-society side – let us call this domain of hybridity *discourse*, to distinguish it from purified language – "the cheat and abuse of words," which embrace ambiguous, unstable and shifting meanings, rhetoric, and intertextuality, transformed words into sources of misunderstanding and vehicles for undermining the rationality and independence of thought. Writing in the unsettled period following the English Civil Wars, Locke thus identified discourse as the major source of social disorder, religious factionalism, and political conflict. The stakes for keeping language separate could not be higher. At the same time, the manner in which Locke hybridized language still affects us in profound – and often profoundly negative – ways. Deeming education to be requisite to gaining linguistic precision, he then decreed that women, the poor, and laborers were so immersed in concrete, localized concerns that they needed little access to pedagogy. He helped to make the linguistic forms that he championed – precise, plain and unadorned, rational ways of speaking – markers of social status and key gatekeeping mechanisms that would shape who would be accorded the right to participate in politics or to speak, as Jürgen Habermas (1989) suggests, in the public sphere. And at the same time that he apologizes repeatedly for bringing up linguistic concerns in a political work, the little-read first *Treatise* sets up the project for the second by providing a textual demolition of a leading Royalist political statement.

So there you have it – a separate domain of language and the work of purification, carried on faithfully to this day by linguists (such as Noam Chomsky), grammar teachers (remember Miss Fidditch?), and such modern-day defenders of linguistic purity as William Safire (see Silverstein 1996). Add to this the constant production of hybrids by advertisers who tie words and phrases to commodities, political propagandists who make words like "crime," "drugs," or "welfare mothers" stand for race, and educational professionals who make non-standard dialects into markers of irrationality, ignorance, school failure, and suitability for dead-end service jobs. All of which makes it possible to keep producing constructs of science and society.

Our book fills in this hitherto largely unrecognized chapter in the story of modernity, how language came into being and the work of purification and hybridization that makes it a crucial means of structuring social relations. We are interested, on the one hand, in how language is like science and society – the way that all three realms are continually constructed through purification and hybridization. But, on the other hand, we also want to show how language is unlike the other two domains. While purification and hybridization render society and science visible and seemingly omnipotent, these processes measured their success in constructing language and managing discursive practices by the degree to which they could render language unimportant – only worthy of attention by linguists and grammar teachers. Locke only thought to worry about language, he tells us, when it got in the way.

Latour misses language, that is, the role of its construction as autonomous and the work of purification and hybridization this entails in making modernity. For him, the philosophical construction of language and semiotics plays a secondary, derivative role in articulating the relationship between society and nature. In his own view, language is best understood as mediating between the two primary domains, and he casts attempts to render language as an autonomous domain as secondary moves to fill the gap created by the purifying efforts of modernizing philosophers (Latour 1993: 63). Latour is simply modern here, having succumbed to the definition of language as real and its relegation to the role of carrying out particular modernist functions, such as conveying information. This comes in spite of his attention to the role of language in constructing science through laboratory practices (see Latour and Woolgar 1979).

Now, informed readers will probably be quick to point out the parallels between our project and the classic account of modern epistemologies that Foucault (1970) provides in *The Order of Things*. Indeed, one of the major foci of that influential work is on the transformation in thinking about language that took place in the sixteenth and seventeenth centuries. In the former period, words were seen as indissolubly interwoven with things, and they provided natural signs of the hidden properties of the world. This view gave way, according to Foucault, to a conception of language as constituting a separate epistemological realm. Language was simultaneously demoted, losing its status as an embodiment of truth and becoming a neutral and transparent medium for finding and conveying it. At the same time, by characterizing signs as arbitrary or conventional human constructions, the distinctions that drive language hold the key for unlocking the analytical and ordering operations that lie, in Foucault's view, at the heart of the "Classical episteme." Since all knowledge depends on representation, demoting language to mere representation simultaneously promoted it to the status of a quintessentially human sphere (1970: 86). Unlike Latour, Foucault suggests that "the experience of language belongs to the same archaeological network as the knowledge of things and nature" (1970: 41); that is, rather than being a tool for constituting science and society, the construction of an autonomous realm of language in the seventeenth century provided a key force for making modern knowledge possible. Indeed, Foucault seems to grasp that the success of this construction is evident in the degree to which language could subsequently be generally regarded as self-evident and epiphenomenal.

At the heart of Foucault's analysis, however, lies the contention that language was viewed in a unified fashion in the Classical period. Language, he claims, was generally accorded the status of being neutral, representational, and autonomous. This linguistic "episteme" included efforts to fashion artificial languages and to construct language as rhetoric. At this point in Foucault's analysis, the power of language's role in the modernist drama is largely lost, a vast scenario of contestation and domination turned into a single dramatic event that resolves all tensions, contradictions, and complications. Our objection is not a mere historical quibble. The issue, rather, lies at the very core of the process involved in creating language and rendering it a powerful means of creating social inequality. What interests us about Locke's view of language, for example, is not the way it embodies a unified episteme but rather the way he positioned it *vis-à-vis* opposing linguistic ideologies and practices – and the perceived failure of most of the people on the globe to embrace the linguistic discipline he advocated. Most people's language was not credited with being transparent, neutral, representational, or autonomous; the regimes for the surveillance of language practices that Locke helped put into place played a key role in empowering the legislators that Zygmunt Bauman (1987) describes and in structuring social inequality right through to the present.

In short, the idea of a single, unified conception of language in the Classical episteme short-circuits our awareness of the powerful work of purification and hybridization in which Locke was engaged and which prepared the ground for Foucault's monolithically conceived Classical episteme. At the same time, however, we want to be alert to alternative ways of reimagining language as part of the work of imagining modernity. Indeed, much of our attention in the chapters that follow will be devoted to tracing an ideological orientation that does not set language apart as an autonomous domain in Lockeian fashion, but assimilates it rather to the dual epistemology that is central to Latour's argument. Emerging out of eighteenth-century classical philology and coalescing in the philosophy of Johann Gottfried Herder was a discursively founded framing of the advent of modernity that viewed language as a radically hybrid formation (though also susceptible to purifying inflections), inherently both natural and social, but in shifting proportions over the long course of human social evolution. This conception of language is the basis, for example, on which Herder can assert that "While still an animal, man already has language," while claiming at the same time that "Language originated through intercourse and not in solitude; through conversation every expression is sharpened and polished" (Herder 1966 [1787]: 87; Ergang 1966: 158). While Foucault's account of language thus provides an excellent starting point for discerning how reimagining language was crucial for imagining modernity, we suggest that the story needs to be retold if its broader significance – particularly for understanding how modernity produces and structures inequality – is to become more intellectually and politically accessible.

Tradition, orality, and the discourse of others

To this point, our critique of Latour has centered on the identification and calibration of the epistemological domains that set the terms for the construction of modernity, and we have argued for the full recognition of language as a domain co-equal in this enterprise with Latour's society and nature. Our turn to language, however, and to the forces of purification and hybridization that shape the ways that it has been conceived and aligned in the construction of modernity, attunes us as well to another dimension of Latour's argument, namely, the conceptualization of temporality in the constructional process.

Latour certainly recognizes that any discussion of modernity – its formation or conformation – implicates temporality, both the succession and the contrast or opposition between past and future. As with modernist approaches to language, Latour sees modern temporality as derived from the primary epistemological separation of nature and society: "The asymmetry between nature and culture becomes an asymmetry between past and future. The past was the confusion of things and men; the future is what will no longer confuse them" (1993: 71). In these terms, the hybridity highlighted by his title, *We Have Never Been Modern*, arises out of a mediation of past and future as well as of epistemological domains. Not surprisingly, however, given his preoccupation with nature (or science) and society, the terms most relevant to his primary mission of developing a charter for science studies, Latour devotes scant attention to past–future purification and hybridization. Moreover, his persistent use of the label "pre-modern" for the antecedent side of the Great Divide represents the very historicist usage that assimilates history everywhere to the temporality of Western "progress" and thus runs counter to the agenda of reprovincializing Europe that Chakrabarty and Chatterjee articulate.

But when we turn our attention to the role of language in the construction of modernity, we enter an intellectual field that is permeated by concern with temporal continuities and discontinuities in language. And a key rubric under which the figures we examine engage that concern is *tradition*. When used in the service of articulating a purified, modern conception of language, as we shall see, that is, when it is used to differentiate the past from the present, tradition becomes a mode of discourse that is diagnostic of the past; it is an archaic language-society hybrid characterized by all of those indexicalities of time and place and interest and intertextuality that Locke worked so hard to clear away. It is the opposite of the modern, rational, decontextualized language that he advocated so strongly in the *Essay*. In its mediational guise, tradition becomes the intertextually constituted continuum of reiterations by which the language – and thus the thought – of the past survives into the present, the mechanism that bridges the historical juncture represented by the advent of modernity. A central concern of our book, then, is the construction, articulation, and ideologization of a conception of tradition founded on language and its alignment in the field of forces represented by the purifying and hybridizing operations to which it has been subject in the creation and maintenance of modernity. Or, we should say, of *modernities*, for we will argue that there are significant differences between a conception of modernity as dependent upon a decisive, irreversible break with the past and an understanding of modernity as continuous with the past, though there are also convergences between the two.

There are important and enduring issues here. No concept has been more central to the formation of the social disciplines than tradition (see Bauman 2001). The durability of the problem – is tradition superseded by modernity or does it persist into the present, linking the present to the past? – is attested by the current debates surrounding "detraditionalization," in which the proponents of what is characterized as "the radical thesis," that is, the basic modernist notion that modernity is progressively and irrevocably rolling back tradition as it advances, face off against advocates of "the coexistence thesis," in which detraditionalization "is seen as competing, interpenetrating or interplaying with processes to do with tradition-maintenance, rejuvenation and tradition-construction" (Heelas 1996: 2–3). We will have much more to offer that bears on this debate in the chapters that follow. Especially important to our explorations will be the ways in which tradition, as classificatory concept or mediating force in the alignment of premodernity to modernity, consistently lends itself to the articulation of other asymmetries that have been useful in the construction of modernity and social inequality: female/male, rural/urban, working class/bourgeois, unsophisticated/educated, oral/literate, European/Oriental.

Closely linked to tradition, both as an order of communication and as a mediator between past and present, is the communicative technology by means of which the chain of iterations that is held to constitute tradition is realized, that is, the spoken voice. Concomitantly, one of the principal moments that comes to mark the threshold between past and present is the advent of print; the transformative force of the printed word looms large in the epoch-defining formulations of seventeenth- and eighteenth-century ideologues of modernity. Francis Bacon, to cite but one prominent example, identifies printing in the *Novum Organum* as one of the "discoveries," "unknown to the ancients," that "have changed the whole face and state of things throughout the world" (Aphorism 129, p. 118). John Aubrey, whose antiquarian program we examine in detail in the pages that follow, echoes Bacon in more concrete terms that register the profound epistemological and expressive transformation that Weber identified two centuries later as "the disenchantment of the world": "Before printing, Old-wives Tales were ingeniose," Aubrey observes, but "the divine art of Printing and Gunpowder have frighted away Robin-good-fellow and the Fayries" (Aubrey 1972a: 290).

The transposition of the word, then, from speaking to print, was assimilated to the Great Divide that defined the historical juncture between past and present, and it has remained central to modernizing understandings to this day, providing a frame of reference not only for the advent of modernity but for futurist imaginings in our own day of a new epochal shift to be brought about by digital technology. Indeed, one of the intellectual fields in which the development and propagation of print technology currently holds considerable sway is Latour's own: a burgeoning line of inquiry in science studies focuses on the epistemological and social consequences of "print culture" (Elizabeth Eisenstein's term), on the history of the book (stimulated by the French *histoire du livre*), and allied concerns relating to the nexus of print, authorship, and authority. At the same time that contemporary digital forecasters wonder what will happen when "the author, once the fount of imagination . . . has been divested of *authority*" (Birkerts 1994: 184, italics in the original), or, more colorfully, "What is to become of the priests of literature, as their temples are abandoned?" (Gore Vidal, quoted in Heim 1999: 3), historians of print culture are looking back to the seventeenth and eighteenth centuries, when the modern concept of authorship first took firm root, when "the vocabulary of 'authorship' was, quite literally, a vocabulary of 'author-ity,' and the word 'author' was a word of power" (Jaszi 1991: 270; see also Johns 1998; Kernan 1987; Woodmansee 1984; Woodmansee and Jaszi 1994). If, as Adrian Johns argues, "the very identity of print has had to be *made*," it becomes necessary to "reappraise where our own concept of print culture comes from, how it developed, when it took hold, and why its sway continues to seems secure" (Johns 1998: 2–4).

Investigations of how print culture was made focus, understandably, on the constructional processes by which the printed word, especially the book, was invested with authority and value, shaped for the pursuit and publication of certain kinds of knowledge, aligned with certain emergent commercial and class interests, organized into certain structures of production and consumption, and so on (see, e.g., Chartier 1994; Johns 1998; Kernan 1987; Woodmansee and Jaszi 1994). And within a broader historical frame of reference, these processes are identified with the advent of modernity, as reciprocally related to such forces – long recognized as diagnostic of that epochal transformation – as the rise of mercantile (or print) capitalism, the formation of the bourgeoisie, and the ascendancy of a naturalistic worldview as the foundation of scientific epistemology.

The scholarly project to which we refer has a decidedly revisionist cast. Prominent among the announced goals of those engaged in discovering the history of the book is to provide a critical corrective to conceptions of the printed word that view its purported capacities for social transformation as inherent in the medium itself or its purported cognitive, epistemological, and social correlates as determined by print technology. Insofar as print culture must be recognized as the emergent construction of diverse and often competing parties who are economically and politically interested, socially positioned, and institutionally sited, it is not simply "culture" in some value-neutral sense, but ideology (Schieffelin, Woolard, and Kroskrity 1998; Kroskrity 2000). Accordingly, it has become increasingly difficult to sustain a consideration of print culture (in the singular) as a unitary phenomenon. What emerges from the works we have cited is a more complex and contested arena of print cultures and ideologies, rooted in the particularities of time and place.

Illuminating and productive as this work may be, however, it gives us only half the picture by focusing on only part of the constructional work necessary to the authorization of the printed word and the discursive transformations that were effected by that process. What is missing from the scholarly project devoted to the constructional history of print culture and the authorization of print discourse, we would suggest, is the focused investigation of concomitant processes by which print and its attendant discursive formations are constructed in *symbolic and ideological opposition* to other technologies of communication and modes of discourse. It is a commonplace, not only of histories that focus on transformations of the word associated with the production and reception of print discourse, but of far more sweeping lines of social, cultural, philosophical, and cognitive theory, to contrast the printed word with the spoken word, literacy with orality. But if print culture had to be made, as we are now coming to recognize, so too did its symbolic opposite; if discursive formations associated with the printed word had to be invested with authority, so too did discursive formations associated with the spoken word need to be divested of it. And, importantly, if cultures of the printed word are also ideologies of print, so too are cultures of the spoken word ideologies of orality. Essentialist conceptions of the spoken word and determinist understandings of how it shapes society, culture, or thought are as much in need of critical examination as corresponding conceptions of print. Still further, we would offer, the ideological construction of modernity in terms related to print culture and its associated discursive formations is more fully and clearly explainable as part of a more comprehensive process that depended upon the construction of a contrastive past, characterized by contrastive technologies and modes of communication. This latter process is one of the main foci of this book, and the ways that the dimensions of contrast that took shape during its long course of development were extended to provide an ideological warrant for modern relations of social inequality.

As part of the larger process of making modernity, the making of orality and literacy, as we would expect, involved the same kinds of purifying work that characterizes all Great Divide schemas. The eighteenth-century philologist, Robert Wood, for example, whose writings on Homer were of benchmark importance in establishing orality and literacy as contrastive typological categories, built into this framing of the Great Divide an opposition between the "language of nature" and the "language of compact" (1971 [1775]: 282–84) resting precisely on the fundamental nature–society opposition that Latour identifies as foundational to modernizing epistemologies. After drawing the distinction between the two, however, Wood goes on to identify a critically important zone of mediation.

The language of nature for Wood, as for other eighteenth-century philologists whom we consider at length in the first section of our book, is poetry, and it is the durability of poetic forms from the past and their persistence into the present that constitutes oral traditions as the domain of discursive mediation in modern life. Perhaps the most important consideration in this historical process of ideological construction is the siting of the relic area constituted by oral tradition, for it is by this locational process that oral tradition acquires the associations that allow it to serve as a diagnostic element in the measure of modernity. The process by which oral tradition became the foundation of a poetics of Otherness, a means of identifying the premodern Others both within modern society (uneducated, rural, poor, female) and outside it (savage, primitive, "preliterate"), is a vital part of the story we have to tell. This poetics of Otherness, at the same time that it provides for oppositional contrasts between

Others and moderns, also lays the ground for two broadly hybridizing processes, one founded on cultural relativism, the other on vernacularization. Cultural relativism comes into play as a hermeneutic orientation to the literature of the exotic Other, the Homeric Greeks, the ancient Hebrews, the American Indians. Relativism, in Latour's suggestive formulation, renders alien worlds *commensurable* (Latour 1993: 113–14). It provides a standard of measure, a mensural framework, that mediates between cultures, allowing for epistemological translation from one to another. The philological perspective that we trace from the early eighteenth century to the mid-twentieth, from Thomas Blackwell to Franz Boas, offers a hermeneutic vantage point on exotic Others that renders their literature – and through their literature, their culture – intelligible and meaningful to Western readers, through the mediation of those intellectuals who can guide the translation process. Vernacularization, by contrast, involves a refiguration of the domestic Other through the dual processes that Sheldon Pollock terms *literization*, in which local languages are admitted to literacy, and *literarization*, in which the oral, traditional forms of vernacular expression are accommodated to "literature," worthy of being cultivated, read, and preserved (Pollock 1998a, 1998b, 2000). Vernacularization, like relativism, foregrounds the provincial – dispersed, peripheral, local – but always in dialogue with the cosmopolitan and the universal. One of the principal tasks we undertake in the chapters that follow is to chart the zone of mediation in which this dialogue takes place.

But it is not only ideology that concerns us here. The intellectual engagement with the words of Others in the construction of ideologies of modernity gave rise – from the early nineteenth century onwards – to an interventionist project of very broad reach and enormous political consequence, centering on the collection and publication of oral traditions. This project, in turn, demanded the development of metadiscursive regimes for the conceptualization, management, and rendering of oral traditional texts, sets of practices adapted to the achievement of ideologically founded ends.[3]

The task involved, first of all, a consideration of how such texts were made, as a basis for determining how they might be recognized, appropriated, and managed in the modern world. At one level, this is a matter of elucidating the formal, constructional properties of those oral, traditional texts as they are produced and circulated by those Others among whom they remain current, a poetics of entextualization, circulation, and preservation as constitutive of oral tradition. This is likewise a poetics

---

[3] The discussion that follows draws on Bauman and Briggs (1990) and Briggs and Bauman (1992); see also Silverstein and Urban (1996).

of contextualization and recontextualization, insofar as traditionality is conceived of as a chain of iterations, within "premodern" social and situational milieux, of archaic texts – all of these features and processes, of course, contrasting with "modern" modes of entextualization and circulation. The chief question here has to do with the relationship between how oral traditional texts are made and what endows them with the capacity to perdure, to bridge the epochal gap between antiquity and modernity.

But there is a second order of text-making and recontextualization implicated here as well. One of the most persistent and vexing problems confronting those intellectuals engaged in the collection and publication of oral texts revolves around the production of the text-artifact (Silverstein 1993: 38), the written rendition of an oral text for a modern, literate audience. This is a key moment in the vernacularization process, what Pollock calls "literization," the commitment of oral and vernacular poetic forms to writing, as forms of literature (Pollock 1998a: 41, 1998b: 9). In significant part, this is a task of translation: both intersemiotic translation – that is, rendering oral discourse in written form – and often interlingual translation as well, the transposition of discourse from one language into another. It is also, however, a problem of decontextualization and recontextualization: how to lift the oral text from its "traditional" oral context and recontextualize it in a printed work.

The questions here are many. What constitutes the oral-traditional "text" in the first place? What and how much of its originary context should it carry with it into the new context of the printed page? To whom should the print-mediated text-artifact be addressed? To what extent should it be re-entextualized to accommodate to its new context? How is the relation of the text-artifact to the source text to be conceived and framed?

These are not simply minor matters of "mere" form and ancillary framing. To the contrary, we would maintain, it is precisely in the conception, calibration, and rhetorical framing of the intertextual relationship between what are taken to be primary oral texts and the text artifacts published by intellectuals that the politics of hybridization are played out. There will inevitably be an intertextual gap between the source text, however conceived, and the text-artifact. Most importantly, the source text is conceived as oral, collectively shaped by the traditionalizing process, premodern in form and provenance, while the text artifact is written, individually rendered, and presented in a printed book, a quintessentially modern venue. And it is precisely in the space of hybridity defined by these contrastive qualities that the politics of authenticity – one of the key tropes of modernity – are contested. It is here too that the tensions between the Enlightenment pull towards a linguistic cosmopolitanism that transcends the particularities of time and place and a vernacularism that foregrounds the indigenous and the traditional comes into heightened relief. In Pollock's terms, these are "practices of literary communication that actualize modes of cosmopolitan and vernacular belonging" (Pollock 2000: 595). Accordingly, the metadiscursive regimes that organize intellectual interventions in oral tradition must be recognized as key elements in the symbolic construction of modernity. Or, again, modernities – for the framing and calibration of those metadiscursive regimes are multiple and contested, and they may serve interests as varied as colonialism, national liberation, ethnic cleansing, the rationalization of education, and academic discipline formation. Thus, the second section of our book, dealing with the tensions of purification and hybridization in the recording and editorial efforts of three influential nineteenth- and early twentieth-century scholars, adds to our earlier focus on seventeenth- and eighteenth-century language ideologies an equal emphasis on metadiscursive practices, "practices of literary communication that actualize modes of cosmopolitan and vernacular belonging" and calibrating and recalibrating the balance between them (Pollock 2000: 595).

Ultimately, sweeping generalizations about the nature of modernity seem less useful to us than discovering how social categories, texts, contexts, forms of knowledge, and social relations are produced and reproduced, legitimized, denigrated, challenged, superseded, and often revived in discourse-oriented terms. Just as discovering how science was made involves learning how air pumps were operated (and by whom), tracing how tradition and language were created and mobilized in the symbolic construction of modernity demands the close examination of discursive, textual, and traditionalizing practices and the texts in which they were articulated. Ways of speaking and writing make social classes, genders, races, and nations seem real and enable them to elicit feelings and justify relations of power, making subalterns seem to speak in ways that necessitate their subordination.

We are interested in people who created new regimes of metadiscursive ideology and practice, who seized new opportunities for imagining and naturalizing language and tradition. Beginning in the seventeenth century with Francis Bacon and ending in the twentieth with Franz Boas, we have sought to identify authors and texts that carved out modes of purification and hybridization that dominated their competitors, shaping economies of social inequality. We want to examine in detail how they achieved their influence, but also at the contradictions of the regimes they sought to promote. In selecting particular examples, we have not focused on the traditional historiographic task of tracing explicit lines of historical influence, though many such lines do in fact link the figures and works we examine and we take explicit note of them in developing our argument.[4] We have rather chosen examples that appear to us to have had a substantial impact on the way that language is conceptualized and used. We have attempted to select authors and issues that are of foundational importance to a wide range of disciplines, including anthropology, folklore, linguistics, literary criticism, and sociology as well as such cross-disciplinary fields as cultural, ethnic, science, and women's studies. It has been necessary to select only a few writers from among the plethora of figures that we would have liked to treat, and it will be easy for readers to challenge our omissions. We can rightly claim, though, that the authors on whom we have focused shaped the politics of language and, to varying degrees, the language of politics in significant ways and played key roles in fashioning the metadiscursive practices that constructed, legitimated, and regulated social inequality in Europe and the United States and many of the regions they dominated for more than two centuries. In particular, they used language to construct and sustain an epochal gap between premodern Others, both internal and foreign, and modern subjects, thereby legitimating the social and political ascendancy of the latter and the practices that held social inequality in place.[5]

---

[4] Fortunately, we can rely on the work of a wide range of intellectual historians in most of the cases we detail. For example, Hans Aarsleff (1982) details relationships between authors who present ideologies of language, as the title of his work suggests, *From Locke to Saussure*. We can also rely on the extensive historical research of George W. Stocking, Jr. (1968, 1974, 1992) for information on Franz Boas and his generation.

[5] We do not mean to imply, however, that these writers explicitly and in every case argued in favor of the exclusion or exploitation of their social subordinates. In particular, Franz Boas sounded a clear anti-racist voice in academic and public life in the United States. The story is thus far more complex, involving the construction of difference and its connection with metadiscursive practices that privilege certain modes of producing, circulating, and receiving discourse while at the same time stigmatizing and controlling other modes; we suggest that this process has real social and political effects.

2 Making language and making it safe for science and society: from Francis Bacon to John Locke

For writers who like to tell the story of modernity in terms of a powerful rupture that took place in the seventeenth century, Francis Bacon provides a compelling point of departure. Not given to modest claims, Bacon entitled one of his works (published in 1620) the *Novum Organum*, seeking to pull the mantle off Aristotle's *Organon* (1949) and to displace "ancient philosophy" and the way it was used in colleges and universities of the day as a basis for inquiry, thereby establishing his own claim to fashion knowledge "anew from the very foundations" (1860b: 52). Bacon played a key role in the invention of nature, in the carving out of a domain that excluded humans and simultaneously seemed to be made just for them – to harness and control for their own mental and material progress. Providing a social and philosophical charter for experimental work, Bacon argued that nature tends to hide or obscure some of "her" properties; it is accordingly best to observe nature "under constraint and vexed; that is to say, when by art and the hand of man she is forced out of her natural state, and squeezed and molded" (1860b: 246). Experiments are thus needed to isolate the property in question and to force nature to reveal "her" secrets; the role of sense data could be limited to judging the results of the experiment. Thus, both nature "herself" as well as the masculinized experience of "her" must be rendered "artificial," as Bacon puts it, carefully controlled and decontextualized *vis-à-vis* the way they intersect in daily life. Bacon's vision promised to bestow material prosperity by letting "the human race recover that right over nature which belongs to it by divine bequest" (1860b: 115); in other words, only by separating nature and society could people get down to the real work of producing useful hybrids. Beyond engendering technological advances, scientific knowledge could lay the basis for a utopian patriarchal and rational society that would enjoy the dominion over nature that had been lost in the expulsion from paradise. Evelyn Fox Keller (1985) and Carolyn Merchant (1980) argue that Bacon's epistemology amounts to a sexualized cartography that grants men dominion over nature – and women.

Even if Bacon may not have been thoroughly modern, in Latour's terms, he played a key role in bringing modernity into being. Bacon inspired the men who half a century later formed the Royal Society, inspiring them to chart nature and to create the experimental tools they would need to do it. He pioneered the magic of scalar effects, the notion that experiments conducted with finite materials in particular times and places could yield knowledge that applied to nature everywhere and at all times. His vision was technologically and industrially oriented – it provided a blueprint for playing these scalar effects in reverse – in the course of embodying general principles in specific devices that could perform concrete works of material advantage for their owners. This is not to say, however, that Bacon's enormous success sprung from his own scientific discoveries or even providing guidance to future experimenters. Randall Collins (1998: 564) suggests that Bacon rather opened up "an autonomous attention space" that was carefully distinguished from past and other contemporary approaches. He became an exemplary "propagandist for the future development of science" by proclaiming that the crucial means and end lay in "the art of discovery" itself (ibid.).

What theorists of modernity have failed to see, however, is that Bacon did not contribute directly to a modern construction of language, that is, to its containment in an autonomous realm set apart from things and social relation. Indeed, he seemed to think that language – at least in its "natural" state – could not become part of the modern project. His contribution to modernizing language was rather to depict it as perhaps the greatest *obstacle* to modernity and progress. Linking perceived linguistic disorder closely with the political threats to the royalist order with which he was so closely identified, Bacon not only alarmed succeeding generations regarding language's anti-modern character but convinced many natural philosophers that the only solution lay in creating a philosophical grammar and universal language – an artificial code that would circumvent the defects of its natural cousin.

Francis Bacon and the scientific mistrust of language

As is well known, Bacon advances the claim that knowledge is gained through the senses. Far from championing the importance of sensory experience of the world, however, Bacon's epistemology asserts that "the sense by itself is a thing infirm and erring" (1860b: 58). The senses constitute a "false mirror" (1860b: 54) in that an individual's character, education, and social interaction distort the nature of things. In short, the reflexive character of sensory experience renders it unreliable; only by decontextualizing one's experience of the world *vis-à-vis* specific situational, discursive, personal, social, political, and historical circumstances could it become a reliable means of obtaining scientifically valid information.

Bacon then propounds a new method of induction that groups "particulars" derived from observation and experimentation into levels of abstraction that stretch from lesser axioms to middle axioms and then to general axioms. Contrary to simplistic readings of Bacon, he specifically argues against the notion that knowledge can be produced by simply adding one particular to another; he rather asserts the need for a "closer and purer league" between the experimental and the rational (1860b: 93). Mary Poovey (1998) argues that Bacon did much more than simply promote empiricism or a new way of relating facts and theory. Rather, he envisioned particulars as standing apart from both the way they were commonly experienced and from theories at the same time that he elevated patient observation of the particulars of natural phenomena to the status of evidence that could prove or disprove theories. In other words, he played a crucial part in creating the modern fact.

In presenting his new mode of acquiring knowledge, Bacon specifically rejects the use of logic and rhetoric alone as means of generalizing from sense data. He cautions repeatedly against the use of syllogisms, "For syllogisms consist of propositions, and propositions of words; and words are but the current tokens or marks of popular notions of things" (1860c: 411). While sense data are susceptible to distortion, they are the fundamental source of authoritative knowledge, and they are perfectible. Words, on the other hand, are *intrinsically* unreliable instruments; they can only distort – not contribute – to knowledge.[1]

Natural language could not, for Bacon, be isolated within its own autonomous domain, because it was deeply connected to that "most troublesome" of the "idols" that beset men's minds, the market-place. Rather than being faithful servants of understanding, words can subvert reason and block efforts to bring thought and observation more in line with nature (1860b: 61). "The juggleries and charms of words" cloud reason by providing names for things which do not exist or by creating confused and ill-defined relations between things. Even when they do not create distortion, words are ineffective as tools for representing the world in that "the subtlety of nature is so much greater than the subtlety of words" (1860c: 411). Clear definitions are of little help, as they simply consist of *more* words. As Robert Stillman (1995) argues, Bacon opened up a breach between words and things by equating natural philosophy with reason and natural divisions derived from the nature of things – in opposition

---

[1] See Lisa Jardine (1974) and Robert Stillman (1995) for lucid accounts of Bacon's approach to discourse.

to rhetoric, false philosophies, and language, which were rather tied to imagination and desire.

A strong element of class antagonism emerges in Bacon's rejection of language. For Bacon, standing near the top of the social and political elite of English society (having served as the Chancellor of the Exchequer) not only do words simply codify "popular" or "vulgar" notions of things, but they can prevent "a more acute intellect" from making progress in philosophy and science (1860c: 433). The rebellion of words, according to Bacon, "has rendered philosophy and the sciences sophistical and inactive" (1860b: 61), and "This evil stands in need therefore of a deeper remedy, and a new one" (1860c: 433), namely, a *Novum Organum*, an epistemology in which knowledge derives its authority from experiments and sense data, not deduction, dialogue, or debate. Bacon does not attempt to sever links between language and nature. At the same time that he imagines language as posing perhaps the greatest threat to the work of purification, the crucial task of separating nature/science and society, he suggests that the only hope for containing this powerful source of epistemological disorder is to transform words into direct extensions of the nature of things.

Bacon's view of language is still intrinsically social; language consists of both words and larger units of speech (*contra* Locke's more atomistic view), and both are shaped by social interaction. This social constitution is, of course, precisely the source of Bacon's beef with language. As Stillman (1995) argues, Bacon was specifically concerned with the power of language for reimagining society in ways that were incompatible with the Royalist order that he defended and specifically with the challenges that the House of Commons were issuing to James's rule. Bacon's view of speech as intrinsically prone to licentiousness and conspiracy informed his interventions as James's main guardian over public discourse in the Commons, courts, city, and church. As attorney general, he prosecuted many cases that criminalized unlicensed words.

This is not to say, however, that Bacon did not contribute in any way to the modernization of language. Indeed, he laid out a number of paths that would be pursued later in attempts to make language into a cornerstone of modernity.

First, Bacon anticipated a later locus of modernist views of language by attacking rhetoric. Insofar as he specifically criticized its use in stylistic ornamentation, Bacon's attitude reflected the degree to which rhetoric had been reduced to ornament by the early seventeenth century (see Poovey 1998: 85). Bacon displaced the value of rhetoric in providing conceptual and analytic frameworks for understanding social life and a means of *generating* knowledge; he rather accorded this privilege of place to systematic observation and experimentation. Barilli (1989: 78–80) suggests that although Bacon recognized the practical value of rhetoric, especially in civic affairs, he played a key role in the epistemological relegation of rhetoric to the marginal zones associated with fancy, wit, and imagination. As Lisa Jardine (1974: 218–19) points out, however, Bacon asserted that rhetoric and imagination could work together with reason: "[T]he duty and office of Rhetoric, if it be deeply looked into, is no other than to apply and recommend the dictates of reason to imagination, in order to excite the appetite and will" (1860c: 455). Rhetoric could fulfill its subservient function, however, only when it stayed within its bounds: "The end of rhetoric is to fill the imagination with observations and images, to second reason, and not to oppress it" (1860c: 456). Uday Singh Mehta (1992) argues that controlling the imagination was a central preoccupation of seventh-century English elites. Bacon sought to render rhetoric useful by enlisting it as a tool for submitting the imagination to surveillance and control – thereby curbing dissent.

Bacon's treatment of rhetoric was tied into the same concerns with social, political, and sexual order that shaped his views of nature and mechanical philosophy. Civil conflict could be suppressed as virile men eschewed political and religious disagreement and joined in dominating a feminine and passive, if resistant nature: "Nor is mine a trumpet which summons and excites men to cut each other to pieces with mutual contradictions, or to quarrel and fight with one another; but rather to make peace between themselves, and turning with united forces against the Nature of Things," to storm and occupy her castles and strongholds, and extend the bounds of human empire, as far as God Almighty in his goodness may permit (1860c: 372–73). Bacon's narrative constructs science as a "divine" or "holy" quest undertaken by mature men who progressively "penetrate" "the womb of nature" (1860b: 100), a realm that is as secret and obscure as it is feminine; finding a way through "the outer courts of nature" and "into her inner chambers" (1860b: 42) becomes as much a secular analogy for "entrance into the kingdom of heaven" (1860b: 69) as it is a sexual metaphor. Note that rhetoric and intertextuality as well as science get sexualized in Bacon's work; while science is accorded a solid masculinity, as evident in its ability to beget offspring, rhetoric is impotent at the same time that it is feminine and sensuous.[2]

Second, Bacon attempted to limit the function of speech to reference, to serve as a neutral means of conveying information. Roman Jakobson

---

[2] We do want to distance ourselves, however, from any attempt to literalize obligatory grammatical gender markings in the Latin as indicating a sexualization of philosophical or social domains.

(1960) suggested that language can be used to draw attention to the speaker or writer, the addressee, the acoustic and psychological contact between them, the form of a message (the "poetic function"), and elements of the linguistic code itself in addition to reference. Later writers, such as Dell Hymes (1974), have suggested that other functions are possible. But Bacon sought to define language in terms of the referential function alone. He similarly decried the use of intertextuality in the process of discovery, whereby "a man ... first seeks out and sets before him all that has been said about it by others" (1860b: 80). Intertextuality is nothing more than a series of "contentions and barking disputations," "endless repetitions" (1860b: 84). By building discourse intertextually, scholars not only become incapable of making new contributions to knowledge – they surrender their capacity for independent thought and investigation; they are, to paraphrase Jameson (1972), locked in the prison house of rhetoric.

Third, privileging reference went hand-in-hand with the attack on reflexivity. Language is unavoidably reflexive, in that it embodies the discursive properties that it seeks to regulate. Following Derrida (1974, 1988) we can argue that it constantly generates a surplus or excess, providing a range of messages about linguistic conduct by virtue of its own textual features as well as its referentially coded assertions. Thus, the goal of providing decontextualized, reliable, universal knowledge about the world can never be entirely divorced from society due to the way that language unavoidably comments on itself and its social surround – through such features as tense and aspect forms and deictics (pronouns, demonstratives, and so forth). When authors talk about how their texts were created or tell their readers how they should approach them, works become explicitly reflexive, increasing awareness that narratives about the world are intertwined with the linguistic and social processes in which they are told. Insofar as scientific knowledge is rooted in language, the purification process will accordingly always be problematic, partial, and even self-defeating.

Bacon indeed laid a crucial cornerstone in the modern construction and regulation of language by suggesting that to retain even a foothold in the new order generated by science, language must deny its reflexivity, seeking to draw attention to nature and never to itself. Discourse can only be trusted when it consists of "plain and simple words." As Poovey (1998) suggests, Bacon argued that this simplified language would be maximally functional, economical, and transparent, thereby eliminating conflicts over meaning. Here Bacon reflected a royal linguistic ideology that combined divine linguistic right with a model of the king's speech as bearing an almost pre-Babel transparency (see Stillman 1995). This call for simplifying language, which Locke incorporated into his theoretically quite different perspective, was to constitute one of the foundations of linguistic modernity through to the present. Bacon's lionization of linguistic parsimony provided a central gate-keeping mechanism for controlling which linguistic concepts and practices would be discarded with the worthless ancient philosophies and which would be placed among the modern "foundations" that were providing the basis for an emerging scientific and social order. Bacon accordingly characterized his own discourse as "plain and simple words" (1860b: 92), a model of a purified language that would present less of an obstacle to modernity and progress. In other words, Bacon inaugurated a transformation not only of the content of linguistic ideologies and practices but the conceptual and social basis by which they could be produced and legitimated. Only by becoming alienated from itself could language find a place in the emerging reconfiguration of knowledge and society.

There is a strong element of irony, if not of bad faith, in Bacon's attack on rhetoric, even if it may have been more tempered than that of many of his followers. At the same time that he criticized accepted rhetorical practices, denigrated language, and urged his readers to direct their attention instead to nature, Bacon's success largely lay in providing a new rhetorical model. As we noted, Bacon's innovation did not lie primarily in new techniques of experimentation or modes of writing. Bacon's construction of natural philosophy rather achieved its aura of novelty and secured discursive authority for itself and its author by providing a rhetorical model that defined modern knowledge and regulated how individuals could create and deploy it. At the same time that Bacon depicted the production of knowledge as involving individuals interacting with nature, his schema "both supported and required an entire set of state-sponsored institutions" (Poovey 1998: 102). Bacon's attempt to confine language to a marginal space seems to add up to a return of the repressed, in that the purported weaknesses in language seem to have provided him with the major positive features of his epistemology (Stillman 1995: 94).

Bacon's most sweeping proposal for closing the gap between words and things lay in creating an artificial body of signs that emanated from the nature of things and reflected natural laws and relations in rational and transparent ways. This perfected, universal language would provide a logical model for natural philosophy, a means of controlling the imagination, and a vehicle for preserving political – read monarchical – order. In *De augmentis scientarium* (1860e), Bacon outlined his proposal for such an artificial language based on real characters whose signification will be apparent to speakers of different languages, signs that would be connected by a logical grammar. Nevertheless, he largely left the construction of this model for modern communication to others, including members of the Royal Society (see Stillman 1995).

In the wake of Bacon's works, language continued to be seen as one of – if not the – major stumbling blocks to natural philosophy, knowledge, and modernity. Bacon's artificial language, even if was designed to be insulated from political and religious controversy, was not framed as an autonomous domain – it was directly wedded to nature and to society – that is, to the power of the monarch to designate which speech was authoritative, which was authorized, and which was forbidden. Although he sought to purify natural language of particular sorts of hybrids, those that threatened the king's power, Bacon saw language as too intrinsically connected to things and society to ever become the object of a thorough-going campaign of purification. Indeed Bacon's most lasting contribution, beyond his celebration of "plain and simple words" and his anti-rhetorical rhetoric, may have been to have cast language in such a villainous role that someone would have to come along and rescue it. But language was to face even more ardent and persistent enemies before its savior, John Locke, would appear.

Language and civility in seventeenth-century science

Steven Shapin and Simon Schaffer (1985; Shapin 1994) have illuminated the epistemological and discursive turn that emerged from the experimental approach to mechanical philosophy that was so prominently embodied in the person and work of Robert Boyle. In the *Leviathan*, Thomas Hobbes (1968 [1651]) drew on mechanical philosophy and geometry, in addition to psychological extrapolation from the society in which he lived (see C. B. MacPherson 1962), in claiming to have deduced the principles that underlie the motion of human bodies in political relations. As Latour (1993) suggests, Boyle won and Hobbes lost – science and society came to be defined as separate spheres, each possessing its own set of operating principles. It is important to note that the battle was waged on textual as well as epistemological grounds. Boyle rejected the sort of claim to deductive certainty and overt textual authority advanced by Hobbes in favor of a constructed image of the modest experimenter. As Shapin (1994: 179–80) suggests, Boyle used a range of rhetorical tropes to distance himself from his own texts, reluctantly accepting the role of author only as a means of presenting fragmented and imperfect observations. Rather than framing his work as a coherent theory or definitive interpretation, his experiments were presented as "matters of fact." In doing so, however, these matters of fact came to dominate an emerging public sphere of scientific discourse in which experiments were subjected to the critical

eyes of a number of observers. The public space admitted by the Royal
Society's quarters at Gresham College afforded an epistemological domain that was purportedly depersonalized, such that experimenters and
witnesses performed disinterested personae, rejected personal authority,
and distrusted interpretation in favor of participating in the collective adumbration of matters of fact. Hobbes, who had been excluded, pointed
out that this "public" consisted only of members of the Royal Society and
their guests (Shapin and Schaffer 1985: 113). Shapin (1994) argues that
this process of gate-keeping followed class lines.

In keeping with Bacon's blueprint, Boyle advanced his knowledge
claims in the guise of plain, descriptive, unpretentious prose that contributed to a civil conversation. Discussions within the Royal Society
were presented as models of disinterested, depersonalized exchanges that
could include disagreements but eschewed the sort of dispute and contention that might lead to disorder and conflict. As Shapin (1994) points
out, this metadiscursive regime achieved the dominance in scientific circles that it enjoys through to the present by displacing other practices –
including the Scholastics' celebration of intertextuality and dialogue and
Hobbes's non-experimental and deductive natural philosophy – in favor
of imposing a model of civil conversation that elevated an emergent model
of the Protestant Christian gentlemen to the status of a social and communicative norm. The experimentalists' preeminence in the process of
constructing modernity emerged as much from their success in casting
the discursive and social relations they projected as a model for restoring
social order to a war-torn society as from the particular content of their
discoveries. Their work modeled the need to control language by keeping
its role to a minimum in order to purify science and make it a reliable
basis for modern knowledge.

Even as the discourse that took place under the aegis of the Royal
Society became a privileged social model, language's admission into the
Royal Society was tenuous, begrudging, and contested. Bacon had argued
that the fundamental failing of concepts and words is grounded in their
inferiority to scientific observations and mathematical models as means of
representing the "the nature of things." Distrust of language and textual
authority were inscribed onto the Royal Society by virtue of the adoption
of its motto, *Nullius in verba* "On no man's word." Thomas Sprat went
on in his *History of the Royal Society* to claim that Society members would
free philosophy "not so much, by an solemnity of Laws, or ostentation of
Ceremonies; as by solid Practice, and examples: not, by a glorious pomp
of Words; but by the silent, effectual, and unanswerable Arguments of real
Productions" (1958 [1667]: 62). Rhetoric no longer simply plays second
fiddle to reason, as for Bacon, but becomes its enemy; Sprat asserts that to

dispel falsehoods and reveal truths about nature, Royal Society members "have indeavor'd, to separate the knowledge of *Nature*, from the colours of *Rhetorick*, the devices of *Fancy*, or the delightful deceit of *Fables*" (1958 [1667]: 62). The place of words in the presentation of scientific findings could be taken directly by "Inventions, Motions and Operations" (1958 [1667]: 327).

For a group that wished to distance itself so clearly from language, the Society's activities and publications focused to a surprising degree on language, and this part of their program constituted a key means by which the Fellows sought to demonstrate their usefulness to king and society. The Committee for Improving the English Tongue endeavored to show how natural philosophy could provide a basis for ameliorating the problems that language posed for social, political, and economic order. John Wilkins, who was assigned to supervise this committee, was one of the greatest promoters of the new science in England. He referred to language as one of the "two general curses inflicted on mankind" after the fall from the Garden of Eden (quoted in Aarsleff 1982: 241). Wilkins was also assigned the task of setting forth basic principles for a philosophical language that would not only be universal but, consisting of marks that were tied reliably to the nature of things, would avoid the natural imperfections of languages. His *An Essay Towards a Real Character and a Philosophical Language* (1668), an important Royal Society publication, is advertised in the Epistle Dedicatory, as offering "universal benefits" not only to natural philosophy but to resolving differences in religion, fostering commerce between nations, and promoting social and political order. This artificial language offers a model for decontextualizing and dehistoricizing speech, for transforming what is contextual, shifting, customary, and historically grounded into points in a timeless, universal grid and "to harmonize with the Restoration gentry's ideal of a free commerce of negotiable rights, contracts, and obligations" (Stillman 1995: 17). Wilkins's language amounts to a sort of display of epistemological insecurity, as if natural language did not provide a sufficiently powerful basis for deprovincializing Europe. Even Wilkins's artificial language, which went far beyond Bacon's ambivalent proposal, is cautiously framed as a sketch; it thus amounts to a more elaborate deferral that sustains the idea that language could never really become a solid basis on which to establish modernity.

The preceding discussion of the positions of Bacon and such members of the Royal Society as Sprat and Wilkins underlines the need for more precision with regard to the role of language in the emergence of modernity. These authors can be seen as having modernized language in two senses: as having placed language at the core of problems of order, knowledge, science, and politics and as having fostered a profound distrust of language among elites who endeavored to align themselves with the modern project. Proposals for reducing speech and writing to "plain and simple words," the emergence of an anti-rhetorical rhetoric, and the quixotic ideal of an artificial, universal language promoted a set of pragmatic principles for decontextualizing and dehistoricizing discourse, for making utterances seem to stand apart from the social, political, and historical conditions of their creation. These writers advertised their partial attempts to purify language of its social base as a means of creating more effective hybrids of words and things, and such proposals seemed to further indict language as being intrinsically and problematically social. The threat posed by "the juggleries and charms of words" to reason and order was so fundamental that it could only be controlled; short of adopting an artificial and universal code, language could never stand alongside natural philosophy as being thoroughly modern. In the end, the path to modernity seemed to lie in circumventing language, in connecting the mind more directly to nature. Thus, what Latour identified as the crux of modernity – techniques for purifying relations between nature and society – did not lead automatically and inexorably to a modern view of language. The emergence of a purportedly autonomous realm of language, one that provided the political technologies needed for projecting a cartography of the modern subject of liberal theory, required a substantially different point of departure.

The mission of Locke's *Essay*

Thus, Locke certainly had his work cut out for him in the *Essay Concerning Human Understanding*, a book that attempts to make language a cornerstone of modernity. Locke finished the first two drafts of his *Essay* in 1671, eleven years after the Royal Society was formed (Aarsleff 1982: 45) and some three years after Locke became a member (Cranston 1957: 116). According to the royal charter which it received in 1662, the Royal Society was intended "to be imployed for the promoting of the knowledge of natural things, and useful Arts by Experiments" (quoted in Sprat 1958 [1667]: 134); its members included such luminaries as Robert Boyle, Christopher Wren, Robert Hooke, and Isaac Newton. In his *Essay*, Locke refers to Newton's *Principia* as a "never enough to be admired book" (IV. vii. 11). Aarsleff (1982: 56) suggests that Locke knew and admired Boyle's work more than that of any other individual. After receiving assurance from Christiaan Huygens that Newton's mathematics was reliable, Locke helped to create an image of Newton as a prominent philosopher (A. Rupert Hall 1963: 297, 319). The *Essay* was dedicated to Thomas Herbert, Earl of Pembroke, who was president of the Royal Society when the work appeared in 1690.

Locke prefaces the *Essay* by telling a story of its origin:

> I should tell thee, that five or six friends meeting at my chamber, and discoursing on a subject very remote from this, found themselves quickly at a stand, by the difficulties that rose on every side. After we had awhile puzzled ourselves, without coming any nearer a resolution of those doubts which perplexed us, it came into my thoughts that we took a wrong course; and that before we set ourselves upon inquiries of that nature, it was necessary to examine our own abilities, and see what *objects* our understandings were, or were not, fitted to deal with. (1959 [1690] I: 9).[3]

As Cranston (1957: 117) suggests, Locke seems to have found it more productive to organize a small philosophical circle that met in his quarters on a regular basis than to take an active part in the experimental work of the society; Lord Ashley, later the first Earl of Shaftesbury, appears to have been a prominent member of Locke's circle.

Locke's origin narrative seems to have been designed to rhetorically align Locke with readers who were likely to be skeptical of the virtues of language; he could thereby invite them along with him on an intellectual journey headed in the direction of giving language a positive public face. That it was language that had thrown civil discourse into disarray was a conclusion that Locke's readers were quite likely to accept. Rather than confirming the exclusion of language from modernity, however, Locke used this story in providing a rhetorical opening for an effort to find a secure space for language *within* modernity – and a central one at that. He seeks to legitimize his project by linking it to a master narrative of seventeenth-century England – the story of the individual male philosopher/scientist who finds himself surrounded by disorder and uncertainty. Virtually compelled by these circumstances to set out on a mission to provide a new conceptual foundation, he proposes a model for creating linguistic order and exhorts his readers to promulgate it, or at least to proclaim its legitimacy. As readers, we are placed in the middle of not only the group of "five or six friends" but also in the company of those enlightened souls who are crusading to uproot confusion and disorder. Failing to climb aboard would place us in the position of contributors to misunderstanding and disorder; having been presented with an alternative, we would become willing and knowing promulgators of mayhem.

---

[3] We will cite the *Essay* by placing the book number in upper-case Roman numerals, followed by the chapter number in small Roman numerals, followed by the section number in Arabic numerals. All emphasis is in the original.

In tying the mission of the *Essay* to a discussion that arose in this group, Locke creates an imaginary space that denies its own historical and textual location within writings about language and epistemology; the book seems to spring from a reasoned encounter with the nature of things, not from a relationship with other texts and writers. Nevertheless, in his Epistle to the Reader, Locke suggests that his efforts were prompted by a widespread conviction that the abuses of language had degraded philosophy to such a degree that it impeded the advance of knowledge and "was thought unfit or incapable to be brought into well-bred company and polite conversation" (Epistle I: 14). Locke thus characterizes his *Essay*, a founding document of linguistic and semiotic inquiry and a major epistemological statement, as an effort to make language and human understanding safe for science – and society. He begins by admitting his readers' skepticism and the immensity of the task that confronts him.

While Locke may have inherited the fundamental problem with which he struggled, his proposed solution was brilliant and largely original. If language was to be saved, it must be made to function like more authoritative or "certain" forms of knowledge. Turning this notion on its head, Locke argues that the value of language for acquiring knowledge lies in its fundamental *difference* from the means by which we could come to know nature; reforming language thus involves developing a greater and more systematic appreciation of its particular nature rather than trying to make it look more like mechanical philosophy. He similarly asserts that language can – and must – be separated from society; purifying language of ties to particular social positions, interests, and from differences between human beings in general is a central mission of the *Essay*. *Contra* many of his fellow members of the Royal Society, Locke claims that language is essentially reliable, or at least that it can become so; its well-established dangers arose from the production of hybrids, from attempts to embed language either within nature or society. By investigating the "original" of ideas in an effort "to show what *knowledge* the understanding hath by those ideas" (Introduction I: 28), Locke sought to provide a foundation for his efforts to chart a new province of the emerging world of modern knowledge. The practices of purification that lie at the heart of the *Essay*, tools for stripping language of direct connections to things or social forms, would come to form some of the most important bases for constructing modern subjects in terms of their rationality and their ability to speak within the public sphere – and thus for evaluating each individual and community and determining his or her proper place in the emerging social order. Ironically, Locke thus simultaneously modeled the production of language–nature–society hybrids that would naturalize power and inequality as differences of linguistic ability.

The *Essay* – and the modernization of language in general – sought to do far more than to change the ideologies of language constructed in learned texts. Locke created a new regime that required each individual to closely monitor his or her own linguistic repertoire and each and every utterance. Individuals who had submitted themselves to his linguistic regimen earned the right to regiment the speech of others, to model linguistic precision and constancy and to point out the errors of their fellows. Following Foucault (1991), we can say that Locke created a powerful set of practices of purification that constructed a new form of governmentality, a metadiscursive regime that drew on assertions regarding the nature of language in regulating linguistic conduct and imbuing some ways of speaking and writing with authority while rendering other modes a powerful source of stigma and exclusion. Since this regime seemed to flow directly from the essential properties of language, it became a powerful means of naturalizing emergent forms of social inequality. Having constructed language as a separate and self-contained domain of human conduct, Locke could then draw on his linguistic program as an undisclosed basis for shaping economic, religious, scientific, and political principles and for requiring individuals to internalize them – if they wished to be considered modern subjects. Locke's work is thus brilliant, turning a denigrated subject into a seemingly independent source of power and using it to transform other means of constructing and regulating modern forms of inequality. Much of Locke's legacy has simply become common sense, even for individuals who challenge his political program or attempt to divorce themselves from modernity itself. Indeed, Hans Aarsleff's (1982) history of linguistic thought takes Locke's project as constituting the basis for scientific knowledge of language, and he measures each subsequent author in terms of his or her contribution to the work of purification – as culminating in the work of that modern prophet of linguistic modernism, Ferdinand de Saussure (1959). The emergence of language as a modern domain in the *Essay Concerning Human Understanding* is seldom perceived – since its existence and legitimacy are generally taken for granted. It is accordingly crucial to examine Locke's anti-rhetorical rhetoric in detail if we are to gain critical awareness of how another dimension of consciousness has been colonized by a modern formulation, Lockean linguistics.

Towards a doctrine of signs

Perhaps the clearest announcement of Locke's goal in the essay of establishing language as a modern domain lies in the *Essay*'s final sentence:

For a man can employ his thoughts about nothing, but either, the contemplation of *things* themselves, for the discovery of truth; or about the things in his own power, which are his own *actions*, for the attainment of his own ends; or the *signs* the mind makes use of both in the one and the other, and the right ordering of them, for its clearer information. All which three, viz. *things*, as they are in themselves knowable; *actions* as they depend on us, in order to happiness; and the right use of *signs* in order to knowledge, being *toto coelo* different, they seemed to me to be the three great provinces of the intellectual world, wholly separate and distinct one from another. (IV. xxi. 4)

Having declared a new cartography for the modern world, one that grants language the same importance as nature/science and society/politics and yet grants it autonomy, Locke defines his "doctrine of signs" as concerned with "the nature of signs, the mind makes use of for the understanding of things, or conveying its knowledge to others" (ibid.). How can he reach this point, knowing that his readers believed that language could not be extricated from either nature or society?

Locke begins by turning efforts to make words stand directly for things on their head. He argues that we can never know the internal constitution of things, what he refers to as "real essences"; the common view that words stand "for the reality of things" is accordingly mistaken. In building his theory of conventional and arbitrary associations between words and ideas, Locke distinguishes words that stand for simple ideas and general words. Simple ideas are products of sensation, "those impressions objects themselves make on our minds" (III. iv. 11). Their meaning is accordingly determined by sense experience, not defined through language. While the mind is more passive in forming simple ideas, it does not simply reflect things or sensations. A simple idea of an apple is abstracted from any set of particular apples; in its formation, information is selected from the available range of sensory impressions. Even in this limiting case, a modern theory of language divorces words from things, particularly from singular objects as viewed in terms of their uniqueness and sociohistorical location.

Most words are, in contrast, general terms, which are created by the mind through combining a number of simple ideas. Since the mind is free to combine simple ideas that are not associated in nature, it necessarily selects certain sensory characteristics and rejects others. "Mixed modes" refer directly to "ideas in the mind" rather than to things in the world, even though the process of construction is ultimately retraceable through reflection. This conception allows Locke to retain a Baconian commitment to the primacy of sense data while at the same time suggesting that they play a vastly different role in language than in knowledge of "*things* themselves." It also provides him with an epistemological foundation on which to base his claim for the autonomy of language from nature and mechanical philosophy; language can be purified only by appreciating the way that words are abstracted from the world, not by learning more about the physical properties of things themselves or the laws that govern them. Hans Aarsleff (1982) stresses the importance of Locke's theory of language in countering premodern views of words as signs of the inner nature of things, as thereby tied to mysticism, magic, and alchemy. Locke's notion that signs are arbitrary, tied to ideas in the mind rather than directly to things, provided a powerful means of asserting the primacy of modern knowledge – grounded in the autonomy of language and nature – over the conflations of language and nature generated by mystical, premodern perspectives and practices. Here Locke's purification project helped discredit supposedly premodern views of the nature of things, thereby making a major contribution to a modern epistemology that relegated some ideologies and practices to the realm of magic and tradition and declared their defeat and displacement by the scientific perspective championed by his fellow members of the Royal Society.

Locke repeatedly discusses the central role of abstraction in the creation of general names. The abstract ideas that mediate between simple ideas and general names are derived by factoring out the particulars through which each simple idea differs and "retaining only those wherein they agree" (III. iii. 9). Locke points specifically to the crucial importance of abstraction from physical, social and linguistic contexts: "Words become general by being made the signs of general ideas: and ideas become general, by separating from them the circumstances of time and place, and any other ideas that may determine them to this or that particular existence" (III. iii. 6). Truth and abstraction are one: "Truth, then seems to me . . . to signify nothing but the joining or separating of Signs" (IV. v. 2). Locke repeatedly turns to mathematics as a model for language in view of its ability to use economical, basic terms with precisely defined values in generating universal, certain propositions (see for example 1966: 70, 91). The equation of language with abstraction is rationalized in part by the need for economy. Noting that "the true end of speech . . . is to be the easiest and shortest way of communicating our notions" (III. vi. 33), Locke argues that the ability to encompass a number of particulars within a general class enables us to avoid wasting "our time and breath in tedious descriptions" (III. vi. 30). In privileging abstraction, Locke goes on to argue that "*things* themselves" are only particulars; directly contemplating things is accordingly incapable of yielding universal knowledge. Words, on the other hand, are signs of general classes created by the mind; once general terms have been combined in propositions, it is possible to derive conclusions that are universal, certain, and eternal, which Locke sees as the goal of philosophy.

Experimentation did not provide Locke with a means of elevating language to a privileged status or marking it as quintessentially modern, as was the case for mechanical philosophy. To make the passage into modernity – and to create a purified language that could serve as means of mapping social inequality – language had to match the power of experimentation and the prestige of Boyle's air pump for turning isolated particulars into universal icons. Separating words from things and placing abstraction, decontextualization, and generalization at the heart of language provide Locke with a means of matching the claims of mechanical philosophy while at the same time declaring language's autonomy and purity. In the end, words are not intrinsically pure *or* hybrid. The task of purification rather lies in metadiscursive practices, techniques for controlling and modifying it in ways that make speech seem to stand apart from the circumstances in which it was produced and received as well as from any particular things. This is, of course, a quintessentially cosmopolitan view, in that it sought to free language from any connection to concrete circumstances and parochial concerns. Locke's construction of language fashions it into a necessary foundation for cosmopolitanism.

Purification functioned like Boyle's air pump and other laboratory equipment in enabling Locke to tackle the problem of scale. Latour (1988) argues in the case of Pasteur's work on microbes that scientists remove the tremendous complexities that surround problems by relocating them in the laboratory, in which they are reduced to a few basic entities and processes; they then make the results seem universal by projecting these simplifications back out into the world. Locke similarly tackled the problem of scale, of making observations that reflected individual experiences seem universal, by virtue of the way he defined signs (as abstracted from sense data), the purification practices that extirpated any remaining connections to particular things or people, and the dissemination of purified signs through pedagogy.

Paradoxically, the importance of language once it has been purified lies both in its autonomy and in its centrality to any question for attempts to derive truth, universality, and certainty in any other domain of knowledge. Rather than providing the downfall of science, language becomes the necessary foundation for scientific discovery. Locke frames his work in the Epistle with a disclaimer of performer, a humbling assertion that his role was confined to that of "an under-labourer in clearing the ground a little, and removing some of the rubbish that lies in the way to knowledge" (1959 [1690] I: 14) for such "master-builders" in "the commonwealth of learning" as Boyle, Huygens, and Newton. But this show of humility seems to lure readers into the clutches of a garden-path argument that leads them to the conclusion that only by adopting Locke's ideology of language and practices of purification can the stars of the Royal Society hope to provide certain, universal knowledge. The language that comes to be autonomous and, in the end, to form a necessary basis for scientific discovery is one that, Locke asserted, did not yet exist – it not only had to be invented but had to be constantly disciplined by metadiscursive practices of purification.

The "cheat and abuse" of words

Locke may have taken a step towards solving the problem of the conflation of language with nature, but the embeddedness of language in society posed an equally important challenge to language's legitimacy. Purifying language from society involved a complex process of redefining language in such a way that its social embeddedness could be construed as peripheral, pathological, and suppressible at the same time that a purified core could be elevated to the status of the privileged mode of generating knowledge.[4]

Like any effective rhetorical program, Locke needed a succinct and morally charged phrase that could be used in encapsulating all the elements that he sought to purify. Whether or not Locke had read Hobbes on this point, he based his attack on what Hobbes referred to as "abuses" of words, which he traced (*inter alia*) to semantic "inconstancy" and to metaphor (Hobbes 1968 [1651]: 102). Hobbes (1968 [1651]: 109) argued that "the diversity of our reception" of words "gives everything a tincture of our different passions"; we must accordingly be leery of speech in that words "have a signification of the nature, disposition, and interest of the speaker" (ibid.). While Hobbes saw the tension between passion and reason at the heart of his nominalist political linguistics, Locke sought to expunge desire from the domain of language. For Locke, "the cheat and abuse of words" became a central focus of the essay and a rhetorical catch-all for aspects of language that seemed to be intrinsically

---

[4] We differ here with Taylor's (1990b) suggestion that Locke viewed language as fundamentally flawed. While Locke clearly had misgivings about language, his goal was precisely to identify a core of language that escaped these natural imperfections and to create a reformist movement and to develop pedagogical strategies capable of creating subjects who possessed a perfected language. Similarly, while Locke's ideology of language is certainly individualistic, we attempt to show that he viewed language as playing a crucial role in constituting society and social institutions. In short, it is necessary to see how he helped create schemes for the production of hybrids as well as how he advocated purism. See also Formigari (1988, 1993) on Locke's philosophy of language and its historical context.

tied to society. Locke equates the use of one word in several senses and contextual variation with cheating and misrepresentation in the marketplace; this analogy becomes particularly provocative in the light of the moral and legal sanctions Locke was to recommend in *Further Considerations concerning raising the Value of Money* (1714 [1695]a) for counterfeiting and other types of fraud that challenged the authority of the state to ensure contracts (see Caffentzis 1989).

Locke perceived that the effort to wrench language from society, as from nature, hinged on a process of decontextualization. Insofar as words were explicitly tied to particular speakers and writers, hearers and readers, contexts of production and reception, and other social activities, the work of purification could not begin. In imagining how language is built from sensations by individual minds – the construction he used in extracting it from nature – Locke placed a crucial constraint on "the free choice of the mind" in creating signs. Words must be used identically by producer and receiver in order "to convey the precise notions of things." Maintaining a rigid one-to-one correspondence between sound and meaning is, accordingly to Locke, requisite for communication: "It is plain cheat and abuse, when I make [words] stand sometimes for one thing and sometimes for another" (III. x. 5). Locke's purification efforts here paralleled contemporary efforts to overcome widespread distrust of books with respect to questions of authorship, authenticity, and the reliability of texts (see Johns 1994).

The thrust of Locke's project here can be usefully characterized in terms of Charles S. Peirce's (1932) famous trichotomy of signs, which distinguishes *indexes*, which are tied to contextual relations, *icons*, which link sign vehicles and their objects through perceptual similarity (such as the word *oink* and the sounds produced by pigs), and *symbols*, which revolve around arbitrary, context-free referential relations between sign vehicles and objects of representation. Locke attempted to reduce language to symbolic meaning. Indexicality constituted the primary source of language's problematic links to society; he argued that indexicality was not a part of language's basic constitution but rather was introduced through human action, thereby undermining communication and social order. To reduce language to the symbolic mode thus became the central means of purifying it – and of making modernity possible.

One of the reasons that Bacon saw speech as intrinsically social is that he imagined language as comprised not just of words but of larger discursive units as well. Locke saw atomism as crucial to declaring the autonomy of language and seeking to purify it of any intrinsic link to society. His definition of the linguistic domain reduced language to signs by fiat. *Contra* Latour's (1993: 88) assertion that modernity constituted language as the domain of stories, texts, and discourses, Locke asserted that when relations between words became even relatively fixed as metaphors, figures of speech, or texts, trouble was sure to follow. The importance of this foundational step for constructing a theory of speech that was not tied to particular languages, speakers, rhetorical forms, poetic or narrative genres, or historical circumstances is profound. While genres, stories, and widely circulated texts seem to be intrinsically connected to social units, words provided good candidates for purification. Language was powerfully reimagined as a question of individual words spoken by individual speakers.

What is the chief source of language's contamination? As for Bacon, intertextuality lies at the core of unacceptable metadiscursive practices. Although Hobbes and Boyle clashed centrally on the role of deduction *versus* experimentation in generating authority, they both condemned, as Hobbes put it, the way that words become "the mony of fooles, that value them by the authority of an Aristotle, a Cicero, or a Thomas, or any other Doctor whatsoever, if but a man" (1968 [1651]: 106). Hobbes denigrated persons who rely on intertextuality and distinguished them from the virtuous followers of science: "So that in the right Definition of Names, lyes the first use of Speech; which is the Acquisition of Science: And in wrong or no Definitions, lyes the first abuse; from which proceed all false and senslesse Tenets; which make those men that take their instruction from the authority of books, and not from their own meditation, to be as much below the condition of ignorant men, as men endued with true Science are above it" (ibid.). Intertextuality is thus closely connected with semantic imprecision and instability, that is, with indexicality. Laslett (1960: 87) suggests that Locke copied this quotation, without citation, onto the flyleaf of a volume in his library.

Locke argues that discourse produced through explicitly intertextual links is grounded indexically in particular texts, persons, and activities. Beyond being incapable of producing the abstract, general thinking that constitutes knowledge, such practices simply provide a cover for semantic indeterminacy, shifting definitions, weak arguments, and imperfections of knowledge. Locke strongly attacked textual authority itself. When texts become authoritative, he asserted, they encourage uncritical repetition at the expense of knowledge and comprehension. While textual authority is dialogic, involving social and discursive relationships, knowledge is monologic, individual, rational, and universal. Intertextual connections embedded language inextricably in society. Banishing intertextuality from the province of language and creating practices designed to suppress it were thus necessary not only for legitimating Locke's claim for language's autonomy and practices of purification but also for consolidating a modern ideology of knowledge as produced by individual men as they pressed the world around them to yield its secrets.

Accordingly, Locke believed that the chain of signifiers must be broken and ideas derived from texts indexically severed from the author's authority and the discourses articulated by other people and in other times (III. ix. 9–10). Locke's rejection of the notion of innate ideas was similarly tied to the conviction that a set of central, innate notions would constitute a fixed intertextual basis for the production and interpretation of discourse. Knowledge must rather be internalized by each individual through rational reflection at the same time that it is externalized by connecting it, through observation and sense perception, with reality. Otherwise, individuals will be discursively dependent on others "without being steady and settled in their own judgments" (1966: 67). A person's reading "makes his understanding only the warehouse of other men's lumber" (1966: 93), a capitalist metaphor that relates cognitive and economic forms of productivity. Locke suggested that it is particularly difficult to extirpate intertextually based practices because people learn new words in conversation without being certain of their meaning; language socialization fundamentally involves the interpersonal transmission of linguistic knowledge. The words then retain these unthinking assumptions through the force of "custom," depriving "men" of their common sense and filling their heads with "some independent ideas, of no alliance to one another, [that] are, by education, custom, and the constant din of their party, so coupled in their minds that they always appear there together" (II. xxxiii. 18). Language socialization thus becomes a site of danger for modernity, a space into which tradition naturally creeps and in which the intrinsic dangers of language are naturally reproduced and even extended. An educational program was thus needed to break this process, becoming a crucial foundation for modernity; we will examine Locke's pedagogical proposals in a moment.

The discursive practices promoted by members of the Royal Society were modeled on the civil conversation of gentlemen. Gentle speech was reliable due to the disinterested demeanor of its author and his – and we do mean his – freedom from being constrained by or needing to rely on the will of other individuals. Authorizing one's own work by citing another writer and text thus not only diminished its credibility but located the author in an inferior position within a class-based hierarchy. In a similarly individualistic and utilitarian metaphor, intertextuality is compared to "borrowed wealth" and "fairy money," which cannot be used as currency and "make no considerable addition to [one's] stock" (I. iii. 24). Recall Bacon's (1860a: 14) metaphor of sexual reproduction in disparaging the "barren" lack of "issue" associated with Scholastic discourse. Ironically, Locke spent many many hours engaged precisely in acts of intertextuality – his large collection of notebooks were largely filled with citations of other men's books; Laslett (1960: 87) tells us that these intertextual labors were "referenced and arranged with monumental carefulness." Locke's quarters thus seem to have been a vast "warehouse of other men's lumber"! The work of purification thus involved rendering intertextual endeavors invisible, carefully decontextualizing one's writing and speech from its connections with other texts.

Society was not the only hybridizing threat posed to language's autonomy through intertextuality. As we will argue in Chapter 3, a key opposition between modern subjectivity – including nature/science, society, and language – was tradition. The modern production of knowledge as the product of individual men reflecting on individual objects in order to create universal, abstract, general knowledge that could be conveyed – largely through written texts – to cosmopolitan modern subjects was contrasted with its nemesis, tradition. Locke conceived of tradition as intertextually constituted, a chain of testimonies, each successive link of which stands at a farther remove from the experiential base of true knowledge. He suggests:

[A]ny testimony, the further off it is from the original truth, the less force and proof it has. The being and existence of the thing itself, is what I call the original truth. A credible man vouching his knowledge of it, is a good proof: but if another equally credible, do witness it from his report, the testimony is weaker; and a third that attests from hearsay of an hearsay, is yet less considerable. So that *in traditional truths, each remove weakens the force of the proof*: and the more hands the tradition has successively passed through, the less strength and evidence does it receive from them. (IV. xvi. 10)

Locke perceives that traditional authority rests on a metadiscursive foundation – in the course of denying its legitimacy. This is a resonant moment in the advent of modernity, as Locke advances the "rational man" as the arbiter of "authentic truths," displacing "men… [who] look on opinions to gain force by growing older" (ibid.). Drawing on English law as an evidential model, Locke imposes a standard, which he refers to as "the original truth; each step away from personal, direct knowledge in the direction of intertextuality constitutes a move away from 'assurance' in the direction of belief, conjecture, guess, doubt, wavering, distrust, disbelief, &c." (ibid.). Intertextuality thus posed a double obstacle to making language autonomous, modern, and cosmopolitan, embedding it both in society and parochial tradition. Small wonder that for Locke, as for Bacon, intertextuality was high on the list of threats to language and modernity.

Linguistic reform and social inequality

In Locke's view, language becomes somewhat schizophrenic, possessed of a pure core that is firmly rooted in modernity but beset on all sides by human practices that threaten to embed language in nature, society, and tradition; language, when it becomes compromised in this fashion, poses a threat to social and political order. But even as Locke pretends to wrest language from society, his model reinserts language and the work of purification into a powerful social cartography, creating hybrids that mark myriad forms of social inequality. Some people, it turns out, seem to gravitate naturally towards the pure and modern side of language, while others are inextricably enmeshed in the "cheat and abuse of words." As Locke creates a reform program for language, he asserts – in advance – that its unfolding will serve to widen this social chasm.

Locke suggests that language operates distinctly in civil and philosophical spheres. While the *civil use* of words "may serve for the upholding of common conversation and commerce, about the ordinary affairs and conveniences of civil life," their *philosophical use* revolves around communicating "the precise notions of things" and general propositions regarding "certain and undoubted truths" (III. ix. 3). Locke suggests that the requirements for semantic precision and referential constancy are more stringent in the philosophical domain, while "vulgar notions suit vulgar discourses.... Merchants and lovers, cooks and tailors, have words wherewithal to dispatch their ordinary affairs" (III. xi. 10).[5] While Locke notes with respect to the process of stabilizing and strictly delimiting significations that "it would be well, too, if it extended itself to common conversation and the ordinary affairs of life" (III. xi. 10), he seems to doubt that individuals who must devote themselves to "ordinary affairs" are likely to benefit directly from linguistic reform. The task of purifying language, of severing its ties to nature and society, is thus marked from the start as an elite enterprise, one that is to be undertaken by the elite for their own benefit; Locke clearly projects that while the fruits of this process for the elite will be substantial, other classes will largely be left out in the cold.

Locke's treatment of understanding and language provide a strong cognitive and linguistic foundation for his doctrine of natural rights. All persons are born with "faculties and powers" that would enable them to

---

[5] Shapin (1994: 207–8) quotes Locke's words to the effect that a conventional approximation of epistemological certainty is all that is needed "in the ordinary affairs of life" (IV. xi. 10). Locke seems less interested in accepting a general lowering of standards for referential specificity and verifiability, however, than in privileging philosophical – and gentle – discourses by placing them in a separate, privileged epistemological domain.

cultivate their understanding and heighten their linguistic precision. Not everyone subjects himself or herself, however, to the "much time, pains, and skill, strict inquiry, and long examination" (III. vi. 30) required for this process of linguistic reflection and reasoning. Locke makes it clear that social class, occupation, and gender create sharp differences in the ability of individuals to reason, the breadth of their understanding, and the degree of verbal competence they achieve. "The day labourer in a country village has commonly but a small pittance of knowledge because his ideas and notions have been confined to the narrow bounds of a poor conversation and employment" (1966: 39); "men of low and mean education" are similarly "no more capable of reasoning than almost a perfect natural" (1966: 50). One of Locke's clearest statements in this regard appears in *The Reasonableness of Christianity*:

> The greatest part of Mankind have not leisure for Learning and Logick, and superfine Distinctions of the Schools. Where the Hand is used to the Plough and the Spade, the Head is seldom elevated to sublime Notions, or exercised in mysterious Reasoning. 'Tis well if Men of that Rank (to say nothing of the other Sex) can comprehend plain Propositions, and a short Reasoning about Things familiar to their Minds, and nearly allied to their daily Experience. Go beyond this, and you amaze the greatest part of Mankind: And may as well talk Arabick to a poor day Labourer, as the Notions and Language that the Books and Disputes of Religion are filled with. (1714 [1695]b, II: 540)

Ever a student of how class differences are written on the body, Locke mobilizes the opposition between physical labor and mental activity in arguing that "the greatest part of mankind" is only capable of an elementary form of reasoning that is confined to immediate, concrete phenomena that surround him – and her.

Philosophers, truth seekers, and gentlemen, on the other hand, *must* develop their understanding, rationality, and verbal skills. The relevance of gender as well as social class is clear. Locke notes that women, like men whose business is confined to common life, can appropriately develop verbal skills entirely by rote; gentlemen and philosophers, on the other hand, should master grammatical rules and perfect the stylistic features of their speech (1989 [1693]: 224). As we ascend the social ladder in terms of both class and rank, consciousness of linguistic structure and language use becomes not only more possible but increasingly necessary. The development of reasoning and linguistic precision are limited by the range of experiences gained through one's occupation and the amount of leisure time available; laborers have little or no spare time that can be devoted to reflecting on and practicing precision in language and reasoning. Locke argues that "We are born with faculties and powers capable of almost anything...; but it is only the exercise of those powers which give us ability and skill in anything, and leads us towards perfection" (1966: 41–42). Locke observed long ago that social class is inscribed on the body as much as it is on the tongue in suggesting that it is training and practice that create differences in "carriage and language" between a middle-aged plowman and a gentleman (1966: 42). People's ability "to reason well or speak handsomely" are limited by the extent to which they have access to the metadiscursive practices that instill such competence. Thus for Locke, the task of purifying language cannot be left to a few writers and confined to treatises – it rather becomes a central question of modern discipline and governmentality, a constant focus of daily life.

This self-disciplining process must be extended interpersonally: "In discourse with others, (if we find them mistake us,) we ought to tell what the complex idea is that we make such a name stand for" (III. xi. 24). The inverse is true as well, such that the linguistically unreformed pose a conceptual if not social danger: "He that uses words without any clear and steady meaning" may "lead himself and others into errors," and thus "ought to be looked on as an enemy to truth and knowledge" (III. xi. 5). While Locke stresses linguistic self-discipline, he makes it clear that the purifying process accords individuals the right to discipline others; bonding together in a joint effort to make our words clear and ensure that we use them identically, we are "not to be unwilling to have them examined by others" (III. v. 16). The linguistically enlightened can also play a special role in policing the language acquisition of children, "diligently to watch, and carefully to prevent the undue connexion of ideas in the minds of young people" (I: 531); linguistic surveillance becomes a key dimension of the pedagogical program that Locke advocates. Purification emerges both as hegemony, the internalization of discipline, and as linguistic coercion.

In the Epistle Dedicatory to *Some Thoughts Concerning Education*, Locke argues that the most care should be devoted to the education of gentlemen, "For if those of that Rank are by their Education once set right, they will quickly bring all the rest into Order" (1989 [1693]: 80). We might thus say that Locke pioneered a "trickle down" theory of education, asserting that affording linguistic advantages to elites will eventually provide direct benefits to even the least advantaged. Like other trickle down theories, it was designed to fail. Locke's new imagination of language as a stable, autonomous, referential core that was surrounded by practices amounting to cheat and abuse and his creation of techniques for suppressing the latter provided a powerful device for generating and naturalizing social inequality. Practices of linguistic purification ironically became key social hybrids in that they placed a vital aspect of the creation of modernity in the hands of the elite and designated its fruits as a means of ensuring the reproduction of their social, political, and economic capital. Women, the poor, country people, and non-Europeans were excluded from the contexts and practices needed to participate in this reproduction process; epistemological assertion that all humans possessed language and the capacity for rational thought, the reformist claim that everyone should participate in purification, and the ideological individualization of the process ensured that the perceived failure of most of the people in the world to rationalize their linguistic practices could be blamed on these individuals themselves. Language became a key means for creating new forms of exclusion and their ideological conversion into means of explaining the perceived intellectual and moral failure of women, the poor, country people, and non-Europeans. The task of purifying language created language-society hybrids and networks that continue to play a key role in creating and sustaining social inequality and exclusion. As the sinister effects of differential access to educational resources in keeping with social class, race, gender, and immigration status are felt more and more acutely around this world, it seems worthwhile to reflect for a moment on the location of Locke's influential call for education – as a means of counteracting the way that language socialization multiplied the "natural imperfections" of language – in reproducing and extending social inequality.

Extending the attack on rhetoric

For Locke, as for Bacon, the discursive practices that are antithetical to rationality and science are embodied in language's *bête noire*, rhetoric, particularly as it emerged in the Scholastic "art of disputation." Locke's *Essay* greatly extends Bacon's theoretical demotion of rhetoric, even seeking to limit severely the *practical* value of rhetorical training. Bacon uses rhetoric in confirming his view of language as essentially flawed; for Locke, on the other hand, the exclusion of rhetoric serves as a foil to bring into high relief what he viewed as the core of language. According to Locke, rhetoric fosters unexamined, imprecise uses of language that are ordered through intertextual and other types of indexical linkages. Since it confounds meaning, "the admired Art of Disputing hath added much to the natural imperfection of languages" (III. x. 6) and kept "even inquisitive men from true knowledge" (III. x. 10). While the use of such epithets as "the admired Art of Disputing" are hardly original to Locke, in post-Civil War England they must have evoked powerful moral and political associations between discursive and civil disorder, and Locke seems to have mustered these overtones in advancing his program of linguistic purification.

Rhetoric becomes the foe of rationality and knowledge through its connection with interest, passion, emotionality, and belief. Locke's ideal discursive type – plain speech that conveys information with maximum economy through referentially stable signs – actively engages the rational capacity of the mind. Rhetoric and its devices (metaphor, figurative meaning, dialectic, syllogisms, and the like) rather renders the mind passive and fosters an emotional attachment to the words of others. As we noted above, subordination was a marker of social inferiority. Like intertextuality, with which it is closely associated, rhetoric stands for practices that embed language in society and thus all that endangers the autonomy and modernity of language. As Barilli (1989: 78–81) notes, Locke echoed the Baconian dichotomy that opposes the universality of logic *versus* the particularity of rhetoric. Reason needs only the discursive common denominator, stable signs, to convey it, and it is accordingly free from all of the indexicality that links rhetoric to personal authority and discursive interactions – in short, to society. Discourse must be purified of interest – that is, from individual agency, social location, and history. Locke uses the trope of the racial Other, which he also exploits extensively in his *Second Treatise of Government*, in suggesting that men can reason quite adequately in Asia and America "who yet never heard of a syllogism" (IV. xvii. 4). By spatializing and temporalizing rhetoric, Locke casts reason as universal, as part of man's fundamental nature, while rhetoric is extracted from human nature and the nature of language.

Locke marginalizes rhetoric by aestheticizing it as verbal ornamentation, and he locates it in the realm of "wit and fancy" (III. x. 34). Since it strives for entertainment and pleasantry, rhetoric can be tolerated "in discourses where we seek rather pleasure and delight than information and improvement" (ibid.). He condemns rhetoric not only for being an art but for being a false one at that – "the art of rhetoric" really amounts to the "arts of fallacy," exchanging truth for "Rhetorical *Flourishes*" (1714 [1697]: 594). The discursive realm to which rhetoric is relegated must be tabooed not only in that it thwarts reason and knowledge and is directed towards "popular" audiences but due to the seductive power of its beauty. The emergent discursive realm of modernity, on the other hand, is marked by its rejection of rhetoric: "in all discourses that pretend to inform or instruct, it is wholly to be avoided" (ibid.). Uday Singh Mehta (1992) argues that the fundamental concern of Locke's work is to use reason in harnessing the imagination and thus avoiding the disorder that ensues when it is not disciplined. The preceding passages from Locke suggest that he located the dangers of rhetoric not only in creating dialogue and semantic ambiguity and decreasing linguistic economy but in opening up domains in which the imagination was unrestrained.

The opposition between "fancy" and "reason" and the attack on rhetoric can thus be read as an expression of Locke's anxiety regarding the effects of the collapse of the *ancien régime* and the rise of individual freedoms in unleashing the imagination. Rhetoric was, of course, also the embodiment of the another great evil of the imagination – slavish reliance on the authority of others, which left the individual no space to imagine.

Rhetoric is feminized and forbidden. By way of anticipating charges of "great boldness, if not brutality" for speaking against rhetoric, Locke notes: "Eloquence, like the fair sex, has too prevailing beauties in it to suffer itself ever to be spoken against. And it is in vain to find fault with those arts of deceiving, wherein men find pleasure to be deceived" (III. x. 34). Here Locke creates a powerfully seductive analogy, sexualizing his dichotomy between knowledge, truth, universality, rationality, agency, and science *versus* passion, beauty, belief, passivity, particularity, error, deceit, and rhetoric. Linguistic purification is, once again, cast as masculine, active, and powerful, while language-society hybridization becomes feminine, passive, and socially subordinating. Paradoxically, Locke denies women access as skilled practitioners into the feminine realm of rhetoric. Learning to speak and write in the "plain Natural way," that is by rote, will suffice for women and for those engaged in "the common Affairs of Life and ordinary commerce" (1989 [1693]: 224, 225). The way Locke connects gender and class in this assertion becomes more explicit as he goes on to suggest that all gentlemen should be taught grammar and rhetoric "since the want of Propriety, and Grammatical Exactness, is thought very misbecoming one of that Rank, and usually draw on one guilty of such faults, the censure of having had a lower Breeding and worse Company, than suits with his quality" (1989 [1693]: 225). Both the work of purification as well as the production of hybrids is thus as thoroughly sexualized as it is structured in terms of class and race. While the essences of things may be excluded from language, Locke seems to think that the essences of social positions should be hardwired into communicative practices and institutional means of reproducing them.

Locke allowed even less space for poetics. Poetry, for Locke, is simply referential redundancy; if the use of words is confined to the expression of clear and distinct ideas through stable significations, large tomes "would shrink into a very narrow compass; and many of the philosophers (to mention no other) as well as poets works, might be contained in a nutshell" (III. xi. 26). In *Some Thoughts Concerning Education*, Locke argues that poetry is useless, a waste of time that squanders estates rather than produces wealth and places one in "bad company and places" (1989 [1693]: 230). Poetry should thus be expunged from education, or at least from the teaching of gentlemen; parents whose children possess a "Poetic Vein, . . . should labour to have it stifled, and suppressed" (1989[1693]: 230). In likening poetry to gaming, Locke would seem to muster religious overtones in linking aesthetics with frivolity, desire, and sin.[6] Poetry, like rhetoric, embodies for Locke the excesses of language, the points at which language steps beyond "the true end of speech, which is to be the easiest and shortest way of communicating our notions" (III. vi. 33); in celebrating form for form's sake, poetry inverts the proper means–ends relationship between form and content. Keller (1985) and Merchant (1980) note how early modernist thought feminized and subordinated nature as a locus of masculine desire and domination. But other feminized domains were more severely attacked – at the same time that Locke feminizes rhetoric and poetry, he attempts to expel them altogether from social life. Herein lies a clear limit to the autonomy of language. The reflexivity of language, explicitly "metalinguistic" (Jakobson 1960), "metacommunicative" (Bateson 1972), or "metapragmatic" (Silverstein 1976) uses of language to comment on or draw attention to itself, must be suppressed. Autonomy can only extend as far as the referential function allows – language must remain a means to convey ideas in as parsimonious a fashion as possible. The "intervention of words" (III. ix. 21) should rather be strictly limited, leading us as quickly as possible out of language and into universal knowledge.

We hasten to note a fascinating exception to Locke's dismissal of rhetoric and his celebration of purification, one that emerges in *Some Thoughts Concerning Education*. There he is concerned with an aspect of "ill-breeding" that springs from failing to show "Respect, Esteem, and Good-will" for one's interlocutors (1989 [1693]: 203). According to Locke, the appearance of disrespect can spring from several factors. A "natural roughness" precludes consideration of the "inclinations, tempers, or conditions" of interlocutors (1989 [1693]: 201). Other sources of interpersonal friction are displaying contempt or censoriousness toward others or, on the other hand, flattery and excessive formality ("Ceremony"). Locke would seem to have anticipated Bakhtin, Goffman, and reception theory by observing that only clowns and brutes fail to perceive "what pleases or displeases" their interlocutors or to "bend to a compliance and accommodate themselves to those they have to do with" (1989 [1693]: 201). The seemingly contradictory character of Locke's call for dialogicality in conversation goes hand-in-hand with his assertions

---

[6] Locke (1989 [1693]: 253) similarly notes that music ranks last on the list of educational priorities in view of the amount of time consumed in mastering an instrument, its lack of productivity, and the way it places an individual "in such odd Company."

that such sensitivity will not only display good breeding but "bespeak the more favourable Attention and give great Advantage" (1989 [1693]: 205). More "Credit and Esteem" will be accrued by offering even an ill argument or ordinary observation "with some civil Preface of Deference and Respect to the Opinions of others" than to present a clever argument "with a rough, insolent, or noisy Management" (1989 [1693]: 203). Locke specifically argues for the centrality of discursive interaction here – "*Good-Breeding*" is not essentially a matter of taking off hats and holding one's legs properly: "*Civility* being, in truth, nothing but a care to show any slighting, or contempt, of any one in Conversation" (1989 [1693]: 203). Locke astutely observes the range of channels that shape the conversational encounter: "Looks, Voice, Words, Motions, Gestures" (1989 [1693]: 200). Locke seems to anticipate a bit of both Benjamin Lee Whorf and sociolinguistics in arguing that such fashions of speaking are "as peculiar and different, in several Countries of the World, as their languages" (1989 [1693]: 204).

Locke's prescription for civil conversation contradicts his privileging of truth, referential precision and consistency, parsimony, and monologicality and his rejection of intertextuality and the indexical grounding of speech. Locke advances linguistic purification as the salvation for language and the only route to modernity. He creates powerful language–society hybrids all along the way, distributing both stigmatized and modern linguistic practices according to gender, class, and space and marking particular discursive styles and forms as privileged; nevertheless, as is the case with Latour's science–technology–society hybrids, the work of purification suppresses awareness of practices of hybridization. But in pushing for conversational civility, it would seem that Locke encounters an upper limit to the values of purification. In asking gentlemen to adapt their discourse to context and social encounter, Locke seems to admit that connections between language and society can only be entirely suppressed at the cost of civility.

Language reform and social order

Locke's model for civil conversation is gentle speech, the discursive ways associated with gentlemen. By rejecting intertextuality, speakers more closely approximate the image of the gentleman – autonomous, free, disinterested, and not dependent upon anyone. We noted earlier Shapin's (1994) suggestion that gentlemanly speech, as embodied in Boyle's work, was presented by the Royal Society as a model for scientific discourse. At the same time, Boyle and his fellows helped to reshape the conversational practices and social dispositions of gentlemen, drawing them away from a chivalric model that centered on the pursuit of pleasure and towards a pious, Protestant, and rational model. Locke extends the hegemony of rationalized elite language in three ways. First, he presents it not as a means of escaping the vices of a problematic communicative medium but as the embodiment of its true, rational core. Second, he presents it explicitly as being a model not just for science but for speech in civil society in general; it becomes, in short, a communicative and social standard. Third, since women, the poor, laborers, and Others in general can never hope to develop their linguistic skills as fully as gentlemen, language becomes a means of systematically evaluating individuals and social sectors in terms of their linguistic precision and parsimony and the social qualities that speech ideally embodies – rationality and independence. These are precisely the qualities that figure so squarely in *The Second Treatise of Government*, as we will suggest shortly. Given his advocacy for developing tight gate-keeping mechanisms over the means of acquiring communicative competence (see Bourdieu 1991), the contest that Locke sets up is clearly rigged.

In providing a charter for linguistic standardization, Locke's writings vividly announce the profound irony that makes language such a powerful means of organizing social inequality: while everyone's speech will be evaluated with respect to the norms established by elite males, all others are condemned in advance to failure (in varying degrees). Gentleman can aspire to purification, but others can only mouth the hybrids Locke condemns as the "cheat and abuse of words." Thus, that which joins (all humans possess language) ultimately separates – just as social class and gender restrict access to the practices that enable speakers to dominate this standardized code, an individual's speech closely indexes and legitimates her or his location in the social structure. Since speaking properly is tied to understanding, rationality, agency, truth, and social order, linguistic competence *à la* Locke provides a powerful synecdoche of one's suitability and authority as a member of civil society. Dipesh Chakrabarty (1992: 21) argues that the irony of modernity is evident in "the undemocratic foundations of 'democracy.'" While Chakrabarty had modern medicine and public health in mind, we might argue that his rich phrase captures the way that Locke fashions discourse into a promise of universal accessibility and a practice for creating social inequality. What makes Locke's vision all the more powerful is that he is not talking about an existing cartography that mediates between supposedly separate planes of linguistic features and categories of inequality but rather creating a reformist vision of a world that must materialize if modernity is to restructure reality. The insidious nature of language-hybrids in structuring and naturalizing social inequality to this day points to the horrific genius of Locke's imagination.

One of the primary motives for Locke's distrust of rhetoric and his general attack on the "cheat and abuse" of words was his conviction that such discursive practices generate conflict, even to the point of undermining the social order. As usual, "learned men" exemplify the dangers of unconstrained dispute and the disruptive potential of indexically grounded speech. Locke asserts that the learned men who "had the advantage to destroy the instruments and means of discourse, conversation, instruction, and society... did no more but perplex and confound the signification of words" (III. x. 10). In areas that concern morality and ethics, for example, "Nothing can be so dangerous as *principles* thus *taken up without questioning or examination*" (IV. xii. 4). Locke projected the abuse of words directly on to the larger social stage, arguing that confused, indeterminate, and shifting meanings, illogical relationships between ideas, and particularly the metadiscursive practices associated with disputation "establish the irreconcilable opposition between different sects of philosophy and religion" (II. xxxiii. 18) and "hath invaded the great concernments of human life and society; obscured and perplexed the material truths of law and divinity; brought confusion, disorder, and uncertainty into the affairs of mankind; and if not destroyed, yet in a great measure rendered useless, these two great rules, religion and justice" (III. x. 12). On the other hand, when language is purified – restored to its true nature as shared, arbitrary, and decontextualized signs – it provides a crucial social glue, "without which laws could be but ill made, or vice and disorders repressed" (II. xxii. 10). The exception to his dismissal of rhetoric revolves around precisely this issue – conversation's potential for generating conflict must be defused. While the right to disagree with opinions and to correct matters of fact must be preserved, objections must be raised "in the gentlest manner, and [with the] softest words [that] can be found" in order to preserve civility (1989 [1693]: 202).

Locke capitalizes on the success that he and his fellow members of the Royal Society had achieved for imbuing post-Civil War England with peace and order:

I leave it to be considered, whether it would not be well for mankind, whose concernment it is to know things as they are, and to do what they ought, and not to spend their lives in talking about them, or tossing words to and from; whether it would not be well, I say, that the use of words were made plain and direct; and that language, which was given to us for the improvement of knowledge and the bond of society, should not be employed to darken truth and unsettle people's rights. (III. x. 13)

The rational, gentle speech modeled by Boyle and the Royal Society was linked to social order largely through its effects – producing consensus and restricting differences of opinion to amicable disagreements. In constructing a civil-and-rational-discourse-as-social-harmony model in explicit, systematic, and theoretical terms, Locke increases the power of language as a tool for creating social order. Having invested language in signs and distinguished them sharply from "*things* themselves," he elevates "the doctrine of signs" from the status of a threat to science and society to the status of an attribute of scientific and gentlemanly comportment, a distinct source of knowledge, and a powerful force for social order. Locke becomes the scholar and prophet of a new and equally important branch of "the commonwealth of learning."

The fruits of linguistic purification provide a basis for discerning the limits of human knowledge. Part of the promise that experimental work in mechanical philosophy held for Restoration England was to provide a sphere of knowledge that lay beyond dispute, the matter of fact (see Shapin and Schaffer 1985). Locke's program offered two additional mechanisms. First, he argued that many debates were not really about things at all but about unknowing divergences in the definitions of words; only purifying and standardizing language, not experiment, could remove a vast source of disagreement and disorder. Second, if attempts to exceed the limits of what is knowable are a major source of intellectual and social disorder, confining discourse to areas that can be subjected to reason and to metadiscursive practices that promote linguistic order is necessary: "If we can find out those measures, whereby a rational creature . . . may and ought to govern his opinions, and actions depending thereon, we need not to be troubled that some other things escape our knowledge" (I: 31). The rational interrogation of words in terms of their relations to sense data can reveal the lexical domains that cannot be rooted in knowledge of the world. What cannnot be said in a rational, dispassionate, and disinterested fashion through the use of context-free signs and sharply delimited meanings had best not be said at all. Locke hoped to prevail upon his readers "to sit down in a quiet ignorance of those things which, upon examination, are found to be beyond the reach of our capacities" (ibid.). These metadiscursive controls thus provided a basis for what could be thought, discussed, and enacted by modern subjects. Locke's writings on politics, economics, and religion suggest that he hardly wished to confine this program to epistemology and mechanical philosophy alone.

Those men, literally, who have submitted their own speech to the discipline Locke prescribes constituted a discursive elite, arbiters of epistemological and social order. Locke clearly counts himself among this linguistic elect. Being in a position to inspire others to discipline themselves, Locke offers his *Essay* as a self-help manual for those who seek linguistic self-improvement. Not content simply to tell people what to do, Locke seeks to model the metadiscursive practices he advocates in the *Essay*. He asserts that he has avoided intertextuality in the construction of his text, boasting that "I shall not need to shore . . . up [this Discourse] with props and buttresses, leaning on borrowed or begged foundations" (Epistle I: 18). Locke believes that his example of purification will further social as well as intellectual order: "I shall imagine I have done some service to truth, peace, and learning if, by any enlargement on this subject, I can make men reflect on their own use of language" (III. v. 16).

It seems worthwhile to point out that "language" here means English. While gentlemen should learn Latin and scholars would be wise to study Greek, it is the ability to convey one's thoughts in English that really counts. Locke faults teachers who taught rhetoric and logic in Latin and Greek "but yet never taught [their pupils] how to express themselves handsomely with their Tongues or Pens in the Language they are always to use" (1989 [1693]: 242). In deriding those who exalt Latin and Greek, deeming English to be "the Language of the illiterate Vulgar," Locke cautions that unnamed neighboring countries "hath not thought it beneath the Publick Care, to promote and reward the improvement of their own Language," as institutionalized through colleges and stipends (1989 [1693]: 244). But Locke's focus was hardly limited to English or England; he claims to speak for the nature of all languages, and the practices of purification he promotes create cosmopolitan subjects who can speak for truth and rationality in universal terms.

The *Essay vis-à-vis* the *Two Treatises*

Locke's *Essay* is commonly seen as epistemology, while *Two Treatises of Government* is read mainly as political theory. Having presented a reading of the discursive politics that emerge in the *Essay*, it is incumbent upon us to cross the borders established by disciplines and Lockean textual specialization in commenting on the relationship between the *Essay* and the *Two Treatises*. This task embodies the thrust of the larger argument we have undertaken in this book – an exploration of the often hidden way that ideologies of language and metadiscursive practices are linked to constructions of social and political spheres in the making of modernity.

In his Introduction to an edition of the *Two Treatises*, Peter Laslett (1960: 96) argues against seeing the work as an extension of the general philosophy of the *Essay* into politics. He suggests that "the implications of Locke's theory of knowledge for politics and political thinking were very considerable and acted quite independently of the influence of the

Two Treatises" (1960: 97). Laslett ties this purported lack of intertextuality to circumstances surrounding publication of the two works. While Locke signed the preface to the *Essay*, he published the *Treatises* anonymously, which he vehemently denied writing; his authorship was only established by a statement that he made in a codicil to his will just a week or two before his death (see Laslett 1960: 16–17). Laslett attributes two motives to Locke's denial of authorship. The *Treatises* first appeared in 1690, and the first essay in particular was a response to the reprinting of *Patriarcha*, a Royalist apologia by Robert Filmer; Locke's attack on Filmer helped legitimate the position of the Whig Exclusionists in the Revolution of 1688 (even though the text had been written much earlier). Closely aligned with Anthony Ashley Cooper, the first Earl of Shaftesbury, Locke might have been afraid of landing in an even more precarious political position if he acknowledged being, as many suspected, the author of the *Treatises*. Laslett (1960: 79) also suggests that Locke may have been reluctant to face criticism over what might be construed as important epistemological contradictions between the two texts.

But Locke's efforts to separate the two texts would seem to be fundamentally rooted in his declaration of the autonomy of language and society; to link them closely, particularly to suggest that the same principles operated in both texts, would have potentially undermined the work of purification. We would assert that modern readers' efforts to keep them separate provide a striking indication of the power of Locke's purifying strategies. By the same token, the importance of hybridization to rendering his visions of language and society authoritative and placing them at the center of mechanisms for generating and naturalizing social inequality require us to refuse Locke's metadiscursive directions and read the works against one another.

The comparative lack of attention to the first *Treatise* has greatly enhanced modern readers' ability to sustain the work of purification. Explicit intertextual relations with the *Essay* are far more apparent there than in the second *Treatise*. Even before we get to the first *Treatise*, The Preface that precedes both *Treatises* clearly reflects the spirit of the *Essay*:

I suppose, no Body hereafter will have either the Confidence to appear against our Common Safety, and be again an Advocate for Slavery; or the Weakness to be deceived with Contradictions dressed up in a Popular Stile, and well turned Periods. For if any one will be at the Pains himself, in those Parts which are here untouched, to strip Sir Robert's Discourses of the Flourish of doubtful Expressions, and endeavour to reduce his words to direct, positive, intelligible Propositions, and then compare them one with another, he will quickly be satisfied there was never so much glib Nonsense put together in well sounding English. (Preface)

Here Locke clearly signals that purification is going to be mustered to the task of disarming Filmer and the Royalists.

Locke seems to lavish praise on Filmer's virtuosity as a writer: "I never, I confess, met with any Man of Parts so Dexterous as Sir Robert at this way of Arguing" (I. xi. 137), and he calls Filmer a "Master of style" (I. xi. 110).[7] Having set up plain speech as a model of truth and rationality in the *Essay*, however, this is faint praise indeed. Locke criticizes Filmer repeatedly for failing to define his terms and for using words in multiple and shifting senses. Locke suggests that this practice is no oversight but a means of hiding objectionable notions in fine words (I. ii. 7). Locke places arguments and reason on one side of a dichotomy that lumps fancy, passion, imagination (I. vi. 58), and the "intricacy of words" (I. vi. 21) together on the opposing side; "Fancies of ones own Brain" are similarly opposed, in terms befitting a member of the Royal Society, with the "Matter of Fact" (I. xi. 145).

Locke argues that once reason has given way to nonsense dressed up in rich stylistic garments, fashion converts it into custom, imbuing it with a sacredness that renders it resistant to critical examination (I. vi. 58). In short, Locke accuses Filmer of rhetorically hybridizing language not only to society but to tradition. The displacement of reason by fancy, passion, and imagination has so distorted the "Governments, Religions, and Manners" of "the Nations of the World" that the impartial observer cannot but wonder if "the Woods and Forests, where irrational untaught Inhabitants keep right by following Nature, are fitter to give us Rules, than Cities and Palaces, where those that call themselves Civil and Rational, go out of their way, by the Authority of Example" (I. vi. 58). Here Locke's political and literary foes are damned by comparison with the objects of his alteric fascination, the peoples of the Americas, at the same time that they seem to be linked implicitly with those reliable straw men of early modernity, the Scholastics.

Locke thus returns in the first *Treatise* to his central hobby horses – intertextuality and rhetoric. Filmer is placed in the company of authors who embrace "Tenets and Parties" rather than reason, defending them "with the Words and Sense of Authors, they would fit to their purpose, just as Procrustes did with his guests, lop or stretch them, as may best fit them to the size of their Notions: And they always prove like those, so served, Deformed, Lame, and useless" (I. vi. 60). Here Locke musters a classical allusion and a rather witty verbal flourish of his own to the task of discrediting Filmer's linguistic excess – while at the same time declaring himself "To speak less Learnedly, and more Intelligibly"

---

[7] References to the *Two Treatises* will consist of book, chapter, and page numbers.

(I. iii. 19) than his opponent, invoking his anti-rhetorical rhetoric. Locke associates rhetoric with political interest, deeming it to be a tool utilized to "flatter princes" (I. i. 3). Rhetoric goes together with attempts to mislead readers (I. xi. 141) just as naturally as "clear and distinct Speaking" (I. iv. 23) is tied to "the force of reason and argument" (I. ii. 13). The former will only be effective with people who have an interest in believing, meaning in this context a political interest in Absolute Monarchy, while it is naturally repugnant to the minds of rational and disinterested men. Here epistemology and political theory are tightly interwoven as Locke asserts that clarity, precision, and semantic stability serve as markers of the political importance and advisability of a position (see I. xi. 108, 109), while imprecise and shifting terms, intertextuality, and rhetorical flourish signal a lack of adequate rational foundations – and the potential to create disorder and destroy government (I. vi. 72; I. xi. 106). In the name of purification, Locke creates fascinating hybrids between textual and political strategies. This critique is not merely rhetorical, as it were, but constituted a broadside against a text that had been recently reprinted in order to provide a Tory charter for defending the monarchy against Shaftesbury and the Whig Exclusionists – who in turn claimed Locke as a crucial theoretician and propagandist (see Cranston 1957: 208; Laslett 1960: 64).

Interestingly, Locke apologizes at several points for introducing metadiscursive criticism into the *Treatises*. He addresses his audience directly in the first *Treatise*:

I fear I have tired my Reader's Patience, by dwelling longer on this Passage [of Filmer's] than the weightiness of any Argument in it, seems to require: but I have unavoidably been engaged in it by our A[uthor]'s way of writing, who hudling several Suppositions together, and in that doubtful and general terms makes such a medly and confusion, that it is impossible to shew his Mistakes, without examining the several Senses, wherein his Words may be taken, and without seeing how, in any of these various Meanings, they will consist together, and have any Truth in them. (I. iii. 20)

Contra Laslett's more radical separation of the *Essay* and the *Treatises*, Locke clearly states that exposing language-society hybrids constitutes a necessary precursor to political criticism. In the second *Treatise*, Locke again apologizes for his anti-rhetorical rhetorical analysis: "It may perhaps be censured as an impertinent Criticism in a discourse of this nature, to find fault with words and names that have obtained in the World: And yet possibly it may not be amiss to offer new ones when the old are apt to lead Men into mistakes" (II. vi. 52). Having created a hybrid form of linguistic and political criticism, Locke must apologize to his readers in order to maintain the autonomy of language and society and the legitimacy of purification. Locke recognizes that here purification serves a most impure function.

This passage suggests an additional factor that may have prompted the suppression of explicit intertextual links between the *Treatises* and the *Essay*. If we read his reference to "a discourse of this nature" to refer to treatises that address political issues, then the statement would seem to suggest that generic rules limit the amount of explicit metadiscursive criticism that can be invoked. At the same time, these expressions of regret can be read as reflecting the basic constraints on metadiscursive criticism that he outlined in the *Essay*. Drawing explicit attention to words, their meanings, and their relations is positively valued when used by gentlemen as precursors to effective discourse. Otherwise, explicit metadiscourse signals that something is wrong. When written or spoken discourses call attention to their own verbal means, we slip into the realm of the "cheat and abuse" of words. Note that while metadiscursive criticism lies at the heart of the first *Treatise*, it appears only rarely in the second, wherein Locke lays out his own political program. Since he does not need to work metadiscursively in the second *Treatise*, we can presume that clarity, simplicity, semantic stability, and truth reign supreme – language/society hybrids have already been stripped away.

Locke had gained admission to the first of "the three great provinces of the intellectual world" through his training as a physician, membership in the Royal Society, and his dabblings in medical and scientific research. Nevertheless, Locke laid no claim to authority over this province in his published writings, and he seems to concede this domain, in the Epistle to the *Essay,* to Boyle, Huygens, and Newton. The *Essay* constructs the third domain, "the right use of *signs*," as being "*toto coelo* different" (IV. xxi. 4) from the first two, charts its topography, establishes Locke's epistemological control over it, and dismisses competing claims, such as those that could be mustered by the Scholastics. The *Second Treatise*, in turn, metadiscursively regiments the second terrain, that of society/ politics, and, once his authorship became known, extends his authority to it as well. Attempting to assimilate politics to epistemology would have undermined his intellectual cartography, rendered the work of purification impossible, and diminished the scope of his textual and political authority, rendering him master of one domain alone. We should not allow Locke's claim for the epistemological independence of the three provinces to keep us from examining the way that seventeenth-century contributions to these realms helped provide the central foundations for a larger project, which we now call modernity. The metadiscursive practices that Locke advocates and undertakes in the second and third spheres involve parallel sorts of moves.

At the same time that Locke incorporates some of the moral assumptions regarding the sanctity of life and natural equality that had been rejected by Hobbes, Locke argues that both contemporary society and the putative state of nature comprised individuals who possess rights to their lives, liberty, bodies, and labor. Locke follows Bacon in suggesting that God confers upon human beings the right and the moral obligation to subdue the earth by making it serve human ends, thereby appropriating it. While the earth was given to "men" collectively, inequality seems to have been divinely decreed in that "He gave it to the use of the Industrious and Rational" (II. v. 34). Once money is created through general agreement, inequities in the appropriation of land and other property are not limited by the moral injunction against spoilage and waste; subsequently and consequently, the English land mass – in Locke's historical imaginary – becomes entirely appropriated. At that time, those individuals who possess inferior "degrees of Industry" (II. v. 43) fail to appropriate land and must sell the only form of "property" that they have left – their labor. Locke contends that the landless retain "that equal Right that every Man hath, to his Natural Freedom, without being subjected to the Will or Authority of any other Man" (II. vi. 54), since they are free to act as individual agents in selling their labor; in so doing, Locke hides from view the power relations over laborers that he, as a landowner, enjoyed. Inequality thus emerges in the state of nature as a result of individuals' own actions; society and its laws, which simply enlarge freedom (II. vi. 57), do not produce nor can they be blamed for inequality.

Many commentators had seen property, as embodied in substantial differences in the circumstances of rich and poor, as morally and politically problematic, and popular protests challenged its legitimacy. The *Treatises* attempt to strip property of these negative connotations, thereby removing a constraint on the development of capitalism and construing it, like language, as the quintessential embodiment of modernity. This argument runs in parallel to the one presented for language in the *Essay*. Both language and property become key means of marking the positionality of individuals, classes, and nations in terms of rationality, morality, and modernity and thus their access to the full rights of citizenship. Having become key markers of the failure to assimilate emergent codes of pious gentility, a lack of property and the "cheat and abuse" of words display an inability to embrace the modern code – or an attitude of resistance.

Reason plays a key role in both arguments. Reason renders all humans naturally equal, being the law of nature (II. ii. 6) and "the Rule betwixt Man and Man, and the common bond whereby humane kind is united into one fellowship and societie" (II. xv. 172). But Locke goes on to note that while the law of nature teaches all who heed it, some do not: "Thus we are born Free, as we are born Rational; not that we have actually the Exercise of either" (II. vi. 61). While this passage deals specifically with the ontogenetic emergence of reason through education and maturation, both texts provide ample evidence that Locke deemed gentlemen to carry the process of acquiring reason to such a different extent quantitatively that it results in profound qualitative differences. In the case of the majority of human beings, individuals live in circumstances that tie them to concrete interests and/or leave them too little leisure time to develop their reasoning. The arguments for both property and language thus begin with a notion of natural equality and end in a vision of radical social differentiation that includes two distinct – and distinctly unequal – types of rationality, relations to property and language, and types of consent (tacit and partial *versus* explicit and full). Arguing that Locke's notions of the state of nature and of society were abstracted from a reading of his own society, as aided by his historical imagination and his fascination with travel literature, C. B. MacPherson (1962: 245) suggests that Locke's image of natural equality reflects the self-image of the English bourgeoisie, while his vision of observed inequality is grounded in the bourgeoisie's image of society as a whole.

In Locke's view, the development of reason and understanding, rooted both in ownership of property and linguistic purification, are needed if an individual is to govern himself by his own free will (II. vi. 63), and both are prerequisites to full participation in civil society. Locke thus uses them in distinguishing degrees of citizenship. The landless, the linguistically unrefined, and women are thus *in* society, subject to the power of the state, without being *of* society (see C. B. MacPherson 1962: 223–24). Carole Pateman (1980, 1988) has written eloquently on the way that Locke's universal subjects of political participation were sexless, thereby rendering women – who always bear a specific and subordinate gendering marking – subject to political society without forming part of it. Just as individuals who have rationalized their speech must serve as models for and correct their verbal inferiors, the landless must accept the governance of their superiors: "he that understands for him must will for him too" (II. vi. 58). Violence provides the only form of political participation that is open to the landless: "The labourer's share [of the national income], being seldom more than a bare subsistence, never allows that body of men, time, or opportunity to raise their thoughts above that, or struggle with the richer for theirs, (as one common interest), unless when some common and great distress, uniting them in one universal ferment, makes them forget respect, and emboldens them to carve to their wants with armed force" (quoted in C. B. MacPherson 1962: 223). Nevertheless, unlike the efforts made by the landed to uproot governments that violate natural and civil law, uprisings by laborers do not constitute legitimate attempts to gain political power. According to Locke, class position entails respect for superiors and precludes class struggle.

Conclusion

If John Locke embodies modernity, then a closer look at his approach to language yields a deeper understanding of what we mean by that phenomenon and what made it possible. In rescuing language from the disrepute into which it had fallen, Locke sought to wrench it from nature/science and society. In severing the links between purified language and tradition, Locke made the former stand for modernity itself. But language could only become modern and be freed of its "natural imperfections" once it was redefined as the center of a new realm of governmentality – practices of purification that became the measure of each individual's modernity. Purportedly stripped of ties to particular social locations and interests and freed of all forms of social difference and conflict, language came to constitute the abstract, general, and certain basis for generating knowledge, a perfect embodiment of logic and rationality. Tying purification to governmentality rendered language a perfect vehicle for constructing and naturalizing social inequality. Since linguistic forms were (in theory) stripped of all ties to material and social worlds, how individuals spoke seemed to spring from deep within the self, to depend solely on the way they had disciplined their minds, not on the wealth they possessed; language could thus perfectly embody the liberal ideology that purportedly judges individuals on the basis of their own individual actions. Locke's regime of decontextualization seemed to free some individuals from their social circumstances and from the chains of tradition and render them cosmopolitan subjects, able to speak to and for the world, for "man."

Roy Porter (2000) has recently suggested that over the course of forty years, Locke "had undergone a profound radicalization, one indicative of how bold minds were driven by darkening times into enlightened convictions" (2000: 29). Interpreters who remain under the spell of Locke's practices of purification will probably find this formulation to be a good description of his linguistic theory, since he sought to explode the hybrids that linked language to nature–science, society–politics, and tradition. But such naiveté is the essence of modernity, because it blinds us to Locke's success in creating one of the greatest schemes for the production of hybrids that history has known – and that is no less effective today. Locke's framework has remained powerful because he did not promote a particular set of hybrids, most of which would have quickly lost their currency. (Note, however, that the plain, unadorned speech that he and Bacon promoted gains new champions and is placed at the center of new reform movements periodically.) Rather, Locke created a winning formula: attack existing hybrids in the name of purification and then create new ones – under the banner of purification! By defining language as purely referential and declaring its separation from the material and social worlds, the powerful social indexicality and performativity of new hybrids can be rendered ideologically almost invisible even as they are stamped on people's voices and bodies. Making the reflexivity of language, the way it calls attention to discursive patterns and functions, a no-no, Locke made it easier to keep these hybrids beneath the radar screen of people who might challenge their powerful role in creating and naturalizing social inequality.

We have stressed how deeply schemes of purification and hybridization were written into social practices. Access to education provided some individuals with prestigious tools for attacking some hybrids and for appropriating the symbolic capital proffered by others. Now, more than three centuries later, the "savage inequalities" identified by Jonathan Kozol (1991), within schools (in tracking systems), between schools (particularly when tied to racial segregation), and between school systems (especially in segregated communities) replace a binary process of inclusion in or exclusion from education with a system that creates myriad positions in relationship to the distribution of prestigious and stigmatizing language-society hybrids. Language standardization, whose ideological charter Locke provided by promoting linguistic self-help, pedagogy, and criticism of the errors of others, still helps to extend spatially the ability of individuals to use hybrids and classify others through their speech as well as to place hybrids beyond the reach of debate and resistance. By locating language and its purification in individuals, Locke helped to make these hybrids just seem like part of the self. Insofar as people speak or inscribe the linguistic forms that are currently designated as rational and cosmopolitan, it is presumed that their thinking and conduct reflect these properties.

In Locke's schema, language bears a double value as means of defining modernity and regulating access to it, in that language enters into all other social fields as well as constituting its own province of knowledge. With regard to religion, he claimed that his effort to purify language could serve as a means of reforming Christianity in two ways. First, the subject of the discourse that engaged the five or six friends who met in Locke's chambers – thereby reportedly giving rise to the *Essay* – was, according to one of the participants, "the principle of morality and revealed religion." This prompts Roger Woolhouse to suggest that "Perhaps, then, the questions about which 'difficulties rose on every side' concerned the manner in which the principles of morality are discovered and known to be true, and the role and authority of religious revelation as a source and foundation of morality," hotly debated issues in the tumultuous public sphere of mid-seventeenth-century England (Woolhouse 1997: xi). Locke asserted that the principles expounded in his *Essay* could transform religious conflict into civil discourse. A purified language could thus transform religion from a key source of social and political cataclysm into a subject of polite debate. Locke seems to condemn most theological discourse in asking "What have the greatest part of the comments and disputes upon the laws of God and man served for, but to make the meaning more doubtful, and perplex the sense?" (III. x. 12). The atomizing and decontextualizing thrust of Locke's logic is at work here as well in his efforts to extract a set of basic religious principles that would be free from "such learned, artificial, and forced senses of them, as are fought out, and put upon them, in most of the systems of divinity, according to the notions that each one has been bred up in" (1997 [1695]: 5). Locke made the metadiscursive basis of his approach to theology clear in an essay that responded to strident criticism of *The Reasonableness of Christianity*.

A second implication lies in the different way that this reform would map for working-class subjects. Locke attempts to reform Christianity by setting aside the "learned, artificial, and forced senses of [the words and phrases of the Bible], as are fought out, and put upon them, in most of the systems of divinity, according to the notions that each one has been bred up in" in favor of reducing Christianity to a small number of easily comprehensible articles of belief based on "the written Word of God . . . , a Collection of Writings, designed by God for the Instruction of the illiterate bulk of Mankind in the way to Salvation; and therefore generally and in necessary points to be understood in the plain direct meaning of the Words and Phrases, such as they may be supposed to have had in the Mouths of the Speakers, who used them according to the Language of that Time and Country wherein they lived" (1714 [1695]b: 474). In *A Second Vindication of the Reasonableness of Christianity, &c.*, Locke rhetorically asks a critic of *The Reasonableness of Christianity* if the basic articles of faith "are all plain and intelligible, and such as may be understood and comprehended . . . by every illiterate Countryman and Woman capable of Church-Communion?" (1714 [1697]: 583). Providing an answer to his own question, Locke asserts that linguistic complexity would exclude most humans from real access to Christianity. The rational earned the right to instruct "the illiterate bulk of mankind."

As Constantine Caffentzis (1989) suggests, Locke extended this brand of reasoning into economics in his *Some Considerations of the Consequences of lowering the Interest and raising the Value of Money* (1714 [1691]) and *Further Considerations concerning raising the Value of Money* (1714 [1695]a). In countering proposals that would have officialized the economic effects of the activities of coin clippers and counterfeiters, Locke presented a theory of money based on the nature of currency and its role in promoting trade. Since such individuals committed "cheat and abuse" against not just coins but the basic principles of monetary semantics, Locke promoted penalties that were more severe than those reserved for persons who resisted the linguistic order – clipping and counterfeiting constitute acts of treason against the state and should be punished accordingly (Caffentzis 1989: 46–47). Locke's role here was not of merely philosophical significance, so to speak; in following his patron, Lord Shaftesbury's appointment as Chancellor of the Exchequer in 1672, Locke served on the Council of Trade. Newton was charged with prosecuting these crimes once Locke secured his appointment as Warden of the Mint.

The process of purifying language also intersects with that of purifying mechanical philosophy in a number of ways, several of which we have pointed out in the course of this chapter. As Gruner (1977: 114) notes, the mode of scientific inquiry that emerged in the seventeenth century is distinguished less by the kinds of objects it investigated than by its methods. Behind the differences that separate deductive from inductive approaches and rationalism from empiricism lie a host of shared assumptions. Perhaps the most basic of these is the role of atomization, abstraction and idealization in gaining knowledge of the natural world. As Hall (1963: 235) suggests, the main object of the mechanical philosophy associated with such figures as Galileo, Boyle, and Newton is the principle of the simplicity of physical structure. In order to understand things scientifically, the experienced complexity and diversity of phenomena must be broken up into their basic components. Understanding nature thus entails discovering universal elements and discerning their motions or relations.[8] Locke's atomistic and decontextualizing approach to language runs a parallel course. As Shapin and Schaffer (1985; Shapin 1994) suggest, the civil, dispassionate, truth-seeking discourse of the scientist provided a model for the sort of civil discourse and interaction that could protect social order in Restoration England – and the social privileges of the elite. Particular forms of speech had to become models of rational thought before they could become emblems of science.

---

[8] There were, however, important differences in the degree to which mechanical philosophers sought to frame their findings as universal and context-free, as Shapin and Schaffer (1985) suggest.

Locke's language purification program provided a crucial prerequisite for constructing a key feature of modernity, one that Jürgen Habermas (1989 [1962]) terms "the public sphere." Habermas quotes Locke's assertion of the need of men "to accommodate themselves to the opinions and rules of those with whom they converse" (II. xxviii. 12), thereby creating a "law of fashion, or private censure" that parallels the law of God and that of the state (II. xxviii. 13). But Habermas falls far short of appreciating the extent of Locke's role in the emergence of public spheres during this period and their importance in shaping civil society. Locke distinguishes three public spheres in the guise of his cartography of "the three great provinces of the intellectual world, wholly separate and distinct from one another" (IV. xxi. 5). "Philosophical" realms can similarly be distinguished from the world(s) occupied by "Merchants and lovers, cooks and tailors." Locke stratifies these domains in terms of the degree to which rationality could be achieved in them, noting frequently that different discursive rules apply in each. Moreover, Locke systematized the metadiscursive regulation of what could be said – and what couldn't be uttered – by whom, in which contexts, and in what ways. Beyond setting up the rules for defining the political subject and deciding which classes and individuals would be granted this designation, Locke provided a theoretical base that helped to legitimate these practices for a very long period of time.

The concept of disinterested speech, which Habermas seems to accept, played a crucial role in Locke's vision of the sort of speech that belongs in scientific and political arenas. Poovey (1998: 86) argues that this notion presupposes the work of constructing society as an intersection of competing interests advanced by individuals in the absence of an institution that can structure and negotiate those interests. We might add that to become a disinterested speaker presupposes one's prior status as an interested individual, as a subject who is capable of conceptualizing, articulating, and advancing his or her own particular interests, apart from the authority and influence of others. Surprise – one first has to be a Lockean liberal subject! While becoming an interested subject thus involves a substantial degree of mastery of Locke's linguistic program, being designated as "disinterested" requires a sort of advanced certification in making one's speech seem decontextualized and dehistoricized. Let us not forget that Locke spelled out the social and geographic limitations on membership in this elite group. A closer reading of Locke thus suggests the extent to which frameworks that draw on notions of disinterestedness in defining "public" or "political" spheres reproduce a cornerstone of the "undemocratic foundations of 'democracy'," to reinvoke Chakrabarty's rich phrase. This element of Locke's autonomous sphere of language presupposes – and thus naturalizes and hybridizes – the political theory of possessive individualism, Locke's metadiscursive regime, and the gatekeeping mechanisms that he proposed for restricting access to it.

Olivia Smith's (1984) discussion of how linguistic ideologies entered into political life a hundred years after Locke's *Essay* was published provides a sense of just how deeply the language purification program shaped the grounds for political debate. The expansion of pedagogical programs included substantial attention to language; dictionaries and grammars provided different models of English for use by shopkeepers or servants *versus* members of the elite, thereby helping to institutionalize class-based language-society hybrids and naturalize assumptions about the depth of class differences. Following Locke, language tied to specific times and places was deemed to be vulgar or primitive, while a refined or civilized English attempted to erase the rootedness of language in time and place and to tie words to permanent and universal ideas (1984: 24–25). As pressures mounted for broader franchise and political participation, the supposed coarseness of political petitions provided a key rationale for rejecting them, thereby protecting elite power and shielding the state from criticism. In enforcing censorship laws, both an inexpensive price and a popularly accessible style rationalized prosecution for "malicious intent" by demonstrating that the book was addressed "to the ignorant, to the credulous, to the desperate" (1984: 64). Ironically, the valiant attacks launched by such writers as Paine, Hooke, and Cobbett against elite hybrids were often rationalized on Lockean grounds. These writers attacked the elite for using elegant styles that thwarted independence of mind, and they urged simplicity, clarity, and the rejection of rhetorical and poetic elaboration. Smith (1984: 247) suggests that in the eyes of these writers, "obscurity in the grammar is the *modus vivendi* of oppression." In attempting to resist Locke's program of purification, critics were doomed to extend it in attempting to undermine the hybrids it had created.

Our point here is not simply to point out parallels in the purifying practices that Locke uses in reformulating these domains or to help reveal the powerful language-society and language–science–technology hybrids and networks that link them, as important as these goals may be. We want to argue that the work of purifying language played a key role in creating practices for producing and naturalizing forms of social inequality. Locke argues that how people think and act is an individual matter, in that we have free will and the capacity to determine our own thought and actions. How individuals act is contingent on how they think, which can be measured in terms of its rationality, independence, and the degree to which individual thought is based on sound, certain, empirical grounds.

How individuals think is a product of their own efforts to discipline their thought. Theoretically, everyone has the ability to undertake this process but only some actually pursue it. The observed social inequalities are the effects of this fundamental difference. Thus, the wealthy and powerful have earned their position, while the poor and powerful can be blamed for theirs.

Language is doubly privileged in this process. First, it provides the key model of rationality, precision, empirical groundedness, abstraction and generalization, civility, and political order; insofar as individuals master the purification process, they will be able to order their thoughts and deeds in other areas. Building these notions in the *Essay* provided Locke with a key means of constructing his view of society – and justification for social inequality – in the second *Treatise*. Second, such arenas as science, society, economics, and religion require a purified language for their successful functioning. Locke emphasizes the role of language as the source of the understanding, agreement, and social order that are needed in order to enable society and the state to create and enforce laws. He cautions that the development of concepts and words in "business of mankind" is vital, "without which laws could be but ill made, or vice and disorders repressed" (II. xxii. 10). The law ultimately depends upon language, that is, speech that conforms with Locke's linguistic reform project. If language exceeds these bounds, not only knowledge but the social contract itself are threatened: "language, which was given to us for the improvement of knowledge and the bond of society, should not be employed to darken truth and unsettle people's rights" (III. x. 13). Order can only be established and chaos and conflict avoided in the various arenas of society if Locke's project of linguistic purification is systematically undertaken. On an individual level, linguistic purification defines the citizen and establishes who can claim this status.

Latour's view of modernity fails to recognize the importance of Locke's constitution of language as a separate "province" and the centrality of the practices he promoted for purifying language from its connections with nature/science and society to modernity. We have shown just how key a role these purification and hybridization processes played in creating and sustaining social inequality; this aspect of Latour's (1993) analysis strikes us as being greatly underdeveloped, thereby rendering his framework less useful as a tool for political analysis. He seems to suggest that purifying connections between nature–science and society came to characterize modern societies starting in seventeenth-century England, but that other societies (the "premoderns") did not undertake this process. While both types generate hybrids, premoderns are characterized by their "*inability to differentiate durably*" between hybrid social-scientific-technological "networks" on the one hand and the conception of society and nature as autonomous on the other (1993: 133; emphasis ours).

Our exploration of Locke suggests that there are two serious flaws in this formulation and that they preclude grasping the centrality of purification and hybridization processes to social inequality. The laboring classes, shopkeepers, and, largely, women, were excluded in advance from significant access to practices of purifying science, society, and language or, especially in later generations, provided less prestigious types of entrée, and their positions were marked by their association with stigmatizing hybrids. Recall the way that Locke often lumps together "merchants and lovers, cooks and tailors" (III. xi. 10), "the day labourer in a country village" (1966: 39), and women with the people of Asia and the Americas in terms of their inability to undertake the purification practices he promotes. Focusing on a contrast between modern and premodern societies misses the role of purification in constructing and naturalizing social inequality within each.

Second, framing the effects of the work of purification as a cognitive problem (an "*inability* to differentiate durably") extends the naturalizing processes that Locke, Boyle, and others promoted; phrasing the problem in terms of the subaltern's perceptual and/or cognitive state played and continues to play a key role in creating and legitimating modern forms of inequality. The poor, women, country people, and non-Europeans were deemed to have failed in advance, and their perceived inability to engage in the work of purification – and to identify themselves with the prestigious hybrids claimed by elite modern males – could be located deep within the self, turning it into a global moral, intellectual, and behavioral failure for which they themselves were to blame. Educational practices were then instituted to make sure that this prophesy would be self-fulfilling. To his credit, Latour suggests that hybrids are material and have material effects on people's lives – he does not locate modernity exclusively in the mind. A radical critique of modernity and its role in creating and sustaining social inequality would seem to require, however, systematic and sustained analysis of notions that reduce differential access to property and prestigious social forms to the ability to grasp modernity. Given the power and durability of these ideologies and practices, allowing their premises to slip into one's argument quickly places one in complicity with Locke and his successors.

Nevertheless, having established the centrality of social inequality and exclusion to the work of purification and hybridization, this connection can help understand the power of Locke's work to create modern forms of social inequality. It is not the case that Locke simply pushed a particular set of hybrids. C. B. MacPherson (1962) seems to suggest, for example, that Locke promoted a view of the poor as irrational and promoted the position of the bourgeoisie. Beyond Locke's obvious affinity for the landed gentry, he went far beyond theorizing the position of any particular set of hybrids by creating a theory of the modern subject that was not limited to a particular relationship to property but was rooted simultaneously in social, legal, economic, political, educational, and linguistic orders and guaranteed by the state. He thereby created a powerful mechanism for constructing, legitimating, and regulating regimes of social inequality, one that far outlived the particular class contours on which it was modeled, which were, in any case, very much in transition as he wrote. Purification and hybridization played a key role in this process.

Similarly, David Goldberg's (1993) suggestion that Locke played a key role in theorizing racial difference can similarly be extended along these lines. While Locke certainly justified the ownership of African slaves – and profited from their exploitation – it seems far from clear that his contribution lay specifically in tying inequality to skin color, an approach that does not seem to be a dominant idiom in Locke's day or in his writings. Goldberg (1993: 28) draws attention to Locke's assertion that an English boy is likely to think that all men are "white or flesh-colour" and to therefore conclude that "a negro is not a man" (IV. vii. 16), suggesting that this passage constituted a justification of slavery and racial inequality in general. Locke uses this example in characterizing the provincial subject, the way that semantic categories shift in relationship to limited experiences of the world; he accordingly uses it as a means of arguing the need to produce cosmopolitan subjects whose experience is not limited in this way.

This is not to suggest, however, that this example is unmotivated, that the selection of white versus Negro was not tied into forms of racial domination. Race seems to enter more directly and more centrally in his theory through his passion for travel literature; as we have noted, references to inhabitants of the Americas are common in both the *Essay* and the *Treatises*. Locke's interest in these sources was shared by other members of the Royal Society; one of the tasks of its Correspondence Committee was to assemble travel books. By supposedly providing evidence regarding a natural state as it exists apart from "society," these references enabled Locke to make assertions about human nature and to devise linguistic and political-economic measures of rationality. Linking allusions regarding Americans and Asians to characterizations of women, laborers, the poor, children, and other subalterns, Locke seems to have helped legitimate in advance schemes of racial inequality to a greater extent by virtue of the way he theorized practices for *producing* pervasive schemas of inequality than by promoting the idea that difference is color coded. Locke's emphasis on distinct fashions, morals, customs, and discursive practices renders him more similar to "cultural" racists of the late twentieth century (see Balibar 1991) than to proponents of biologically based inferiority of the intervening centuries. Much more than shaping the content of particular racial categories, especially on the basis of skin color, Locke helped establish the practices by which racism and other forms of subordination could be developed, legitimated, and converted into everyday practices.

Grasping the connection between purification, hybridization, and social inequality provides us with a powerful tool for discerning the fundamental importance of cosmopolitanism in modernity. At the same time that he helped loosen the hold of premodern Latin-based cosmopolitan regimes in arguing for the need to speak English in political and civil communication (see Mignolo 2000; Pollock 2000), Locke saw himself as advancing a new cosmopolitan project, modernity. As redefined by Locke, language became a perfect means of deprovincializing knowledge – the "cheat and abuse of words" must be expunged in order to overcome the way that explicit hybridization ties speakers and writers irrevocably to particular circumstances and prevents them from looking beyond their presumed local horizons. Only a cosmopolitan language is suitable for producing modern knowledge and modern subjects, and only those individuals who undertake Locke's purifying regime could hope to achieve this status. By denying women, the poor, country people, and others educational rights, Locke excludes them by fiat from the promise of cosmopolitanism. This magical sleight of hand draws on practices of generalization, abstraction, and decontextualization in seeming to make some forms stand for knowledge that is not tied to any place or time – and thus can speak to and for all humans – all the while producing hybrids that place every individual and community in hierarchical schemes. This juxtaposition of explicit practices of purification and largely implicit hybridization lies at the heart of efforts to elevate elite, male European forms to the level of supposed universals. Grasping Locke's linguistic program of linguistic purification and its lingering and powerful effects thus provides a crucial means of taking up Partha Chatterjee's (1993) and Dipesh Chakrabarty's (1989, 1992) challenge to see how Europe came to be "deprovincialized," how ideologies and practices tied to a specific gender, race, class, and time were reframed as a universal, timeless knowledge of "man." Locke's linguistic epistemology provided a key means of constructing the concept of the universal liberal subject that legitimated the projection of European ideologies on a global basis. His anti-rhetorical rhetoric engendered a process of stylistically marking discourse that had passed through practices of purification. In other words,

Locke's program for rendering language autonomous and subjects rational and disinterested provided the discursive machine for the work of deprovincialization. Simply by opening their mouths or puting pen to paper, individuals and populations seem to provide their own measure of the extent to which they had succeeded in deprovincializing themselves.

At the same time, the way that linguistic purification became a key means of creating and naturalizing social inequality within English society points to the narrow distribution of "Western knowledge" within the social and historical locus of its production. Purification thus helped to fuel new schemes of sexual, spatial, and class discrimination at the same time that it helped provide a foundation for colonialism. In the end, not much of Europe got deprovincialized. The project of "reprovincializing" Europe thus seems necessarily to entail challenging the power of practices of purification rather than simply attacking a particular set of hybrids they have generated.

3 Creating modernity's others in seventeenth- and eighteenth-century England: antiquarian and philological inflections

Introduction

Francis Bacon has a secure place in the pantheon consecrated by intellectual historians to the makers of modernity. As we have discussed in Chapter 2, Bacon's bold heralding of the charter for his Natural Philosophy insistently proclaims the need for a decisive break with the past if the quest for genuine knowledge is to be placed on its proper course. An essential part of Bacon's scientific program, we recall, is the necessity of direct experience and the exercise of individual reason in the pursuit of true knowledge, and the concomitant distrust of traditional authority, mediated by texts and testimonies: "First, then, away with antiquities, and citation or testimonies of authors, and also with disputes and controversies and differing opinions – everything, in short, which is philological" (Bacon 1968 [1857–74] IV: 254). By oft-cited pronouncements such as these, Bacon created – or portrayed himself as creating – the kind of gap between the past and the present that is constitutive of the advent of modernity, in this instance between a supernaturalist worldview resting on traditional authority and a naturalist worldview resting upon the exercise of reason.

In the preceding pages, we have traced some of the linguistic inflections of Bacon's proclaimed epistemic break in science, and followed them as they were extended and transformed through the work of John Locke and others. In this chapter, we depart from what most intellectual historians of linguistics, like most historians and philosophers of science, see as the historical mainstream by tracing other channels that descend, at least in part, from the Baconian source.

The image of Bacon as creator of the break that separates the old and the new science derives largely from the core documents of his *Great Instauration*, especially the *Novum Organum* and the *Preparative Towards a Natural and Experimental History*, the charter statements of Natural Philosophy. It is worth remembering, however, that in the larger context of Bacon's classification of knowledge, as outlined in the *Advancement of*

Learning and developed further in the *Dignity and Advancement of Learning*, Natural Philosophy occupied only a portion of the domain of philosophy, which was itself but one of three principal domains of human learning, each deriving from one of the three intellectual faculties. History, which is grounded in memory, is "properly concerned with individuals, which are circumscribed by place and time"; poesy, issuing from the imagination, consists of "feigned history or fables," "an imitation of history at pleasure"; and philosophy, "the office and work of Reason," discards individuals; neither does it deal with the impressions immediately received from them, but with abstract notions derived from these impressions" (Bacon 1968 [1857–74] IV: 292).

As in the domain of philosophy, Bacon is concerned in both history and poesy with the gap between past and present, but his rhetorical stance towards the fissure in these latter domains is markedly different. Rather than portraying himself as proclaiming or creating the gap in regard to history and poesy, Bacon simply recognizes that such a gap inescapably exists and suggests the need to transcend it. Consider, for example, Bacon's characterization of Civil History,[1] "whereof the dignity and authority," he maintains, "are pre-eminent among human writings" (1968 [1857–74] IV: 302). "But the difficulty is no less than the dignity," he continues, "For to carry the mind in writing back into the past, and bring it into sympathy with antiquity . . . is a task of great labour and judgment – the rather because in ancient transactions the truth is difficult to ascertain, and in modern it is dangerous to tell" (1968 [1857–74] IV: 302). In the pursuit of historical knowledge, then, the difficult task is to use what remains of the historical record in an effort to bridge the gap of place and time between past and present. Or consider Bacon's program for the study of "Poesy Parabolical" that serves in fables to disguise true meaning, such that they are "seen as it were through a veil" (Bacon 1968 [1857–74] IV: 317). Again, the task is to penetrate the veil of time and secrecy in order to arrive at true meaning, all the more difficult because "the writings in which these fables are related are, next to sacred story, the most ancient of human writings, and the fables themselves are still more ancient" (Bacon 1968 [1857–74] IV: 317).

In this chapter, we will examine two intellectual projects of the late seventeenth and eighteenth centuries for which Bacon's programs for the pursuit of knowledge in history and poesy provided frames of reference, namely, antiquarianism and philology, the very pursuits that Bacon excludes so vehemently from natural philosophy in the passage quoted

---

[1] Bacon divides History into Natural History and Civil History: "Natural History treats of the deeds and works of nature; Civil History those of men" (1968 [1857–74] IV: 293).

above. Both of these enterprises were as strongly involved in the construction and comprehension of modernity as was the new science; the identification and scrutiny of antiquated custom and belief and the interpretation and evaluation of classical texts constituted twin fields in which the symbolic construction of modernity was especially salient. We are interested most centrally in how discursive forms and practices figured as resources in this constructional process. If the advent of modernity is characteristically framed in terms of a historical fissure or gap separating contrastive social formations, technologies, ideational systems, or other features of human existence considered to be diagnostic of epochal change, what sort of gap was conceived in ways of using language and regimenting discourse? And how did those notions about language and discourse relate to conceptions of society? While John Locke focused primarily on creating ideologies and practices that positively modeled the shapes that modernity should assume, as we suggested in Chapter 2, a vision of internal and external Others also provided him with a negative image of how modern subjects should *not* think, speak, write, and act. In this chapter we specifically take up writers who played a key role in defining modernity through this negative or alteric process.

Antiquarian constructions of modernity and the discursive Other

Antiquarianism coalesced as a field of inquiry in England in the latter half of the sixteenth century, under the convergent influence of Renaissance humanist historiography, the doctrinal and institutional dislocations of the Reformation, and the emergent national consciousness of a burgeoning imperial power (Dorson 1968: 1–43; Evans 1956; Parry 1995). Characterized from the beginning by an admixture of nostalgia for a vanished past and a growing ideological commitment to progress, antiquarian inquiry centered its attention on remnants of the past – documentary, material, behavioral, or ideational indices of past ways of life – in an effort to construct and comprehend a contrastive present.

In the course of its development in the seventeenth century, antiquarianism tended to be the province of the socially more conservative classes (Parry 1995: 17), drawing its patronage and practitioners from the nobility and gentry, which helps to account for the generally local, county-based focus of antiquarian research. These were the people who were most likely to fear the iconoclasm of the Puritan zealots and to have both the motivation to regard the past with nostalgia and the interest to claim intellectual control over the definition of the future. Antiquarian investigations formed a significant, if minor, part of the program of the Royal

Society in its early years, consistent with its Baconian charter, and the empirical rigor of the new science contributed a measure of systematization to antiquarian inquiry.

Typical in all of the above respects – gentleman, Royalist, early member of the Royal Society, devoté of Wiltshire antiquities, synthesizer – was John Aubrey. Aubrey has come to be seen by intellectual historians of a number of disciplines as a foundational figure, variously credited as a pioneer of modern archeology, social history, ethnology, and folklore (Dorson 1968: 5–7; Hunter 1975: 155–59; Kite 1993: 21, 41). He is thus a fitting figure with whom to begin.

John Aubrey (1626–1697)

John Aubrey was born into the upper levels of England's landed gentry in 1626, and although he was conspicuously – even disastrously – inept at the management of his practical affairs and had to depend in his later years on the hospitality and patronage of those who valued his friendship, he lived throughout his life in a milieu of wealth and privilege. Aubrey moved in the highest intellectual circles of his day. Educated at Oxford and the Middle Temple, he was a prominent early member of the Royal Society and his friends and acquaintances included such luminaries as Thomas Hobbes, John Locke, Robert Boyle, William Harvey, Isaac Newton, and Christopher Wren. He was an energetic and prolific – if undisciplined – writer, who managed to see only one of his books through to publication, two years before his death in 1697. While his voluminous manuscripts have been mined by scholars for 300 years, and various of his works have been published since his death, it is only recently that comprehensive assessments of his intellectual career have been possible.[2]

Beneath the apparent untidiness of Aubrey's career and writings and the diffuseness of his scholarly production, his work takes on a significant measure of overall coherence within the context of the intellectual program outlined by his intellectual idol, Francis Bacon. While the titles of some of his works suggest his Baconian orientation – *Natural History of Wiltshire* reflects the Baconian emphasis on natural history, *Brief Lives*

---

[2] On Aubrey's life and work, see Britton (1845), Buchanan-Brown (1972), Dick (1949), Hunter (1975), Kite (1993), Tylden-Wright (1991). Aubrey's only work published during his lifetime was *Miscellanies* (1972a [1695]). Aubrey tended to expand and revise his writings over extended periods of time and left much of his work in an unfinished state. Dating his work is, accordingly, a complex task. We have cited published versions by date of publication; the reader interested in when Aubrey was at work on particular writings should consult the table of Events in the Life of John Aubrey, compiled by Buchanan-Brown in Aubrey (1972: xiii–xv). Aubrey (1972a) contains three works: *Miscellanies*, *Remaines of Gentilisme and Judaisme*, and *Observations*.

accords well with Bacon's call for the individual life as an organizing focus for one type of civil history – virtually none of Aubrey's works maintains a systematic and unified focus on a single aspect of the Baconian program. In this chapter, we want to examine only one significant aspect of Aubrey's intellectual vision: the role of discursive forms and metadiscursive practices in his lifelong engagement with antiquities.

Bacon, we recall, divided civil history into three kinds, "Memorials, Perfect Histories, and Antiquities," comparing them, respectively, with three kinds of pictures or images: "some are unfinished, and wanting the last touch; some are perfect; and some are mutilated and defaced by age." Thus, "Memorials are history unfinished, or the first rough draughts of history, and Antiquities are history defaced, or some remnants of history which have casually escaped the shipwreck of time" (1968 [1857–74] IV: 303). Antiquities, or "Remnants of History," he goes on, are "like the spars of a shipwreck; when, though the memory of things be decayed and almost lost, yet acute and industrious persons, by a certain persevering and scrupulous diligence, contrive out of genealogies, annals, titles, monuments, coins, proper names and styles, etymologies of words, proverbs, traditions, archives and instruments as well public as private, fragments of histories scattered about in books not historical – contrive, I say, from all these things or some of them, to recover somewhat from the deluge of time" (1968 [1857–74] IV: 303–4). In these terms, antiquities, by definition, can only exist in a damaged state. They are emblems of absence, decay, and loss, constructing and underscoring the gap between past and present. Antiquarian research is an effort of salvage – from the shipwreck, or rescue – from the deluge of time.

Reflecting on his intellectual career, Aubrey recorded in 1670 that "I was inclined by my Genius from my childhood, to the love of antiquities" (1862: 314). His definition of antiquities echoes Bacon's own: "These Remaynes are 'tanquam tabulata naufragii' (*like fragments of a Shipwreck*) that after the Revolution of so many yeares and governments have escaped the teeth of Time and [which is more dangerous] the hands of mistaken zeale" (1862: 4). The work of the antiquary is to restore to presence the way of life of which the antiquities are remnants: "the retrieving of those forgotten things from oblivioun in some sort resembles the Art of a Conjuror who makes those walke and appeare that have layen in their graves many hundreds of yeares: and represents as it were to the eie, the places, customs and Fashions, that were of old Time" (1862: 4). The antiquary bridges the gap between old Time and the present, conjuring the past into presence.

Aubrey's sensitivity to temporal disjuncture permeates his writings. Historical gaps may be opened by the inexorable passage of time, as events

fade out of memory and are "drowned in oblivioun"; they may be the
consequence of world-transforming discoveries, such as "the divine art of
Printing and Gunpowder"; or they may be caused by catastrophic events,
such as the "Civil Warres" of his own era. Historical rupture was not at all
an abstract or distant phenomenon for Aubrey – it was a matter of lived experience, revolving around the radical overturnings of mid-seventeenth-
century England. His personal sense of temporal dislocation runs like a
leitmotif through his writings. Again and again, Aubrey frames an account
of some now vanished or disappearing custom with a recollection of its
currency "when I was a boy before the Civil Wars." Consider the following observation: "When I was a child (and so before the Civill Warres)
the fashion was for old women and mayds to tell fabulous stories night-
imes, of Sprights and walking of ghosts, &c. This was derived downe from
mother to daughter, &c. from yᵉ Monkish Ballance which upheld Holy
church, for yᵉ Divines say, 'Deny Spirits, you are an Atheist'. When yᵉ
warres came, and with them Liberty of Conscience and Liberty of inquisition, the phantoms vanished. Now children feare no such things having
heard not of them; and are not checked with such feares" (1862: 15).
Elsewhere, Aubrey provides further elaboration: "Before Printing, Old-
Wives Tales were ingeniose: and since Printing came in fashion, till a little
before the Civil-warres, the ordinary sort of People were not taught to
reade: now-a-dayes Bookes are common, and most of the poor people
understand letters: and the many god Bookes, and variety of Turnes of
Affaires, have put all the old Fables out of dores: and the divine art of
Printing and Gunpowder have frighted away Robin-good-fellow and the
Fayries" (1972a: 290).

What is significant about the historical characterizations that emerge
from these passages is that Aubrey reads historical and cultural disjunction out of a change in discursive and metadiscursive practices; the displacement of particular speech forms and speech practices becomes an
index of a fundamental contrast between the old time and the present,
marked by the disruptions of the Civil Wars. Indeed, there is a concomitant break in historical discourse itself: "In the old ignorant times, before
woomen were Readers, the history was handed down from Mother to
daughter, &c: and W. Malmesburiensis pickt up his history from the time
of Ven: Bede to his time out of old Songs: for there was no Writer in
England from Bede to him. So my Nurse had the History from the Conquest down to Carl. I in Ballad" (1972a: 289–90). Let us consider more
closely how this discursive disjunction is manifested.

First, the "fabulous stories" of sprites, ghosts, fairies, Robin Goodfel-
low, and other "phantoms" are no longer told. What accounts for their absence? Aubrey attributes the demise of these stories and the supernatural

beliefs to which they give voice to "Liberty of Conscience and Liberty of inquisition," which is to say the freeing of belief and knowledge from the traditional authority of Catholicism and custom, the broadening of the sphere of individual agency – even for children. In addition, print technology, the increased availability of good books, and the extension of literacy brought reliable, secular knowledge to a formerly credulous populace.

Clearly, in Aubrey's characterization, this discursive realization of Weber's (1946: 155, 350) "disenchantment of the world" through the silencing of stories is also a deeply gendered process: what is also displaced is the authority of women and their role as custodians of traditional knowledge and as agents of socialization. There is a disruption and diminution of specifically female modes of cultural transmission, from mothers to daughters, from women to children, features of the "old ignorant times" that extend back to classical antiquity – Aubrey links old wives' tales to discursive practices documented in Ovid's *Metamorphoses*, his warrant for including them among the "remains of gentilism." It is not that men play no role as custodians of oral tradition. Aubrey recalls of his youth that "When a boy he did ever love to converse with old men as Living Histories" (Britton 1845: 16), but the significant factor is that he finds no need to discredit their discourse and authority as he does those of women.

In addition to gender, Aubrey's characterization of discursive transformation is heavily inflected by class. It is the tales and ballads of servants (such as his nurse), "the ordinary sort of People," "poor people" that have lost their currency and cultural importance, displaced by the "good Bookes" written, presumably by their intellectual and social superiors.

The passages we have been examining are couched in a purifying rhetoric of clear contrast between the "old ignorant times" and the present. It is evident, however, from the bulk of Aubrey's writings, that the discursive forms and practices that he identifies with the earlier era had not fully disappeared. Indeed, it is precisely their survival into the "modern" era – Aubrey uses the term (1898: 10) – as "remains" that constitute them as antiquities. That is to say, the antiquity is a hybrid form, mediating between past and present. It is rooted in the old time, but persists in appropriately distressed form into the new. In part, this persistence is a matter of memory, the "remembrance" of people like Aubrey himself, whose lives span the gap between historical epochs. Thus Aubrey can record old usages held "within my own Remembrance, or within the Remembrance of some Persons worthy of Belief in the Age before me" (1972a: 6). But his copious collections also included numerous items that were still current. To cite but one apt example, once again clearly inflected by gender and class, Aubrey reports "An old filthy Rhythme used by base people, *viz.*:

"When I was a young Maid, and wash't my Mothers Dishes,
"I putt my finger in my Cunt, and pluck't-out little Fishes.
See Burchardus . . . where there is an interrogatory; if she did even *immettere pisculos in vulvam*, and let it die there, and then fry it, and give it to her Lover to eate, *ut in majorem modum exardesceret amor*? The Lord Chancellor Bacon sayes – thus the fables of the Poets are the Mysteries of the Philosophers: and I allude here, that (out of fulsome Ribaldrie) I have picked-out the profoundest natural Magick, that even I met with in all my Life. (1972a: 254–55)

Note here that it is the rhyme alone which remains, a piece of ribald speech-play, severed from its original role in an act of sympathetic magic – thus, a fragment. Antiquities may be fragments in another sense as well, that is, drastically diminished currency; what was the "fashion" in former times becomes an isolated and etiolated remnant.

The question must arise of why the antiquary should devote himself so assiduously to rescuing the remains of the old ignorant times from their destiny of loss, especially as the ignorance to which they give voice has been discredited by the epistemological rigor of reasoned inquiry. Certainly, this was a question that Aubrey's contemporaries, including some of his intellectual associates in the Royal Society, were not hesitant to ask. Even Bacon, who provided a clear charter for antiquarian research, was somewhat dismissive of the enterprise (1968 [1857–74] IV: 304). Aubrey's defense of antiquarian pursuits is highly suggestive. "Old customs, and old wives fables are grosse things," he concedes in the Preface to his *Remaines of Gentilisme*, his fullest compendium of such materials, but he goes on to caution that "there may be some truth and usefulness to be elicited out of them: besides 'tis a pleasure to consider the Errours that enveloped former ages: as also the present" (1972a: 132). The pleasure he takes in the work is not insignificant as a motivating factor; we have already noted his acknowledgment of his "Strong and early impulse to antiquities." But the stronger intellectual argument appeals to "truth and usefulness," those twin goals of Baconian Natural Philosophy. Where might this truth and usefulness lie?

At one level, there is a very pragmatic appeal to practical utility, as in the apparent efficacy of certain curative "Receipts" recorded in the section on Magick in the *Miscellanies* (1972a). Aubrey goes further, however. As many intellectual historians have argued, the Natural Philosophy of the late seventeenth century contained a significant admixture of supernaturalism in various guises, from Hermetic occultism to religious orthodoxy to Deism. While the nature and location of the boundary between the natural and the supernatural were the focus of active investigation, testing, and negotiation, few were ready to deny entirely that the boundary existed. It is in this context, above all, that Aubrey found his firmest grounds for arguing the potential for discovering some degree of truth and usefulness in "Old customs and old wives-fables." In the dedication of the *Miscellanies*, an avowed exploration of "Hermetick Philosophy," Aubrey writes, "The Matter of this Collection is beyond Humane reach: We being miserably in the dark, as to the Oeconomie of the Invisible World, which knows what we do, or incline to, and works upon our Passions, and sometimes is so kind as to afford us a glimpse of its Praescience" (1972a: 5). Aubrey's preoccupation with these epistemological hybrids, then, is in the interest of that broader task to which Latour (1993: 32–35) alerts us: where to position the brackets that set God at a sufficient distance from science and society to allow us to treat them as essentially autonomous, but close enough to appeal to when one threatens to overpower the other.

But the discovery of truth and usefulness, of course, has its complement in the exposure of error – they are twin tasks. While the old wives' tales and oral traditions that give voice to error may persist in the present as remains of "former ages," in larger scope the rhetorical thrust of Aubrey's argument for the study of these discursive remains centers on their value in constructing and maintaining the essential contrast between the old ignorant times and the modern present. "I know that some will nauseate these old Fables," he writes in his *Monumenta Britannica* (1692), "but I profess to regard them as the most considerable pieces of Antiquity I collect: and that they are to be registered for Posterity, to let them understand the Encroachments of Ignorance on Mankind: and to learne, what strange Absurdities Man can by Custome & education be brought to believe" (quoted in Buchanan-Brown 1972: xxxi). This argument makes clear the rhetorical efficacy of oppositional, Great Divide cultural and historical contrasts, the powerful trope of constructing a contrastive past as a means of defining the present. Note, too, the appeal to posterity as a warrant for antiquarian research; we rescue and record the old tales of the past to fill the needs of the future in sustaining the symbolic opposition of old and new times. What we want to underscore here is the pride of place that Aubrey assigns to the words of Others – especially women and the lower classes – in constructing and authorizing this program: "the most considerable pieces of Antiquity I collect."

The discursive gap constructed and sustained by Aubrey's characterization of oral traditions is, of course, traversed by those very antiquarian researches. The antiquary is an intermediary, traveling back and forth between the old ignorant times and the new era. We have already registered the depth of Aubrey's engagement with the living sources of oral tradition, such as his nurse, who "was excellent at these old stories" (1972a: 445) and the old men of his neighborhood whom he saw as "Living Histories." But there was a negative element to this engagement as well, and here again it was the experience of the Civil Wars that heightened Aubrey's sensitivity to the discursive disjunction between his worlds.

As discussed briefly in Chapter 1, Aubrey's education at Oxford was twice interrupted by his Royalist father's calls to return home for fear of the war's dangers. Of the second occasion, Aubrey records that "my father sent for me into the country again, where I conversed with none but servants and rustiques.... It was a sad life to me then, in the prime of my youth, not to have the benefitt of an ingeniose conversation; and scarce any good bookes" (Britton 1845: 14). On his return to Trinity College, Aubrey experienced "great joy: was made much of by the fellows, had their learned conversation, lookt on books, musique. Here & at M.[iddle] T.[emple] ... I for the most part enjoyed the greatest felicity of my life" (Britton 1845: 14). In his treatise on the education of gentlemen, Aubrey is more explicit about the disadvantages of "being bred at home": "their minds are advocated with continual suggestions of trivial divertisements as coursing, hawking, setting and conversation with their sisters and relations, domestic differences" (1972b: 19). He goes on to recommend that "Gentlemen are the fittest to breed gentlemen, and youths of this quality ought to be bred up amongst their equals.... A cobbler's son may have a good wit and may perchance be a good man, but he would not be a proper friend for a person of honour" (1972b: 20). Note the convergence here between the work of Aubrey and Locke, both of whom were concerned with questions of education. Their programs for educational reform revolved around providing the sons of gentleman with competence in the metadiscursive practices of modernity, thereby affording them exclusive access to the emergent public domain; expunging "traditional" discursive practices was much less important in the case of sisters, cobbler's sons, and – in brief – most of English society.

In these observations, then, Aubrey draws a clear contrast between the stultifying and trivial conversation of servants, rustics, domestic relations (specifically including sisters), artisans, and the ingenious, elevated, intellectual conversation of the educated upper classes. Aubrey extols "the modern advantages of coffee-howses" in London as a venue in which to "indulge my genius wth my friends," and it is clear that he treasured his involvement in the activities of the Royal Society so highly chiefly for the fellowship of discourse it afforded him (1898: 10; Britton 1845: 16; Dick 1949: 100–1). A gentleman may converse with uneducated people, the lower classes, and women for the purposes of antiquarian research, he may even value such conversation as a means of collecting the remains of oral tradition, but the ultimate value lies in elevated conversation with one's fellow gentlemen, and the fables and old wives' tales are of value as recontextualized resources for this learned discourse.

Notice here the contrastive siting of the two discursive domains, their social and spatial ecology. Home, domestic relations, and the company of women constitute the domain from which Aubrey yearns to escape. The learned, "ingeniose," intellectual, "modern" conversation in which he delights is to be found in the elite male fellowship of the university and the coffeehouse. The latter, of course, is a prime site as well for the coalescence of that other great formation of modernity, Habermas's bourgeois public sphere.

Henry Bourne (1696–1733)

While Baconian Natural Philosophy provided one of the principal intellectual charters for antiquarian research, as exemplified by the career of John Aubrey, it did not stand alone as an epistemological frame of reference for the burgeoning antiquarian enterprise. A second motivating impulse driving the search for antiquities derived from the reformist program of Protestant religion, the arena in which the recalibration of God's place in the universe – a task in which we have seen Aubrey engaged as well – was of paramount importance. An influential exemplar of this second line of antiquarian research was the Newcastle-upon-Tyne clergyman Henry Bourne (1696–1733), whose *Antiquitates Vulgares, or the Antiquities of the Common People* (hereafter *Antiquities*), published in 1725, became the nucleus of an extended series of subsequent antiquarian works.[3] Bourne, the son of a tailor, was initially apprenticed to a glazier, but the sponsorship of influential friends who recognized his intellectual talents secured his release from his apprenticeship and directed him to Cambridge University where he received the BA and MA degrees. He returned to Newcastle in 1724, where he was appointed curate of All Hallows Church, a position he retained for the remainder of his life.

Consistent with the rhetoric of modernity that we have traced in our consideration of Aubrey, the polemical thrust of Bourne's *Antiquities* rests upon a vision of historical disjunction, marked in this case by the epochal importance of the Protestant Reformation. Before this juncture lay the benighted ages of heathenism and Roman Catholicism, succeeded, after

---

[3] We have used the 1977 facsimile reprint edition. In this edition, all nouns are capitalized, but in quoting from Bourne we have reduced them to lower case. On the uses, reuses, and abuses of Bourne's work, see Dorson (1968: 10–43). On Bourne's life, see Sutton (1963).

the turning point of the Reformation, by the enlightened era of Protestant faith. At the conclusion of a chapter exposing the heathen foundations of the fears surrounding burial places, Bourne portrays the gap between the age of heathenism and the current era in a parallel series of contrasts: "But now with us, God be thanked, the scene is changed, we live not in the darkness of error, but in the light of truth; we worship not *daemons*, but the God of the whole earth; and our temples are not the temples of idols, but the temples of the Holy God" (1977 [1725]: 64). Thus, the historical disjunction between the old and the new might be constructed with heathenism or Catholicism or both on the one side of the historical divide and pure Protestant Truth on the other. Bourne traces the belief in fairies, for example, as having been "handed down" from "the times of heathenism" (1977 [1725]: 83), but goes on to draw the decisive break in terms of the Reformation: "This opinion," that is, the belief in fairies, "in the benighted ages of Popery, when hobgoblins and sprights were in every city and town and village, by every water and in every wood, was very common. But when that cloud was dispell'd, and the day sprung up, those spirits which wander'd in the night of ignorance and error, did really vanish at the dawn of truth and the light of knowledge" (1977 [1725]: 84). In other instances, the origin of error lies with "the ignorance and superstition of the Romish Church" alone (1977 [1725]: 85).

As we have noted in our earlier discussion, an antiquity, by its very nature, bridges the historical gap between the ancient and the modern epochs. The religious standard of relevance by which Bourne identified and assessed antiquities directed his attention to elements of "heathen" or "Romish" or "Popish" religion that were handed down to the present by "custom," "tradition," "hearsay," the mechanisms by which antiquities mediate between past and present. These were, for the most part, "ceremonies" and "rites" – elements of practice – and "opinions" or "traditions" – elements of belief – but Bourne recognizes as well the discursive means by which antiquities are "talk'd of": "conversation," "discourse," "tales," "stories" (1977 [1725]: 82, 83, 87, 219). Indeed, he devotes an entire chapter (1977 [1725]: 76–90) to the custom of telling stories about ghosts, apparitions, fairies, haunted houses, and the like in "country conversations in a winter's evening," a discursive focus that allows him to attend jointly to custom and belief.

Bourne characterizes the antiquities that form the core of his collection not only in epistemological and historical terms, but in sociological terms as well. In this, he is far more direct than Aubrey. The very title of his book, *Antiquitates Vulgares, or the Antiquities of the Common People*, foregrounds the sociological dimension of the work, and the opening lines of the Preface make this focus still more explicit: "The following sheets are a few of that vast number of ceremonies and opinions, which are held by the common people; such, as they solely or generally observe. For tho' some of them have been of national and others perhaps of universal observance, yet at present they would have little or no being, if not observed among the vulgar" (1977 [1725]: ix). Thus antiquities, the detritus of cultural forms that were widely current in past eras, are at present to be found in the lower – vulgar, common – strata of society. Bourne goes on to specify more closely the kinds of people among whom antiquities are current. He directs attention, first of all and most frequently, to "country places" (or, variously, "country villages," "country parishes") and thus, by implication, preeminently to the peasantry, the "common people" of "country places." In complementary terms, he assigns the currency of the ceremonies and opinions with which he is concerned to "the ignorant part of the world," "ignorant people," the "uneducated part of the world," that is, to the unsophisticated and unrefined populace among whom "the politeness of the age hath made no great conquest" (1977 [1725]: x, 29, 115, 188). Beyond class (vulgar), location (rural), education (ignorant), and refinement (lacking politeness), the social currency of antiquities is further inflected by gender and age. It is "the fables of nurses," the "legendary stories of nurses and old women," that are the vehicles for maintaining the old beliefs (1977 [1725]: 41). Likewise, it is "the generality of old people among the commonalty" (1977 [1725]: 29) who observe the old customs most persistently.

Now, it is true that Bourne does note the currency of certain old Christmas customs at the universities (1977 [1725]: 136, 152), and of rogation days (walking the bounds and limits of the parish) "here and there in the towns and cities" as well as in country places, but these are occasional and exceptional departures from the normative center of Bourne's sociology of antiquities. As constructed by Bourne, the proper province of those customs and beliefs left over from the pre-Reformation eras of heathenism and Roman Catholicism was among the uneducated, unpolished, rural lower classes, especially the female and the elderly among them. So clearly does Bourne establish the association between these social categories and antiquities that there is no need for him to spell out the sociological lineaments of post-Reformation modernity in quite such detail. There is a consistent and revealing rhetoric of authorization, however, by which he claims authority for those whose interpretations support his own: a "great and learned man" who delivers his opinion with "strength of reason and argument"; "men of good learning and knowledge"; "an author of good credit" (1977 [1725]: 82, 88). A clear, if less detailed, profile of authority emerges from these characterizations; authority is male, educated, literate, rational, persuasive.

Thus, when Bourne delineates the break between the darkness of the heathen and papist past and the light of the modern Protestant era in historical terms, he does so in the purifying rhetoric of Great Divide oppositional contrast. But when the mediating force of antiquities translates the historical opposition into social terms, modernity itself is revealed as hybrid, insofar as these Others within retain the persistent remnants of the past in the modern era. We will return to this important point later in the chapter.

Bourne's religious vocation, as we might expect, demanded more than a mere compilation of heathen and Catholic antiquities "observed among the vulgar." His ideological principles commanded him as well to an attitude and a strategy. The Reformation marked a new religious order in which the remnants of earlier belief and practice were not merely anachronistic, but spiritually dangerous. Whatever legitimacy these antiquated forms may have had in "the early ages of the world," the light of truth imposes a new spiritual standard: "they were only peculiar to those times. We have no warrant for doing the like" (1977 [1725]: 74).

Bourne's interventionist program, however, turns out to be more complex and flexible than his religious office might lead us to expect. The foundations of his program are clearly expressed in the following extended passage from the Preface to *Antiquities*:

Some of the customs they hold, have been originally good, tho' at present they retain little of their primitive purity; the true meaning and design of them, being either lost, or very much in the dark through folly and superstition. To wipe off therefore the dust they have contracted, to clear them of superstition, and make known their end and design, may turn to some account, and be of advantage; whereas observing them in the present way, is not only of no advantage, but of very great detriment.

Others they hold, are really sinful, notwithstanding in outward appearance they seem very harmless, being a scandal to religion, and an encouraging of wickedness. And therefore to aim at abolishing these, will I hope be no crime, tho' they be the diversions of the people.

As to the opinions they hold, they are almost all superstitious, being generally either the produce of heathenism; or the inventions of indolent monks, who having nothing else to do, were the forgers of many silly and wicked opinions, to keep the world in awe and ignorance. And indeed the ignorant part of the world, is still so aw'd, that they follow the idle traditions of the one, more than the word of God; and have more dependence upon the lucky omens of the other than his Providence, more dread of their unlucky ones, than his wrath and punishment. (1977 [1725]: x–xi)

The first paragraph of this passage offers an illuminating statement of Bourne's antiquarian perspective and method. It is in the very nature of religious antiquities, as etiolated remnants, that their true meaning and purpose have been obscured. The antiquarian's task is to restore them from obscurity to clarity, to recover and reveal their true meaning, purpose, and functional effects. What is surprising, perhaps, is Bourne's concession that some of these obscure and misunderstood practices may originally have been good. If practiced in ignorance, however, they can only be detrimental; the revelatory efforts of the antiquarian are necessary if they are to be recuperated and turned to advantage. These same efforts, to be sure, will reveal which remnant customs are intrinsically sinful and inevitably conducive to wickedness, though they might appear on the surface to be harmless or benign.

While Bourne leaves open the possibility that certain customs might be beneficial once restored to their true meaning and design, he finds little redemptive potential in the antiquated beliefs he records. These vulgar opinions, in his view, are worthy only of condemnation, as the products of ignorance, wickedness, and folly, bequeathed to subsequent ages by heathens or foisted upon a credulous populace by indolent monks with too much idle time on their hands and an official policy of keeping the people in ignorance and awe.

The antiquary emerges from this passage, then, as the moral guardian of the common people, impelled by his religious duty and enabled by his intellectual superiority to police and purify the beliefs and practices of the vulgar, who are too ignorant and uncritical to look after themselves. Contrary to Dorson's assessment, however (1968: 13), Bourne was no zealot. There are clear indications in *Antiquities* that his antiquarian researches were the subject of some controversy, as Bourne is at pains to make clear that he "would not be thought a reviver of old rites and ceremonies to the burdening of the people, nor an abolisher of innocent customs, which are their pleasure and recreation" (1977 [1725]: x, xi). Apparently, Bourne's critical stance, which allowed for the retention of customs that could, with proper understanding, be construed as consistent with proper spiritual standards, while it demanded abolition of those that are revealed to be detrimental to spiritual well-being, attracted censure from both sides.

For his own part, Bourne deplores most the forces that might lead to the loss or elimination from organized religion of all ceremonial. "But, alas!" he laments, "We are fallen into times of such irreligion and prejudice, such contempt of antiquity, and such too great Reformation, that what with indolence on one hand, and ignorance on the other; what with no zeal on this side, and too false a one on that, we either neglect the most decent ceremonies of religion, or we think it is religion to have no ceremonies at all" (1977 [1725]: xi). This appearance of moderation notwithstanding, contrasting significantly with the purifying rhetoric of "darkness of error" versus "light of truth," it remains the case that Bourne assumes the authority to intervene in the culture of the vulgar populace. His aim, he insists in the Preface, is "regulation": "The regulating... of these opinions and customs is what I propos'd by the following compositions, whatever has been suggested to the contrary" (1977 [1725]: xi). By formulating his program of regulation in terms of antiquities, moreover, Bourne helps to lay the foundations of a political sociology of culture that has remained a key element in the ideological construction of modernity.

John Brand (1744–1806)

Bourne's *Antiquities* appears to have been highly regarded by his fellow antiquaries, with copies fetching high prices some decades after its publication (Brand 1777: 18–19n.). The ultimate reach of Bourne's work was expanded enormously, however, by its whole-cloth incorporation, a half-century after its first appearance, into a work of benchmark importance in antiquarian studies, John Brand's *Observations on Popular Antiquities* (1777; hereafter *Observations*). Brand (1744–1806) extended Bourne's collection by adding entries to each of Bourne's chapters and including an appendix made up of his own articles on subjects not treated in the earlier work.

Brand's career was parallel to Bourne's in many ways.[4] As with Bourne, Brand's intellectual abilities attracted the support of patrons who secured his release from his apprenticeship to a cordwainer in Newcastle and assisted in his further education. Bourne attended Oxford University, where he received his BA in 1775. Beginning in 1773, he held a succession of church appointments, culminating in 1784 in the office of rector of two united parishes in London under the patronage of the Duke of Northumberland. In the same year, he was elected resident secretary to the Society of Antiquaries, an office he retained until his death in 1806.

Brand's *Observations* reflects the maturing of antiquarian studies in England. This maturity is manifested, in one respect, by Brand's decision to construct his *Observations* on the foundation of Bourne's earlier work, acknowledging the existence of a scholarly tradition on which to build. And although Brand feels it necessary, like Aubrey and Bourne before him, to anticipate and respond to the critical dismissal of antiquarian studies as "trivial" or of "seeming unimportance," he can appeal with confidence to the growth and institutionalization of the antiquarian enterprise: "The English antique has become a general and fashionable study; and the discoveries of the very respectable Society of Antiquaries

---

[4] On Brand's life, see Cooper (1963).

have rendered the recesses of papal and heathen antiquities easier of access" (1777: iii, vi, ix). In more intellectual terms, Brand echoes Aubrey's rationale for antiquarian research: "The antiquities of the common people cannot be studied without acquiring some useful knowledge of mankind. By the chemical process of philosophy, even wisdom may be extracted from the follies and superstitions of our forefathers" (1777: ix).

The reader who encounters Brand after reading Aubrey and Bourne will find much in the *Observations* that rings familiar. Not only does Brand incorporate the body of Bourne's earlier work into his own, but central aspects of his conceptual and rhetorical framework follow on the approaches of his predecessors. His designation of his subject matter, "popular antiquities," "vulgar rites and popular opinions" (1777: i, iii), echoes Bourne's terminology, and his antiquarian orientation, in its general outlines, has much in common with both Aubrey and Bourne. Antiquities, in Brand's treatment, are elements of custom and belief whose origins lie in "remote antiquity"; they exist now only in a damaged state, "mutilated," their "parts... awkwardly transposed," "the very causes that gave rise to them" forgotten (1777: iii). Their damaged nature notwithstanding, they have "preserved at least some form and colour of identity" and "the principal traits, that distinguished them in their origin" (1777: iii). The antiquary's task is to "rescue" their lost origins and causes "from oblivion" (1777: iii). Their ultimate origin, Brand concedes, may be impossible to recover, but by tracing antiquities back as far as possible, we can make significant discoveries nevertheless (1777: iv). The key operation, as we have come to expect, is to locate the origins and the full realization of the "superstitious notions and ceremonies of the people" (1777: iv) on the other side of a historical divide that separates antiquity from modernity.

For Brand, as for Bourne, it is the "times when Popery was our established religion" (1777: iv) that gave their "first direction" to the popular antiquities we seek to understand, while the Protestant Reformation marks the point of historical disjunction between the past and the present eras. Brand recognizes that "Papal Rome borrowed her rites, notions, and ceremonies, in the most luxurious abundance from ancient and heathen Rome," but his principal concern is to mark popular antiquities with the taint of Catholicism, which was sufficient to condemn them as morally corrupt. They were part of the "yoke which Holy Church... has imposed on her servile devotees," a "countenance to sinners," "a profusion of childish rites, pageants and ceremonies [that] diverted the attention of the people from the consideration of their real state," and so on (1777: v–viii). Then, in an epochal turning point, came the Reformation, in which "our sensible and manly forefathers... had spirit enough" to throw off the

Catholic yoke (1777: viii). Before was "dark" and "gloomy superstition"; after was "enlightened understanding" (1777: vii). In Brand's historical vision, this act of spiritual liberation and purification takes on a national cast, with manly Englishmen throwing off the shackles of "spiritual merchandise from the Continent" (1777: viii).

As we have emphasized in our earlier discussions, it is in the nature of antiquity that it transcends the historical rupture that reduced it to a damaged remnant. Brand places greater emphasis on this element of continuity, which he identifies as "tradition," than either Aubrey or Bourne: "Tradition has in no instance so clearly evidenced her faithfulness, as in the transmitting of vulgar rites and popular opinions" (1777: iii). This is tradition, then, in its mediating guise, as bridging past and present. One of the factors to which Brand attributes the persistence of antiquated forms introduces a metadiscursive dimension into the making of antiquities. The popular rites and superstitions, he suggests, "consecrated to the fancies of men by a usage from time immemorial, though erased by public authority from the *written word*, were committed as a venerable deposit to the keeping of *oral tradition*" (1777: iv). This, of course, has proven to be an extremely durable notion, that the oral, or spoken, is the vehicle of conservative tradition, while writing is the medium of enlightened change and intellectual liberation.

Having identified tradition as the process by which antiquities bridge the gap between past and present, Brand goes even further in emphasizing the persistence of these cultural forms: "They have indeed travelled down to us through a long succession of years, and the greatest part of them, it is not improbable, will be of perpetual observation" (1777: iii). This concession, that the popular rites and opinions are not simply transitory remains from an earlier era, but are likely to be of perpetual observation, marks a highly significant departure in the conception of popular antiquities: it suggests that these old practices and understandings constitute a permanent part of the culture of the common people. Brand thus advances a conception of the sociology of culture in which there are two strata: one class of the "learned," "enlightened," "sensible" – and thus modern – people, who have thrown off the old forms, and a second class made up of the "multitude," "the common people," the "vulgar," who are disposed to retain them. This latter class is bound by tradition, Brand explains, "for the generality of men look back with superstitious veneration on the ages of their forefathers: and authorities, that are grey with time, seldom fail of commanding those filial honours, claimed even by the appearance of hoary old age" (1777: iii). In Brand's view, then, the advent of enlightened modernity is, in social terms, a partial process: the common people continue to be tied to the past. To paraphrase Latour, they will never be modern.

What makes Brand's sociology of culture still more noteworthy, however, is the political program that follows from it. Brand is strongly critical of the policy he attributes to the Catholic Church of instituting "A profusion of childish, rites, pageants and ceremonies [which] diverted the attention of the people from the consideration of their real state" (1777: viii). The church authorities are "forgers of shackles," fabricators of a "yoke which the Holy Church...has imposed on her servile devotees" (1777: vii). But with the Reformation, we would expect, all should be different – the new Protestant authorities should be energetic in breaking the shackles that the Catholic Church had imposed. It is striking, then, to find Brand ready to acknowledge that "It is not improbable that, in the infancy of Protestantism, the continuance of many of these was connived at by the state," suggesting a time-honored strategy of gradualism in religious reform, based on the premise that "the Reformation of manners, and of religion, is always most surely established, when effected by slow degrees" (1777: iv–v). Brand is ready, however, to go beyond strategic gradualism, which anticipates a point at which the state will no longer connive in the preservation of vulgar antiquities from the popish past. He proposes, rather, a political strategy not unlike the one he condemns on the part of the Catholic Church. "The common people," he writes, "confined by daily labour, seem to require their proper intervals of relaxation; perhaps it is of the highest political utility to encourage innocent sports and games among them. The revival of many of these, would, I think, be highly pertinent at this particular season, when the general spread of luxury and dissipation threatens more than at any preceding period to extinguish the character of our boasted national bravery" (1777: v–vi). Here is state-sponsored antiquity management in the interest of political control, sustained by antiquarian research. In this program, Bourne's interventionist "regulation" of popular custom and belief is carried to the level of state policy. Brand is at pains to assure the reader, however, that this political intervention on the part of the antiquary is fully, and with the best of humanist intentions, consistent with the nature of the social order: "The people, of whom society is chiefly composed, and for whose good, superiority of rank is only a grant made originally by mutual concession, is a respectable subject to every one who is a Friend of Man.... The beautiful sentiment of Terence: 'Homo sum, humani nihil a me alienum puto,' may be adopted therefore in the place, to persuade us that nothing can be foreign to our enquiry, which concern the smallest of the vulgar; of those little ones, who occupy the lowest place in the political arrangement of human beings" (1777: ix). The intellectual's claim to social and political authority could hardly be more clearly expressed.

Philology, relativism, and conjectural history

As we have seen in our consideration of antiquarianism and the metadiscursive construction of modernity, certain of the cultural forms construed as antiquities had a textual aspect. Supernaturalist beliefs, for example, such as the belief in ghosts or apparitions, might be encoded in legends or narratives of personal experience – old wives' tales – while folk history might be encapsulated in ballads. By the same token, texts like Aubrey's "filthy rhyme" of the little fishes might be understood as the surviving remnants of larger complexes of custom and belief. And certain customary practices, such as Bourne's winter-night storytelling, might consist in the performance of traditional texts. Notwithstanding the presence of textual forms in antiquarian corpora, however, the antiquarian paradigm was not at all concerned with textuality *per se*, but rather with those aspects of the texts that constitute them as antiquities, that is, as remnant survivals of earlier wholes. The primary focus of antiquarian inquiry is on relics of past ways of life, formerly coherent, that have survived in distressed form into the present. Notwithstanding the operation by which antiquities are entextualized for inclusion in the antiquary's collections – a significant part of the very process of constituting them as antiquities–textuality is only incidental to antiquarian inquiry.

In philology, however, texts are primary. The lines of intellectual inquiry that we identify as philological have their roots in the concern of Renaissance humanism to make the cultural heritage of classical antiquity accessible to contemporary readers. As a practical program, the philological enterprise consists of a range of text-centered operations. One set of such operations revolves around the textual object itself: constructing a standard out of variant texts, authenticating particular texts, tracing genetic relationships among texts, and like authorizing tasks. A second set has to do with the search for meaning: glossing, interpreting, commenting upon the text. The work of philology thus rests on a combination of linguistic expertise and critical skill, oriented towards the understanding and evaluation of texts as cultural expressions – if not as cultural monuments. In classical and biblical philology, the authorization of particular texts as cultural monuments is very much to the point – philology grew up quite literally in the service of canon formation. In the following section, we will trace in the work of philologists Thomas Blackwell, Robert Wood, and Robert Lowth an emergent reorientation in the eighteenth century towards the understanding and evaluation of the most canonical of literary works, the Homeric epics and the Old Testament, framed in terms of the semiotics and rhetoric of modernity.[5]

Thomas Blackwell (1701–1757)

As with Aubrey, but to a more limited extent, the ideas of Francis Bacon had a shaping influence on the writings of Thomas Blackwell (1701–57), Professor of Greek at Aberdeen University from 1723 to 1757.[6] Most relevant, as being most often cited in Blackwell's major writings, is Bacon's *Of the Wisdom of the Ancients*, in which Bacon attempted to devise an interpretive framework that would render intelligible "the fables of the poets," principally the Greek myths recorded in the works of Homer, Hesiod, and other classical authors. Writing a century after Bacon, Blackwell accepted Bacon's goal of finding meaning in the classical texts, but rejected the master's interpretations and the very interpretive framework he employed (see, e.g., 1970 [1735]: 217). The sociohistorical and cultural approach that Blackwell offered in its stead was ultimately more enduring.

The failure of Bacon's strained attempts to read the Greek myths as parables and to find rational meaning behind their apparent absurdity was symptomatic of a larger tension inherent in the Renaissance humanists' revival of the classics. Blackwell's major works, *An Enquiry into the Life and Writings of Homer* (1970 [1735]) and *Letters Concerning Mythology* (1976 [1748]), may be read productively as attempts to mend the fissure between the exalted, universal, timeless status of the classics, attributed to them by Renaissance humanism, and the sense of strangeness that modern readers experienced in reading the texts (see Levine 1991: 2).[7] His concern in these works is to formulate an interpretive approach to classical texts that will render them meaningful, coherent, and efficacious in terms acceptable to modern readers while remaining true to the historical circumstances and understandings under which they were originally produced.

Blackwell's *Enquiry* was one of the most influential works of eighteenth-century classical philology, an inspiration not only to British scholars but to intellectuals in other countries, principally Germany, as well. The *Enquiry* is framed around one central question, probing the enduring appeal of Homer: "By what fate or disposition of things it has happened,

---

[5] For a survey of Blackwell's, Wood's, and Lowth's contributions, see Lessenich (1989: 134–58).

[6] On Blackwell's life, see Westby-Gibson (1963).

[7] In quoting from Blackwell's works, we have substituted roman for italic type; the alternation between the two in the original is highly idiosyncratic and arbitrary.

that none have equalled him in epic poetry for two thousand seven hundred years, the time since he wrote; nor any that we know, ever surpassed him before" (1970 [1735]: 2). Blackwell immediately rejects one possible explanation: "that Homer was inspired from heaven; that he sung, and wrote as the prophet and interpreter of the Gods" (1979 [1735]: 3). The Greeks may have attributed his achievement to divine inspiration, but, Blackwell argues in good Enlightenment and Baconian fashion, "the happy change that has since been wrought upon the face of religious affairs, gives us liberty to be of the contrary opinion," that is, that his genius derives from "a concourse of natural causes" (1970 [1735]: 4). The task, therefore, is to investigate the full range of natural causes "that can possibly have influence upon the human mind, towards forming it to poetry and verse" (1976 [1748]: 37).

Blackwell assigns the natural circumstances that exercise a formative influence on human activity to two broad categories, public and private (the terms are his). The public factors are those that operate on the collectivity and have "a common effect on the whole generation": "the state of the country where a person is born and bred," the "common manners of the inhabitants," including their civil and religious constitution, their "ordinary ways of living," and "the manners of the times, or the prevalent humours and professions in vogue" (1970 [1735]: 11–12). Note the nationalizing thrust of Blackwell's formulation, in locating the operative sphere of these collective influences in "the country where a person is born and bred." The private factors are "private end" and "the particular way of life we choose and pursue" (1970 [1735]: 12). Blackwell clearly views these factors "That make us what we are" (1970 [1735]: 12) in systemic terms. "A change in any one of them," he argues, "makes an alteration upon us, and taken together, we must consider them as the moulds that form us into those habits and dispositions, which sway our conduct and distinguish our actions" (1970 [1735]: 12).

In developing his argument, Blackwell goes on to assign a critical role to language, which, in his treatment, comprehends not only languages and dialects, in the common senses of the terms, which serve for "the conveyance of our thoughts," but also the language-society hybrids, "discourse," "speaking," "speech," that is, language in social use (1970 [1735]: 36, 43, 44). There is "an inviolable and necessary connection between the dispositions of a nation and their speech," Blackwell maintains; "the fortunes, the manners, and the language of a people are all linked together, and necessarily influence one another" (1970 [1735]: 44, 54). Blackwell traces the linkages most fully in relation to Homeric Greece, drawing more general conclusions as well, and we will consider some of his conclusions below.

Before doing so, however, it will be useful to fill in an additional element of Blackwell's broader approach to language and culture as causal factors in the production of literature, namely, that both the manners and language of a nation are subject to historical change. "The manners of a people seldom stand still," Blackwell observes, and "along with their manners, their language too accompanies them both in their growth and decay" (1970 [1735]: 2, 36). Now, although he allows for both "growth and decay" or "rises and falls" in the history of nations, in "the widest views of human affairs" Blackwell perceives an overall trajectory of "progression" or "growth." This broader developmental process, in turn, provides the basis for a series of oppositional contrasts between the "ancients" and the "moderns." The ancients are characterized as "natural," "simple," and "unaffected" in their manners, unashamed "to avow passions and inclinations, which were entirely void of art [i.e., artifice] and design" (1970 [1735]: 24–36), whereas the moderns are "cover'd . . . from Nature's face," "admire nothing but pomp" and "the produce of wealth" and "luxury," and are distanced from their human nature by "state and form" (1970 [1735]: 24–25). This is no simple and nostalgic exaltation of primitive virtues, however, at the critical expense of modern life. Blackwell freely acknowledges the advantages of a "well-ordered" and "well-governed" state, the "peace, harmony and good order, which make the happiness of a people" (1970 [1735]: 26–27). Then too, he views the earliest stages of primitive life as characterized by "nakedness and barbarity" (1970 [1735]: 35). His concern, we must remember, is with the conditions that are conducive to great poetry. His central argument, then, is that it does not "seem to be given to one and the same Kingdom, to be thoroughly civilized, and afford proper subjects for poetry. The marvelous and wonderful is the nerve of the epic strain. But what marvelous things happen in a well-ordered state?" (1970 [1735]: 26). A well-governed state may be "Happy indeed for the best of ends," namely, "public tranquility and good order; but incapable of giving delight in fiction or poetry" (1970 [1735]: 26). In sum, "peace, harmony and good order, which make the happiness of a people, are the bane of a poem that subsists by wonder and surprise" (1970 [1735]: 27). It is then at a stage between the truly primitive state of "nakedness and barbarity" and "times of wide policy and peace . . . when private passions are buried in the common order, and established discipline" (1977 [1735]: 35) that conditions are most conducive to great national poetry. Such conditions may be dominated by violence and misery or by peace and prosperity; what is essential, though, for the inspiration of epic, is an openness to wonder, heroism, and simplicity, without the routinization of institutionalized order (1970 [1735]: 23–27).

As with culture, so with language (Blackwell 1970 [1735]: 40–59). Blackwell's theory of the progress of language begins with simple, "broken, unequal and boisterous" cries of passion, succeeded by an intermediate stage of development, still part of antiquity, as a people advances to a degree of security, and moves from fear expressions of "terror, rage or want" to a language of "admiration and wonder" (1970 [1735]: 42–43). From this intermediate stage, according to Blackwell, "there is a mighty distance" (1970 [1735]: 43) to the polish of modern language, which he characterizes as enervated by "prattle, and little pretty forms . . . over-run with quibble and sheer wit" (1970 [1735]: 55). "A language thoroughly polished in the modern sense," he goes on, "will not descend to the simplicity of manners absolutely necessary in epic poetry" (1970 [1735]: 59). This has important implications for literary taste, Blackwell suggests: "And this I take to be the reason, 'Why most nations are so delighted with their ancient poets.' Before they are polished into flattery and falsehood, we feel the force of their words, and the truth of their thoughts" (1970 [1735]: 55–56). The appreciation of epic poetry, then, locates it at a point in the developmental trajectory of nations between the beginnings of society and language and the modern condition, though nearer the former than the latter. Epic – poetry in general – is an historical hybrid, affecting and powerful but of the past.

Now, Blackwell's unilinear, stagewise developmental schema is a foundational articulation of what Dugald Stewart later termed "conjectural history," an approach that came to characterize the social thought of the Scottish Enlightenment in the latter half of the eighteenth century.[8]

---

[8] The term "conjectural history" was coined by Dugald Stewart in his commentary on Adam Smith's "Considerations Concerning the First Formation of Languages" (1983 [1761]), which Stewart regarded as a fine exemplar of the approach. Stewart's characterization of conjectural history is as follows:

When, in such a period of society as that in which we live, we compare our intellectual acquirements, our opinions, manners and institutions, with those which prevail among rude tribes, it cannot fail to occur to us as an interesting question, by what gradual steps the transition has been made from the first simple efforts of uncultivated nature, to a state of things so wonderfully artificial and complicated. Whence has arisen that systematical beauty which we admire in the structure of a cultivated language; that analogy which runs through the mixture of languages spoken by the most remote and unconnected nations; and those peculiarities by which they are distinguished from each other? . . . On most of these subjects very little information is to be expected from history; for long before that stage of society when men begin to think of recording their transactions, many of the most important steps of their progress have been made. A few insulated facts may perhaps be collected from the casual observations of travellers, who have viewed the arrangements of rude nations; but nothing, it is evident, can be obtained in this way, which approaches to a regular and connected detail of human improvement.

In this want of direct evidence, we are under a necessity of supplying the place of fact by conjecture; and when we are unable to ascertain how men have actually conducted

The antecedents of Blackwell's historical vision lie in seventeenth-century political philosophy, in which conjectural representations of "natural man" establish the origo from which subsequent political formations may be derived and projected onto a trajectory of historical development that culminates in the modern state.[9] Blackwell's formulation is a creative adaptation of such a priori historical models to the origin and development of language and poetry. Consistent with Stewart's characterization of the methods of conjectural history, Blackwell goes on to use "detached facts" derived from travelers' accounts to complement his historical schema, a strategy of decontextualization and recontextualization, of creating intertextual links and gaps, that serves well in the creation of modernity and its opposites. After rejecting grammatical examples as beyond the understanding of most of his readers, though he claims that he could easily produce them, Blackwell presents instead an example drawn in part from Galland's *Arabian Nights Entertainments*, centering on the linkages among manners, expressive style, and poetic discourse characteristic of the intermediate stage of development. "I will only observe," he offers,

That the Turks, Arabs, Indians, and in general most of the inhabitants of the East, are a solitary kind of people. They speak but seldom, and never long without emotion. But when, in their own phrase, they open their mouth, and give a loose to a fiery imagination, they are poetical, and full of metaphor. Speaking, among such people, is a matter of some moment, as we may gather from their usual introductions; for before they begin to deliver their thoughts, they give notice, that they will open their mouth; that they will unloose their tongue, that they will utter their voice, and pronounce with their lips. These preambles bear a great resemblance to the old forms of introduction in Homer, Hesiod, and Orpheus, in which they are sometimes followed by Virgil. (1970 [1735]: 43–44)

themselves upon particular occasions, of considering in what manner they are likely to have proceeded, from the principles of their nature, and the circumstances of their external situation. In such inquiries, the detached facts which travels and voyages afford us, may frequently serve as landmarks to our speculations; and sometimes our conclusions *a priori* may tend to confirm the credibility of facts, which, on a superficial view, appeared to be doubtful or incredible. (1980 [1794] 292–93)

Towards naming the procedure, Stewart states,

To this species of philosophical investigations, which has no appropriated name in our language, I shall take the liberty of giving the title of *Theoretical* or *Conjectural History*; an expression which coincides pretty nearly in its meaning with that of *Natural History*, as employed by Mr. Hume, and with what some French writers have called *Histoire Raisonnée*. (1980 [1794]: 293)

See also Höpfl (1978); Lehmann (1930: 230–32); R. Meek (1976: 230–43).
[9] The political philosopher who had the strongest influence on Blackwell was Shaftesbury. See Whitney (1926). On the relationship between political philosophies of the "natural man" and conjectural history, see Höpfl (1978: 26) and Klein (1994: 200–1).

This is a highly suggestive passage. In it there is a productive perception of culturally based expressive style, of the relationship between explicitly reflexive utterances and communicative practices, and of the adaptability of such metapragmatic devices to poetic performance. The focus here on highly reflexive speech devices and upon the poetic qualities of the utterances they frame directs attention to marked ways of speaking, to performance, not simply to features of texts. And indeed, what emerges from Blackwell's account of Homer is a picture of the poet as performer, accountable above all to an audience: "The people must be entertained.... For his poems were made to be recited, or sung to a company; and not read in private, or perused in a book, which few were then capable of doing; and I will venture to affirm, that whoever reads Homer in this view loses a great part of the delight he might receive from the poet. His stile, properly so called, cannot be understood in any other light; nor can the strain and manner of his work be felt and relished unless we put ourselves in the place of the audience, and imagine it coming from the mouth of a rhapsodist" (1970 [1735]: 118–19). This is one of the most resonant and illuminating passages in all of eighteenth-century classical scholarship, a cornerstone of relativist perspectives on literature, language, and culture, and an influential adumbration of performance-oriented conceptions of oral poetics. To be sure, the image of Homer as rhapsode was not original to Blackwell (Whitney 1924: 366), but he was the first to extend the idea to a consideration of form–function interrelationships in the singer's performance, tying Homer's style to the context of his performance before an audience. "Put ourselves in the place of the audience": in that phrase, Blackwell articulates the relativist principle of empathetic projection and epistemological shift that is crucial to an understanding of the relationship between form and function.

Blackwell extends his insights into this nexus of interrelationship still further by casting Homer's performance as founded upon extemporaneous improvisation. He centers his attention upon "the habit which the poet must acquire by singing extempory strains" (1970 [1735]: 119). Blackwell finds support for the principle that speech practices regularly employed become habitual and thus fluent "in every art and employment." "An inclination indulged turns to a habit," he argues, "and that, when cultivated rises to an ease and mastery in the profession. It immediately affects our speech and conversation; as we daily see in lawyers, seamen, and most sets of men who converse with ease and fluency in their own stile, tho' they are often puzzled when forced to affect another" (1970 [1735]: 119). Thus, the poet's improvisatory style becomes in Blackwell's formulation a species of occupationally grounded performance register, a conventionalized manner of speaking that grows out of regularity in practice characteristic of a particular group within a heterogeneous speech community. In the formulation of these ideas, Blackwell launched the intellectual tradition that led, in the twentieth century, to the hugely influential oral-formulaic theory of Milman Parry and Albert Lord.

It will be useful to pause at this point to make more explicit what we mean by "relativism" in this discussion. Relativism, as a perspective on the variability of human culture, is founded on the principled recognition of diversity, the understanding that cultural entities (however construed) or their constituent institutions are the unique and historically emergent products of their time and place. By "principled recognition" here, we mean to distinguish the general *experience of diversity* as a condition of social life from the recognition and articulation of a *doctrine of relativism*.[10] Relativism may be manifested in a merely descriptive emphasis on cultural uniqueness and diversity, but at a more profound level it involves a recognition of experiential, phenomenological diversity, that is, the recognition that culture provides the lens through which experience is refracted and that truly relativist understanding demands the kind of empathetic projection captured in Blackwell's phrase, "Put ourselves in the place of the audience." And this kind of projection, to be sure, implies commensurability, the potential for translation from one culture to another (Latour 1993: 113–14).

In more abstract terms, a doctrine of relativism represents the foregrounding of the particular – or the "provincial" – as opposed to the general, the broadly normative, or the universal in the conceptualization of culture, but the two tendencies – particularization and generalization – are not at all incompatible. In practice, a doctrine of relativism may be – usually is – combined with generalizing operations, such as classification or typology. Certainly, in the early coalescence of the doctrine of cultural relativism, as in the thinking of Blackwell, Wood, and Lowth, the relativist perspective may be in tension with received or concurrently emergent generalizing schemas. In the case of the literary explorations of Blackwell, Wood, Lowth, and Blair (with whom we will deal in the next chapter), the doctrine of relativism involves on the one hand a critical corrective to the normative universalizing of classical models, stemming from Renaissance humanism, and on the other hand a dialogue with emergent philosophies of universal progress based upon the ascendency of reason, inspired by Bacon, Locke, and other foundational thinkers of the seventeenth century. What they offer, then, is a hermeneutic relativism in which literary forms are to be interpreted against the ground of the

---

[10] We draw here upon the illuminating work of Schiffman (1992). See also Foerster (1947) and Wellek (1941).

cultures, times, and places in which they were produced – that is, provincialized – coupled with a historicist universalism in which societies and culture may be ranged in a developmental series in terms of their progress towards a rationally founded social, economic, and political order. At the same time, relativist rhetorics form fundamental elements of a number of schemas, such as Blackwell's, for the creation of the modern through the construction of its opposite. Far from a creation of twentieth-century anthropology, as Balibar's (1991) treatment of cultural reasoning would seem to suggest, relativism has formed a commonly used resource for modernist schemes at least from the time of the Enlightenment; it is, as such, part of projects for constructing and reifying social inequality.

One final point. Having distinguished the experience of diversity from the doctrine of relativism, we must also distinguish the latter from what we might call the *ideology of relativism*, that is, the moral commitment to the equal legitimacy and value of each distinctive culture. This commitment figures not at all in the thinking of Blackwell, Wood, Lowth, or Blair.

Returning, then, to the specifics of Blackwell's arguments, we may observe that in foregrounding the "public," social, collective factors that Blackwell identifies as shaping poetic production – culture, language, expressive style, social relations, performance contexts, and the like – we should not lose sight of his announced theme, namely to account for Homer's unsurpassed greatness as an *individual* poet. Blackwell argues that Homer's greatness is attributable to the "united influence" or "conjunct powers" of the *special* qualities of culture, language, subject matter, and other factors that came together in his time and place and enabled his distinctive genius. "It is no wonder," Blackwell maintains, "that such a production should appear but once in three or four thousand years" (1970 [1735]: 334–35).

What was most influential about Blackwell's book, however, was not his delineation of what was distinctive about Homeric Greece or unique to Homer, bur rather the more general sociohistorical and relativist perspective on literary production and interpretation that he offers. His insistence that one cannot comprehend any poetic work, exalted or undistinguished, without due regard for the "public" factors – cultural, social, linguistic – that have a formative influence on the poet and the audience, and his identification of these factors as operating at the level of a people or a nation, represents a foundational, systematic articulation of the relativist poetics that was to achieve widespread currency in European social and literary philosophy in the latter half of the eighteenth century.

We must note, however, that Blackwell's relativism has its limits; it is constrained by a more generalized, proto-evolutionary framework that identifies a progression from primitive "nakedness and barbarity" through an intermediate stage of relatively greater security and understanding to a "well-ordered state." This process operates at two levels: it shapes the historical development of particular peoples, such as the Greeks, and in "the widest view of human affairs" it characterizes the overall history of humankind. When Blackwell attempts to illuminate Homer's poetry by reference to the expressive style of Arabs, Turks, and Indians, thereby assimilating these *contemporary* peoples to the *ancient* Greeks in terms of their ways of speaking, he is operating at the more particular of the two levels; though separated widely in time, the contemporary peoples of the East are at a stage of historical development corresponding to that of Homeric Greece: no longer in the primitive state of nakedness and barbarity, not yet in well-ordered states of "peace, harmony, and good order."

Both, however, are a "mighty distance" from modernity, in the larger scope. By identifying poetry at its most natural and vital as a product of a premodern phase in a larger developmental framework, and by offering a relativist standard for its interpretation, Blackwell fashioned what proved to be a highly attractive and durable bridge to span the fissure between the ancients and the moderns mentioned at the beginning of this discussion. On the one hand, this solution accepts the basic rationalist principle that reason, the philosophical perfection of language, and other features of modern life are inimical to poetry, which is projected back upon a more primitive antecedent stage of development – more passionate, disorderly, even violent than the modern age. Thus displaced, it can nevertheless be claimed as part of a cultural and linguistic heritage at the same time that it is used as a measure of having transcended that past. Moreover, by establishing the linkage between one's own national past and the contemporary culture of others, one can easily claim a warrant for dominion over those others, by virtue of having attained a higher stage of development. Likewise, the feeling of nostalgia and loss that attends radical social change can be assuaged by estheticizing and valorizing the expressive culture of our ancestors and their developmental (if not historical) co-equals at the same time that we distance ourselves from it.

Strong continuities are apparent in Blackwell with the work of the antiquaries in terms of the role of intertextuality in the construction of the Other, despite the change from contemporaneous, domestic Others to those who are seen as being remote in time and nationality as well as in custom. Both Blackwell and the antiquaries claim to have discovered discursive contrasts that corresponded with distinctions between social formations. Their success in this regard was certainly enhanced by their role in *creating* the very gaps that they so masterfully bridged. While the logic of otherness played a role in Locke's efforts to construct modernity in particular ways, he actually contributed fairly little – in spite of his fascination with travel accounts – towards developing processes for generating and naturalizing imaginatively rich and fully formed images of Others. The antiquaries and Blackwell, in their own ways, developed techniques of intertextual projection that are still going strong in culturalist discourses today.

Robert Wood (1717?–1771)

Robert Wood sets his *Essay on the Original Genius and Writings of Homer* (1971 [1775]; hereafter *Essay*) within the context of the ongoing debate concerning the relative value of poets "ancient and modern" (1971 [1775]: vi), focusing on the problem of how to achieve an understanding of ancient works that will serve as a reliable basis for judgments of value. The immediate subject is Homer, but as with Blackwell, Wood's interpretive perspective and conclusions have a far broader reach; Wood was arguably the first scholar to formulate a systematic typological contrast between orality and literacy as a basis for discriminating between types of societies and between stages of cultural development (cf. Harbsmeier 1989), and his ideas were foundational to the understanding of Homer as an oral poet.

Wood proposes that the most significant impediment to understanding and thus to informed evaluation of Homer is "his representation of customs and manners so different from our own" (1971 [1775]: 144). Accordingly, like Blackwell, whom he cites in the *Essay* (1971 [1775]: 117), Wood argues for a historically and culturally relativist interpretive perspective: "If we would do the poet justice, we should approach, as near as possible, to the time and place, when and where, he wrote" (1971 [1775]: ix). Again, this perspective is relativist insofar as a consideration of "the character of the times," the "reigning virtues and vices, their state of police, and degree of civilization, their modes and tastes, in short, the great basis and leading pleasures of life" in Homer's Greece is necessary to an adequate understanding of his poetic works (1971 [1775]: xii–xiii). Wood's thesis, framed in terms of Homer's "mimetic powers," or powers of "imitation," is that the Homeric epics present an accurate reflection of "the manners and customs" as well as the language of his time and place, a "faithful transcript" of "his period of society" (1971 [1775]: vii, xiii).

Wood acknowledges, however, that his relativist interpretive method is susceptible to a number of impediments in its own right. First, there is the sheer exoticism of Homer's epic world: "To reconcile ourselves to usages and customs so very opposite to our own, is a task too difficult for the generality of mankind; and therefore Homer's manners must ever be liable to exceptions in proportion to their difference from those of his readers" (1971 [1775]: 145). Still further, there is the great historical gap that separates Homer's time from our own: "many beautiful allusions to the times, for which he wrote, are irretrievably lost, even to the most conversant in antiquities" (1971 [1775]: 145). How, then, to bridge those gaps of cultural difference and historical loss, to render Homer's world commensurable with our own? Wood's solution builds upon and extends Blackwell's suggestive foray into the comparative method, but adds to it an element of great methodological and rhetorical significance for the authorization of his scholarly project.

Wood was an impressively well traveled and well connected individual, with an abiding interest in classical antiquities. Of his early life and education, little is known: he was born in Ireland around 1717, and possibly educated at Oxford. His early travels appear to have been in the capacity of a traveling tutor. From the mid-1750s to the end of his life in 1771, he enjoyed a very public political career, including lengthy service in Parliament and a term as Pitt's Under-Secretary of State. He was notably active in the Society of Dilettanti, an elite association of gentlemen dedicated to classical studies, which sponsored important archeological investigations of classical antiquity (Kopff 1996: 1037–38). Wood's own scholarly reputation derives principally from a well-endowed and fully equipped expedition that he undertook with several companions in 1750–51, in the course of which he visited the islands and mainland countries of the Aegean and Eastern Mediterranean, including Greece, Turkey, Syria, and Egypt.[11] Wood's most significant publications were based upon that voyage, including *The Ruins of Palmyra* (1971 [1753]) and *The Ruins of Balbec* (1971 [1757]) as well as the *Essay*.

One of the chief objects of Wood's voyage was "to read the Iliad and the Odyssey in the countries, where Achilles fought, and where Ulysses travelled, and where Homer sung" (1971 [1775]: v; cf. 1971 [1753]: ii). Such direct, immediate experience, which stimulates the imagination and enhances our enjoyment of the poet or historian, also "helps us to understand them better" (1971 [1753]: ii). These pleasures, Wood argues, "the traveller can only feel, nor is it to be communicated by description" (1971 [1753]: ii).

But what is it that the traveler will discover? Certainly, the vivid concreteness of place adds verisimilitude to the poetic accounts of events that

[11] Constantine (1984: 66–84) provides an excellent account of this expedition; see also Eisner (1991: 72–74). On Wood's public career, see Courtney (1963).

occurred there and provides a measure of Homer's mimetic accuracy. More importantly, though, especially for bridging the gap between a distant past, obscured by time, and the exoticism of cultures very different from our own, is the discovery of living peoples whose way of life is revealingly analogous to the world mirrored forth in the *Iliad* and the *Odyssey*. Thus, Wood offers a powerful antidote to the doubts engendered by the apparent strangeness of Homer's epic world and to the loss of contextual reference through the erosion of time: "we found the manners of the Iliad still preserved in some parts of the East, nay retaining, in a remarkable degree, that genuine cast of natural simplicity, which we admire in his works and the sacred books" (1971 [1775]: 145). Wood himself finds it extraordinary "That so many of the customs of Homer's age, and still more of the antient Jews should be continued down to the present times" (1971 [1775]: 146). It was on his travels through Arabia, Wood observes, that he and his companions found the resemblance most striking, and it was in Syria that they encountered the "pristine inhabitants" of the region, "with their customs, manners, language, and, what is more extraordinary, their traditions" (1971 [1775]: 149). These traditions included oral poetry. Wood records of the Arab horsemen who accompanied his expedition to Palmyra that "When the business of the day was over, coffee and a pipe of tobacco made their highest luxury, and while they indulged in this, sitting in a circle, one of the company entertained the rest with a song or story, the subject love, or war, and the composition sometimes extemporary" (1971 [1753]: 35).

In effect, then, Wood constructs an interpretive framework to illuminate the Homeric epics and measure the accuracy of Homer's mimetic powers based on a "comparison of the Heroic, Patriarchal, and Bedouin manners" (1971 [1775]: 156). The latter play a critical role in this schema, because it was among the Bedouins, Wood claims, that "I had the opportunity of collecting the most authentic information" (1971 [1775]: 154). That is to say, Wood claims authority for his interpretations on the basis of first-hand observation of living cultures – in short, on the basis of being there. Authenticity resides in immediacy. The inclusion in the comparison of the ancient Jews is warranted by the geographical contiguity of their country to that of the contemporary Arabs. The Arabs of Wood's direct observations, then, like Blackwell's peoples of the East, bridge the temporal gulf between the ancient cultures of the Old Testament Hebrews and Homeric Greeks and those of modern Europe. They exist in the present, but live in the past, mediating between the two. Wood attributes the "perpetual and inexhaustible store of the aboriginal modes and customs of primeval life" that he finds in "the interior of Arabia" to the isolation of the region, the inaccessibility of these ways of life "to the varieties and fluctuations, which conquest, commerce, arts, or agriculture, introduce in other places" (1971 [1775]: 155). The forces of change and development have passed them by – they are out of time, inhabitants of a historical relic area.

What, then, does Wood find in the life of these Bedouins of Arabia that illuminates his reading of Homer? He produces a catalog of characteristic "manners" that will capture the eye and ear of the traveler in the East: a predisposition to "dissimulation and diffidence"; "scenes of cruelty, violence, and injustice"; a contrasting "spirit of hospitality" greater than that of Europe; "a loss of female society," with a concomitant "licentious style of pleasantry"; "persons of the highest rank employed in the lowest domestic duties"; and a "general turn of wit and humour" that is "either flat and insipid or coarse and indelicate" (1971 [1775]: 157–58). All of these he finds as well in the Heroic life of Homeric Greece and the Patriarchal life of Old Testament Israel, making clear that "they are not the capricious singularities of a particular age or country; but that they may be traced up to some common causes" (1971 [1775]: 158).

One possible cause, Wood suggests, is environmental, "the nature of soil and climate" (1971 [1775]: 158). Another, more striking, possibility rests on factors of culture and character common to the region, namely, "the spirit of that unequal legislation, to which Oriental timidity has hitherto indolently submitted; not daring to assert the natural rights of mankind" (1971 [1775]: 158). Thus, Wood's observations of contemporary Arab culture and the comparative data provided by the Old Testament serve to confirm Homer's mimetic powers and to provide an interpretive frame of reference for reading the *Iliad* and the *Odyssey* as accurate reflections of the culture in which they were produced. That culture has both a regional and a historical reach; it encompasses both the ancient and the archaized contemporary peoples of the East. Most importantly, it stands in deep contrast to European modernity, not simply in terms of neutrally conceived cultural differences, but in moral, ideological terms as well. The European traveler will be "surprised," "shocked," "disgusted," "offended" by most of the characteristic Oriental traits that Wood enumerates, even as he is occasionally "charmed" by the general spirit of hospitality. Moreover, the differences that engender these negative reactions are grounded in significant part in contrastive political principles: despotism versus the "the natural rights of mankind" (1971 [1775]: 159).

Wood's perspective on Homer, then, is relativist insofar as it posits that the *Iliad* and the *Odyssey* become maximally intelligible to the extent that they are viewed as accurate reflections of Homeric Greece, but it is far from morally or ideologically neutral. Nor does it rest on fine discriminations of cultural difference. Rather, it is constructed in terms of gross distinctions between the pejoratively framed and archaized culture of the unchanging East and the enlightened modern culture of Europe. What Wood finds, then, is modernity – the Enlightenment's construction of knowledge, rationality, and individualism and its marginalization of rhetoric – by virtue of the absence of these purportedly universal features in the Orient.

One of the characteristic traits of the East that Wood enumerates in his comparison of Heroic, Patriarchal, and Bedouin manners warrants our further attention: the "dissimulation and diffidence" of Oriental expression. "There is nothing more remarkable in the manners of the East," Wood observes,

especially to an English traveller, than the degree of refinement to which profound dissimulation is carried in all ranks, but especially among those in power. In the visits and common intercourse of the Great, more attention is paid to the looks than to the words of the company: and the speaker generally weighs, what he is to say, by the countenance of the person he converses with, rather than by his own sentiments or opinion of the question. He accommodates his language much less to truth and matter of fact, than to the private purposes of his hopes or fears. In short, all confidence is destroyed by the despotism of the East. Suspicion begins with the prince, and from him a general diffidence spreads through every rank and order, ending only in the man, who has nothing to fear, because he has nothing to lose. The arts of disguise are in those countries the great arts of life; and the character of Ulysses would form a perfect model for those, who wish to make their way in it with security and respect. (1971 [1775]: 158–59)

Here, Wood's ethnographic observation of an interactional style characteristic of his Arab hosts illuminates the character of Odysseus and confirms for Wood once again the mimetic accuracy of Homer's compositions. Wood's observation, of course, is baldly ethnocentric, reading the contextual orientation of speakers to their interlocutors in the shaping of conversational interaction in negative terms, as dissimulation, disregard of truth and fact, and craven suppression of one's own sentiments or opinions. That is to say, Wood's own language ideology, consistent with the "elocutionary revolution" of mid-eighteenth-century Britain valorizing self-expression, plain truth, and objective fact (Fliegelman 1993), casts a negative shadow on the expressive manners of the East, darkened still further by his Englishman's contempt for "the despotism of the East" and the "Oriental timidity" to which it gives rise. What is most significant, for our purposes, is that Wood uses communicative style and its social and political correlates as primary criteria for differentiating rational, rights-oriented, politically enlightened, individualistic modern England from the emotional, dissimulating, suspicious, despotic cultures of heroic and partriarchal antiquity on the one hand, and the contemporary but archaic cultures of the Orient.

Wood uses language and communicative style in similar fashion to define the gap between antiquity and modernity in an extended consideration of Homer's language. Dismissing most treatments of Homer's language as anachronistic because they fail to consider "the poet's age and manners," Wood proposes a more historically and culturally relativist perspective, revolving around what was to become one of the most powerful and enduring articulations of the ancient/modern contrast: orality versus literacy. Developing upon Blackwell's suggestive opening, Wood insists that the *Iliad* and the *Odyssey* stem from an age before writing and that they were therefore not to be read, but performed before an audience (1971 [1775]: 294–95). In Homeric Greece, Wood proposes:

all was effected by memory; and the histories of ancient times were commemorated in verses, which people took care faithfully to transmit to those, who came after them. They were also preserved in temples, where, upon festivals, the priests and priestesses used to chant them to the people. There were also bards, whose sole province it was to commemorate the great actions of their gods and heroes. Their law was entrusted to verse, and adapted to measure and music. From all which we learn, that all was consigned to memory; and that there was no written record. (1971 [1775]: 253–54).

Wood, in effect, attributes to early Greece a civil and religious culture of poetic performance, in which "there were no compositions in prose" (1971 [1775]: 239–40), the priests, as lawgivers, and the bards, as historians, were also poets and musicians, and "all instruction... was wrapt in Melody and Verse" (1971 [1775]: 287).

Homer, then, "left no written record of his works"; the full, written texts of the *Iliad* and the *Odyssey* were assembled later out of "scraps and detached pieces" in oral tradition (1971 [1775]: 278). It is worth noting here that Wood likens this process of text-making to the achievement of James Macpherson in the composition of the Ossianic epic of *Fingal*, in Scotland, which we will consider at length in the next chapter. Wood suggests that if those who assembled the Homeric epics out of "what had been before only sung by the Rhapsodists of Ionia, just as some curious fragments of ancient poetry have been lately collected in the northern parts of this island, their reduction to order in Greece was a work of taste and judgment," and they are entitled to "claim the same merit in regard to Homer, that the ingenious Editor of Fingal is entitled to from Ossian" (1971 [1775]: 279).

Conceding the difficulty his modern readers might experience in "conceiving how Homer could acquire, retain, and communicate, all he knew, without the aid of letters," Wood suggests that understanding Homer's art becomes less difficult when we realize that "the fidelity of oral tradition, and the powers of memory" in Homeric Greece were much greater, and "the poet's knowledge" much less, than we are apt to consider (1971 [1775]: 259). This is a call, once again, to historical relativism: "the oral traditions of a learned and enlightened age will greatly mislead us, if from them we form our judgment on those of a period, when history had no other resources" (1971 [1775]: 259–60).

Wood goes on to offer a series of formal and functional – and at the same time, historical and developmental – correlates of orality and literacy which laid the foundations of an enduring typological opposition. The oral culture of performance, he maintains, "is agreeable to that rude state of society... when civilization was addressed more to the passions than the understanding" (1971 [1775]: 269). Here, Wood correlates early, oral society with emotion, modern society – by implication – with understanding.

In regard to the style of oral performance, Wood suggests that "When the sense was catched from the sound, and not deliberately collected from paper, simplicity and clearness were more necessary. Involved periods and an embarrassed style were not introduced until writing became an art, and labour supplied the place of genius. The frequent repetition of entire passages... was not only more natural, but less observable, therefore less offensive" (1971 [1775]: 281). Here, Wood adds new dimensions and their correlates, tying orality to naturalness, innate genius, clarity, formal simplicity, and repetition on the one hand; writing to artifice, labor, obscurity (by implication), involved periods, and embarrassed style on the other. Still further:

If [Homer's] language had not yet acquired the refinements of a learned age, it was for that reason not only more intelligible and clear, but also less open to pedantry and affectation. For as technical and scientific terms were unknown, before the separation of arts: and till science became the retired pursuit of a few, as there was no school but that of Life, and no philosophy but that of Common Sense; so we find in Homer nothing out of the reach of an ordinary capacity, and plain understanding. (1971 [1775]: 285–86).

In these passages, Wood counterposes an earlier (oral) stage in the development of human knowledge in which common sense, the language of common life, experiential learning, and plain understanding prevail, with a later, learned (literate) stage, in which philosophy and science become separate, specialized, esoteric pursuits, characterized by their own special registers.

Finally, in more general terms, Wood distinguishes the language of
Nature from the language of Compact, in a classically modernist formulation that elaborates the separation of nature from society:

The language which we bring into the world with us is not confined to the organs
of speech; but it is made up of voice, countenance, and gesture. And had not
our powers of articulation, that distinguishing mark of our social constitution,
suggested a more convenient mode of conveying our ideas, the simple tones of
Nature, with the varieties of modulation, which are now assigned to the province
of music, might have been applied to the purposes of common life. . . .
    Such is the language of Nature, without which there could be no language
of Compact, the first supplying that communication of ideas which was absolutely necessary to establish the latter; though afterwards falling into disuse, in
proportion to the progress and improvement of what was gradually substituted
in its stead. But, though banished in great measure from common use, it still
retains its powers in the province of Poetry, where the most finished efforts of
artifical language are but cold and languid circumlocution, compared with that
passionate expression of Nature, which, incapable of misrepresentation, appeals
directly to our feelings, and finds the shortest road to the heart. (1971 [1775]:
282–84)

Homer, Wood goes on to say, "lived before the language of Compact and
Art had so much prevailed over that of Nature and Truth" (1971 [1775]:
284).
    The oppositions in this passage are clearly articulated: the language of
Nature, which Wood sees as developmentally prior, simple, keyed to the
emotions and to expressive performance, and truthful, versus the language of Compact, which is artificial, developmentally later, cold, and
keyed to circumlocution. Most significant here is the linkage that Wood
establishes between modes of communication and the structure of social
relations. In counterposing the language of Nature and the language of
Compact, Wood is invoking those currents of eighteenth-century political
philosophy that posit a stage of social development in which relationships
are based wholly on the "natural" bonds of procreation and kinship, succeeded by a stage in which relationships are based upon the rationally
motivated bonds of contract (compact). It is this linkage above all that
allows the typological opposition between orality and literacy to stand
more broadly for contrastive social formations and to mark the historical
juncture that separates them.
    Note the importance here of Wood's construction of intertextuality in
antiquity. His description of memory and oral transmission as modes of
reproducing knowledge is, of course, maximally contrastive with the stress
in European modernity on refusing the authority of texts and persons in
favor of social reproduction through the critical, rational, disinterested

reflections of individuals and the need to break with traditional structures. The elevation of constructions of metadiscursive practices into means of reading the cognitive, social, and even political characteristics of peoples and nations, framed in terms of the differences between "oral" and "literate" cultures, has remained a feature of modernist discourse right into the twentieth century, as the work of Milman Parry (1971), Albert B. Lord (1960), Eric Havelock (1963, 1982, 1986), Walter J. Ong (1967, 1982), and Jack Goody (1977) attests.

Setting out these contrasts in tabular form reveals more clearly the terms in which Wood builds the typological opposition between the past and the present upon the communicative technologies of speech and writing, orality and literacy.

Orality	Literacy
Antiquity	Modernity
Performance	Writing
Passion	Understanding
Language of nature	Language of compact
Nature as basis for social relations	Compact as basis for social relations
Language of common life, common sense	Language of philosophy and science
Memory	Learned and enlightened knowledge
Simplicity, clarity, repetition	Involved periods, embarrassed style

Interestingly, the typological opposition that Wood constructs is not perfect. While the communicative gap between oral and literate societies that emerges from Wood's effort to establish an interpretive foundation for a relativist reading of Homer would seem to consign poetry to the far side of the historical divide, he does allow a place for poetry in modern life. "The province of poetry," set apart from contemporary "common use," represents for Wood a holding area for the language of Nature in modern life. Poetry thus mediates between the past and the present, providing a critical vantage-point on those aspects of modern, literate society and the language of Compact that may remind us that the transition from orality to literacy entails a dimension of loss, the sacrifice of the simplicity, clarity, directness, and passion that distinguish the language of Nature.

It is also worth noting that Wood's oral/literate typology is at odds in at least one significant respect with his characterization of ancient Greek, ancient Hebrew, and Arab cultures as exemplars of the premodern stage of historical development. In enumerating those features of Arab culture that capture the traveler's attention, we recall, Wood places dissimulation at the head of the list – the Arabs, like Odysseus, have no regard for truth. A predisposition to deception, however, should be incompatible with the language of Nature and Truth, which Wood attributes to Homeric Greece and, by extension, to the Bedouins of Syria. We gain little, however, by holding Wood to a standard of rigorous consistency. It is ultimately more productive to recognize Wood's comparative method and his oral/literate dichotomy as parallel but only loosely coupled devices to establish relativist perspectives for the interpretation and evaluation of Homer, based upon discursive and metadiscursive ways and means. One perspective derives its authority from the reliability of direct, proto-ethnographic observation and the discovery, by means of detailed comparison, of sociocultural correspondences. The second is more analytical, drawing its rhetorical efficacy from the logic of oppositions in the construction of binary typologies. Both, however, use discursive and metadiscursive practices as potent means of contruing the historical gap between antiquity and modernity.

Robert Lowth (1710–1787)

The science of biblical poetics

In 1741, six years after the publication of Blackwell's *Enquiry*, Robert Lowth (1710–1787), then Professor of Poetry at Oxford, commenced the series of lectures that were eventually published in 1753 as *De sacra poesi Hebraeorum praelectiones*, and in English translation in 1787 as *Lectures on the Sacred Poetry of the Hebrews*. Lowth resigned his professorship in 1750 and went on to a distinguished career as a churchman, eventually attaining the office of Bishop of London.[12]

The influence of Lowth's *Lectures* on biblical form criticism has been enormous; his work has generated an extensive, often polemical literature on the poetics of the Old Testament (Cripps 1953; Gillingham 1994; Hrushovski 1971; Kugel 1981; Watson 1984). He is best known to linguists for his *Short Introduction to English Grammar* (1979 [1762]) and to students of poetics for his foundational work on parallelism, presented in the *Lectures*, further elaborated in his English translation of the Book of Isaiah (1995 [1778]), and celebrated by Roman Jakobson as foundational to structuralist poetics (1960). *Lectures* is also recognized as a classic precursor to the full-blown Orientalist project of the nineteenth century that is the focus of Edward Said's well-known critique (Said 1978: 17; see also Olender 1992: 29–31). And students of nineteenth-century

---

[12] On Lowth's life and works, see Hepworth (1978).

literature credit the inspirational role of Lowth's ideas concerning the nexus of poetry and prophecy in the development of romanticist ideology (Harshbarger 1995; Prickett 1986; Roston 1965). For our purposes, Lowth's widely read and influential works on Hebrew poetry offer an illuminating complement from biblical philology to the classical scholarship of Blackwell and Wood.

Lowth's *Lectures* represented an important departure in biblical scholarship: a study of the Old Testament not as theology, but as literature. Lowth was certainly not the first to direct attention to the literary properties of scriptural texts, but even in the enlightened era of mid-seventeenth-century England, to treat the Bible as literature required careful justification in the face of widespread belief that scriptural texts were above such considerations of verbal craft or judgments of aesthetic value, let alone all appeal to the earthly pleasures of aesthetic experience.[13] Lowth's justification for taking up this problematic line of inquiry is suffused with the spirit of the Enlightenment: he naturalizes the poetry of the Old Testament (much as Blackwell naturalized the poetry of Homer) and then proceeds to bring it under the aegis of naturalistic, scientific study. Is it only the writings of the classical authors, he asks, that "should be reduced to method and theory," while "those which boast a much higher origin, and are justly attributed to the inspiration of the Holy Spirit, may be considered illustrious by their native force and beauty, but not as conformable to the principles of science, nor to be circumscribed by any rules of art?" Certainly, he contends, sacred poetry is, in its origins, "far superior to both *nature* and *art*," but if we are to understand its efficacy in "exciting the human affections" we must comprehend what those affections are and how they are excited.

In Lowth's classically Aristotelian view, the function of sacred poetry – indeed, of all poetry – is to instruct its hearers or readers in truth and virtue, exploiting the aesthetic pleasure that poetry affords (1995 [1778] I: 7). "Since...it is the purpose of sacred Poetry to form the human mind to the constant habit of true virtue and piety," he offers, "and to excite the more ardent affections of the soul, in order to direct them to their proper end; whoever has a clear insight into the instrument, the machinery as it were, by which this end is effected, will certainly contribute not a little to the improvement of the critical art" (1969 [1787] I: 44–46). Much of his argument, then, centers on the machinery – in the mechanistic idiom of Enlightenment science – of form–function interrelationships, and his investigative method draws its charter from science as well: "Moreover, as in all other branches of science, so in poetry, art

---

[13] For a summary and discussion of these issues, see Sternberg (1985).

or theory consists in a certain knowledge derived from the careful observation of nature, and confirmed by practice and experience; or men of
learning, having remarked in things what was graceful, what was fit, what
was conducive to the attainment of certain ends, they digested such discoveries as had been carefully made, and reduced them to an established
order or method" (Lowth 1969 [1787] I: 45). In bringing sacred poetry under scientific scrutiny, Lowth anticipates further challenges, both
from the ideologues of natural science, who consider poetry too "light
and trifling" for serious inquiry, and from religious zealots, who consider
it "profane or impious" to cast the holy scriptures as poetic art (1969
[1787] I: 49). The poetry of the Old Testament, he contends, "Poetry in
its very beginning," possesses "from its birth . . . a certain maturity both
of beauty and strength." Its originary functions, "to commend to the
Almighty the prayers and thanksgivings of his creatures, and to celebrate
his praises," and "to display to mankind the mysteries of the divine will,
and the predictions of future events," Lowth proposes, are "the best and
noblest of all employments" (1969 [1787] I: 47–48). Thus, the sacred
writings of the ancient Hebrews, as "the only specimens of the primeval
and genuine poetry to be found," are of antiquarian as well as spiritual
value, a key to the origins of religious expression (1969 [1787] I: 50).
Lowth's turn to science, we should emphasize, is not simply a ploy to
add rhetorical weight to his investigation by appealing to the intellectual
cachet of natural science. It is, in fact, a methodological benchmark in the
study of discourse structures, though its potential was not fully realized
until well into the twentieth century. Indeed, it is Lowth's scientific perspective that allowed him to discover the "machinery" of Old Testament
poetry, by investigating the sacred texts in their own terms, as a system,
without being constrained by a priori conceptions of what constitutes
poetry. For Lowth, the poetic structures of the texts are to be discovered,
by naturalistic investigation.

The productiveness of Lowth's perspective emerges especially clearly
in the Preliminary Dissertation to his translation of Isaiah, in which he
frames his own approach against what he sees as the universal understanding "that the Prophecies of Isaiah are written in prose." The alternative
possibility, "that they are written in verse, in measure, or rhythm, or whatever it is that distinguishes, as poetry, the composition of those book of
the Old Testament which are allowed to be poetical . . . has never been
supposed, at least has not been at any time the prevailing opinion" (1995
[1778]: ii). Lowth goes on to survey various attempts – all unsuccessful
in his view – to capture Isaiah under the regularities of one or another
poetic patterning principle already familiar to scholars. Even those books
of the Old Testament that were recognized as "written in verse" were

adjudged to be imperfect and crude by the formal standards of Western, classically shaped poetics. Lowth's perspective not only allowed him to discover the poetry of Isaiah, but to elucidate the poetics of much of the Old Testament.[14] Within the context of eighteenth-century philology, it offered a new scientific foundation to the older strains of historical and cultural relativism, derived from Renaissance humanism.

Lowth proceeds to his elucidation of Hebrew poetry by offering a semantic analysis of two Hebrew words, namely, *Mizmor* and *Mashal*, that might serve as "general terms" for "poem." We should acknowledge that the semantics of *Mizmor* and *Mashal* are far more complex than Lowth's treatment – let alone our own simple summary – would indicate. James Kugel argues strongly that there is in fact "no word for 'poetry' in biblical Hebrew," and that "to speak of 'poetry' at all in the Bible will be in some measure to impose a concept foreign to the biblical world" (1981: 69). But here again, we are less concerned with the substantive accuracy than with the rhetoric and semiotics of Lowth's argument.

Mizmor, according to Lowth, denotes "a short composition cut and divided into distinct parts. It is thus called in reference to the verse and numbers." This is significant, in Lowth's view, "since it appears essential to every species of poetry, that it be confined to numbers, and consists of some kind of verse, (for indeed wanting this, it would not only want its most agreeable attributes, but would scarcely deserve the name of poetry)." Accordingly, Lowth feels called upon to demonstrate "that those parts at least of the Hebrew writings which we term poetic, are in a metrical form, and to inquire whether any thing be certainly known concerning the nature and principles of this versification or not" (1969 [1787] I: 56). A direct demonstration, however, is impossible to achieve, because the "sound and pronunciation" of ancient Hebrew have been obscured by "extreme antiquity" (1969 [1787] I: 57); the poetics of the Hebrew sacred texts is thus something of an antiquarian problem as well as a formal one. There remain, nevertheless, certain "vestiges of verse" or "artifices of poetry" discernible in the texts, including the addition or subtraction of syllables, the use of special particles, ellipsis, "frequent change of persons," "more frequent change or variation of the tenses than occurs in common language," and other "new and extraordinary forms of expression" (1969 [1787] I: 58–62, 309–30), all components of a special register of heightened language that characterizes – to varying degrees – the scriptural texts. The most important such vestiges mark those passages which "treat one subject in many different ways, and dwell upon the same sentiment; when they express the same thing in different words, or different

---

[14] For a discussion of a similar discovery process, see Hymes (1981: 309–41).

things in a similar form of words; when equals refer to equals, and opposites to opposites" (1969 [1787] I: 68–69). The resultant "conformation of the sentences," which Lowth subsequently terms "parallelism," provides evidence of the poetry in the scriptural texts, though it alone is not constitutive of poetry, according to the argument of the *Lectures* and, to a lesser extent, of the introduction to the translation of Isaiah.

Mashal, which Lowth sees as the more important of the two terms, is usually translated as "parable," but "if we investigate its full and proper force, we shall find that it includes three forms or modes of speech, the sententious, the figurative, and the sublime" (1969 [1787] I: 76–78). These three styles, or modes, are systemically related formal dimensions of all Hebrew sacred poetry, operating with varying degrees of salience from one genre to another, but always present in some measure in each. The sententious style resides in the terse, aphoristic, parabolic quality of the scriptural texts, the figurative in the characteristic use in the texts of figurative language, and the sublime in those features that heighten and intensify the style, "that force of composition . . . which strikes and overpowers the mind, which excites the passions, and which expresses ideas at one with perspicuity and elevation" (1969 [1787] I: 309). This latter mode is intrinsic to all poetry, as "the language of the passions," which "are naturally inclined to amplification," to expression that is "animated, bold, and magnificent" (1969 [1787] I: 309). As all the formal and figural devices that Lowth treats under the rubrics of *Mizmor* and the sententious and figural styles are likewise in the service of sublimity, we will concentrate our attention on the latter two stylistic dimensions, which are, in any event, most relevant to the broader considerations of this work.

Lowth defines the sententious style as the "primary characteristic of Hebrew poetry, as being the most conspicuous and comprehensive of all"; it pervades all of the poetry of the Hebrews (1969 [1787] I: 98–99). The principal "instrument," the formal "machinery" of the sententious style, Lowth identifies as grammatical and semantic parallelism, the elucidation of which remains the contribution for which he is best remembered. "Each language," he suggests, "possesses a peculiar genius and character, on which depend the principles of the versification, and in great measure the style or colour of the poetic diction" (1969 [1787] I: 101). What imparts to Hebrew poetry its distinguishing character, Lowth discovers, is that "The Hebrew poets frequently express a sentiment with the utmost brevity and simplicity, illustrated by no circumstances, adorned with no epithets . . .; they afterwards call in the aid of ornament; they repeat, they vary, they amplify the same sentiment; and adding one or more sentences which run parallel to each other, they express the same or a similar, and often a contradictory sentiment in nearly the same form

of words" (1969 [1787] I: 100). In more formal terms, the chief characteristic of Hebrew poetry consists in "a certain equality, resemblance,
or parallelism between the members of each period; so that in two lines
(or members of the same period) things for the most part shall answer
to things, and words to words, as if fitted to each other by a kind of rule
or measure" (1969 [1787] II: 34).[15] Framed in these terms, parallelism
is a device of textual cohesion, tying adjacent lines together into distichs
and representing the constitutive patterning principle of many entire texts
and a characterizing feature of others (Hymes 1981: 177–78). But it is
simultaneously in the service of coherence: Lowth points out that close
attention to parallelistic structures is of great assistance to the interpretive reader, "and will often lead him to the meaning of obscure words and
phrases" (1995 [1778]: xxxvii). Still further, the repetition with variation
that characterizes parallelism imparts rhetorical emphasis and closure to
the propositional content of the text. It is precisely these mechanisms of
cohesion, coherence, and rhetorical emphasis that enhance the memorability, repeatability, and persuasiveness of the sacred texts and so render
them useful for didactic purposes.

Lowth's discovery, typology, and systematic formal analysis of semantic and grammatical parallelism in Old Testament poetry is a benchmark
achievement for which he is justly celebrated, but it is important to recall
in this connection that his analytic concerns are not restricted to formal
considerations alone. As noted earlier in our discussion, Lowth is ultimately interested in functional considerations – the religious uses and
ritual efficacy of sacred poetry – and his close attention to poetic form is
in the service of illuminating form–function interrelationships. This latter
focus finds expression in his works in regard to two principal functional
dimensions, one having to do with the relationship between poetic form
and rhetorical efficacy, the other with the relationship between poetic
form and structures of performance.

We have already suggested the former dimension of function, in connection with the didactic thrust of the sententious style: its capacity to
capture attention, to focus perception, to arouse emotions, to enhance
memorability and repeatability. Lowth also attends to the particular effects of the various types of parallel construction, by which these formal
devices are adapted to different uses: "the sort of parallelism is chiefly

---

[15] Another formulation, from the Preliminary Dissertation to the translation of Isaiah:

> The correspondence of one verse, or line, with another, I call parallelism. When a propo-
> sition is delivered, and a second is subjoined to it, or drawn under it, equivalent, or con-
> trasted with it, parallel in sense; or similar to it in the form of grammatical construction;
> these I call parallel lines; and the words, or phrases, answering one to another in the
> corresponding lines, parallel terms. (1995 [1778]: x)

made use of, which is best adapted to the nature of the subject and of the poem." For example, "synonymous parallels have the appearance of art and concinnity [i.e., harmonious adaptation of parts] and a studied elegance; they prevail chiefly in shorter poems. . . . The antithetic parallelism," on the other hand, "gives an acuteness and force to adages and moral sentences" (1995 [1778]: xxvii).

While Lowth acknowledges that little is known concerning the liturgical uses of sacred poetry among the ancient Hebrews, he attempts to identify several related modes of performance from contextual evidence in the sacred texts themselves. These characteristically involved an arrangement of "opposite choirs" who sang in responsive alternation to each other. In one such arrangement, for example, one of the choirs sang the first line of a distich to which the other responded with the second. "Now if this were the ancient and primitive mode of chanting their hymns, as indeed appears highly probable," Lowth reasons, "the proximate cause will be easily explained, why poems of this kind are disposed in equal stanzas, indeed in equal distichs, for the most part; and why these distichs should in some measure consist of versicles or parallelisms corresponding to each other" (1969 [1787] II: 32). This formal pattern, he suggests further, well adapted both to musical patterning and to "the genius and cadence of the language," was "easily extended . . . into the other species of poetry, though not designed for the same purpose," until, ultimately, "it pervaded the whole of the poetry of the Hebrews" (1969 [1787] II: 32–33). Taken as a way of accounting for the pervasiveness of syntactic parallelism in Old Testament poetic genres, Lowth's claims are far too speculative to be fully persuasive. Taken as an attempt to link poetic form to structures of performance in certain genres of sacred poetry, it appears far more productive.

Relativist perspectives on figurative language

The relativist dimension that we noted earlier in relation to Lowth's discovery of grammatical parallelism as the dominant patterning principle of ancient Hebrew sacred poetry is, if anything, more explicit in his treatment of what he terms the figurative style, that is, the figurative component of the poetic system. To open his consideration of the figurative style, Lowth returns to the Hebrew word, *Mashal*, which, in its most common meaning, "denotes resemblance, and is therefore directly expressive of the figurative style, a far as the nature of figures consists in the substitution of words, or rather of ideas, for those which they resemble" (1969 [1787] I: 100). His approach, he explains, is "in some degree remote from common use," a departure from that of "the Rhetoricians" in their dependence on Greek terms and distinctions, useful though these may be "in their proper place." "Our present concern," he insists, "is not to explain the sentiments of the Greek but of the Hebrew writers" (1969 [1787] I: 104–6), and though he goes on to use rhetorical terms derived from the Greek, it is clear that he intends his investigation once again to be based on the Hebrew corpus as a textual system in its own right, as "the nature of the subject itself obviously indicates to us" (1969 [1787] I: 111), and as free as possible from a priori assumptions.

Lowth distinguishes four types of figure: metaphor, allegory, simile, and prosopopaeia; his examination of the workings of these figures, which we will not recapitulate in detail, is based upon the premise that the design of figurative language in Hebrew sacred poetry is to portray objects with enhanced clarity and force, to make them more striking or sublime. Accordingly, the term that is employed to illustrate and elevate another subject should be "familiar and obvious" and "at the same time as grand and magnificent as possible." The images that are best suited to the purpose are those "with which both the writers and the persons they address are well acquainted, and which have been constantly esteemed of the highest dignity and importance" (1969 [1787] I: 111–12).

Interpretive difficulties will arise, however, if the reader's understandings are different from those of the author; what may be well and felicitously expressed in terms of the author's "habits of life" will strike the reader from another culture as "mean and obscure, harsh and unnatural." The greater the distance in terms of "time, situation, customs sacred or profane," Lowth postulates, the greater the gap in understanding, and in a classic instance of Orientalist othering, he proposes that the ancient Hebrews are maximally foreign to his eighteenth-century British audience.

Here we encounter once again the familiar epistemological gaps in history and culture that the classical philologists, Blackwell and Wood, strove to transcend. "Not only the antiquity of these writings forms a principal obstruction in many respects," Lowth warns, "but the manner of living, of speaking, of thinking, which prevailed in those times, will be found altogether different from our customs and habits." We as interpreters must be on our guard, then, "lest viewing them from an improper situation, and rashly estimating all things by our own standard, we form an erroneous judgment." It is not enough, Lowth cautions, "to be acquainted with the language of these people, their manners, discipline, rites and ceremonies; we must even investigate their inmost sentiments, the manner and connexion of their thoughts." The charge is this: "we must see all things with their eyes, estimate all things by their opinions: we must endeavour as much as possible to read Hebrew as the Hebrews would have read it" (1969 [1787] I: 113). More specifically, "he who would perceive and feel the peculiar and interior elegancies of the Hebrew poetry, must imagine himself exactly situated as the persons for whom it was written, or even as the writers themselves; he must not attend to the ideas which on a cursory reading certain words would obtrude upon his mind; he is to feel them as a Hebrew, hearing or delivering the same words, at the same time, and in the same country" (1969 [1787] I: 114).

We quote this passage at length as representing a remarkably clear and explicit adumbration of a relativist strategy for the achievement of cross-cultural, historical, and cross-linguistic understanding, in a word, for commensurability. But the crucial element of Lowth's formulation, the feature that makes it especially apt for our present purposes, is that it is framed not simply in terms of "habits of life" in general, but in terms of ways of producing and receiving discourse. What Lowth offers is a relativist perspective on discourse – in this case, poetic discourse – insisting that if we are to comprehend what it is, what it means, and how it works, we must strive to do so in terms of the understandings and experiences of the people who produce and receive it. Still further, this interpretive process demands attention not only to language, but to the "manner of speaking" by which discourse is given voice. Fascinatingly, the use of the metadiscursive practices in constructing relativist readings is authorized, in part, by invoking a methodology drawn from the natural sciences.

The translation of Isaiah

Lowth's *Lectures* had a powerful impact on scriptural studies, not only in England, but on the continent as well, especially in Germany. Within a few years of the work's publication (in Latin), in 1753, Johann Michaelis published a German translation with his own annotations (later incorporated into subsequent editions of the *Lectures*), and Hugh Blair drew heavily from Lowth in his own lecture on Hebrew poetry. The accessibility and currency of Lowth's ideas, however, broadened considerably with the publication of *Isaiah: A New Translation*, in 1778, nine years before the translation of the *Lectures* into English. *Isaiah* attracted a broad readership, and its popularity extended well into the nineteenth century. The translation allowed Lowth to demonstrate "the use and application" of his close formal analysis of Old Testament poetics, so that the non-specialist reader "may not think his pains wholly lost, in labouring through this long disquisition concerning sentences and members of sentences; in weighing words, and balancing periods," as he offers in the Preliminary Dissertation to the work.

In providing a warrant for his translation, Lowth feels no need to justify the task of translation itself; his is, after all, only the latest in a long series of translations from the Old Testament Hebrew, including translations into English.[16] He is certainly concerned, however, to make clear his own standards for translational adequacy and the necessity of his methods for meeting them. The opening sentence of the Preliminary Dissertation sets out Lowth's aims: "The design of the following translation of Isaiah is not only to give an exact and faithful representation of the words and of the sense of the Prophet, by adhering closely to the letter of the text, and treading as nearly as may be in his footsteps; but, moreover, to imitate the air and manner of the author, to express the form and fashion of the composition, and to give the English reader some notion of the peculiar turn and cast of the original" (1995 [1778]: i). The two parts of the design, Lowth offers, are quite compatible with each other, but while many attempts have been made to provide a literal translation of Isaiah, "a just representation of the Prophet's manner, and of the form of his composition, has never been attempted, or even thought of, by any translator, in any language whether antient or modern" (1995 [1778]: i).

Both parts of the design demand rigorous source criticism. Authority resides in what is conceived to be the "original" source, the first full entextualization of the text by its putative author. This is all the more true, of course, of sacred texts, considered to have been produced by divine inspiration. Each successive link in the intertextual chain of scribal transmission represents a recontextualization of the text, which Lowth considers inevitably a re-entextualization. Insofar as each of these links enlarges the textual gap between successive copies and the authoritative Ur-text, new textual elements constitute "errors," "impure" etiolations of the text. The task of the text-critic, therefore, is to remove the textual impurities introduced by the history of recontextualization and re-entexualization and to restore once more the original "true" and "perfect" text. Clearly, the rhetoric of originary purity and intertextual error that Lowth employs, a legacy of Renaissance humanism, is motivated in significant part by the established authority of the scriptural texts and the epistemology of the Judaeo-Christian tradition. Nevertheless, this metadiscursive ideology of the authority of originals and the corruptive force of intertextual mediation was clearly susceptible to extension and secularization; it provided the frame of reference that dominated the origin-oriented investigations of oral texts throughout the nineteenth and well into the twentieth century.

---

[16] For a discussion of Lowth's approach to translation, within the larger historical context of Bible translation, see Prickett (1986).

Although Lowth emphasizes the perfection of the source text as a foundation for accurate, literal translation, it is equally important to the fulfilment of the second component of the design he outlines at the beginning of the Preliminary Dissertation, that is, "to imitate the air and manner of the author, to express the form and fashion of the composition, and to give the English reader some notion of the turn and cast of the original." The second responsibility of the translator, beyond literal accuracy, is to produce an "expressive resemblance of the original" (1995 [1778]: xxxv). "In a work of elegance and genius," Lowth insists, "the translator is not only to inform: he must endeavour to please; and to please by the same means, if possible, by which his Author pleases. If this pleasure arises in a great measure from the shape of the composition, and the form of the construction, as it does in the Hebrew poetry perhaps beyond any other example whatsoever, the translator's eye ought to be always intent upon this: to neglect this, is to give up all chance of success, and all pretension to it" (1995 [1778]: xxxvi). If aesthetic effect and rhetorical efficacy depend upon textual form in the original work, then it is incumbent upon the translator to exploit the same formal machinery in the shaping of the translation.

Lowth's notes to the translation suggest how his concern with formal structures (as well as textual criticism) shaped his translation. To take a typical example, Lowth renders Isaiah XXIV.15 as follows:

Wherefore in the distant coasts, glorify ye JEHOVAH.
In the distant coasts of the sea, the name of JEHOVAH I, the God of Israel.
(1995 [1778]: 59)[17]

In his note on this verse, Lowth justifies the reading "coasts" (or rather, of course, its Hebrew source-term) by noting that it is "in a great degree justified by the repetition of the word in the next member of the sentence, with the addition of [the Hebrew word for "of the sea"] to vary the phrase, exactly in the manner of the Prophet" (1995 [1778] Notes 136n.[18]). Here, the core pattern of parallelism – repetition with systematic variation – selects for a particular textual form from among the variant and contested possibilities.

Lowth also uses the notes, we might add, to facilitate that perspectival, recontextualizing shift demanded by the relativist engagement with the text that he insists upon in the *Lectures*. At the end of Isaiah XXII, for instance, Isaiah, quoting Jehovah, catalogues the ways in which he

---

[17] In the Authorized King James version, "Wherefore glorify ye the LORD in the fires, *even* the name of the LORD God of Israel in the isles of the sea."
[18] The Notes are paginated separately.

will impose the government of his servant Eliakim on the inhabitants of Jerusalem. Lowth translates verse 23, in the middle of the passage, as:

And I will fasten him as a nail in a sure place;
And he shall become a glorious seat for his father's house.

(1995 [1778]: 55)[19]

Feeling the need to justify the image of the nail, an apparently insignificant object, as a term by which to convey Eliakim's importance, Lowth offers a lengthy interpretive note in which he provides an impressive range of contextualizing information to allow his modern English readers to comprehend the figure as the ancient Hebrews would have understood it: ethnographic information from a traveler's account concerning the nature and use of the referent of the figural term, textual references from other prophetic books of the Old Testament, a possible parallel from the Koran, and interpretive analysis in support of the appropriateness of the figure. Nor is this Lowth's longest contextualizing note; the line "And falsely setting off their eyes with paint" (from Isaiah III.16)[20] occasions a two-and-a-half page disquisition on the cosmetics and dress of ancient Hebrew women (1995 [1778] Notes 32–34n.).

For all the eloquence of his exhortation to relativism in the *Lectures* and his painstaking cultural contextualization of the Book of Isaiah, Lowth's relativism proves strikingly impossible for him to sustain in the second volume of the *Lectures*. Having devoted the first volume to the identification and elucidation of the three stylistic modes characteristic of ancient Hebrew poetry, Lowth turns in volume II to a consideration of the poetic character of the "different classes," or genres, represented in the Hebrew scriptures (1969 [1787] II: 3). In setting forth this task, Lowth is especially emphatic in his insistence that he will not be guided by the testimony of the Hebrews themselves, who are unequipped to recognize or discover the fine distinctions that organize their poetic discourse:

In forming this arrangement it will hardly be expected that I should uniformly proceed according to the testimony of the Hebrews, or on all occasions confirm the propriety of my classification by their authority; since it is plain that they were but little versed in these nice and artificial distinctions. It will be sufficient for the accurate explanation of the different characters of the Hebrew poetry, if I demonstrate that these characters are stamped by the hand of nature, and that they are displayed either in the subject itself, the disposition of its constituent parts, the diversity of style, or in the general form and arrangement of the poem. (1969 [1787] II: 4)

---

[19] In the Authorized King James version, "And I will fasten him *as* a nail in a sure place; and he shall be for a glorious throne to his father's house."
[20] Rendered as "wanton eyes" in the Authorized King James version.

By naturalizing the generic organization of the sacred corpus and insisting that the differentiating features among genres are manifest and discernible in the poems themselves, Lowth argues, in effect, that they will yield to the discovery procedures of modern natural science what the ancient Hebrews themselves had no way of knowing, notwithstanding the rigorous training in poetry and religion that he attributed to the office of prophet (1969 [1787] II: 11–14). Altogether abandoned here is the principle that "we must see all things with their eyes, estimate all things by their opinions: we must endeavour as much as possible to read Hebrew as the Hebrews would have read it." Clearly, science and cultural relativism are not fully reconciled in Lowth's perspective. Rather than using the "manner of living, of speaking, of thinking which prevailed in those times" as a frame of reference for the systematic investigation of genre categories, Lowth grants primacy to the "science" of his own scholarly perspective (1969 [1787] II: 435).

Still, Lowth's *Lectures* and the translation of Isaiah that put the findings reported in the earlier work into practice established a benchmark in the emergent development of philological perspectives and practices oriented to the words of others. Lowth's works articulate and embody a metadiscursive regimen for the presentation, representation, and interpretation of the discourse of Others in such a way as to bridge the gap of linguistic and cultural difference and historical change that render it obscure to the modern reader. The *Lectures* argue powerfully for science as the basis for authoritative methods of investigation and the authority of expert scientific knowledge, and the translation of Isaiah models a method of re-entextualization and recontextualization based upon these methods of discovery. Jointly, they exercised an influence that resonates throughout the remainder of this work and beyond – from Blair to Boas to the critical perspectives of contemporary ethnopoetics and ethnography.

Conclusion

We have explored in this chapter two lines of inquiry, antiquarianism and philology, in which discursive forms and practices served as diagnostic features in the definition of modernity. The rhetoric of modernity is characteristically framed in terms of discontinuity and succession, most commonly of techno-economic systems (from agrarian production to mercantile and industrial capitalism) or epistemological systems (from supernaturalist to naturalist worldview) or social formations (the emergence of new social classes and the transition from sacred to secular forms of authority). We have argued here that the philosophical discourse of modernity was also framed in certain quarters in terms of discursive forms and practices, taken as diagnostic of epochal change. More specifically, we have established that both the antiquaries and the philologists were centrally concerned with transformations in ways of using language and regimenting discourse in social life that could be conceived as marking a disjunction between the historical past and the modern present and that these discursive gaps bore close and significant relation to contrastive social and cultural formations. Each, however, constructed these discursive contrasts and their correlative social and cultural formations in semiotically different terms.

In our consideration of the antiquaries, Aubrey, Bourne, and Brand, we have identified two different, but not unrelated, ideological motivations for antiquarian research. Aubrey, the seventeenth-century gentleman, drew the intellectual framework for his antiquarian investigations from Baconian Natural Philosophy, and saw the Civil Wars as marking the point of disjunction between the old times and the new. Bourne and Brand, by contrast, both ministers of the established Church, undertook their antiquarian researches in a spirit of Protestant reform, identifying the Reformation as the event that created the break between the heathen and Romish past and the spiritually enlightened present.

Regardless of differences in motivating ideology and historical periodicity, however, all three of our antiquaries shared an understanding of the semiotic constitution of the "antiquity" as a cultural object that is an etiolated fragment or remnant of what was formerly a larger integrated whole. The antiquity mediates between modernity and the past, stripped of those associated constituents of the antecedent whole that formerly rendered it coherent and intelligible, that is to say, stripped by the disjunctive forces of radical historical change from its former context of cultural and social meaning. An antiquity is an indexical puzzle created by historical decontextualization, the true significance of which must be sought on the other side of the historical divide, such as the romantic divination that was formerly tied to Aubrey's ribald rhyme concerning the extraction of little fishes. The key to the puzzle lies in the contextual coherence of a supernaturalist worldview and a structure of traditional authority, both now displaced by the advent of modernity. The antiquary's task is the interpretive recontextualization of the decontextualized fragment.

For the most part, the antiquaries directed their attention to ideational and behavioral elements of old custom and belief, but some of those elements were encoded in or associated with textual forms – tales, songs, rhymes, sayings – and all are sustained to some degree by discursive means: "talk'd of," exchanged in "conversation," expressed in "discourse." These are the discursive practices that the antiquaries saw as appropriately displaced from their prominent and coherent role in the communicative economy, together with their epistemological, functional, and sociological correlates.

Epistemologically, they were the vehicles for the preservation and transmission of supernaturalist knowledge and imperfect history; they were instruments of error, within a rhetorical arena of error and truth, of corruption and purity. Functionally, they were the instruments of traditional authority, serving for the socialization of children, the regulation of behavior, the intergenerational transmission of knowledge. And sociologically, the discursive forms and practices that the antiquaries saw as displaced were associated preeminently with women, the lower classes, the illiterate, country people, the elderly, formerly the agents of socialization and the transmission of knowledge. The antiquarian vision thus contributed to the symbolic construction of a sector of British domestic society occupied by premodern "Others," characterized in part by antiquated discursive practices. Because these Others are uneducated, illiterate, unsophisticated, they are unable to comprehend the ignorance or even blasphemy of their own beliefs and practices, and this, in turn, licenses intervention in their lives by the modern, rational, cultivated scholars who have identified the antiquities in their midst. Such intervention may consist in collecting and interpreting the antiquities as a monument to the ignorance of which the human species was formerly capable, or in imposing official measures to stamp out the harmful remnants, or even in the selective management of antiquities in such a way as to control the lower orders, who, after all, will always be with us, an impediment to the full attainment of modernity.

While the discursive forms and practices that the antiquaries included under the rubric of antiquities were commonly entextualized, the primary concern of antiquarian inquiry was with epistemology and with the sociology of knowledge, and the textuality or poetics of the old wives' tales, supernatural legends, ballads, or rhymes that attracted their interest did not figure in their considerations. For the philologists, by contrast, whose interests were centrally literary, form did matter, because it was systematically related to function and was thus one of the keys to interpretation. The problem that the philologists addressed was an outgrowth of the debates surrounding the relative authority of the Ancients and the Moderns that raged in British literary circles around the turn of the eighteenth century. At issue for Blackwell and Wood, whether under the guise of accounting for the greatness of Homer or as a test of Homer's mimetic powers, or for Lowth, in demonstrating the poetic qualities of the Old Testament, was how to find meaning, coherence, and value in literary works across the gaps of time and space that separated eighteenth-century England from Homeric Greece or ancient Israel and rendered such interpretation problematic. The philologists' effort to recontextualize the ancient works by recuperating their original context of meaning and use is ultimately more complex than that of the antiquaries, resting upon a relativist semiotics of culture, of language, and of the culture of language, all viewed within a larger framework of progressive development. That is to say that for the philologists, a literary work must be interpreted and evaluated as systematically grounded in and shaped by the manners and customs, the ways of life, of a people, the semantic and expressive capacities of their national language, and their ways of speaking, all of which, individually and in combination, exhibit a protean variation from one nation to another. In addition to variations of place, these formative factors are also subject to variation in time, as all are in a constant state of change.

There are significant differences, however, between the approaches of Blackwell and Wood, on the one hand, and Lowth, on the other, in their efforts to restore the Homeric and biblical texts to their ancient contexts of cultural meaning. In broadest scope, the Homeric scholars are able to discern typological regularities amidst all the variability, corresponding to developmental stages in the growth of human culture. For the consideration of literature, this conjectural history allows Blackwell to posit a developmental stage in human history – not the earliest, but still ancient – in which society has achieved a degree of stability while remaining close to nature; language has achieved a concomitant degree of structure while still being suffused with passion, wonder, and metaphorical density; and expressive style has been domesticated to regularity of form while retaining the immediacy, the lack of artifice, and the affecting power of oral performance. It is this stage, in Blackwell's scheme, that constitutes the fertile seedbed of poetry at its most vigorous and affecting. And, for Blackwell's rhetorical purposes, it is this stage as well that contrasts most tellingly with modernity, characterized by good order, alienation from nature and emotion, over-refined language, artificiality of expression, and so on – all the factors that preclude the appearance of another Homer, or a contemporary national literature of the caliber of the *Iliad* or the *Odyssey*, though they are maximally conducive to the happiness of a people.

In Wood's conjectural formulation, a more purifying abstraction from the historical process than Blackwell's processual schema, the great historical trajectory of culture, language, and society is delineated largely in terms of oppositional contrasts that define the poles of antiquity and modernity. Articulated in terms of discursive and metadiscursive practices, the most potent and enduring typological contrast that Wood employs to bring order to the variability of peoples is orality versus literacy. These communicative technologies become indices of contrastive sets of additional features having to do with communicative and epistemological modalities, contexts, forms, and functions that collectively distinguish antiquity from modernity in discursive and metadiscursive terms.

Significantly, however, Blackwell's and Wood's developmental schemas can be uncoupled from strict historical chronology; not all nations at the same developmental/typological stage as Homeric Greece are coeval with it. Some, in fact, like the Arabs, Turks, and Indians of Blackwell's famous example, or the Arabs of Wood's account, are the scholars' own historical contemporaries. These contemporary peoples of the East, then, are assimilated to ancient Greece, developmentally behind their modern British contemporaries in culture, language, and expressive style. To be sure, there is a degree of ambivalence in this philological schema: the developmentally more backward peoples are celebrated as better equipped for poetry, at the expense of the moderns, whose language and culture and expressive style are detrimental to great poetic achievement. Nevertheless, the modern, compact-based, well-governed state is ultimately doubly privileged: it is higher on the developmental scale of happiness, refinement, reason, understanding, and good order, while it can still appropriate and – properly prepared by the philologists – appreciate the great poetry of the ancients.

In aligning the contemporary peoples of the East with Homeric Greece – and, in Wood's case, with the ancient Hebrews as well – both of our philologists employ a standard technique in eighteenth-century conjectural history, as described by Dugald Stewart, drawing on travelers' accounts for examples of peoples on a developmental par with ancient societies. In Wood's work, however, the travel experience is his own, which represents a vitally important methodological innovation. When Blackwell introduces information taken from Galland's *Arabian Nights Entertainments*, the authority of his examples is doubly mediated through Galland to the travelers' accounts on which the French scholar drew. Wood, by contrast, appeals to immediate personal experience and observation; the authority of his account derives from the epistemological power of presence, of being there, prefiguring the authorizing rhetoric of ethnography. Both Blackwell and Wood, however, contribute to the construction of an exotic, premodern Other, culturally and discursively primitive, who exists in symbolic contrast with the peoples of modern nations.

While Blackwell and Wood devote major attention to the historical process of progressive development that separates Homeric Greece culturally, linguistically, and metadiscursively from modern England, Lowth simply takes for granted the distancing effects of great spans of historical time without feeling the need to formulate a general theory of historical

development. Likewise, he cites without explanatory justification contemporary "oriental" analogues to the elements of ancient Hebrew culture as a basis for fleshing out the latter, with the tacit implication that
the contemporary cultures of the East are archaic, unchanged by history.
Nevertheless, several interrelated orders of change figure importantly in
Lowth's work: the death of Hebrew and the consequent obscurity of the
phonology and prosody of the language; the loss of knowledge concerning Hebrew poetics, especially meter; the steady corruption of biblical
texts, due to the cumulation of scribal error; and broad changes in ways
of life, including the meanings and values attached to elements of culture.
Together, these dimensions of change produce a widening gap between
scriptural antiquity and the present, an obstacle to true understanding of
the Old Testament.

There is yet another element of change, however, which compensates
for the cumulative loss of knowledge brought about by the factors we have
already considered, namely, the radical shift in epistemology represented
by the advent of natural science. The systematicity and rigor of scientific
discovery procedures enables the recuperation of parallelism as a key to
the poetics of the Hebrew scriptures, the restoration of textual accuracy,
and the relativist comprehension of ancient Hebrew culture. On the basis
of the expert knowledge that scientific investigation yields to the modern
scholar, Lowth goes one step further than Blackwell and Wood in their
common task of making ancient and authoritative – though obscure –
literary texts accessible and intelligible to the contemporary reader:
he produces a translation of Isaiah into English, simultaneously a re-
entextualization and recontextualization of this canonical work. Lowth's
translation, by using the parallelistic organization of the text as a key to
the didactic and pleasurable effects it produces and the meanings it conveys, argues more immediately than the analytical works of Blackwell and
Wood for the critical principle that form, function, and meaning are inextricably interrelated. Thus Lowth augments the authority of the language
ideologies and metadiscursive practices that he promotes by creating a
textual model that embodies them.

Taken together, there is a powerful complementarity between the antiquaries and the philologists in the social construction of modernity.
Both delineate an Other which then stands as an inverse icon of modern
man – and we use the term "man" advisedly. The antiquaries, highlighting women, country people, the elderly, and the uneducated, create a
composite Other within; the philologists, turning to the "primeval" and
"rude" people of the East, create an Oriental Other without. Significantly,
both construction projects use discursive forms and practices as building
blocks.

The antiquaries concentrate their attention on the encoding and transmission of antiquities, the decayed remnants of an earlier, ignorant age, in an effort to reveal the ignorance and error of the past as a measure of how far mankind – more specifically, the modern enlightened elite – has progressed. Their goal is to discredit these etiolated survivals of an earlier time by revealing their origin in the compromised past of pagan and papist tradition. While the antiquarian program anticipates the ultimate purification of the human mind from those remnants of past error, it holds forth the more immediate prospect of an intellectually stratified society divided between an enlightened, educated elite and the ignorant, vulgar classes still in thrall to the ignorance of the past. Overall, the antiquaries' vision of the advent of modernity tends to be framed in terms of a binary, oppositional Great Divide between past and present, couched in a rhetoric of purification, by reason or religious reformation or both. At the same time, however, the antiquarian project rests on the mediating force of the antiquity, which bridges the Great Divide, neither fully consonant with the past nor a living part of the present – a hybrid, in Latour's terms. Those sectors of contemporary society among whom antiquities remain current – the Other within – are likewise hybrid: living on the modern side of the historical divide, in the present, but constituting a holding area for anachronistic customs, beliefs, and discursive practices that stem from the past.

The philologists, for their part, focus their attention on the form, function, and meaning of canonical literary works in order to reaffirm and strengthen the enduring value of these ancient works, which may be obscured by the great cultural and historical gulf that separates their place and time of origin from modern life. Their value is qualified, however, by being relativized, assimilated to a more primitive era characterized by the rule of passion, conceived as the faculty of poetry. Both have given way to reason in the modern world, and while the spirit of poetry is thereby diminished, the loss is compensated by the capacity that reasoned and disciplined scrutiny affords us to understand the creation, efficacy, and value of the Homeric epics or the Old Testament far better than the creators of those works could achieve.

By contrast with the antiquarian construction, the conception of history that underlay the philological perspective was less oppositional, insofar as it was framed in evolutionary rather than Great Divide terms and rested centrally on a relativistic orientation towards cultural difference. Accordingly, the philologists were less inclined than the antiquaries towards a rhetoric of purification. As Latour observes (1993: 113–14), ethnological relativism is a way of postulating commensurability between cultures, bridging the epistemological gaps that divide them, and it is fundamentally an operation of translation, that is to say, a mediating operation. Lowth's translation program is the most comprehensive of those we have reviewed, drawing together within one unified frame of reference linguistic, formal, functional, and cultural commensurability.

Nevertheless, the philologists were characteristically drawn towards a broad oppositional contrast between peoples in the early stages of evolutionary development and their own society as the most advanced. This opposition was summed up most systematically in Wood's typological contrast between orality and literacy, which created an epistemological gap that was operationally as wide as the historical juncture posited by the antiquaries. Again, like that of the antiquaries, the vision of modernity that the philologists constructed yielded space to two additional zones of hybridity. The first of these was poetry, now reduced from its primitive dominance over all human expression to a limited – and perhaps anachronistic – sector of the speech economy of modern society. The second zone of hybridity was occupied by the Oriental Others without, who embodied the past in the present more fully than the antiquaries' Other within, insofar as their way of life was not suffused with distressed survivals from the past, but was a living embodiment of it. And of course, as we have suggested, relativistic interpretation is itself a mediating strategy, the establishment of commensurability that bridges the gap between cultures, resulting in an epistemological hybrid that blends the ancient and the modern in a single interpretive construction.

Finally, the philologists and antiquaries converge in both manifesting the features of an emergent social role that Zygmunt Bauman identifies as distinctively modern – the expert or specialist intellectual. According to Bauman, the expert claims authority to arbitrate matters of knowledge, taste, and value on the basis of "superior (objective) knowledge to which intellectuals have a better access than the non-intellectual part of society" (Z. Bauman 1987: 4–5), and, one might add, than the non-intellectual part of humankind in general. We will deal again with Bauman's suggestive formulation later in this volume. At this point, however, we would emphasize the part played by the late seventeenth- and eighteenth-century antiquaries and philologists, not only in assuming authority over the non-intellectual Others, but also in the prior task of *constructing* the non-intellectual Others. Both lines of inquiry were oriented towards the construction of a metadiscursive regime of intellectual authority, constituted in terms of ways of speaking as well as ways of knowing. In the chapter that follows, we examine a highly influential synthesis of the two perspectives.

4   The critical foundations of national epic and the rhetoric of authenticity: Hugh Blair and the Ossian controversy

> Is it not strange that, at a time when we have lost our Princes, our Parliaments, our independent Government, even the Presence of our chief Nobility, are unhappy, in our Accent & Pronunciation, speak a very corrupt Dialect of the Tongue which we make use of; is it not strange, I say, that in these Circumstances, we shou'd really be the People most distinguish'd for Literature in Europe?   David Hume[1]

Introduction

Hume's paradoxical query, posed in 1757 and often quoted in histories of eighteenth-century Scotland, expresses well the deep ambivalence of mid-eighteenth-century Scottish intellectuals towards their political condition, their language, and their literature. While Hume's own writings contributed in no small measure to Scotland's – and especially Edinburgh's – literary and philosophical reputation as "a hotbed of genius," he was also closely involved in the production, publication, and promotion of a series of literary works that followed soon after he penned the above observations and that did indeed mark Scotland as the nation "most distinguish'd for Literature in Europe."[2] Between 1760 and 1763, James Macpherson offered to an increasingly receptive public three volumes of translations from the Gaelic poetry of Ossian, a third-century Celtic bard: *Fragments of Ancient Poetry* (1760), *Fingal* (1762), and *Temora* (1763)[3]; these three works were collected in two volumes in 1765, under the title *The Works of Ossian, The Son of Fingal, Translated from the Galic Language by James Macpherson* (1765). Taken all together, the

---

[1] Letter from Hume to Gilbert Elliot, 2 July 1757 (Hume 1932 I: 255).
[2] On Hume and Ossian, see Mossner (1970 [1954]: 414–20) and Raynor (1991).
[3] Full titles: *Fragments of Ancient Poetry, Collected in the Highlands of Scotland and Translated from the Galic or Erse Language* (hereafter *Fragments*); *Fingal, and Ancient Epic Poem in Six Books, together with Several Other Poems composed by Ossian, the Son of Fingal* (hereafter *Fingal*); *Temora, an Ancient Epic Poem in Eight Books, together with Several Other Poems composed by Ossian, the Song of Fingal* (hereafter *Temora*).

publication of Macpherson's works constituted an extended literary event of momentous historical importance which shaped Western understandings of the language and poetry of Others from that day to this.[4]

Macpherson presented his Ossianic texts as English translations from Gaelic originals purportedly composed in the third century by Ossian, son of Fingal, King of Morven, in what was later Argyllshire. Macpherson frames Ossian's poems as the compositions of the bard's last years, in which he recalls in blindness the glories of his youth and laments the passing of the heroic order of his father's day. In style, the translations are rendered in a distinctive register of measured prose (Macpherson's own term), marked by heavy use of paratactic cumulation, simple syntax, grammatical parallelism, descriptive epithets, genitives of description ("brook of the hill"), and syntactic inversion (Fitzgerald 1966). These features all have resonances with Gaelic ballad style, but Macpherson points as well to correspondences with the style of the Homeric epics and the Old Testament.[5] For readers unfamiliar with Ossian, here is the opening passage of *Fingal*, which Macpherson revised slightly from one of the *Fragments* (Macpherson 1996: 28, 55):

Cuchullin sat by Tura's wall; by the tree of the rustling leaf. – His spear leaned against the mossy rock. His shield lay by him on the grass. As he thought of mighty Carbar, a hero whom he slew in war; the scout of the ocean came, Moran the son of Fithil.

Rise, said the youth, Cuchullin, rise; I see the ships of Swaran, Cuchullin, many are the foe: many the heroes of the dark-rolling sea.

---

[4] The best contemporary work on Macpherson is Stafford (1988), which combines biography with critical readings of his Ossianic *oeuvre*; see also Stafford (1996a). Trevor-Roper's widely read critique (1983), while original and suggestive in regard to the invention of Highland tradition, oversimplifies the genesis and character of Macpherson's Ossianic works.

[5] Macpherson draws attention to these correspondences in his notes. For example, he notes the correspondence between the line in "The Death of Cuchillin," "his spear never returned unstained with blood, nor his bow from the strife of the mighty" (Macpherson 1996: 137) and the passage from 2 Samuel.i.22, "From the blood of the slain, from the fat of the mighty, the bow of Jonathan returned not back, and the sword of Saul returned not empty" (Macpherson 1996: 450n.). In a footnote to the passage in Book I of *Fingal*, in which a character says of another's words, "They are like the calm shower of spring" (Macpherson 1996: 62), Macpherson observes that "Homer compares soft piercing words to the fall of snow [*Iliad* 3.222f.]." That is to say, Macpherson modeled his style in part on the Old Testament, most likely with additional guidance from Robert Lowth's influential *Lectures on the Sacred Poetry of the Hebrews*, published in Latin in 1753 and translated into English in 1787 (1969 [1787]; see Stafford 1988: 89–91), and upon Homer in order to impart to it an archaic and epic cast. We should also note that Macpherson draws connections as well between passages in his Ossianic texts and Virgil's *Aeneid* and Milton's *Paradise Lost*.

In the nearly two and a half centuries since the first appearance of Macpherson's Ossianic translations, they have been the subject of a highly polarized critical literature. Some critics have praised the work extravagantly as sublime and inspiring, others have condemned it vigorously as vapid and fraudulent, and still others – especially recently – have considered it more dispassionately as a compelling product of its time and place.[6] Pride of place among the commentaries on Ossian belongs to *A Critical Dissertation on the Poems of Ossian, Son of Fingal*, by the Reverend Hugh Blair (1718–1800), published first in 1763, soon after *Fingal*, and in a revised version in 1765 (hereafter *Critical Dissertation*).[7] The *Critical Dissertation* served well into the nineteenth century as the authoritative guide to the cultural meaning and literary value of Ossian. In certain respects, the *Critical Dissertation* is analogous to Blackwell's *Enquiry* and Wood's *Essay*: all are guides to the reading and interpretation of particular works of epic poetry as expressions not only of their individual authors, but of nations in history.[8]

Blair's own critical reputation, as we might expect, has tended to rise and fall with the critical assessments of Macpherson's work, but the *Critical Dissertation* was also notably influential in its own right as a work of literary and cultural theory and as a charter for artists and intellectuals engaged by the relationship between literature and nation.[9] It is Blair's work that will occupy our attention in this chapter, specifically his theories concerning the origin and historical development of poetry in relation to language and culture-history, and the use of vernacular traditions in the creation and authorization of a national literature. Blair's theoretical vision, we argue, is fruitfully understood as a fusion of antiquarian and philological perspectives on popular discursive practices, and anticipates in significant ways the grander synthesis offered by Herder, who deeply admired and learned from Blair's work.[10]

---

[6] Reassessments especially relevant to the interests of folklorists and anthropologists include Haugen (1998), Haywood (1986), McKean (2001), Porter (2001). See also Ferguson (1998: 237–49), MacCraith (1996).

[7] We have used the Garland Publishing facsimile reprint edition (1970) of the second edition (1765) of the *Critical Dissertation*. This edition contains pagination errors that must be noted: the pages following page 120 are misnumbered 209–12, followed by 113, followed by 214–24, after which the correct pagination resumes, beginning with page 137. In citations, we have cited page numbers as they appear in the volume.

[8] Simonsuuri (1978) considers the Ossian phenomenon vis-à-vis eighteenth-century notions of Homeric epic, including those of Blackwell and Wood.

[9] David Hume considered it a "self-evident truth" that Blair's *Critical Dissertation* was "incomparably the best piece of criticism in the English language" (Hume to Blair, 6 April 1765, Hume 1932 I: 497). See also Phillipson (1981: 34).

[10] The principal biography of Blair is Schmitz (1948). The most illuminating treatment of Blair's public career is Sher (1985); see also Sher (1982).

Hugh Blair

Hugh Blair (1718–1800) was a prominent figure in the remarkable efflorescence of intellectual life in eighteenth-century Scotland that has come
to be known as the Scottish Enlightenment. Blair had a distinguished
career as a minister of the Church of Scotland, officiating at the High
Kirk of St. Giles, the most prestigious parish in Edinburgh, beginning in
1758. His scholarly career was equally distinguished: he began his lectures in rhetoric and literature at Edinburgh University late in 1759, was
appointed Professor of Rhetoric the following year, and was elevated to
the position of Regius Professor of Rhetoric and Belles-Lettres in 1762, a
position he held until his retirement in 1783. His published sermons were
immensely popular, and his lectures on rhetoric and belles-lettres, published after his retirement, had an extensive influence in both the United
Kingdom and the United States well into the nineteenth century.

The intellectual and social circles in which Blair moved give substance
to Matthew Bramble's observation in Smollett's *Humphrey Clinker* (1771)
that Edinburgh, at that day, was "a hot-bed of genius." Blair's close associates – regular dining partners, members of the same clubs – included
his colleagues in the ministry, Adam Ferguson, William Robertson, John
Home, and Alexander Carlyle, but also Adam Smith, David Hume, Lord
Kames, and Lord Monboddo. The intellectual range of the Edinburgh
literati was truly impressive in its breadth, but one of their principal concerns, stimulated by the rapid development of capitalism and commerce
taking place around them, was political economy in historical perspective. There was a strong moral component in the economic thought of
the Scottish Enlightenment, centering on the implications for society of
economic growth insofar as it might lead to excessive materialism and
luxury, aggressive self-interest, alienation, and ultimately even to social
breakdown (Sher 1985: 188).

Another common interest, not unrelated to political economy and
morality in ways that we hope to demonstrate, was the development of
poetry, which figures not only in Blair's writings, but also in the work of
Adam Smith, Adam Ferguson, Monboddo, Kames, and many of their
contemporaries.[11] And central to that interest in the origin and progress
of poetry we find the shadowy but powerfully affecting figure of Ossian,
the subject of Blair's *Critical Dissertation*.

We will focus primarily on the *Critical Dissertation* as the work most
closely bound up with Ossian, but we will take account as well of two

---

[11] Grobman (1974) is a valuable survey of eighteenth-century Scottish precursors of
folklore research.

other writings by Blair, the unattributed Preface to the *Fragments* (Blair 1996 [1760]), which adumbrates some of the larger themes developed in the *Critical Dissertation* and anticipates the recovery and translation of *Fingal*, and his *Lectures on Rhetoric and Belles Lettres* (1970 [1785]), which developed his ideas on the history of poetry. The *Lectures* were not published until after Blair's retirement from his professorship of rhetoric and belles lettres at Edinburgh University, but their composition dates from the very period when Blair was most heavily engaged with the Ossianic project.[12]

The publishing history of the *Critical Dissertation* is somewhat complex (Jiriczek 1935), but as it will have some bearing on points raised later in the chapter, it may be well to sketch its major contours here, before turning in more detail to the substance of the work. The first edition of the *Critical Dissertation*, as we have noted, was published in 1763, by the same London publisher that had issued *Fingal* in 1762. Although the work was published anonymously, Blair's identity as author was generally known in literary circles. In its first version, the *Critical Dissertation* was largely a commentary on *Fingal*, and so it remained through its subsequent revision. Blair had a substantial proprietary interest in *Fingal*, as we will detail below; he expresses hope for the recovery of the full epic from oral tradition in his Preface to the *Fragments* and even goes so far as to anticipate its plot in terms that prefigure closely the epic narrative that Macpherson ultimately produced:

The subject is, an invasion of Ireland by Swarthan King of Lochlyn; which is the name of Denmark in the Erse language. Cuchulaid, the General or Chief of the Irish tribes, upon intelligence of the invasion, assembles his forces, councils are held; and battles fought. But after several unsuccessful engagements, the Irish are forced to submit. At length, Fingal King of Scotland, called in this poem, "The Desert of the hills," arrives with the ships to assist Cuchulaid. He expels the Danes from the country, and returns home victorious. (Blair 1996 [1760]: 6)

With the publication later in 1763 of *Temora*, the last of Macpherson's Ossianic works, Blair recognized the need for a revised edition of the *Critical Dissertation* to take account of this second epic, though in the end he gives it relatively slight attention. *Fingal* remained the far more important work of the two, and other concerns came to demand more of his attention in the revision process. By 1763, the critical challenges to

---

[12] Macpherson contributed prefaces and other introductory statements to several of his collections in their various editions, in which he discusses a range of issues treated by Blair in the writings under examination, including prominently the antiquity of the Ossianic poems. It remains the case, however, that of the two, Blair was the acknowledged literary theoretician, while Macpherson was recognized – or criticized – for his poetical accomplishments.

the authenticity of Macpherson's translations – and, in fact, to the very existence of his purported Gaelic originals – were mounting, and David Hume urged Blair to gather and present to the public convincing proof of the poems' authenticity (Hume to Blair, 19 September 1763, Hume 1969 I: 398–401). Blair accordingly undertook an extensive correspondence with individuals in the Highlands and Islands who were native Gaelic speakers, seeking their "real opinion of the translations published by Mr. Macpherson" (Blair 1970 [1765]: 137). He reported the results of this inquiry in an Appendix to the edition of the *Critical Dissertation*, published in mid-1765. The second edition carries the expanded title, *A Critical Dissertation on the Poems of Ossian, The Son of Fingal, The Second Edition, To which is added an Appendix containing a variety of Undoubted Testimonies establishing their Authenticity*, and identifies the author of the work for the first time as "Hugh Blair, D.D. One of the Ministers of the High Church, and Professor of Rhetorick and Belles-Lettres in the University of Edinburgh." Several months later, in the latter part of 1765, a combined edition of Macpherson's three Ossianic works was published in two volumes; this edition included Blair's revised *Critical Dissertation*, which accompanied all subsequent authorized editions of *The Works of Ossian* published in Macpherson's lifetime and most nineteenth-century editions as well (Macpherson 1996: 542n.).

The beginnings of society and the origin of poetry

Blair opens the *Critical Dissertation* by setting out two complementary bases for the appreciation of ancient poetry, one historical, the other literary. He begins with history, posing an essentially antiquarian problem: how can we come to know "the ancient state of nations," the "beginnings of society," across the gulf of time? Perhaps the most valuable source of illumination, he suggests, is poetry:

Among the monuments remaining of the ancient state of nations, few are more valuable than their poems or songs. History, when it treats of remote and dark ages, is seldom very instructive. The beginnings of society, in every country, are involved with fabulous confusion; and though they were not, they would furnish few events worth recording. But, in every period of society, human manners are a curious spectacle; and the most natural pictures of ancient manners are exhibited in the ancient poems of nations. These present to us, what is much more valuable than the history of such transactions as a rude age can afford, The history of human imagination and passion. They make us acquainted with the notions and feelings of our fellow-creatures in the most artless ages; discovering what objects they admired, and what pleasures they pursued, before those refinements of society had taken place, which enlarge indeed, and diversify the transactions, but disguise the manners of mankind. (Blair 1970 [1765]: 1–2)

Here, Blair reverses the critical agenda pursued by Blackwell, though his overall perspective owes much to Blackwell's pioneering work. For Blackwell, as we recall, it was the ancient poetic works – the Homeric epics – that were resistant to interpretation, with culture-history providing the clarifying element. For Blair, however, it is ancient history that is obscure and confused, with poetry offering the means of illumination.

In advancing this methodological thesis, Blair draws a highly significant distinction between a history of "events" and a history of "manners." The former, he argues in effect, is of negligible importance in the study of early society, because little occurs in that state of human existence that is worthy of recording, that is, consequential enough to claim our attention. We do not, then, look to the ancient poems and songs for historicity, for events that really happened. Rather, what we want to discover about the ancient state of nations, and what their poems and songs can best provide, is the most natural picture of their manners, their human imagination and passion. The poems and songs, in good antiquarian fashion, allow us to penetrate the veil of obscurity between remote antiquity and the present.

It is not only historical value, though, that commends the ancient poems and songs to modern readers; they have literary appeal as well:

Besides this merit, which ancient poems have with philosophical observers of human nature, they have another with persons of taste. They promise some of the highest beauties of poetical writing. Irregular and unpolished we may expect the productions of uncultivated ages to be; but abounding, at the same time, with that enthusiasm, that vehemence and fire, which are the soul of poetry. For many circumstances of those times which we call barbarous, are favourable to the poetical spirit. That state, in which human nature shoots wild and free, though unfit for other improvements, certainly encourages the high exertions of fancy and passion. (Blair 1970 [1765]: 2)

This is a classic statement of the ideas concerning the beginnings of poetry held by the so-called school of Scottish primitivists, eighteenth-century literary and social theorists who, in various guises, promoted the notion that the unbridled passion, the unfettered imagination, the youthful naturalness of primitive society are maximally conducive to poetic expression at its most essential.[13] This natural propensity towards poetry "in the infancy of societies" (Blair 1970 [1765]: 2) stems from two basic conditions, one residing in the primitive, "barbarous" condition of life, the other in the early state of language.

Primitive man, Blair suggests, lives in a state of "wonder and surprize," excited by the beauties of nature, constant encounters with new and

[13] The authoritative work on primitivism in the Scottish Enlightenment is Whitney (1924); see also Pearce (1945), Foerster (1950), Stafford (1996b).

strange phenomena, "sudden changes of fortune occurring in their unset-tled state of life," and free of restraints on their passion and imagination. Relations are "without disguise," action and conversation are conducted in "the uncovered simplicity of nature" (Blair 1970 [1765]: 2). As the passions of men in this state of life are strong, "so their language, of it-self, assumes a poetical turn. Prone to exaggerate, they describe every thing in the strongest colours; which of course renders their speech pic-turesque and figurative" (Blair 1765: 2–3). This "poetical spirit" that Blair derives from the conditions of primitive life shapes the expression of rude ages naturally into poetry, which Blair defines as "the language of passion, or of enlivened imagination, formed, most commonly, into regular numbers" (Blair 1970 [1785] III: 85). It would appear, then, that Blair subscribes to the notion, also held by Blackwell and Wood, that the language spoken "in the infancy of societies," is poetry, the quintessential language–nature hybrid.

In Blair's treatment, however, the idea is turned in a far more nuanced and suggestive direction. "There never, certainly, was any period of soci-ety," Blair concedes, "in which men conversed together in Poetical Num-bers. It was in very humble and scanty Prose, as we may easily believe, that the first tribes carried on intercourse among themselves, relating to the wants and necessities of life" (Blair 1970 [1785] III: 87–88). Never-theless, "the first *compositions transmitted to posterity*, beyond doubt," Blair maintains, "were in a literal sense, poems; that is, compositions in which imagination had the chief hand, formed into some kind of numbers" – that is, metricalized – "and pronounced with a musical modulation of tone" (Blair 1970 [1765]: 4, emphasis added). These were "praises of their gods, or of their ancestors," he goes on, "commemoration of their own warlike exploits; or lamentations over their misfortunes," pro-duced in the state of emotional excitement that attends such experiences. "And before writing was invented, no other compositions, except songs or poems, could take such hold of the imagination and memory, as to be preserved by oral tradition" and handed down through time (Blair 1970 [1765]: 5). Blair's observations, then, are as much or more about textu-ality than they are about language. He is concerned with the durability of discourse, what it is that endows expression with the capacity to be transmitted to posterity, to be preserved by oral tradition: it must appeal to the imagination and it must be memorable.

In Blair's conception, poetry is the expression of heightened emotion and imagination. This state of arousal, in turn, gives form to the act of ex-pression; the poet's "mind is supposed to be animated by some interesting object which fires his Imagination, or engages his Passion; and which, of course, communicates to his Style a peculiar elevation suited to his ideas;

very different from that mode of expression, which is natural to the mind in its calm, ordinary state" (Blair 1970 [1785] III: 85–86). More specifically, Blair identifies two principal stylistic features that would distinguish poetry from conversation "on the common occurrences of life; namely, an unusual arrangement of words, and the employment of bold figures of speech." Poetic language "would invert words, or change them from that order in which they are commonly placed, to that which most suited the train in which they rose in the Speaker's imagination; or which was most accommodated to the cadence of the passion by which he was moved." At the same time, because emotion colors perception and makes us see things "as passion makes us see them," poetic language takes on a strong figurative cast, assuming "those turns of expression, which we now distinguish by the learned names of Hyperbole, Prosopopoeia, Simile, &c. but which are no other than the native original language of Poetry, among the most barbarous nations" (Blair 1970 [1785] III: 89). Stylistically marked in these ways – grammatically, prosodically, figuratively – poetic utterances become texts, "compositions," that are striking, memorable, and thus durable, with the capacity to be transmitted to posterity, preserved by oral tradition. Blair thus adds a further element to the functional correlates of poetic form suggested by Blackwell and Wood, who note the importance of poetic regimentation as an enabling factor in performance.

There is yet another factor that Blair adduces as part of this formal and functional complex that links poetic expression to oral tradition. "From the very beginnings of Society," he observes, "there were occasions on which they met together for feasts, sacrifices, and public assemblies; and on all such occasions, it is well known, that music, song, and dance, made their principal entertainment" (Blair 1970 [1785] III: 88). These public events are a stimulus to poetic expression: "Here we see the first beginnings of Poetic Composition, in those rude effusions, which the enthusiasm of fancy or passion suggested to untaught men, when roused by interesting events, and by their meeting together in public assemblies" (Blair 1970 [1785] III: 87–88). In the Durkheimian effervescence of such collective rites, people are moved to poetry; the public nature of these performances ensures the public currency of the songs, which in turn enhances the likelihood that they will be passed on.

Blair's prototype of the "first tribes," on which he drew in creating his theory of poetic origins, was the American Indians, based on "the particular and concurring accounts of Travellers": "It is chiefly in America, that we have the opportunity of being made acquainted with men in their savage state" (Blair 1970 [1785] III: 88), he observes, noting that "incredible degree of enthusiasm" with which the Native Americans engage "at all their meetings" in the public performances that give voice to the poetic spirit. In outlining the ritual and celebratory functions of these performances, Blair emphasizes that "the Chiefs of the Tribe are those who signalize themselves most on such occasions" and that prominent among the celebratory themes of their songs are "the great actions of their nation, and their heroes" (Blair 1970 [1785] III: 88).[14] In these observations, Blair builds into his conception of poetic origins an essentially political function, proposing that primitive poetry is from the beginning an instrument of political power which rests in equal parts on heroic action and songs that publicize, celebrate, and assimilate it to the national interest. Here, Blair establishes a foundation as well for the contemporary nationalist uses of ancient poetry, claiming those "great actions of their nation and their heroes" as the principal theme of poetry in its originary form. We will deal further with this issue below. Blair's invocation of American "savages" recalls John Locke's fascination with travelers' accounts; once again, American Others provide a powerful trope for constructing modernity and imagining a human nature in its most basic form.

In his identification of contemporary Amerindian peoples as representing the "very beginnings of Society," as in those other statements we have quoted in which he speaks of "the infancy of societies" or "the first tribes" or "periods," "ages," or "states" of society, Blair aligns his ideas with the stadial developmental schemas that we have recognized in the philological explorations of Blackwell and Wood.[15] Blair is far more explicit than Blackwell or Wood, however, in developing the implications of this developmental framework for the comparative study of primitive poetry. Having established that "we may expect to find poems among the antiquities of all nations," he goes on to offer a general comparative hypothesis:

It is probable too, than an extensive search would discover a certain degree of resemblance among all the most ancient poetical productions, from whatever country they have proceeded. In a similar state of manners, similar objects and passions operating upon the imaginations of men, will stamp their productions with the same general character.... What we have been long accustomed to call the oriental vein of poetry, because some of the earliest poetical productions have come to us from the East, is probably no more oriental than occidental; it is characteristical of an age rather than a country; and belongs, in some measure, to all nations at a certain period. (Blair 1970 [1765]: 5–6)

Blair's move in this passage is of the utmost significance in broadening the scope of the philological perspective developed by Blackwell and Wood.

[14] See n. 17, below, on the use of travel accounts as a complement to conjectural history.
[15] On the prominence of stadial models of progress in the social thought of the Scottish Enlightenment, see Bryson (1945) and R. Meek (1976); on the relation of such models to literary theory, see Rubel (1978).

These scholars, we recall, are primarily concerned with the development of a relativist perspective for the understanding and evaluation of Homer. Where they draw in other cultures, ancient or contemporary, they do so within a broadly areal Orientalist framework that allows them to assimilate Homeric Greece to other nations of the East – ancient Hebrews, Arabs, Indians, Turks – at what they see as corresponding stages of development. The significance of Blair's hypothesis, however, is that it extends the developmental framework from the cultures of the East to all cultures, thus universalizing it in a more definitive way than Blackwell and Wood find it necessary to do, and – most importantly – explicitly homogenizing the poetry of peoples at the "beginning" stage of social development.

At the same time, though, Blair also provides for cross-cultural variation, "occasioned by climate and genius." This diversity, while minimal "in the beginnings of society," increases with the "subsequent revolutions" in the development of nations (Blair 1970 [1765]: 6). Let us consider first the overall contours of Blair's schema for the historical development of poetic expression, and then turn to the ways in which it allows for diversity as well.

Poetry and progress: Gothic, Celtic, Greek

In many points, as we have suggested, Blair's characterization of poetry in its originary state is quite compatible with those of Blackwell and Wood, and the correspondences, not surprisingly, extend to Blair's characterization of poetry's subsequent development in the course of history. As we would expect, the development of poetry is closely tied to the development of language: "In its antient state, more favourable to poetry and oratory; in its present, to reason and philosophy" (Blair 1970 [1785] I: 157).[16] As Blair delineates the history of poetry, the imagination and enthusiasm which dominate experience and expression during the "infancy of society" give way in the course of human development to understanding and control, but also to a waning of poetic vigor. "In the progress of society," Blair postulates, "the genius and manners of men undergo a change more favourable to accuracy than to sprightliness and sublimity.

---

[16] In his treatment of public speaking, Blair distinguishes three types of eloquence, of which the highest, which he calls "high Eloquence," "is always the offspring of passion. By passion, I mean that state of the mind in which it is agitated, and fired, by some object it has in view" (Blair 1970 [1785] II: 177). Oratory has this in common with poetry, but developed later: "while the intercourse of men was as yet unfrequent, and force and strength were the chief means employed in deciding controversies, the arts of Oratory and Persuasion, of Reasoning and Debate, could be but little known" (Blair 1970 [1785] II: 182–83). The orator aims at persuasion (Blair 1970 [1785] II: 173, "the primary aim of a Poet is to please, and to move" (Blair 1970 [1785] III: 84).

As the world advances, the understanding gains ground upon the imagination; the understanding is more exercised; the imagination less" (Blair 1970 [1765]: 3). With the accumulation of experience and knowledge, the conditions of life occasion fewer surprises and the mind turns more to causality, correction, precision, refinement, and regulation by "method and rule."[17] "Style becomes more chaste, but less animated" (Blair 1970 [1765]: 3–4). Blair draws an analogy here between the progressive development of society and the human life cycle: "poetry, which is the child of imagination, is frequently most glowing and animated in the first ages of society" (Blair 1970 [1765]: 4).

One of the implications of Blair's developmental schema, like Blackwell's and Wood's, is that as society progresses, poetry becomes ever more distanced from its nature as an expression of imagination and passion. On the one hand, this view allows for the valorization of primitive poetry as being closest to its originary essence: "As the ideas of our youth are remembered with a peculiar pleasure on account of their liveliness and vivacity: so the most ancient poems have often proved the greatest favourites of nations" (Blair 1970 [1765]: 4). On the other hand, however, the infantilization of pure poetry and the assignment of poetic expression at its truest to a developmental stage before the refinement of understanding implies that the primitive poet does not understand the poetic process that shapes his or her own expression. Only a member of a more advanced, mature society can understand the nature of primitive poetry or interpret it to others, though his or her own poetic production can only be a diminished expression of the true poetic spirit.

One of the manifestations of the growth of understanding and control in the historical transformation of poetry is the regularization of literary genres. "During the infancy of Poetry," Blair maintains, "all the different kinds of it lay confused, and were mingled in the same Composition, according as inclination, enthusiasm, or casual incidents, directed the Poet's strain. In the progress of Society and Arts, they began to assume those different regular forms, and to be distinguished by those different names under which we now know them" (Blair 1970 [1785] III: 96). In the first ages of society, however, not only were these poetic genres undifferentiated from each other, "but all that we now call Letters, or Composition of any kind, was then blended in one mass. At first, History, Eloquence, and Poetry, were all the same" (Blair 1970 [1785] III: 97). This lack of formal or functional differentiation that characterized expression in the infancy of society Blair correlates with the lack of social differentiation in early

---

[17] In these ideas lie the foundations of the "devolutionary premise" that Dundes (1969) traces in nineteenth-century folklore theory.

society, "when the character and occupations of the husbandmen and the builder, the warrior and the statesman, were united in one person." With progress came "a separation of the different Arts and Professions of Civil Life," which "led also by degrees to a separation of the different literary provinces from each other" (Blair 1970 [1785] III: 97). The process of communicative differentiation and refinement – of classificatory purification – Blair suggests, was further facilitated by the invention of writing, as men "reasoned and reflected upon the affairs of life" and so desired a durable and objective record of events (Blair 1970 [1785] III: 98). Ultimately history, philosophy, oratory, and poetry were differentiated from each other, each formally, functionally, and sociologically distinct. In modern life, then, the sphere of poetry is reduced to a limited domain: "Poetry became now a separate art, calculated chiefly to please, and confined generally to such subjects as related to the imagination and the passions" (Blair 1970 [1785] III: 98).

Within the broad purview of the universal developmental framework he presents to account for the origin and development of poetry, Blair recognizes two principal domains of diversification, one linguistic, the other national. Attuned as he is to poetic form, Blair recognizes that different linguistic structures will lend themselves to different poetic structures. "Every language," he writes, "has powers and graces, and music peculiar to itself; and what is becoming in one, would be ridiculous in another" (Blair 1970 [1785] III: 111). He goes on to offer a brief survey of versification, in terms of prosodic elements (e.g., number and length of syllables, stress) and phonological structures ("the return of similar sounds" (Blair 1970 [1785] III: 112)), with an emphasis on the contrasts among Greek, Latin, and English; the details need not concern us here.

Blair's treatment of cultural differentiation is far more extensive; indeed, the national particulars of Ossianic poetry represent one of the principal foci of the *Critical Dissertation*. As we have noted, Blair hypothesized that there would be a substantial degree of similarity in the poetry of all peoples in the first stages of society: "as we have reason to look for Poems and Songs among the antiquities of all countries; so we may expect, that in the strain of these there will be a remarkable resemblance, during the primitive periods of every country" (Blair 1970 [1785] III: 92–93). He acknowledges, however, that "Diversity of climate, and of manner of living will occasion some diversity in the strain of the first Poetry of nations" (Blair 1970 [1785] III: 94). In his further consideration of this natural diversity, though, climate immediately recedes from view, and "manner of living" comes to the fore. The poetic productions of nations will vary, he suggests, chiefly "according as those nations are of a more ferocious, or of a more gentle spirit; and according as they advance faster or slower in the arts of civilization" (Blair 1970 [1785] III: 94).

In a capsule assessment of Celtic poetry at the time of Ossian, Blair suggests yet another dimension of variation in the poetic productions of primitive societies, namely, "the long cultivation of Poetry among the Celtae" (Blair 1970 [1785] III: 94). In an earlier passage, Blair proposes that notwithstanding the universality of poetry and music, "they have been more cultivated, and, from a concurrence of favourable circumstances, carried to greater perfection in some countries than in others" (Blair 1970 [1785] III: 87). Blair's characterization of Celtic poetry, of course, takes on special importance insofar as it brings the philological and developmental perspectives back home and turns them to the examination of the ancient poetry of his own country.

Following his initial statement of the nature and antiquarian value of primitive poetry, Blair devotes a full fifteen pages of the *Critical Dissertation* to a consideration of "the ancient poetical remains of the northern nations; in order to discover whether the Gothic poetry has any resemblance to the Celtic or Galic [Gaelic], which we are about to consider" (Blair 1970 [1765]: 6). Specifically, he presents an English translation of a Latin translation of the Old Norse funeral song of Ragnar Loðbrók, already established in English literary circles as emblematic of primitive poetry (Farley 1903: 59–76), to establish that "the Scandinavian tribes," known for their ignorance of the liberal arts, nevertheless, "from the earliest times, had their poets and their songs" (Blair 1970 [1765]: 6). On completion of his translation, Blair observes that "This is such poetry as we might expect from a barbarous nation," characterizing it as breathing "a most ferocious spirit," "wild, harsh and irregular," yet "at the same time animated and strong." The style of the original, he notes, is "full of inversions," as well as "highly metaphorical and figured" (Blair 1970 [1765]: 20). Then the contrast:

But when we open the works of Ossian, a very different scene presents itself. There we find the fire and the enthusiasm of the most early times, combined with an amazing degree of regularity and art. We find tenderness, and even delicacy of sentiment, greatly predominant over fierceness and barbarity. Our hearts are melted with the softest feelings, and at the same time elevated with the highest ideas of magnanimity, generosity, and true heroism. When we turn from the poetry of Lodbrog to that of Ossian, it is like passing from a savage desart [*sic*], into a fertile and cultivated country. How is this to be accounted for? Or by what means reconciled with the remote antiquity attributed to these poems?

The answer, Blair argues, lies with the importance of the Druids ("their philosophers and priests") and the Bards ("their poets and recorders of heroic actions") who held high political office "as chief members of the state" among the Celtic peoples from the earliest times. These functionaries cultivated among the Celts "from very remote ages a system of discipline and manners" such that "We must not imagine the Celtae to have been altogether a gross and rude nation" (Blair 1970 [1765]: 21–22). The Celtic peoples had an especially strong attachment "to their poetry and their Bards," Blair maintains, and "clearly appear to have made it so much their study from the earliest times, as may remove our wonder at meeting with a vein of higher poetical refinement among them, than was at first sight to have been expected among nations, whom we are accustomed to call barbarous" (Blair 1970 [1765]: 23–24). Blair considers the Ossianic poems to be the product of a process of refinement, in which the Bards cultivated poetry and ideas of heroism handed down to them and endeavored to perfect both their art and the heroic ethos of which they sang. Such a process, he submits, "would contribute not a little to exalt the public manners" as well, as men strove to emulate the heroes of the songs in the hope that their exploits too would be celebrated in song (Blair 1970 [1765]: 26–27). This process drew poetic expression towards epic, "the recital of some illustrious enterprise in a Poetical Form," and, "of all poetical works, the most dignified, and at the same time, the most difficult in execution" (Blair 1970 [1785] III: 203, 207). It is also, by its nature, "one of the most moral of all poetic compositions," its moral weight arising "from the admiration of heroic actions" which epic produces, "from the virtuous emotions which the characters and incidents raise," and "from the happy impression which all the parts separately, as well as the whole taken together, leave upon the mind" (Blair 1970 [1765]: 48). The great actions depicted and celebrated in epic, as they are aspired to and emulated in life, center around "heroism in war, and magnificence in peace" (Blair 1970 [1765]: 28). In Blair's exaltation of *Fingal* and of Ossian's poetry in general, as in Blackwell's appreciation of Homer, there is an acknowledgment of the necessity of war and violence to the creation of epic, that highest of poetic forms. Ossian "was not only a professed bard," Blair reminds us, "but a warrior also; and the son of the most renowned hero and prince of his age. This formed a conjunction of circumstances, uncommonly favourable towards exalting the imagination of a poet" (Blair 1970 [1765]: 28).

What Blair is proposing in this extended comparison of ancient Gothic and Celtic poetry is that nations will differ in the degree to which poetry is cultivated and raised to the level of a cultural focus and in the related degree to which poets are recognized and acknowledged as cultural specialists, speakers of morally authoritative words. Blair endeavors as well to establish for Ossian, as Blackwell did for Homer, that the manners of his age, especially the interdependent elements of heroism in war, reputation and honor, the prominence of bards, and the cultivation of poetry, "were abundantly favourable to a poetical genius" (Blair 1970 [1765]: 28; cf. Bauman 1986). There is a gendered component to this complex as well, which Blair himself makes explicit in observing of Ossian's age that "The two dispiriting vices, to which Longinus imputes the decline of poetry, covetousness and effeminacy, were as yet unknown" (Blair 1970 [1765]: 28–29).

Clearly, Blair's comparison of ancient Gothic and Celtic poetry is intended to establish and account for the superior cultivation of the latter and its salutary effects on the sensibilities and values of the Celtic peoples, given that both nations are at a barbaric stage of development. "Barbarity, I must observe, is a very equivocal term," writes Blair; "it admits of many different forms and degrees; and though, in all of them, it excludes polished manners, it is however, not inconsistent with generous sentiments and affections" (Blair 1970 [1765]: 25). Nick Groom also argues persuasively that insofar as Percy, who presented an English translation of the same Old Norse poem, claimed that the Goths were the ancient forebears of the English and established the foundations of their national character, Blair's denigration of Gothic poetry and exaltation of Celtic poetic sensibilities amounted to a nationalist claim for the superiority of Scottish over English culture (Groom 1996).

If Blair's first comparison is to establish the superiority of Celtic poetry by raising it above the Gothic in cultivation and sensibility, his second it to maximize its value by placing it on equal ground with the highest poetical achievement of the ancient world, the Homeric epics. "As Homer is of all the great poets, the one whose manner, and whose time come the closest to Ossian's," Blair suggests, "we are naturally led to run a parallel in some instances, between the Greek and the Celtic bard" (Blair 1970 [1765]: 38). In justification of drawing this parallel between Homer and Ossian, Blair reminds his readers once again that it is not strict historical contemporaneity that warrants the comparison, but corresponding stages of social development: "For though Homer lived more than a thousand years before Ossian, it is not from the age of the world, but from the state of society, that we are to judge resembling times" (Blair 1970 [1765]: 38).

In several points, Blair concedes Homer's "manifest superiority": "He introduces a greater variety of incidents; he possesses a larger compass of ideas; has more diversity in his characters; and a much deeper knowledge of human nature" (Blair 1970 [1765]: 38–39). Relaxing a bit the developmental parity he has advanced as the basis for comparing Ossian with Homer, Blair attributes this superiority to the circumstance that Homer lived in a society that was "much farther advanced" than third-century Scotland: "His field of observation was much larger and more splendid; his knowledge, of course, more extensive; his mind also, it shall be granted, more penetrating" (Blair 1970 [1765]: 39). These advantages notwithstanding, however, Blair submits that Ossian too was favored in certain important respects. The more limited life-circumstances of the poet in the infancy of society may well allow for closer, deeper, and richer engagement with those experiences that are available within the more circumscribed lifeworld: "In a rude age and country, though the events that happen be few, the undissipated mind broods over them more; they strike the imagination, and fire the passions in a higher degree; and of consequence become happier materials to a poetical genius, than the same events when scattered through the wide circle of more varied action, and cultivated life" (Blair 1970 [1765]: 39).

Following these general considerations, Blair goes on to a more detailed comparison of Homeric and Ossianic poetry in terms of such factors as tone, descriptive and dramatic style and pacing, dignity of sentiment, and sublimity. In some of these respects, Blair simply registers a balanced contrast between the two; in others, the balance tips in favor of one poet or the other. Interestingly, one of the factors for which Blair awards the advantage to Ossian is his treatment of war and heroism: "There is a finer mixture of war and heroism, with love and friendship, of martial, with tender scenes, than is to be met with, perhaps, in any other poet" (Blair 1970 [1765]: 47–48), a fascinating softening of the epic imperative of violence. The humane sentiment that Blair remarks here is especially worthy of notice because it runs counter to expectation; men in a state of barbarism should not, by common historical understanding, display the tenderness of feeling that characterizes the Ossianic heroes. Homer's heroes certainly do not. But Blair takes this feature of the Ossianic world not as an anachronism, but as striking evidence of the bardic cultivation of moral refinement in ancient Scotland.[18] But of course, Blair's agenda in claiming greatness for Ossian and his poetry extends well beyond a concern for the poet's reputation. Within the terms established by Blackwell, a claim to greatness for Ossian is also a claim to greatness for the nation to whose history and culture his poetry gives voice. For us, after more than two hundred years of romantic nationalist ideology and rhetoric have shaped modern conceptions of the relationship between literature and nation, such a claim appears straightforward, but we must recall that in mid-eighteenth-century Britain it was far less so. Indeed, Blair's rhetoric was foundational to the subsequent coalescence of romantic nationalism in the writings of Herder and other political and literary philosophers.

Let us examine how he constructs his argument. We must bear in mind, first of all, that Blair is addressing readers who have in hand English texts that have just been produced by a contemporary individual, James

---

[18] Dwyer (1991) offers an illuminating analysis of the world of sentiment in Ossian and of critical responses to this play of feeling.

Macpherson, and that their authority rests on their purported status as translations of ancient texts. From these contemporary texts, Blair wants to establish the antiquity of the poetry, their derivation from a Highland Gaelic original, and their connection to the Scottish nation. How does he manage it? And more importantly, what does he hope to gain in the process?

The creation and authorization of a Scottish national epic

One dimension of Blair's complex act of recontextualization, we may observe, rests upon a tacit analogy established by his linkage of Ossian to Homer. A well-established principle, founded in the Renaissance humanist tradition of classical scholarship, tied Homer's greatness in significant part to the superior qualities of Greek culture. This reasoning, as we have seen, was central to Blackwell's relativist argument in the *Enquiry* – Homer was a great poet because his time and place were especially conducive to the production of great poetry – which had a notably strong influence on the literati of the Scottish Enlightenment, including Blair. Blair's argument is closely similar to Blackwell's: high poetic achievement must be grounded in the superior qualities of the poet's cultural milieu. Accordingly, as we have seen, Blair is at pains to establish the special cultural circumstances that characterized Ossian's time and place, specifically the Celtic devotion to and cultivation of bardic expression, which was in turn conducive to the perfection of poetry and public morality. Thus Ossian, as a bard, may be seen as the gifted and cultivated voice of his people and his time.

But this much carries us only part of the way. Having established a basis on which to identify Ossian as standing for third-century Scots-Gaelic culture, there remains the problem of establishing persuasive grounds on which to claim him for the glory of mid-eighteenth-century Scotland. The texts have a history, but the accessible contours of that history blur into indistinctness at the limits of living memory and the documentary record. This frames the texts as an antiquarian problem: how can we transcend those limits and make the past and the present mutually accessible and intelligible?

Both the *Critical Dissertation* and the Preface to the *Fragments* that preceded it begin with textual antiquities. We have already quoted the opening lines of the *Critical Dissertation* earlier in this chapter; the opening of the Preface to the *Fragments* anticipates the later perspective: "The public may depend on the following fragments as genuine remains of ancient Scottish poetry" (Blair 1996 [1760]: 5). But the attribution of antiquity to the texts in both works is already an interpretive construction,

based upon Blair's conjectural history of the origin and evolution of poetry. Even before he first encountered Macpherson's Ossianic corpus,
Blair was committed to the understanding that the most inspired, unfettered, passionate, and thus fully realized poetry was produced in the
infancy of society, that epic was the highest poetic achievement, and that
the poetic spirit declined as society progressed. It followed readily, then,
that the Gaelic heroic ballads from which Macpherson purportedly made
his English translations must be the detritus of a formerly intact heroic
epic.

In the effort to establish conclusively that the poems stemmed from
remote antiquity, Blair relies largely on internal evidence. One species of
internal evidence to which Blair appeals is the mimetic consistency of the
poems: "no modern allusion drops from him; but every where, the same
rude face of nature appears" (Blair 1970 [1765]: 32). "The compositions
of Ossian are so strongly marked with characters of antiquity," Blair insists, "that although there were no external proof to support their antiquity, hardly any reader of judgment and taste, could hesitate in referring
them to a very remote aera" (Blair 1970 [1765]: 29–30). That era Blair
identifies as the earliest of four developmental stages "in the progress of
society," appealing to a stadial progressive schema commonly advanced
by the social philosophers of the Scottish Englightenment, namely, "the
life of hunters." Blair continues, "pasturage succeeds to this, as the ideas
of property begin to take root; next agriculture; and lastly, commerce"
(Blair 1970 [1765]: 30). No traces of the succeeding stages appear in
the Ossianic corpus, Blair points out, "all is consistent" (Blair 1970
[1765]: 32). It is worth noting here that Blair attributes to *Fingal* a high
degree of mimetic accuracy in relation to its period of composition, as
Blackwell does in regard to the Homeric epics. He does not allow for – or
find – reflections of the subsequent historical stages through which oral
tradition has carried the epic down to the present, when Macpherson
recorded the attenuated "oral editions" that he purportedly reassembled
into the complete epic. We will return to this point later, in connection
with the problem of how Blair constructs *Fingal* as a national epic, mean-
ingfully relevant to the contemporary Scottish nation.

As with content, so too with form. Here again, all is consistent:

The manner of composition bears all the marks of the greatest antiquity. No
artful transitions; nor full and extended connection of parts; such as we find
among the poets of later times, when order and regularity of composition were
more studied and known; but a style always rapid and vehement; in narration
concise even to abruptness, and leaving several circumstances to be supplied by
the reader's imagination. The language has all that figurative cast, which, as I
before shewed, partly the sterility of language and the want of proper terms, have

always introduced into the early speech of nations; and in several respects, it carries a remarkable resemblance to the style of the Old Testament. (Blair 1970 [1765]: 33).

Emotional, vivid, figurative, spontaneous, without artifice. On the basis of these definitive attributes, then, Blair feels justified in concluding in the *Critical Dissertation* that "the poems under consideration, are genuine venerable monuments of very remote antiquity" (Blair 1970 [1765]: 36).

Later, as the critical debates intensified, he appealed to two additional orders of evidence to confirm that the songs were not simply productions of the current moment, but that they stemmed from the past. First, the people among whom the songs were current attributed great age to them and attested that they had been sung and resung by successive generations of performers as far back as living memory extended, establishing an intertextual temporal continuum conceived of by Blair and others as oral tradition. Second, texts that were demonstrably (or arguably) similar in form and content were to be found recorded in old manuscripts (Blair 1970 [1765]: 138–39). We will return to these factors shortly.

At the time that he wrote the first version of the *Critical Dissertation*, in 1763, shortly after the publication of *Fingal*, Blair anticipated that "the degree of antiquity belonging to the poems of Ossian" would be a matter "which might bear dispute"; hence his explicit argument, outlined above, that the poems stemmed from a "very remote period" (Blair 1970 [1765]: 221). What he did not anticipate, however, were the doubts expressed by critics, especially in England, concerning their authenticity. It is these critical attacks that Blair addresses in the Appendix added to the revised edition of the *Critical Dissertation* published in 1765. "I had not the least suspicion, when this Dissertation was first published," Blair confesses, "that there was any occasion for supporting their authenticity, as genuine productions of the Highlands of Scotland, as translations from the Galic [Gaelic] language; not forgeries of a supposed translator. In Scotland, their authenticity was never called in question" (Blair 1970 [1765]: 221).

The controversies that swirled around Macpherson's works implicated a number of factors, of which Joep Leerssen provides a cogent summary: "What concerned readers or critics originally was the question of whether or not this text, in its thematic material or verbal substance, was really based on analogous Gaelic originals; whether these originals were really of such antiquity as Macpherson claimed them to be; whether they really were the fragments of a coherent large-scale composition; and whether its alleged author had really walked the uplands of Caledonia in the fourth century" (Leerssen 1998: 1–2). Any of these questions, or any combination of them, might provide a point of attack.

Blair's defense proceeds on a number of fronts, including an expression of his personal confidence and that of other "gentlemen of rank and taste" in Macpherson's honor and integrity, and his conviction that "the manner in which these poems were brought to light, was entirely inconsistent with any fraud" (Blair 1970 [1765]: 221–23). Such confidence, however, could not forestall the charges of imposture put forward by critics "in England," specifically, "That the poems which have been given to the world are not translations of any old Galic Bard, but modern compositions, formed, as it is said, upon a higher plane of poetry and sentiment than could belong to an age and a country reputed barbarous." Blair offers first the reasoned argument that no one would be "so hardy or so stupid" as to claim, as Macpherson had, that the texts offered in his collections were literal translations of ancient, traditional Gaelic poems, that "the honour of them [was] due to Scotland," that they were known by many "in the original," and that they were related to "current tales and stories concerning them," when such claims, if false, could so easily be discredited by those very people among whom Macpherson claimed them to be current (Blair 1970 [1765]: 223–24). Persuaded, however, that reason alone would not suffice to quiet the critics, Blair devotes the principal part of the Appendix to reporting "express testimonies" from "persons of credit and honour, both gentlemen of fortune, and clergymen of the established church, who are natives of the Highlands or Islands of Scotland, and well acquainted with the language of the country" (Blair 1970 [1765]: 137). Blair acknowledges that the responses of his expert consultants vary in specificity and explicitness, but he advances their collective testimony as strong evidence of the authenticity of Macpherson's Ossianic corpus. These authorities – so constituted by wealth, religious alignment, and class – variously attest to or corroborate the quality and accuracy of Macpherson's translations, the genuineness of his putative manuscript sources, and the persistence and currency of the Gaelic originals and other similar poems in oral tradition.

The accuracy of Macpherson's purported translations posed an especially delicate critical issue for Blair, and he was at special pains to establish the linguistic and poetic fidelity of Macpherson's texts to putative originals. (To be sure, Macpherson's reluctance to produce those originals fueled the debates concerning the authenticity of the Ossianic corpus for decades to come.) The central problem, of course, was that Blair based some of his strongest and most extended arguments for the literary greatness of Ossian on superiorities of style, especially in regard to the felicity and affecting quality of figurative language in the poems. Figurative language, we recall, was an identifying feature of primitive language and poetry in Blair's conception of literary history. The density of images in the Ossianic poems, then, provided internal evidence of their antiquity. Blair's extended examination of figurative language in the poems, however, focuses exclusively on Macpherson's English-language texts, as do various other observations concerning formally constituted elements of poetic style, such as concision and rapidity of speeches, exquisiteness of description, and solemnity of tone (1970 [1765]: 45, 59, 85, 93–119). To treat Macpherson's texts as transparent to Ossian's poetic genius, as Blair does in these arguments, demands a very high degree of fidelity in the translation. Blair even goes so far as to attribute a touch of Ossian's genius to Macpherson himself: "To transfuse such spirited and fervid ideas from one language into another; to translate literally, and yet with such a glow of poetry; to keep alive so much passion, and support so much dignity throughout, is one of the most difficult works of genius, and proves the translator to have been animated with no small portion of Ossian's spirit" (1970 [1765]: 218).

The problem is rendered still more complex, however, by the hybridizing force of the translations as such: they are undeniably productions of the present moment, standing in for putatively older originals, though originals absent from public view. Thus, to establish the accuracy and fidelity of the translations is a purifying tactic on Blair's part, though itself further mediated by his need to rely on the testimony of Gaelic-speaking authorities who – on the basis of comparing Macpherson's texts with accessible manuscript sources or "oral editions" performed by contemporary singers – "all, without exception, concur in holding his translations to be genuine," "amazingly literal," "exact," and so on (Blair 1970 [1765]: 137–47).

How, one might ask, could Blair's Gaelic consultants authenticate Macpherson's Ossianic texts as decisively as Blair represents them as doing when subsequent investigations have revealed the poems to contain a substantial admixture of Macpherson's own literary imagination? In retrospect, we may identify several contributing factors. First, it is important to recognize that the text-making effort that Macpherson undertook in reconstructing *Fingal* and the other poems in his collections was at that time completely unprecedented, so readers had no established frame of reference on which to base their assessments. In addition, thanks to the careful investigations of Derick Thomson (1952, 1987, 1998), we know with confidence that Macpherson did in fact draw upon a *bona fide* repertoire of Gaelic ballads, dating in origin from the twelfth to the sixteenth centuries, and of related oral narratives dating back even further, recounting the exploits of heroes such as CùChulainn, Fionn, Oiséan, Osgar, their companions and their foes. Of Macpherson's works, *Fingal* makes the fullest use of Gaelic ballads, but several of the *Fragments* and the shorter poems published with *Fingal* have clear connections to traditional ballads as well. Still further, many of Blair's Highland correspondents were people whom Macpherson had encountered during the trips he made to the Highlands and Islands in 1760 and 1761 to collect materials that would allow him to expand his corpus beyond the *Fragments* and who had direct knowledge of his recording of songs and acquisition of poetic manuscripts. And we must remember as well that Blair's consultants were assessing English-language texts, translations, distanced by their very nature from any original. In these lights, it is less surprising that Blair's authorities were ready to testify to the genuineness of Macpherson's efforts. We also discover, however, that Blair put the best possible construction on the responses he received from his Gaelic consultants, some of whom did in fact question or criticize the liberties that Macpherson took with the ballads as they knew them; the *Critical Dissertation* makes a far stronger case for the authenticity of Ossian than the surviving letters, at least, might warrant (Stafford 1988: 169). What is most telling, of course, is that Blair himself could not evaluate Macpherson's texts himself vis-à-vis any purported source texts, for he knew no Gaelic.

We might say, then, that Blair and his consultants were attempting to orient themselves in an obscure and ambiguous field of unspecified intertextual relations between Macpherson's English-language texts and, variously, purported third-century Urforms of poems composed by the bard Ossian, heroic poems in Gaelic recorded in manuscripts compiled over several centuries, orally performed songs of which these manuscript texts were in some way a record, heroic songs performed by contemporary singers in the Gaelic-speaking regions of contemporary Scotland, and Macpherson's own transcriptions of these contemporary performances. Moreover, the intertextual links might include proper names, narrative motifs, narrative episodes, or elements of style, any one or combination of which might suffice as a warrant of "authenticity" in the judgment of a particular critic. And all of this, we must remember, was refracted through the authority that accrued to wealth and social status. Clearly, authenticity served in this arena – as it does everywhere – as a rhetorical device for the creation of social value, rather than as a precise measure of textual correspondence or transparency.

However useful or persuasive these testimonials might have been in certain quarters, they too did not suffice to quell the suspicions or end the critical attacks that surrounded the question of authenticity. Nor, indeed, did they add anything substantive to the *Critical Dissertation*. But there is, in fact, some news in the Appendix, information gained from his Highland correspondents and presented in response to critical doubts concerning the authenticity of the Ossianic poems that bears as well on their antiquity. The question at issue is "the manner in which the originals of these poems have been preserved and transmitted" (Blair 1970 [1765]: 138). This problem is of critical importance insofar as it centers on the continuity between the third-century Scotland of Ossian and the eighteenth-century Scotland of Macpherson, the textual relationship of Ossian's third-century songs and Macpherson's eighteenth-century translations, and thus ultimately on how an ancient Ossianic tradition might redound to the greater national credit of Scotland in the modern era. Blair's account is worth quoting in full:

> Until the present century, almost every great family in the Highlands had their own bard, to whose office it belonged to be master of all the poems and songs of the country; that among these poems the works of Ossian are easily distinguished from those of later bards by several peculiarities in his style and manner; that Ossian has always been reputed the Homer of the Highlands, and all his compositions held in singular esteem and veneration; that the whole country is full of traditionary stories derived from his poems, concerning Fingal and his race of heroes, of whom there is not a child but has heard, and not a district in which there are not places pointed out famous for being the scene of some of their feats of arms; that it was wont to be the great entertainment of the Highlanders, to pass the winter evenings in discoursing of the times of Fingal, and rehearsing these old poems, of which they have been all along enthusiastically fond; that when assemble at their festivals, or on any of their publick occasions, wagers were often laid who could repeat most of them, and to have store of them in their memories, was both an honourable and a profitable acquisition, as it procured them access into the families of their great men; that with regard to their antiquity, they are beyond all memory or tradition. (Blair 1970 [1765]: 138–39)

A few paragraphs later, Blair offers additional information supplied to him by his Gaelic consultants and bearing further on the issues of preservation and transmission:

> I am also acquainted, that if enquiries had been made fifty or threescore years ago, many more particulars concerning these poems might have been learned, and many more living witnesses have been produced for attesting their authenticity; but that the manners of the inhabitants of the Highland counties have of late undergone a great change. Agriculture, trades, and manufactures, begin to take the place of hunting, and the shepherd's life. The introduction of the busy and laborious arts has considerably abated that poetical enthusiasm which is better suited to a vacant and indolent state. The fondness of reciting their old poems decays; the custom of teaching them to their children is fallen into desuetude; and few are now to be found, except old men, who can rehearse from memory any considerable parts of them. (Blair 1970 [1765]: 139–40)

What these two passages represent in Blair's historical theorizing is a shift from the conjectural history of poetry presented in the body of the

Critical Dissertation (and the *Lectures*) to a more empirically founded and verifiable history, centering around the process of oral tradition. This information concerning how the poems have been preserved and transmitted, sent to Blair by his Highland correspondents, offered him a firm enough poetic link between the ancient epic of *Fingal* and the surviving texts to sustain contemporary claims to credit for a national epic composed in the third century. Blair's argument represents a pioneering, foundational conceptualization of the durability and preservative power of oral tradition, which had a profound shaping influence, together with Wood's arguments for Homer as an oral poet, on subsequent understandings of vernacular poetry, epic, and the history of literature more generally.[19]

The link is provided by the continuity of the bardic tradition that Blair has offered in the *Critical Dissertation* as the principal factor that allowed ancient Gaelic poetry to attain a level of sensibility superior to that of other peoples at a corresponding stage of development. The bards who were in the service of the great Highland families were cultural specialists, custodians of the Gaelic poetic tradition. Blair enumerates as well a series of contextual factors, both of place and practice, that sustained the continuity of the classical poetic corpus. One mechanism that served to keep the songs in awareness was the currency of "traditionary stories" of Fingal and his heroes, a parallel tradition of narratives, indexing the songs from which they were derived. In addition, Blair observes, episodes in the heroic poetry are localized, attached to particular places that serve in turn to evoke the poems in which those episodes occur. The poems are likewise anchored in situational contexts of use, domestic and public, which keep them at the forefront of expressive attention. They are the favored forms of winter evening entertainment, and the centerpieces of bardic competitions held during festivals or other public occasions. And finally, with the introduction of writing to the Highlands, bards and other devotees of the old songs began to write them down, preserving them in manuscript books kept by the great families.

Notwithstanding these conservative factors that serve to sustain the Ossianic tradition, though, there are etiolating counterforces that bring the tradition into decline, producing two major gaps in the historical continuum, with concomitant gaps in the textual continuum. The first of these occupies the broad span of time between the third-century flowering of Ossianic poetry and the turn of the eighteenth century, which marks the point at which the tradition becomes accessible to the living

---

[19] On the development of the concept of oral tradition in the eighteenth century, see Hudson (1996).

memory of Blair's Gaelic consultants. This is first of all the period in which, according to Blair's general theory, the poetic tradition ceases to be maximally productive, as the inexorable process of social development carries Highland society away from its most primitive beginnings, when poetic expression was at its most vigorous and creative. During this period, the governing dynamic of the Ossianic tradition is transformed from poetic production, as the songs are composed, to traditional conservation, as the songs are reproduced by generations of bardic performers. Concomitantly, this is an era of forgetting, as the originary period fades "beyond all memory and tradition," and a period of fragmentation, as the original unitary epic breaks up into shorter poems. This dynamic accords well with the understanding that the vernacular ballad texts are fragments of ancient epic.

The second major gap occurs between the turn of the eighteenth century and the 1760s, the time of Macpherson's and Blair's interventions in the poetic process. These are the years of "great change" in Highland society and culture, during which, as Blair frames it in terms of the modes of subsistence that constitute the stages of his developmental schema, "Agriculture, trades, and manufactures, begin to take the place of hunting and the shepherd's life." That is to say that these decades of the eighteenth century mark the advent of economic modernization in Highland Scotland, when "the busy and laborious arts" – agricultural, mercantile, and industrial capitalism – bring about a consequent abatement of "that poetical enthusiasm which is better suited to a vacant and indolent life." The gradual poetic decline of the earlier period gives way to a more drastic forgetting as old manuscripts are destroyed or lost, taste for the old ballads declines, adults no longer teach the ballads to their children, and the songs become the province of older and older singers. Before the advent of these changes, there was a vigorous ballad tradition, though no longer a full epic tradition. What is left after the changes, with even the ballad tradition in rapid decline, is a still more drastically fragmented corpus of poetic antiquities, fragmentary and distressed remnants of the original Gaelic epics.

Blair is clearly operating here in terms of a historical framework that subordinates concrete historical events to the point of invisibility and foregrounds instead a broad developmental schema within which those sectors of society in which oral poetry remains current are identified as living in a developmentally prior state. Their poetry is inevitably in a state of decay, because that is understood a priori as the trajectory of primitive poetry, and the historical forces and experiences that have brought it to that state of decay are framed once again in terms of a priori and inevitable stages of progressive development. There is no consideration here of the specific historical events that impelled the changes: the decimation of Highland society by the British in the aftermath of the Jacobite Rising of 1745; the suppression of the Gaelic language in the interest of religious and economic domination and political repression; the violent dislocation and forced emigration brought about by the Highland clearances, as those that remained of the "great families" in the Highlands and Islands – the very families that Blair lauded for sustaining the poetic tradition in earlier years – evicted their tenants and leased the cleared lands for the grazing of sheep. Recall that in Blair's view, the early stages of society "furnish few events worth recording" (Blair 1970 [1765]: 1). No need, therefore, to specify the events that make for change in the Highlands; developmental stages will suffice, in which terms the Highlands were consigned to the status of a cultural relic area.

With the epic fragments in hand, then, collected from oral tradition and manuscripts, and the knowledge of what a complete, great epic should look like, based primarily on the Homeric texts and Aristotle's guidelines as canonical frames of reference, Blair finds grounds for hope, expressed in his Preface to the *Fragments*, that "one work of considerable length, and which deserves to be styled an heroic poem, might be recovered and translated" (Blair 1996 [1760]: 6). Indeed, he goes so far as to outline the plot of this anticipated "Epic poem" (Blair 1996 [1760]: 6). The task can only be accomplished, however, by those with the historical knowledge, literary refinement, and sophisticated understanding to do so. The contemporary bearers of oral tradition, living in a developmentally prior state, before the refinement of understanding and reflection, are a priori unqualified for the undertaking; the project demands the intervention, as we have come to expect, of a member of the educated elite.

The task, then, as rationalized by Blair and undertaken by Macpherson, is a philological variant of antiquarian recovery and restoration, akin in a way to Wood's journey to the eastern Aegean to recover *in situ* the integrity of meaning in the Homeric epics. In more specific terms, Macpherson's charge from Blair and the other "gentlemen of rank and taste" who supported his effort, including John Home, Alexander Carlyle, Adam Ferguson, William Robertson, David Hume, and Lord Kames, was to travel the Highlands and Islands collecting old manuscripts and oral variants, or "oral editions" as Blair termed them (Blair 1970 [1765]: 139, 143), of the old heroic fragments and then, by textual comparison to "ascertain the genuine original, to restore the parts to their proper order, and to give the whole to the publick in that degree of correctness, in which it now appears" (Blair 1970 [1765]: 139). The precise reconstructive practices that Macpherson employed, to be sure, are never detailed, and subsequent scholarship has amply demonstrated that he assumed a great deal of poetic license in the production of the reconstituted epics he offered to the public (see especially Thomson 1952, 1987; see also Bysveen 1982; Porter 2000; Stafford 1988: 127–28). A majority of the *Fragments* and of the "several other poems" that accompany *Fingal* have no clear connection with Gaelic ballads, and *Temora* is free of connections to Gaelic sources after Book I. In those texts that do have ties to Gaelic sources, according to Thomson, Macpherson "manipulated plot detail to suit his own ideas, used or omitted detail, and transposed it, Scotticized or Anglicized nomenclature, and sometimes constructed names from Gaelic elements" (1987: 260). Moreover, Thomson observes, "Macpherson's refining and bowdlerizing pen has often changed the atmosphere of the ballads beyond recognition" (1952: 84). And the poetic style, as we have noted, is of Macpherson's own construction, marked by Homeric and Old Testament imagery and Old Testament grammatical parallelism.[20]

Macpherson's actual textual practices aside, however, Blair's *Critical Dissertation*, with its Appendix, offered a framework for the understanding of poetry in national-historical terms. This framework amounted to a conjectural history of poetic entextualization, decontextualization, and recontextualiation; it privileged narrative and epic poetic forms, linked the documentable corpus of folk poetry still current in the oral repertoire or available in manuscript to conjectural epic origins in terms of oral tradition, accounted for the degenerate quality of oral tradition in terms of progressive social and cultural change, and prescribed a program of recuperative intervention in the process, focused on the full documentation of the epic fragments and textual reconstruction of the original, all couched in a rhetoric of genuineness and authenticity, but also of loss. Blair's program, carried out by Macpherson, allows for the bridging of both the temporal and textual gaps that separate third-century Scotland from mid-eighteenth-century Scotland, and thus provides a charter for claims to Ossianic poetry as a national symbol. The Ossianic epics, especially *Fingal*, made whole in symbolic form the long history of Scotland's national culture. They connected mid-eighteenth-century Scotland with an originary period when poetic creativity flourished, when poets gave voice to and cultivated the moral economy of their society, celebrating in epic form and in a pure, emotional, and figurative language heroes who fought to defend the independence of their nation from outside

---

[20] D. Meek (1991: 39–41) suggests that after 1550 the formal distinction between verse and prose in Gaelic balladry was blurred considerably and that the resultant style may have provided a model for Macpherson's style – what he called measured prose. The inspiration of the Authorized Version of the Old Testament and of Lowth, however, are far more obvious in Macpherson's English-language texts.

encroachment. In the *Critical Dissertation*, Blair was the first to provide a charter for the linkage of vernacular song, collected from contemporary oral tradition, to ancient epic, constructed as a national symbol.

And with Blair as a guide, Macpherson was the first to carry the charter into action. To be sure, Blair wrote and revised the *Critical Dissertation* with Macpherson's *Fingal* and *Temora* already in hand, and published his *Lectures* long after the publication of Macpherson's Ossianic works, but it is clear that Blair's ideas had a powerful formative effect on Macpherson's project. At the time that Blair was introduced to Macpherson, late in 1759, he was deeply involved in composing his literary lectures for Edinburgh University on topics such as the "Nature of Poetry – Its Origin and Progress," and the "Origin and Nature of Figurative Language" (Schmitz 1948: 44–45); indeed, familiarity with Blair's ideas among the Edinburgh literati provided the grounds on which colleagues first brought the younger poet to Blair's attention.[21] Moreover, Macpherson was predisposed towards Blair's frame of reference by his familiarity with Blackwell's ideas, gained during his earlier studies at the University of Aberdeen,[22] and he may even have attended Blair's lectures in Edinburgh. Again, this is not to deny that Macpherson had ideas of his own concerning the nature, origin, and development of poetry, and that in some particulars he may have influenced Blair's thinking, but Blair was unquestionably the more developed scholar of the two and clearly took the intellectual lead in the relationship. In any event, there is no doubt that once Blair became acquainted with Macpherson's early productions he committed himself with enthusiasm to providing encouragement and guidance to the great project of recovering and translating that "work of considerable length" that would establish the existence of a Scottish national epic.

With all of the potentiating factors auspiciously in place – the Gaelic texts, the generic model, the historical framework, the support of the influential Edinburgh literati, plus his own literary abilities and ambitions – Macpherson was well equipped to bring the task of epic recovery to fruition, with *Fingal* as its glowing centerpiece. In the *Critical Dissertation*, then, Blair consolidates his own contribution to the great literary enterprise by confirming the canonical status of the national epic that he had helped to bring into being. And it is no difficult task to adduce close similarities between Ossian and Homer along lines provided by Aristotle (Blair 1970 [1765]: 42) and with echoes from Lowth (Blair 1970 [1765]:

---

[21] Blair began his course of lectures at Edinburgh University late in 1759 and was appointed Professor in mid-1760.

[22] Stafford (1988: 28) observes that all but one of Macpherson's teachers at the University of Aberdeen had themselves been students of Blackwell.

33, 112), if these features are anticipated in advance and woven into the fabric of Macpherson's epic work in the very process of composition.

But why, we might ask, should Blair have felt such a strong stake in the restoration of ancient Celtic epic and the defense of its authenticity? A number of recent critics have noted the ways in which *Fingal* and the other poems resonated with the political, moral, and linguistic concerns of Blair's circle, including the military trustworthiness, moral cultivation, and linguistic improvement of Scotland (Ferguson 1998; Phillipson 1981; Sher 1982, 1985: 242–61). How useful, then, to have the stirring example of Fingal and his heroes defending their nation against Danish invaders, celebrated by poets – beginning with Ossian himself – who were the moral guardians of their people, in the pure language of "a country so free of intermixture with foreigners" (Blair 1996 [1760]: 5).

In larger scope, however, as we suggested earlier, the Ossianic epics represented a symbolic embodiment of continuity and wholeness in Scottish national culture, restored from fragments. The restoration of national continuity out of historical disjunction struck an especially plangent chord in eighteenth-century Scotland. Many commentators on the Scottish Enlightenment have remarked upon the preoccupation of the intellectual and political elite of the day with the great changes that had transpired in the political status of their country: the Union of the Crowns in 1603, through which Scotland lost its Court, formerly a center of intellectual and political life; the political and religious upheavals of the seventeenth century, during which Scotland lost its independence for a time through forced membership in Cromwell's Commonwealth and then saw its royal Stuart line displaced in the Revolution of 1689; and the Union of Parliaments in 1707, in which Scotland surrendered its parliamentary autonomy and thus its national independence and sovereignty (Daiches 1964, 1986; Phillipson 1981; Sher 1982, 1985). These political events the Edinburgh intellectuals and political leaders recognized quite clearly in terms of their complex particularities, not in terms of broad stages of progressive development. These are the very political conditions that Hume addresses in the passage with which we began this chapter. The political ruptures had cultural consequences as well, as Scotland was relegated to the status of subordinate and marginal member of the United Kingdom, its literature looked down upon by the English arbiters of taste and culture in London and its language considered inferior even by those who spoke it – as witness again Hume's query at the head of this chapter (cf. Dundes 1985)

In these concerns, we would suggest, lies the principal motivation for Blair's extended defense of Ossian's authenticity and a basis for elucidating the enduring significance of his work. To this point, we have emphasized the affinities between Blair's polemic and the intellectual program of the antiquaries and philologists. There is this great difference, however: where the antiquaries and philologists we have discussed – not to mention Bacon and Locke before them – foregrounded the *discontinuities* between antiquity and modernity, magnifying the gap between epochs, Blair focused his critical energies precisely in the opposite direction, constructing a framework for establishing the *continuities* between past and present. In the view of the Scottish literati, as Hume's reflections express quite clearly, Scotland had experienced all too much historical disjunction, to its political and cultural detriment. Disadvantaged as she might be, however, Scotland did have at least one claim to distinction, as Hume again makes clear, as home to "the People most distinguish'd for literature in Europe." How, then, to cement that claim still more firmly and in such a way as to redound to the glory of Scotland as a distinctive nation, not merely as a northern outpost of England's cultural – as well as material – economy?

Blackwell's influential writings had already established for Scottish intellectuals the preeminence of epic as a mark of high literary achievement, possible only under the rare but powerful confluence of poetic genius and a culturally and historically auspicious moment in time. The discovery of a Scottish epic, then, would extend Scotland's literary greatness back into the past. Establishing links of continuity between the ancient epic and the present would bolster the distinctive national claims of Scotland in an arena of cultural politics that otherwise accorded that country little respect. It is important to bear in mind that beyond bolstering the pride and interests of the Scottish intellectuals, Macpherson's Ossianic productions were addressed to English readers. All of Macpherson's collections were presented in English translations (his Gaelic version, produced in his later years, was not published until 1807, eleven years after his death) and Blair's defense was framed largely as a response to critical attacks from England.

There is a problem here, however. The intellectuals of the Scottish Enlightenment, Scots-speaking, English-writing Lowlanders, were committed to a historical ideology of progress, the stadial evolution of human society from savagery to civilization, and they saw themselves as eminently civilized men. How might their sense of their country's place in the modern era be reconciled with the extension of the primitive past into that present, and in such a way that the perduring elements might appropriately be assigned a strongly positive valence? Macpherson's Ossianic poems, read through Blackwell's theory of the evolutionary history of language and poetry, offered an attractive solution: look to the people of the past in Scotland's present, that is, to the Gaelic-speaking people of the Highlands, as a holding area for poetry that still resonates, however weakly, with the poetic vigor of its originary period in the distant past. These poetic survivals are distressed, to be sure, for poetry declines as society advances; what is left is a hybrid remnant. But with the intervention of learned intellectuals, who alone can recognize the oral poetry and antique manuscripts for what they are, the poetry can be purified once again: reconstituted as great epic, and warranted by the authorizing rhetoric of authenticity, notwithstanding the further mediation of availability only in English translation. This was Blair's achievement, building upon and authorizing Macpherson's own, and though he failed to convince many of the critics – Hume himself came to harbor strong doubts (Hume 1964) – the argument proved powerful, durable, and influential in its own right. We will trace its further inflections in subsequent chapters. The irony that this ideology and rhetoric of authenticity rested on what was substantially a fabrication is provocative, but ultimately beside the point. The constructed edifice proved durable nevertheless.

Conclusion

Blair's *Critical Dissertation*, in its synthesis of antiquarian and philological perspectives on the words of others, was offered as a prolegomenon to the reading of Ossianic poetry. In the century following its publication, however, Blair's work came to serve as a charter formulation of an enormously influential metadiscursive paradigm in the service of romantic nationalism. Notwithstanding Blair's preoccupation with "the ancient state" of society, the paradigm that he constructed served more importantly as a guide to the conceptualization and management of certain contemporary forms of discourse for contemporary political ends.

What Blair offered, more specifically, was a theoretical framework within which vernacular forms of verbal art – songs and stories current among the more backward sectors of national society – could be tied by the historical process of oral tradition to ancient epic poetry, the highest and most authoritative form of literary achievement. This epic, in turn, as a nexus of literary and moral value, served as a potent resource for claims to national distinction. Finally, in completion of the metadiscursive circle, the vernacular forms that are the contemporary remains – and thus the metonyms – of the ancient epic may come to stand as national symbols of an equivalent order.

The intellectual underpinning of this paradigm, of course, was provided by the conjectural history of linguistic and literary development that occupied so central a place in the social philosophy of the Scottish Enlightenment. In this historical schema, the conditions of life, the communicative needs, and the intellectual capacities of "men in their savage state" shaped linguistic expression naturally into poetry. The textual qualities of poetic compositions allowed them to take hold of the imagination and memory of the people and thus to be preserved by oral tradition. The poems and songs became vehicles for the cultivation and transmission of the morals, values, and sentiments of a people, expressions of its distinctive national spirit. The fullest realization of this "poetical spirit" occurs in "the infancy of societies," with a subsequent decline in poetic vigor as the workings of reason tame and regiment human understanding, emotion, language, and expression in the course of social progress.

The logic of this historical schema leads readily to the positing of an intermediary stage of historical development in which society has developed beyond its infancy but has not yet attained the full maturity of modernity, and ancient poetic forms have correspondingly declined from their originary heights but have not yet fully disappeared. In a period of rapid change and marked social transformation – a period like late eighteenth- and early nineteenth-century Europe – this indermediary stage may be seen to characterize a sector of society, developmentally behind the leading edge of modernity: the rural, isolated, unsophisticated, illiterate peasantry. These historically backward Others among us provide a holding area, a medial space, for the remnants of ancient poetry, which the etiolating process of oral tradition has carried down to the present in fragmentary form. Notwithstanding their decayed state, though, these remnant texts retain the qualities of naturalness, enthusiasm, passion, and freedom from artifice that distinguished the ancient epics from which they are descended. By the timely intervention of the cultivated intellectuals who alone can recognize and comprehend their great historic and aesthetic value, the fragments can be recorded, preserved, and perhaps even reassembled into their full epic form. Thus rescued from otherwise inevitable loss, the national epic can be displayed as a sign of national distinction, proclaiming historical continuity, heroic power, artistic sensibility, and high literary achievement. The poetic discourse of the marginal Others within our own nation, who lack a priori the intellectual capacity to understand its importance, to halt its decline, or to restore it to its full epic glory, becomes at the hands of the intellectual elite an instrument of national aggrandizement within the transnational arena of modern nation-states.

This paradigm for the invention of folklore and the symbolic construction of national epics, further refined by Herder, became a central element in the project of romantic nationalism throughout the nineteenth century, and still serves cultural-nationalist movements today, as in the former

Yugoslavia and the former Soviet Union. It gave shape and meaning to
the Finnish *Kalevala*, the Icelandic sagas, the Russian *byliny*, the Serbo-
Croatian oral epics, and a myriad other national epics. Blair's *Critical
Dissertation*, that is to say, was a charter document in the great movement
towards vernacularization of literature in the Western world, which was
fundamental, in turn, to the coalescence of nationalist ideologies and the
formation of modern nation-states.

Vernacularization, according to Sheldon Pollock, is "a process of
change by which...universalistic orders, formations, and practices...
[are] supplemented and gradually replaced by localized forms" (1998a:
41). "A key site for understanding vernacularization," he goes on to suggest, "is literary culture....In vernacularization local languages are first
admitted to literacy..., then accommodated to 'literature' as defined by
preexisting cosmopolitan models" (Pollock 1998a: 41). In certain key respects, the complementary efforts of Macpherson and Blair would seem
to represent a type-case of the process Pollock outlines in comparative
terms. Homeric epic is the "preexisting cosmopolitan model" par excel-
lence, and the assimilation of Ossianic poetry to Homeric epic frames it
as a local realization of the cosmopolitan model. Indeed, as Pollock observes, "The localization of a superposed epic tradition is...a common
step in the elaboration and ennoblement of a regional code" (1998a: 50).

Observe, however, how Ossian ultimately falls short; it is, if nothing
else, an instance of vernacularization manqué. Proclaimed by Macpherson and Blair as translations from the vernacular Gaelic originals,
Macpherson's Ossianic texts existed only in English, whose cosmopolitan
reach was already wide by the mid-seventeenth century, and still growing.
Blair's *Critical Dissertation* defended a vernacular masterpiece for which
there was no vernacular-language text, only the purported translation in
the dominant tongue. In the long run, as we have noted, it didn't matter: the charter for vernacularization that Blair provided turned out to
be enormously productive nevertheless. We will trace some of its further
inflections in the chapters that follow on Herder, the Brothers Grimm,
and Henry Rowe Schoolcraft.

In tracing the lineaments of the metadiscursive paradigm that vernacularization represented, it is important to recognize the sustaining role
played by the purifying rhetoric of authenticity in the elevation of oral
poetry to the status of national symbol. Blair's defense of the authenticity
of the Ossianic corpus was prompted initially by critical charges that the
poems were not what they were represented to be, namely, the epic compositions, in Gaelic, of a third-century Celtic bard named Ossian, now
recovered from manuscript sources and oral tradition and translated into
English. In larger scope, however, Blair's claims to the authenticity of

the Ossianic corpus reached back to encompass the purported qualities of naturalness, passion, freedom, imaginative vigor, rootedness in place, and moral sensibility of the primitive poetry itself, that is, the qualities that distinguished the poems of Ossian from modern productions. It was these primitive qualities, then, that became the more durable touchstones of authenticity in the century to follow. Blair's *Critical Dissertation* was the first work to link the rhetoric of authenticity systematically to oral poetry, construed as an emblem of national identity and distinction.[23]

The present exploitation of past glories in historically founded claims to greatness, the naturalization and essentialization of poetic expression, and the rhetoric of authenticity, taken together, constitute a powerful means of masking the interested character and hegemonic capacities of the process of symbolic construction we have described. We have suggested in our consideration of Blair's *Critical Dissertation* some of the interests of the Edinburgh literati in promoting Ossian and we will attend to similar factors in the chapters that follow. It is noteworthy, however, that whatever the local factors may be that define particular arenas of interest in the shaping of national epics, the authority of intellectual elites in appropriating, defining, and recasting the vernacular poetry of the backward Other is always firmly established. The poems, songs, and tales in the vernacular repertoire are highly valued as national symbols, but in their hybrid state – distressed remnants of the past in the present – they cannot serve this important function without the intervention, mediation, and authorization of intellectuals. Left to the backward classes, who are a priori unable to speak for it, this national heritage can only disappear, as poetry declines in the face of modernity. But this mediation must be masked by a purifying rhetoric of authenticity, because to acknowledge that the shaping – much less the creative – hand of a modern, intellectual individual has transformed this ancient, unreflective, national poetry is to compromise the very qualities for which the purportedly ancient poetry is valued in the first place. There is a special irony in the foundational and inspirational role played by the *Critical Dissertation* as a charter document in shaping the invention of folklore, the romantic nationalist veneration of oral poetry and national epic, and the ideology of authenticity, insofar as Blair's treatise is built upon a work of massive misrepresentation, and insofar as Blair himself knew nothing of the language or the tradition that Ossian purportedly represented. That so many were persuaded by the *Critical Dissertation* testifies to the social power of the metadiscursive paradigm it laid out and to the efficacy of the rhetoric of authenticity.

---

[23] See Bendix (1997) for the subsequent history of this rhetorical resource.

5 Language, poetry, and *Volk* in eighteenth-century Germany: Johann Gottfried Herder's construction of tradition

In his most comprehensive treatise on the relationship of poetry to culture in the course of human history, the great German philosopher, Johann Gottfried Herder (1744–1803), pays tribute to those scholars of ancient poetry who most inspired his own work: "especially and above all, I want to cite only Blackwell's *Enquiry into the Life and Writings of Homer*..., Wood's *Essay on the Original Genius and Writings of Homer*..., Blair's *Critical Dissertation on the Poems of Ossian*" (SW 8: 341n.). The writings of these critical precursors, and Lowth as well, with whom Herder was also closely familiar, had a profound shaping influence on Herder's thought: his understanding of the radical interrelationship of language, poetry, and history, his conception of oral tradition as the touchstone of cultural continuity, his valorization of immediacy and presence in performance, and his recognition of the affecting power of significant form. Herder's debt to the British philological tradition will be clear in the pages that follow, but it was his own great intellectual achievement to render the ideas of his forebears into a metadiscursively founded theory of culture, society, and history, a magisterial synthesis that has served as one of the cornerstones of the project of modernity for the past two hundred years.[1] Building upon Blair's recognition of oral transmission as the engine of textual continuity between ancient bardic song and contemporary oral poetry in the formation of national epic, Herder created a conception of tradition as constitutive of vernacular literature and national identity. Poetic, collective, affecting, infused with the national spirit, tradition, as Herder saw it, is nevertheless always under duress in the modern world, requiring the intervention of intellectuals to preserve it for the health of the nation.

---

[1] On the German influences of Blackwell, Wood, and Blair, see Böker (1991), Constantine (1984: 79–84), Foerster (1969: 108–12), Gillies (1933), Hecht (1993), Hepworth (1978: 182–83, Whitney (1926: 196–97). On Herder, Ossian, and Blair, see Gaskill (1966). On the intellectual forces and influences that contributed to the shaping of Herder's thought, see Aarsleff (1982), Bendix (1997: 29–34), Blackall (1978), Clark (1969), and Zammito (2002). See also Blackall's valuable survey of critical and bibliographical resources (1978: 526–60).

At the heart of this philosophical project, as it was for the philologists who inspired him, was a highly developed ideology of language. It will be useful, then, to begin our consideration of Herder's thought by outlining in broad terms some of the principal aspects of the intellectual context within which his ideology of language was formed.

In his wide-ranging study of *The Emergence of German as a Literary Language* (1978), Eric Blackall traces the intense preoccupation with language that characterized German intellectual life in the eighteenth century to the disastrous and lingering effects of the Thirty Years War (1618–48), the military and political defeats of which engendered as well a widespread sense of cultural inferiority vis-à-vis the brilliance of France. One manifestation of this cultural distress was a deep anxiety about the capacity of the German language as a vehicle for literature, philosophy, and other forms of intellectual expression (1978: 1–2). Importantly, however, as Blackall is at pains to establish, "the dissatisfaction was no passive despair; it was accompanied by a vigorous determination to improve the situation" (1978: 1).

The intellectual stimulus for these efforts at reforming and reconstituting the German language came from such influential figures as Gottfried Wilhelm Leibniz, who tied his program for the promotion of the vernacular to the patriotic need for pride in one's fatherland, and Christian Thomasius, for whom the cultivation of German was part of an Enlightenment vision that demanded liberation from the past habits of thought and from the separation of the world of learning from everyday life, perpetuated by a reliance on Latin for intellectual expression (Barnard 1965: 8; Blackall 1978: 2–18; Clark 1969: 10). But the efforts at linguistic reform became more broadly based as well with the growth of "German Societies," nominally open to "all aficionados of the German language," but in practice made up largely of middle-class intellectuals with links to the universities (priests, teachers, professors, students) (van Dülmen 1992: 45). While programs for language reform followed many lines, both practical and theoretical, we may identify two broad problems in particular that framed the efforts of German intellectuals with their counterparts in other countries, to comprehend the nature of language and its role in the formation of German culture, namely, the origin and evolution of language and the relationship of language and literature to national identity.

Problems of the origin and evolution of language were widely debated in the mid- to late-eighteenth century, deriving considerable stimulus from the influential contributions of Etienne Bonnot Condillac and Jean-Jacques Rousseau in France and Blackwell, Wood, and Blair in England. The engagement of German scholars, like J. P. Süssmilch and J. D. Michaelis, with these issues took place within a broader intellectual arena that transcended political or linguistic boundaries while at the same time allowing for the valorization of particular languages as in some respect or some measure superior to – that is, more highly evolved than – others. (Aarsleff 1982: 146–209; Porter 2000: 235–38). Indeed, one issue which raised the question of the relative capacities and merits of particular languages had to do with the second broad problem that gave focus to debates concerning language reform in eighteenth-century Germany, namely, the relationship between language and literary expression. At one level, the problem might be framed in general, universal terms, as it was by the British philologists, by asking, for example, what stage of linguistic development or type of language is best suited to poetry or prose. For the most part, however, the particularities of specific languages figure prominently in considerations of language and literary expression.

As the debate was joined in eighteenth-century Germany, we find on the one hand the cosmopolitan proponents of Latin or French or even English as superior for literary purposes to German, and, on the other, the vernacularizing champions of some variety of German – past or current, natural or constructed – as the only proper vehicle for an authentic German literature. This may state the terms of the debate in too oppositional a fashion, to be sure, for one of the most prominent figures in the arena, J. C. Gottsched, advocated the German vernacular as a literary language while at the same time advancing French classical drama as a literary standard, thus separating language from genre.

One prominent line of influence on German thought concerning national literatures came from the British philologists, Thomas Blackwell, Robert Wood, and Robert Lowth, treated in Chapter 3. The relativizing thrust of the critical method advanced by these British philologists, taken up by such influential German scholars as J. D. Michaelis and C. G. Heyne, fostered a conception of literature as a national phenomenon and a standard of literary power and authenticity as achieved only through faithfulness to one's own national language and culture.

Language, poetics, and tradition in Herder[2]

Johann Gottfried Herder's early essay, "On Diligence in the Study of Several Learned Languages," published in 1764, signaled his public entry

---

[2] References to Herder's works are keyed to the 1967 facsimile reprint of the standard Suphan edition (Herder 1967 [1877–1913]), cited in the text as SW (for *Sämtliche Werke*). When we have drawn quotations fom published translations, we cite those works as well. We have also drawn upon unpublished translations of the following: *Auszug aus einem Briefwechsel über Ossian und die Lieder alter Völker* (1773), translated by John Cash; *Über die Wirkung der Dichtkunst auf die Sitten der Völker in alten und neuen Zeiten* (1778), translated

into the intellectual arena we have sketched out in the foregoing pages, marking the beginning of a passionate and lifelong engagement with language, literature, and the foundations of national culture. Accordingly, rather than offering a chronological examination of his writings on language, we will endeavor to delineate in general, synthetic terms his ideology of language, as a basis from which to trace, ultimately, his contributions to the construction of modernity, a construction very different from Locke's, but convergent with it in certain important aspects.

We begin, though, with specific attention to his essay *On the Origin of Language* (1772), the work best known to students and historians of linguistics. The essay won the prize competition of the Berlin Academy for 1771, the topic of which was framed in the following terms: "Supposing that human beings were left to their natural faculties, are they in a position to invent language? And by which means will they achieve this invention on their own?" (Aarsleff 1982: 194–95). Herder's victorious submission brought him into full intellectual prominence and established him as a significant participant in the language debates of the day.

Herder opens his essay with a provocative assertion: "While still an animal, man already has language" (SW 5: 5/ Herder 1966: 87). As Herder develops upon this assertion, however, it soon becomes clear that this language that resides in our animal nature is but one species of language, not yet human language. The language that we have "in common with the animals," as sentient beings among other sentient beings, consists of "screams," "sounds," "moans," "wild inarticulate tones," responses to "violent sensations of [the] body" (SW 5: 5–7/ Herder 1966: 87–88). This "language of feeling," to be sure, has communicative power, striking a resonant chord in other sentient beings of like feeling. But true human language, in Herder's view, rests on very specifically human capacities that clearly differentiate us from other animals. These capacities Herder terms *Besonnenheit*, reflection, one of the most fundamental concepts in all of his philosophy.

Besonnenheit is the "entire disposition of man's forces," a complex and unitary human capacity that encompasses "the total economy of his sensuous and cognitive, or his cognitive and volitional nature" (SW 5: 28/ Herder 1966: 109–10; see also Barnard 1965: 42–43). In the concept of *Besonnenheit*, Herder rejects the separation of faculties – reason, emotion, will, etc. – on which Kantian philosophy is built. For Herder, "all such words as sensuousness and instinct, fantasy and reason are after

by Barbara Hummel; *Von Ähnlichkeit der mittlern englischen und deutschen Dichtkunst* (1777), translated by Clover Williams; and *Homer und Ossian* (1795), translated by Peter Bixby. We are grateful to these colleagues for allowing us to use their work. The remaining translations are our own. All italics are in the original.

all no more than determinations of one single power wherein opposites cancel each other out" (SW 5: 31/ Herder 1966: 112); the concept of *Besonnenheit* neutralizes the Kantian antinomies (Clark 1969: 407).[3] In *Besonnenheit* resides "The distinctive character of mankind" (SW 5: 29/ Herder 1966: 110) as well as the capacity for language: "Man, placed in a state of reflection which is peculiar to him, with this reflection for the first time given full freedom of action, did invent language" (SW 5: 34/ Herder 1966: 115).

The process begins with the human animal immersed in a sea of sensations. By exercise of the power of reflection, one set of sensations is singled out, arrested; the sensory image thus selected becomes the focus of alert and conscious attention (SW 5: 34–35/ Herder 1966: 115) and is recognized as a distinguishing characteristic of its source. It is worth noting here the *reflexivity* of the process; *Besonnenheit* is not merely reflection in the sense of focused consciousness, but involves also consciousness of consciousness: in the exercise of *Besonnenheit* man must be "conscious of being attentive" (SW 5: 35/ Herder 1966: 115).

In an extended argument which we need not recapitulate here, Herder concludes that sonic images are the ones most apt to be singled out in this reflective process. His central example is the bleating of a sheep: "The sound of bleating perceived by a human soul as the distinguishing mark of the sheep became, by virtue of this reflection, the name of the sheep, even if his tongue never tried to stammer it." The bleating is "a conceived sign through which the soul clearly remembered an idea – and what is that other than a word? And what is the entire human language other than a collection of such words?" (SW 5: 36/ Herder 1966: 117). By this process, then, "human language is invented" (SW 5: 35/ Herder 1966: 116).

It is important to emphasize that the language thus invented is not merely an abstract set of signs by which the reflective being apprehends the phenomenal world. In Herder's view, it "is in its very origin ... a means of contact," a social instrument: "I cannot think the first human thought, I cannot align the first reflective argument without dialoguing in my soul or without striving to dialogue. The first human thought is hence in its very essence a preparation for the possibility of dialoguing with others! The first characteristic mark which I conceive is a characteristic word for me and a word of communication for others!" whose capacity to comprehend it stems from the innate correspondence of *Besonnenheit* in all individuals

---

[3] Herder was Kant's student at Königsberg but later became a strong critic of Kant's philosophy. On the relationship between Herder and Kant, see Clark (1969: 41–46, 390–413) and Zammito (2002).

(SW 5: 47/ Herder 1966: 128). *Besonnenheit* is thus doubly reflexive: a consciousness of one's own consciousness is inherently bound up with a striving for dialogue with others. Language, thought, and communication are all rooted in *Besonnenheit*.

Clearly, the original human language that consists of onomatopoeic imitations of distinguishing sonic characteristics bears little apparent relation to language as we now know it. From its first emergence in this rudimentary form, language – and with it the human species – embarks upon a process of development towards the full realization of its humanity (*Humanität*) that is intrinsic to its nature. The precise processes of change that Herder sets forth with regard to the formal structure of language need not concern us too closely; they echo the conjectural history of the British philologists that we have encountered in the preceding chapters. In Herder's understanding, for example, grammar is an emergent superaddition to language and "the more primordial a language is, the less grammar there must be in it, and the oldest language is no more than the aforementioned dictionary of nature" (SW 5: 82–83/ Herder 1966: 159). Verbs develop prior to nouns because things are named initially for the actions by which they produce their distinguishing sounds (sheep is "bleater"); primitive languages are characterized by abundant synonymy because they have not yet developed general categories which require the capacity for abstraction; and so on (see, for example, SW 5: 9–10/ Herder 1966: 91; SW 11: 228–29/ Herder 1833 I: 31).

The forces and mechanisms of development that Herder outlines, however, are important to our argument. Herder states these in a series of "natural laws" in the second part of the essay *On the Origin of Language*, focusing on linguistic development in the individual, in social interaction, and in the nation, or *Volk*.[4]

The first natural law is as follows: "Man is a freely thinking and active being whose powers work on in progressive continuity, for which reason he is a creature of language" (SW 5: 93/ Herder 1966: 173). The motive force of this development derives again from the human power of reflection; the more reflective thought is exercised in the apprehension of the world, the more developed language becomes – it grows by experience. Better thinking makes for better speaking in the progressive realization of human potential (*Humanität*).

By the same token, language develops continuously by virtue of our social nature: "Man is by destiny a creature of the herd, that is, of society; and the continuous development of his language is hence natural,

---

[4] The fourth natural law deals with the monogenesis of language and is not relevant to our discussion here.

essential, and necessary to him" (SW 5: 112/ Herder 1966: 173). As explained in *On the Origin of Language*, the social development of language takes place first within the family, as knowledge is shared between spouses and passed on to offspring, thus making for cumulative growth through the generations. But elsewhere Herder generalizes the process: "Language and speech are developed most intensely through conversations.... Language originated through intercourse and not in solitude; through conversation every expression is sharpened and polished" (SW 30: 223/ English translation quoted from Ergang 1966: 158). Thus, for Herder, as for Bacon, the social use of language as an instrument of social interaction is part of the natural essence of language itself. While for Herder the social nature of language constituted the inherent means of its progressive cultivation, Bacon saw this connection as central to language's inherently flawed character.

From the individual to small groups in conversational interaction, Herder's third natural law carries the process of development to social units of still broader scope, namely nations, *Völker*: "As it was impossible for the entire human race to remain one herd, so it could not remain restricted to one language. There ensued the development of diverse national languages" (SW 5: 123–24/ Herder 1966: 173). Indeed, Herder's entire understanding of the social organization of language is founded on a recognition of linguistic diversification at every level of integration from the individual to the international. Because of individual differences of experience and learning, no two individuals speak exactly the same language. In like manner, every family, every group, shapes language in its own distinctive way. In turn, these social forces, in interaction with environmental differences which – Herder believed – induce modifications of the organs of speech, give rise to dialects and eventually to national languages. Indeed, in Herder's conception, it is the possession of its own distinctive language that constitutes the touchstone of a people or *Volk*, the *sine qua non* of its national identity and spirit: "Only through language can a people exist" (SW 18: 387). And it is with this relationship of language to *Volk* that Herder is most centrally concerned.

In one of his earliest writings, Herder articulated this fundamental principle: "Every nation has its own storehouse of thought rendered into signs," he wrote; "this is its national language: a store to which the centuries have added, and that has waxed and waned like the moon, that... has experienced revolutions and transformations ... the treasury of the thought of an entire people" (SW 2: 13/ English translation quoted from Morton 1989: 135). The quotations from Herder's writings marshaled by Robert Ergang establish the radical centrality of language to national identity especially emphatically:

"Has a nationality," a character in one of Herder's dramas asks, "anything more precious than the language of its fathers? In this language dwell its whole world of tradition, history, religion and principles of life, its whole heart and soul" [SW 17: 58]. Language "is the bond of souls, the vehicle of education, the medium of our best pleasures, nay of all social pastimes" [SW 18: 384]; "it expresses the most distinguishing traits of the character of each nationality, and is the mirror of its history, its deeds, joys and sorrows" [SW 11: 225; 18: 337]; "it is generally acknowledged to be the means for transmitting human ideas, inclinations and deeds; by means of it we bequeath the treasure of former times to later generations; through a common language all the members of a social group participate one in another to a greater or lesser degree" [SW 16: 46]. (English translation quoted from Ergang 1966: 149–50)

We will pursue the further implications of all of these dimensions of relationship between language and nation in the course of our discussion, but for the moment we would simply underscore the affirmative tone that colors Herder's observations: the complex anchoring of language in national character, history, and society is to be celebrated. What for Bacon and Locke is an impediment to true knowledge is for Herder a quality to be treasured. Not surprisingly, Herder's understanding leads, ultimately, to a conception of modernity that contrasts strongly with Locke's, founded on the collective, historically situated force of tradition in human existence as opposed to the individual, decontextualized exercise of reason, on which Locke's political and linguistic ideology depend.

In order to comprehend more fully how it is that language comes to be "the treasury of the thought of an entire people," we must consider in some detail Herder's poetics as a central component of his ideology of language. Herder employs the term poetry (*Poesie*) in two related senses. In the first and primary sense, poetry designates a quality of language, intrinsic to its nature; in the second, the term takes on a textual component as well, comprehending all genres of verbal art, including proverbs, fables, *Märchen*, myths, legends, and various dramatic forms as well as forms of verse, such as songs, odes, ballads, and epics.

For Herder, the foundation of poetry, its essence, is inherent in the origin of human language itself, as it was for the British philologists. Let us recall the nature of the first human language: it consisted of "a dictionary of significant names, and expressions full of imagery and feeling" (SW 12: 7/ Herder 1833 II: 7). "Imitation it was of sounding, acting, stirring nature! Taken from the interjections of all beings and animated by the interjections of human emotion! The natural language of all beings fashioned by reason into sounds, into images of action, passion, and living impact!" (SW 5: 56/ Herder 1966: 135). But then, Herder goes on to say, "What else is poetry?" (SW 5: 57/ Herder 1966: 136). That is, this first human language is "a collection of elements of poetry" (SW 5: 56/ Herder 1966: 135).

The identification of feeling as essential to the poetic quality of this first human language stems clearly from the constitution of the language itself as built up of imitations of the natural language of feeling. In this conception, feeling and reference are inescapably joined. But the prominence of feeling in Herder's formulations makes it all the more necessary to emphasize that the original human language – and thus poetry as well – consists of an integration of feeling and form. The sensory impressions that flow in upon the first speaker have discernible form and the first human utterances are shaped by that form as well as by feeling: "From without, the forms of sense flow into the soul, which puts upon them the impress of its own feeling, and seeks to express them outwardly by gestures, tones, and other significant indications. The whole universe with its movements and forms is for the outward intuition of man. . . . Thus what flows in on him from without, according as he feels it and impresses his own feeling upon it, forms the genius of his poetry in its original elements" (SW 12: 6/ Herder 1833 II: 6). Thus, from the beginning, form plays a key role in Herder's philosophy of language. We shall have more to say on this below.

Given the identity of language and poetry, at least in their origins, we must expect that poetry, with language, undergoes transformation over time. One significant developmental factor that affects the role of poetry is the functional differentiation of language, which, in Herder's speculative history of language, is bound up as well with the evolution of grammatical forms: "For as the first vocabulary of the human soul was a living epic of sounding and acting nature, so the first grammar was almost nothing but a philosophical attempt to develop that epic into a more regularized history. Thus it works itself down with verbs and more verbs and keeps working in a chaos which is inexhaustible for poetry, which is very rich – when subjected to a little more order – for the fixing of history, and which becomes usable only much later for axioms and demonstrations" (SW 5: 84/ Herder 1966: 161). First poetry, then history, then formal philosophy, as verb forms (especially past tenses) and noun inflections are progressively systematized (SW 5: 84–85/ Herder 1966: 161–62).

It is not only grammar, however, that evolves in relation to functional differentiation, but communicative style as well. As language develops still further, in Herder's view, the uses to which it is put continue to have a shaping effect on its formal organization. "Then, through poetry," he writes, "come into being syllabic meter, choice of expressive words and colors, order and impact of imagery; through history, come differentiation of tenses, precision of expression, then, through oratory, comes finally the perfect rounding of periodic speech" (SW 5: 88/ Herder 1966: 165). But note that we have here arrived at a transition from the first to the second sense of poetry distinguished just above: features such as meter, order of imagery, or the rounding of periodic speech are features of *discourse*, formal devices that organize the discursive structure. From poetry as a quality of language, Herder's developmental schema has led us to the emergence of poetry as characterized by formal regimentation at the level of discourse. Ultimately, then, in the long course of language development, poetry recedes from being coterminous with language to being one among a range of functional varieties marked by special discursive regimentation. Yet at the same time, poetry (like other functional varieties) is itself multifunctional. With it, the poet "instructs, reproves, consoles, directs, commands, contemplates the past, and discloses the future" (SW 12: 22/ Herder 1833 II: 26).

While the unfolding of this historical process, as Herder envisions it, does expand the communicative capacities of language, it also entails a potential loss. As the sphere of philosophy is extended and reason has an ever-increasing role in the shaping of language, it can impinge upon poetry, leading to increasing formalism, to mechanical "counting of syllables and scanning of verses" (SW 5: 189), to "delicate and overwrought refinement" (SW 11: 230/ Herder 1833 I: 32). Again, it is not formal patterning to which Herder objects (as we shall see in more detail below), but the increasing insistence on formalistic regimentation. In this process, poetry can be distanced from natural feeling, with a concurrent diminution of its expressive capacity, its vitality, its affecting power (SW 1: 53–55/ Herder 1992: 106–7; Kamenetsky 1973: 837). "What is it that works miracles in the assemblies of people," Herder asks, "that pierces hearts, and upsets souls? Is it intellectual speech and metaphysics? Is it similes and figures of speech? Is it art [by which he means artifice] and coldly convincing reason?" These can be effective, but they do not suffice (SW 5: 16/ Herder 1966: 98). Poetry must strive to retain its ties to the language of nature: "even with us, where reason to be sure often displaces emotion, where the sounds of nature are dispossessed by the artificial language of society – do not with us to the highest thunders of rhetoric, the mightiest bolts of poetry, and the magic moments of action come close to this language of nature by imitating it?" (SW 5: 16/ Herder 1966: 97–98). What Herder is expressing here, echoing Blackwell and Wood, is summed up by his distinction between *Naturpoesie* and *Kunstpoesie*, the poetry of nature versus the poetry of art, which is to say, of artifice (SW 32: 73/ Herder 1992: 44; see also Kamenetsky 1973). In poetry, then, the hybrid character of language, implicit all along in Herder's vision, assumes its most critical importance. Rooted in our animal nature, but socialized in the reflexive moment that makes us human, language loses more and more of its attunement to nature as society becomes increasingly culti-vated. In poetry, however, the calibration is open: *Naturpoesie* shifts the balance towards natural expression, *Kunstpoesie* towards the cultivated crafting of artifice.

Nor is it only grammatical, stylistic, and functional differentiation that diminish the vitality and affecting power of poetry. A further critical de-velopment that may work to this end is the advent of writing. "The more distant a people is from artful cultivated thinking, language and letters," he observes, "the less will its songs be written for paper – dead liter-ary verse." What is lost to the written word is the fullness of "animated representation" (SW 14: 105/ Herder 1968: 178), the expressive power of performance. For Herder, the power of poetry resides maximally in the energy and immediacy (i.e., unmediatedness, *Unmittelbarkeit*) of per-formance, both of which are diminished as poetry is dissociated from movement and music and rendered on the printed page (Fugate 1966: 246). The full power of poetry is a power of presence: "the poems of an-cient and savage peoples arise to a great extent from immediate presence, from immediate excitation of the senses, and of the imagination" (SW 5: 185; see also SW 32: 74/ Herder 1992: 45). In Herder's understand-ing, the more expression is informed by immediate sensory experience, the more true, genuine, and effective it will be. In foregrounding sensory experience and presence, Herder's view converges with that of Bacon and Locke. The critical difference, of course, lies in Herder's valorization of the emotional component of sensory experience, in marked contrast with Bacon's and Locke's insistence that sensory experience must be dis-ciplined in the service of reason.

Let us recall that for Herder, the essence of poetry – as of language – lies in the union of feeling and form, born in immediate sensate experience. The external stimuli that flow in upon the senses and the imagination possess a natural form that is answered by the reflexive shaping capacities that render experience into human language and into poetry. From this formative moment, both language and poetry are set upon a course of further human development, but the essence and efficacy of poetry con-tinue to reside in the union of living, present experience and expressive form:

upon the lyrical, upon the living yet at the same time dance-like rhythm of song, upon the living presence of images, upon the coherence yet at the same time upon the demanding urgency of the content, of perception, upon the symmetry of words, syllables, many times even of letters [i.e., of sounds], upon the cadence of the melody, and upon a hundred other things, which belong to the living world . . . upon these, and upon these alone depend the essence, the purpose, all of the wonder-working power, which these songs have, to be the magic spell, the main-spring, the eternal heritage and joy in song of the people! . . . The longer a song should last, the stronger, the more sensual must these wakers of souls be, that they should spite the power of time and the changes of centuries. (SW 5: 164)

This resonant inventory of elements that are constitutive of poetry, with its insistence on the present, living immediacy of inspiration and its balancing of experiential and linguistic form, establishes clearly Herder's conception of *Naturpoesie*.

Herder's idealization of immediacy, presence, performance, derived in part from the language ideologies he assimilated from his British predecessors, finds corroboration in the accounts of travelers among "the savages in North America" (SW 5: 166) and from Wood's stirring experiences in Homer's world. Not surprisingly, however, Herder yearned "to hear the songs of a living people" himself, to experience the affecting power of presence in a more immediate form than literary theory and travelers' accounts could provide. He appeals to two experiences in particular that elevated his engagement with primitive poetry beyond the printed page.

The first of these occurred during his sojourn in Latvia, early in his career, where he ministered to the German community that remained powerful there even after Latvia was ceded by Sweden to Russia. On an excursion from Riga into the countryside, he had "the opportunity to see the living remnants of these old, savage songs, rhythm, dance, among living peoples from whom our ways have not yet been able to take away completely their language and songs and customs" (SW 5: 170). Herder is referring here to Latvian peasants performing *dainas*, the folksong genre subsequently canonized as the key symbol of Latvian national identity in one of the many nineteenth-century romantic nationalist movements informed and inspired by Herder's own philosophy.

The second formative – really transformative – experience was Herder's 1769 sea journey from Riga to Nantes (SW 4: 343–461/ Herder 1969: 63–113), a Wood-like voyage, Ossian in hand, through the very waters "where long ago skalds and vikings with sword and song plied the seas" and "past the far-off shores where Fingal performed his deeds" (SW 5: 169). This experience impressed deeply upon Herder the power of presence, of the affecting resonance of the places sung of in the songs he so admired.

We should note, however, that it is not solely the immediacy of poetic expression that is at issue in the passage we have quoted above, but its durability, its capacity to "spite the power of time" and to constitute "the eternal heritage . . . of the people." But how are the two principles to be reconciled? How can the ephemerality of the living inspirational moment "spite the power of time?"

Strength and genuineness of feeling clearly play a role: "The more true, the more recognizable and stronger the imprint of our sentiments proves to be, and the more genuine the poetry is, the stronger and truer her mark, effect, and duration will be" (SW 8: 339). But feeling alone, of course, will not suffice, however strong it may be. The other necessary element, as we might expect, is form. Celebrating the great poets of all times, the Moses' and Homers, Herder proclaims, "You sang from inspiration! You planted what you sang in eternal metre, in which it was held fast; and thus it could be sung again for as long as men wanted to sing it" (SW 4: 460/ Herder 1969: 85). That is to say, Herder, like Blair and Lowth, recognizes here the entextualizing force of formalization – variously "metre," "rhythm," "cadence," or "symmetry" in his terms – which makes poetic discourse memorable, repeatable, persistent. In like manner, formal patterning renders poetry pleasing and persuasive. In his extended appreciation of parallelism in *The Spirit of Hebrew Poetry*, Herder asks "Does not all rhythm, and the metrical harmony both of motion and sound, I might say, all that delights in forms of sounds, depend upon symmetry?" (SW 11: 236/ Herder 1833 I: 39), observing further that "It changes the figure and exhibits the thought in another light. It varies the precept, and explains it, or impresses it upon the heart" (SW 11: 238/ Herder 1833 I: 41). Most importantly, Herder's observations on translation, one of the central concerns of his *Extract from a Correspondence on Ossian* make clear that he saw form, content, and meaning as mutually constitutive and sustaining. The "meaning" or "internal feeling" of a poetic work depends on "the external...the sensual, in form, sound, tone, melody" (SW 5: 163).

Thus rendered meaningful, memorable, pleasing, and persuasive, the poetic texts created in the moment of inspiration are perfectly adapted for circulation among the people: "they were so shaped that children and the people at large would master them, and would make them into their favorite songs and sayings of wisdom; they were meant to guide the public and preserve it to be true to its origin and aware of the national tradition" (Herder 1985: 14/ Herder 1997: 84). The immediacy of poetic creation and performance thus give rise to an *intertextually constituted tradition*, as the people learn, remember, and pass on the texts. In this process of poetic continuity, form and tradition are mutually sustaining. Formal regimentation makes traditional continuity possible at the same time that particular formal structures – both linguistic structures and the artistic structures of poetry – become traditionalized through "acclimation of the ear," by repetition, imitation, and socialization (SW 5: 165;

SW 18: 462): "He who has the sound of the Italian stanza or the Scottish 'Chevy Chase' song in his ear will, after ninety-nine stanzas and strophes be able to hear the hundredth. His ear desires the repeating cadence" (SW 18: 462). Thus, the poetic tradition is shaped by multiple dimensions of intertextual relationships. Poetic *texts* are passed on in a chain of transmission, while at the same time poetic *forms* become conventionalized and serve as orienting frameworks for the production and reception of new texts.

The poetic tradition thus established was, for Herder, not simply a treasury of artistic diversions, but rather, the very foundation of culture itself and the vehicle of national character: "A people that has no national songs scarcely has a character" (SW 27: 180). The central argument of Herder's essay, "On the Effects of Poetry on the Customs and Morals of Nations in Ancient and Modern Times" (1778), builds upon the conception of poetry that we have traced above:

> If poetry is what she should be, then according to her essence, she is influential. How could she not exert influence when she is the language of the senses and of first powerful impressions, the language of passion and of everything that passion created, of imagination, action, of memory, of joy or of pain, lived, seen, enjoyed, worked, received, and of the hope and fear to do so in the future – how could she not influence? Nature, perception, and man's entire soul flowed into the language and impressed itself into it, into this body, and therefore it affects everything which is nature including all like tuned and compassionate souls. (SW 8: 338–39)

A people's poetry, then, becomes "the whole treasure of their life," giving voice to "teachings and history, law and morality, delight, joy and comfort" (SW 8: 392). Like language, poetry stores up culture; it is "the archive of the folk" (SW 9: 532).

The same process of socialization that imprints the formal patterns of poetic expression upon the mind of successive generations of hearers also imparts to them the culture of their nation: "The ignorant child listens with curiosity to the tales, which flow into his mind like his mother's milk, like the choice wine of his father, and form its nutriment. They seem to him to explain what he has seen: to the youth they account for the way of life of his tribe, and stamp the renown of his ancestors: the man they introduce to the employment suited to his nation and climate, and thus they become inseparable from his whole life" (SW 13: 304/ Herder 1968: 45). Moreover, the traditions become constitutive of a public: "The fathers taught their children, the lawgivers and so-called wise men taught the public, which was called the people" (Herder 1985: 14/ Herder 1997: 84). The tradition, then, molds the worldview, the ways of life, the values, and the aspirations of a people, shaping the lives of children and adults alike. Its reflexive capacity allows a people to "portray themselves, and see themselves, as they are" (SW 9: 532). It is worth remarking – mother's milk notwithstanding – that there is a pronounced masculinizing of tradition in Herder's formulations, as tradition becomes more politically important, in contrast to the tendency on the part of Aubrey and other antiquaries to identify traditional transmission with women.

There are, to be sure, certain fundamental enabling conditions that a poetic tradition must meet in order to be maximally efficacious and authentic. As we have established, true national poetry must be *Naturpoesie*, passionate, inspired, and natural. It must be consonant with the spirit of the people (*volksmässig* [SW 5: 189; SW 9: 529]), with time, and with place; it must be "created for these people and therefore... in the language, the morals, the way of thinking of the people and of no others in no other time" (SW 8: 360). That is to say, once again, that Herder's vision is popular and relativist in its principles, both culturally and linguistically, and firmly anchored in history. Note also that in this regard the true folk poet must articulate a *collective* spirit, a *collective* genius, must give expression to thoughts and feelings deeply shared by all. The folk poet may, it is true, be a named individual; Herder celebrates Moses, David, Homer, Ossian, and Shakespeare as great folk poets who articulate with special power the collective spirit of their people. Nevertheless, the demand of *Volksmässigkeit* foregrounds the shared, collective quality of the folk spirit, and for the most part, Herder speaks of folk poetry as the collective and anonymous expression of a people, notwithstanding the allowance that he makes for individuals. We will return to the further implications of this homogenizing tendency later in our discussion.

The necessary quality of *Volksmässigkeit*, however, which demands that poetry, to be authentic, must be grounded in the historical moment and "no other time," might seem, once more, to be incompatible with the capacity of tradition to "spite the power of time." How can this apparent contradiction be reconciled? The answer lies in Herder's understanding of cultural continuity as shaped not only by the conserving power of tradition, but by a second human capacity as well, what he terms "organic powers." "All education arises from imitation and exercise," he writes, "by means of which the model passes into the copy. What better word is there for this transmission than tradition?" He goes on, though, to observe that, "the imitator must have powers to receive and convert into his own nature what has been transmitted to him, just like the food he eats." Thus, the traditional inheritance is creatively transformed: "Education, which performs the function of transmitting social traditions, can be said to be *genetic*, by virtue of the manner in which the transmission takes place, and *organic*, by virtue of the manner in which that which is being transmitted is assimilated and applied" (SW 13: 347–48/ Herder 1993: 51). That is to say that a viable, productive, active tradition is a dynamic process, insofar as the teachings of the elders are adapted anew by each successive generation. In this manner, tradition itself may be rendered *volksmässig*, consonant with the historical change that was so central to Herder's philosophy of history.

To identify poetic tradition as *the* constitutive cultural process is to vest great responsibility in the poet. Indeed, in Herder's vision of culture, as in those of Lowth and Blair, poets are the culture makers, the figures who create and shape the culture of a people. "A poet is the creator of a nation around him," he writes, "he shows them a world and has their souls in his hand to lead them there. That is how it should be" (SW 8: 433). Not only does the poet create the culture of a nation, but its continued viability rests upon his shoulders: "As long as there were bards, the cultural spirit of [a] people was invincible, their morals and customs could not be extinguished" (SW 8: 392).

Herder recognizes in the role of the poet as culture maker a centrally *political* dimension, in identifying poets as "lawgivers" (*Gesetzgeber*). Thus Moses, for Herder the great poetic founder of the Hebrew nation (on Moses as poet, see, e.g., SW 11: 309–310/ Herder 1833 I: 108), is the "liberator and lawgiver" of the nation. Accordingly, "The greatest part of their poetry, which is often taken to be spiritual, is *political*" (SW 12: 119, emphasis in the original). In ancient Greece, "The oldest lawgivers, judges of secrets and intimate worship, even, according to legend, the inventors of the most beautiful objects and customs made for morality of life, they were all poets" (SW 8: 366); and so on. It follows still further, then, that tradition, the process by which the poetic forms of a culture, once created, "are passed down from the earliest times, from the founders of the tribe" (SW 1: 263/ Herder 1992: 179), is itself an essentially political process. The socialization of the child, the basic mechanism of tradition and cultural continuity, is, accordingly, the foundation of political culture. "Man is born under the very mild government of father and mother," Herder writes, "and since no authority transcends the parental authority, no wisdom the parental wisdom, no kindness the parental kindness, this government in miniature is the most perfect which can be found" (SW 9: 313–14/ Herder 1969: 229). And here again, Herder makes explicit that it is poetic forms, manifested as "powerful sayings and proverbs . . . fables, genealogies, songs celebrating great deeds or virtues," and the like, by which this political authority is established: "all these are imprints of early paternal rule" (SW 9: 313–14/ Herder 1969: 229–30).

Herder regarded the paternal and domestic government of the family, in which authority rests on the acquired wisdom of poetic tradition, as the most natural form of political order, the "most perfect which can be found" (SW 13: 375/ Herder 1969: 317–18). Beyond the stage of family government, nature leaves off and "it was left to man how to construct a polity" (SW 13: 382/ Herder 1969: 322). The best of such polities, in Herder's view, were those in which the natural principles of family government were extended, allowing the people to choose the best and wisest of their number, the poet-legislators, to lead them. Herder admired especially the democracy and freedom of the Greek republic, in which "All public affairs concerning the people were openly discussed and matters were decided on the spot according to the feeling of the meeting. . . . The orator spoke to his own people, to a circle he knew . . . a multitude who were educated through poetry, songs, art, drama in the finest language in the world" (SW 9: 325/ Herder 1969: 236–37). Consider what is being affirmed here: political community, founded in a sense of cultural cohesion – a shared set of understandings, mutual familiarity, and a sense of common purpose, in which political discussion is open and public, and action is based upon consensus, all resting on education through poetry, songs, art, drama, and language, that is, on a poetic tradition. As in all things, to be sure, Herder would not at all insist that any historical or cultural precedent should be erected as a standard for replication in another place or another period. Even the best of the republics he so admired "had aspects which we would not wish to bring back even for the sake of their orators and poets" (SW 9: 377/ Herder 1969: 252). Still, the foundational principles which enabled these earlier polities to flower were, in his view, worthy of emulation in a form adapted to the particularities of German conditions, needs, and aspirations (SW 9: 377/ Herder 1969: 252).

But Herder carries his naturalization of government from familial (and paternal) principles still further:

It is nature which educates families: the most natural state is, therefore, one nation, an extended family with one national character. . . . Nothing, therefore, is more manifestly contrary to the purpose of political government than the unnatural enlargement of states, the wild mixing of various races and nationalities under one sceptre. . . . Such states are but patched-up contraptions, fragile machines, appropriately called state-*machines*, for they are wholly devoid of inner life, and their component parts are connected through mechanical contrivance instead of bonds of sentiment. (SW 13: 384–85/ Herder 1969: 324)

While this is at one level a condemnation of imperial conquest and domination, it is at the same time a clear affirmation of the need for organic purity as the only natural basis for a viable polity. More concisely, "The most natural state is therefore one people, with one national character"

(SW 13: 384). And it is only a nation that "raised itself without foreign as-sistance in the pursuit of its own culture" that will have the national songs that provide the means for this process of national cultivation (Herder 1985: 16/ Herder 1997: 85). The implication is unmistakable: a *Volk*, a nation, a culture, a polity must be homogeneous – diversity is unnatural and destructive of the bonds of sentiment that hold a people together. In this declaration, Herder has suppressed decisively the acknowledgment of diversity within the nation that we find in his essay *On the Origin of Language*. Acceptable diversity, whether linguistic or cultural, begins at the national boundary. Here we encounter once again, this time in stronger terms, the homogenizing, standardizing thrust that we identified earlier as inherent in the principle of *Volksmässigkeit*.

Like all organisms, governments, no matter how perfectly they may be constructed, will ultimately decline, according to Herder's philosophy of history. "Each state has its period of growth, maturity, and decay" (SW 9: 375/ Herder 1969: 250). Philosophical over-refinement and rational regimentation rob language of its expressive vitality; people come to "live on the basis of knowledge" rather than relying on tradition as the "source of wisdom" (Herder 1985: 12/ Herder 1997: 83), artifice, printing, and commodification rob poetry of its "living effect" (SW 8: 411); the advent of despotic hereditary rule makes for a "warping of traditions" (SW 9: 375/ Herder 1969: 251); and ultimately the nation sinks into the oblivion of history.

Now, although Herder envisions the trajectory of growth, maturity, and eventual decay as inevitable in the life-cycle of all nations, it is crucial to an understanding of his philosophy of history and language to recognize that this process, in his view, is neither uniform nor inexorable in its op-eration from one nation to the next. Perhaps most important, the course of development is susceptible to human intervention (SW 9: 360/ Herder 1969: 360), and this, indeed, is what motivates much of Herder's writings on poetry. In the larger interest of cultural revitalization and political re-form, one of his principal instrumental goals was to reinvigorate German literature, weakened not only by an unbalanced reliance on reason at the expense of emotion, but also by the misguided imitation of Greek and Latin literary models and – worse yet – by the adoption of French among the cosmopolitan German intellectuals and nobility, who, by valu-ing these foreign tongues over their own vernacular, distanced themselves from their own national tradition (SW 5: 551/ Herder 1969: 209; SW 18: 136/ Herder 1993: 142–43; cf. Wilson 1973: 824).

Herder's program for the revitalization – which amounted to the ver-nacularization – of German literature consisted of two complementary elements, both centering on folk poetry, *Volksdichtung*: the study and celebration of the poetry of other peoples among whom it displayed its full expressive vigor – the Other without, and the retrieval and revalorization of the remnants of vital poetic expression still to be found in those sectors of his own society least affected by the changes that had robbed cultivated poetry of its emotional power and efficacy – the Other within.

The former enterprise led to Herder's celebration of the language and poetry of primitive peoples, or what, by the lights of his period, he considered primitive peoples, for they included the ancient Hebrews and Greeks as well as Hurons, Brazilian Indians, Iroquois, Eskimos, and Tahitians. "What do you consider the most essential to poetic language?" asks one of the interlocutors in the dialogue that constitutes the first volume of his *Spirit of Hebrew Poetry*. "No matter whether it belongs to the Hurons or Otaheitans. Is it not action, imagery, passion, musick, rhythm?" Pressing the point, he continues, "the language that exhibits these in the highest perfection is the most peculiarly poetical. Now you are aware that the languages of people but partially cultivated may have this characteristic in a high degree, and are in fact in the particular superior to many of the too refined modern languages. I need not remind you among what people Ossian, or at what period even the Grecian Homer sang" (SW 11: 225/ Herder 1833 I: 27). And Hebrew, he insists, is "more poetical than any other language on earth" (SW 11: 230/ Herder 1833 I: 33).

His partner is not fully persuaded: "Is it possible you are speaking of those barbarous and uncouth gutterals? And do you venture to compare them with the silvery tones of the Greek?" (SW 11: 230/ Herder 1833 I: 34).

"I make no comparison," he replies. "Every language suffers by being thus compared with another. Nothing is more exclusively national and individual than the modes of gratifying the ear, and the characteristic habitudes of the organs of speech" (SW 11: 231/ Herder 1833 I: 34). This disclaimer is of the utmost importance. It is, in fact, an expression of Herder's deeply held relativism, his respect for all languages and cultures in their own terms. In fundamental opposition to the universalist aesthetic of Kant, Herder insisted that the language and poetry of every people be assessed "with respect to time and place" (SW 14: 98/ Herder 1968: 172); for each *Volk*, the authenticity and vitality of its poetry rested only on its faithfulness to "The genius of their nature, their country, their way of life, the period in which they lived, and the character of their progenitors" (SW 14: 98–99/ Herder 1968: 172). Only by entering sympathetically into the spirit of a nation can one hope to achieve an understanding of its culture (SW 5: 502/ Herder 1969: 181). This is in fact an extension and full generalization of hermeneutic and text-critical principles developed by the classical and biblical philologists we have considered in the preceding chapters. In this move, Herder provides the charter for the vernacularization of literature as a cornerstone of romantic nationalism.

In accordance with this principle, this insistence on rootedness in time and place as the touchstone of authentic poetic expression and interpretation, Herder did not valorize the poetry of other *Völker* in order to hold them up to his fellow Germans as models for imitation, for this would have undermined the very foundation of an authentic national literature (SW 1: 140–41/ Herder 1992: 94): "if we mimic practices that are borrowed from foreign peoples and times, that are foreign to our inner sense, then we damn ourselves to Hades as we live and breathe" (SW 24: 44/ Herder 1993: 102). Rather, he celebrated the poetic forms of other nations as demonstrations of how such authentic expression might be constituted (SW 1: 444/ Herder 1992: 228); this was the principal motivation for his influential collection of *Volkslieder*, published in 1778–79.

For Germany, the corrective to a poetry of artifice must be sought in the German vernacular tradition itself. Inspired by Macpherson and Blair, Herder found this corrective in German folksongs, folktales, myths, and other poetic forms. "I am familiar with folksongs in more than one province," he proclaimed, "provincial songs, peasant songs, which would certainly hold their own in liveliness and rhythm, in naive character and strength of language; but who is it who collects them? who concerns himself with them? with the songs of the people? in streets, and alleys, and fishmarkets? in the untutored roundelays of the country folk? with songs, which frequently do not scan, and are often poorly rhymed? who would collect them – who would print romances in handsome volumes?" (SW 5: 189). Here, among the peasants and ordinary people of the towns, those "whom our ways have not yet fully deprived of their language and songs and customs, only to give them in return something misshapen or nothing at all" (SW 5: 170), Herder found an authentic German folk voice, crude, perhaps, by the mechanical, formal standards of cultivated critics, but full of the emotional energy and *Volksmässigkeit* he so valued as the essence of poetry (Schütze 1921: 117). These songs are endangered by the privileging of foreign models and standards, as by the encroachments of a mediating literacy, but they must be saved: "I cry out to my German brothers! just now! The remnants of all living folk imagination are rolling precipitously toward a final plunge into the abyss of oblivion. . . . the light of so-called culture is devouring everything about it like a cancer" (SW 25: 11). There is thus a preoccupation with absence, a fear of imminent loss, that suffuses Herder's writings on German folk poetry. The revitalization of German culture, the restoration of its vital balance, demands the recuperation of authentic folk culture to counter the "so-called culture" of a universalizing, cosmopolitan enlightenment rationalism (SW 9: 530). Herder's rallying cry to his German brothers stands as a critical moment in the symbolic construction of what we might call, drawing upon Susan Stewart's felicitous notion, the rhetoric and poetics of distress that has attached to folklore since the idea was first invented (Stewart 1991; see also Briggs 1993). Herder frames the poetry of the peasants, market traders, and country people as multiply distressed: it is formally flawed, survives only in remnants, and these too are tumbling towards oblivion with no one to save them. The implication is that the people who still actively sing the songs cannot themselves hold them back from the abyss; others must intervene, as Macpherson had in Scotland, rescuing the distressed remnants of Ossian from oblivion and restoring their poetic luster to the greater glory of his nation.

We encounter in this context a further dimension of Herder's usage of the term *Volk* that warrants attention (see Barnard 1965: 73–75; Gaier 1990). In its most general sense, *Volk* designates a nation, a people, but it may also designate that portion of a more complex, stratified society that remains most firmly grounded in its inherited language and traditions and still open to feeling, as distinct from those who have been distanced from their roots and their feelings by over-rational refinement or the cosmopolitan adoption of foreign languages and alien ways. Herder is not always consistent in his usage, but in this more marked sense, the *Volk* is "the largest," "most useful," "most venerable," and "most feeling" segment of a populace: peasants, artisans, burghers – essentially, the bourgeoisie [*das Volk der Bürger*] (SW 1: 392, 6: 104, 7: 265, 32: 60). The members of the *Volk* are closer to nature than the intellectuals (SW 32: 41). Intellectuals may remain part of the *Volk* (*das Volk der Gelehrsamkeit*) as long as they remain faithful to the *Volk* character, but the over-rational, over-refined intellectual (*der Grübler*) is removed from the *Volk* (SW 7: 265). Likewise, as also in Justus Möser's conception of *Volk*, which influenced Herder's own, the nobility (*der erste Stand*) are set apart (see, e.g., SW 17: 391; on Möser see Sheldon 1970). Also excluded are the rabble (*der Pöbel*). It is not fully clear what Herder means by this term – perhaps the dispossessed vagrants and urban poor whose numbers were increasing in late eighteenth-century Germany (Braunschwig 1974: 106–16) – though his most explicit statement, "*Volk* does not mean the rabble on the streets, who never sing and create poetry, but shout and mutilate" (SW 25: 323) does differentiate them from the *Volk* in terms of poetic creation and performance. Whatever else they may be, the true *Volk* are the source of authentic poetic expression and the bearers of poetic tradition.

Clearly Herder's extended view of the *Volk* implicates structures of inequality. When he speaks of a *Volk* in general, collective terms as a nation or a people, the discursive and metadiscursive practices by which an authentic, vital cultural tradition is constituted emanate from the social formation as a whole. From the more immediate perspective of his own society, though, the true folk spirit is unevenly distributed. The autocratic and cosmopolitan nobility is detached from folk culture – they speak French! And at the bottom of the hierarchy, the dispossessed rabble are incapable of participation in the authentic poetic discourse of the *Volk*; their discourse is distorted, mutilated, pathological. The discursive practices that are fully authorized by Herder are those of the bourgeoisie, the landed peasants, artisans, people of the market-place.[5] "From the *middle* classes emerges the widely known and principal part of spiritual activity and culture; that which enlivens the whole is bound to effect both high and low" (SW 24: 174). In addition to these members of *das Volk der Bürger*, Herder also provides a place among the true *Volk* for certain intellectuals, those in fully sympathy with the *Volksgeist*, among whom, by implication, he would number himself and those who would join in his mission for the rescue and nurture of German folksong.

But note the interventionist and recuperative role assumed by these members of *das Volk der Gelehrsamkeit*. It is the task of intellectuals to recover, collect, and preserve the folk poetry and to foster the use of the German language, to develop the educational and literary institutions that would sustain the authentic folk culture. It lies also with *das Volk der Gelehrsamkeit* to create the poetry that will renew the folk spirit of the German nation and carry it into the future. This is the foundation of that broad nineteenth-century effort of "all those lexicographers, philologists, grammarians, folklorists," and other intellectuals who provided grist for the mill of print capitalism, grinding out the reading materials for bourgeois readers, that Benedict Anderson identifies as necessary to the coalescence of modern nationalism (1991: 71; see also Hobsbawm 1992: 103–4). The program led, in the latter part of the nineteenth and early twentieth centuries, to the romantic nationalist rhetoric and ideology that Ernest Gellner ridicules in its full *volkisch* guise (1983: 57–62).

The simple folk alone cannot save folk culture from its inevitable decline. They lack the ability to treat their own means of expression analytically, to recognize the reflexive capacity of language, or "to separate the *thought* from the *expression*." "[I]t would appear ridiculous," Herder suggests, "to see a peasant explicating words" (SW 1: 387/ Herder 1992: 197). The unlearned "common man," at least, can be educated to scholarly pursuits; this requires that "I . . . speak *his language* and gradually

---

[5] It is interesting to note, parenthetically, that Herder celebrates in the discourse of the market-place precisely what Bacon and Locke distrust, while Sprat valorizes as "the language of Artizans, Countrymen" for its plainness, not its poetry.

accustom him *to mine*; I must not speak to him as if I were in the clouds, but stand on his level and slowly raise him to my sphere" (SW 1: 390/ Herder 1992: 199). Women, however, differ in this regard. If the woman "is to develop herself into what *she is meant to be*, so that she may enhance her soul and be the delight of the male species, so that she may grow to attain the dignity of the burgher's estate, of motherhood, of a spouse, and of an educator," her "education must not reflect the male view or, still less, the scholarly view." Rather, it "must accommodate her mind," "her sphere," that is, "the good common sense of life...the common sense of the house and kitchen" (SW 1: 393–94/Herder 1992: 201–2). What Herder does, then, in recognizing *das Volk der Gelehrsamkeit* is to authorize, as Blair had before him, a metadiscursive regime of intellectual intervention in folk culture, founded in Herder's case on intellectual and gender inequality, the influence of which continues to be felt to this day.

The potential reach of such metadiscursive intervention is suggested by Herder's late reflections on the Ossian controversy, especially on the nature, extent, and legitimacy of Macpherson's role in the production of the Ossianic texts (SW 18: 451–52). Agreeing with many critics that the best – indeed, the only – way to resolve the debates that continued to swirl around Macpherson's work would be to bring the putative Gaelic originals to light, Herder observes that no matter what the public scrutiny of the originals might reveal, "it cannot hurt Macpherson's reputation." If the songs are all "taken from the tradition," as Macpherson maintains, he remains the one who rescued them from oblivion and rendered them "agreeable to the entire educated world." If, on the other hand, "he merely received the raw materials, and composed with creative hand that which he portrayed, all the more fame for him, and an even greater lesson for us. Here he excluded inferior features; there he supplemented with similar, finer features from the Hebrews, the Greeks, or the Moderns, and gave the noblest and gentlest form to the whole...all the better. He did what an intelligent man must do." The warrant for such textual manipulations, which are framed as an intellectual responsibility, is precisely that attunement to the *Volksgeist* that constitutes Macpherson, an intelligent, educated man, as a member of *das Volk der Gelehrsamkeit*: "the spirit of his fatherland, his forefathers, the spirit of his language and the songs sung in it seized him." This licenses the interpolation into the Gaelic texts of "many beautiful things collected from other ages as well as the feelings of his own heart. That he did this under the mask of Ossian is something for which we should not only forgive him, it was also for him perhaps a duty of gratitude and necessity. He was brought up around such songs; they wakened his most inner self." Macpherson's "holy deception," then, if such it turns out to be, does not detract at all from the authenticity (*Echtheit*) of his work – in fact, it is to his credit, given the combined imperative of refining the raw folk poetry to make it agreeable to educated people everywhere while at the same time remaining true to the spiritual call of the fatherland, its language, and its poetry.

Volksmässigkeit, the essential measure of authenticity for Herder, thus emerges as a remarkably capacious quality. The purifying rhetoric of authenticity allows, we can see, for extensive hybridization. The Ossian texts may be a pastiche of Celtic and cosmopolitan, ancient and modern, collective and individual, traditional and newly created, crude and polished, but Herder can nevertheless insist on their authenticity on the basis that Macpherson was of the culture, was familiar with its language and its songs, and – most importantly – was inspired by the national spirit. An appeal to the spirit, to be sure, may smack a bit of mystification, but it is rhetorically effective: it enhances the aura of purity that suffuses authenticity. But seizure by the spirit of the fatherland may be quite effectively indexed for practical purposes by the very recontextualization of vernacular texts as national expressions, as both Blair and Macpherson were at pains to do.

The rejection of cosmopolitanism was also rhetorically effective, useful though appeals to cosmopolitanism may be in other contexts, as we have just seen. Herder again and again castigates his countrymen for selling out the culture of their fathers for a bloodless and over-refined cosmopolitanism. "Perhaps we could ask the flatterers of this century," he suggests, "what is this greater virtue that Europe is supposed to have acquired through enlightenment? Enlightenment! We know so much more nowadays, hear and read so much, that we have become tranquilized, patient, meek and inactive" (SW 5: 555/ Herder 1969: 212; see also 1774: 192). With bitter irony, he observes that "With us, thank God, national character is no more!... To be sure, we no longer have a fatherland or any kinship feelings; instead, we are all philanthropic citizens of the world. The princes speak French, and soon everybody will follow their example; and, then, behold, perfect bliss: the golden age, when all the world will speak one tongue, one universal language, is dawning again! There will be one flock and one shepherd! National cultures, where are you?" (SW 5: 550–51/ Herder 1969: 209). Herder's censure here of a homogenizing cosmopolitanism as inimical to the authentic national literature he advocates so passionately might remind us once again that the nationalizing thrust of his cultural ideology exerts an equally homogenizing force, but within national boundaries. As Pollock observes, "Vernacular intellectuals define a literary culture in conspicuous opposition to something larger...." The "local" that they define in this process "typically comes to be constructed as dominant and dominating for similar cultural spaces...a further step in the cosmopolitan-vernacular transformation and unthinkable without it" (Pollock 1998b: 8).

Especially pernicious is the neglect of Germany's own national poets in favor of foreign models. Reproaching his countrymen "for the unwavering indifference with which they neglect and ignore the best poets of their own language in their schools and in the education of their young in general" (SW 18: 136/ Herder 1993: 143), Herder warns of the linguistic and cultural consequences of such national indifference: "Through what means is our taste, our style of writing, supposed to develop? Through what means is our language supposed to take on structure and rules? How else except through the best writers of our nation? Through what means are we supposed to acquire patriotism and love of country except through our country's language, except through the most excellent thoughts and feelings that are expressed in this language and lie like a treasure within it?" (SW 18: 136/ Herder 1993: 143). It is in this spirit that Herder hopes that his writings on folk poetry will encourage his readers to recover what is left of the treasure of German folksong, so that Germany will be able to listen again "to the voice of its own poetry" (SW 8: 392; see also 8: 428). The model, again, is Ossian, a true Scottish voice to sound above the English voices imposed from without.

In the political arena, this authentic national voice of the skalds and poets, Herder submits, might offer a powerful, purifying corrective to the enervated political discourse of the present, "corrupted through artifices, slavish expectations, fawning sneaky politics, and bewildering intentions" (SW 5: 181). This critical inventory of political ills, in turn, points us towards the contemporary grounding of Herder's political ideology and reformist program. While we do not have the space here – nor is it our purpose – to describe fully, much less explicate, the broader contours of Herder's political theory in its historical context (see Barnard 1965, 1969), a brief account will help to clarify the grounding and implications of his emphasis on linguistic and poetic traditions as the foundations of an authentic political culture.

Late eighteenth-century Germany existed as a unified entity in name only. Prussia, under Frederick the Great, dominated the political landscape, but in reality, the empire consisted of more than three hundred essentially autonomous states, a significant common feature of which was the personal absolutism of their sovereign rulers. The concentration of absolute power in the hands of the ruling aristocracy diminished the status of the non-sovereign nobility, while the middle classes, lacking economic vigor and unified political consciousness, had no effective political presence.

Absolutism, to be sure, does not preclude political reform; in the aftermath of the Seven Years War, Frederick devoted great effort to reforming
the machinery of government, and the commanding presence of Prussia
in the political environment drew other rulers to emulate his example.
Under conditions of absolute rule, however, reform can only be instituted from above, "enlightened" though it may be. One of Frederick's
own administrators, in suggesting that Frederick's administrative accomplishment "could serve as a model and as an example to be striven
after by the rest of the German states," observes as well that "everything was done by autocracy, there was no Estates constitution and no
active state council to give unifying force; there were no institutions in
which a community spirit, a comprehensive view and fixed administrative
maxims could develop. Every activity awaited initiative from above, independence and self-confidence were lacking" (quoted in Hubatsch 1975:
233). The prevailing thrust of reform efforts centered on the progressive
enlightenment of the rulers; the solutions put forward, founded on solid,
rational, enlightenment principles, recommended such reforms as the acceptance by the rulers of constitutional restraint and the rationalization
of the administrative apparatus of government (Barnard 1965: 19–22;
Hubatsch 1975: 148–68).

The ideology of the German *Aufklärung* accorded well with top-down
programs of political reform. Henri Braunschwig, in his classic study
of the Enlightenment in eighteenth-century Prussia, offers a trenchant
characterization: "In the case of the Aufklärung, culture ... comes from
above and moves downward, for the elite minds at the upper levels are
often barely intelligible.... The enlightened minority is conscious of its
merit; it has 'raised itself' above the crowd, but in doing so it has parted
company with the masses. Its ideal is to radiate above the masses and gradually to penetrate then, not to reflect them. It is not this minority which
expresses the community, but the community which painfully spells out a
new alphabet of ideas which are alien to it" (Braunschwig 1974: 90–91).
Herder, however, placed no faith in the corrective potential of nobility-
down political reform, especially if it amounted to little more than minor
incremental adjustments of the administrative machinery and remained
dependent in the end on the personal will of an autocratic sovereign. He
believed deeply in the moral implications of the principles on which the
reformers based their programs – that government should be based on
consent rather than coercion, that it should be moved by law and reason
rather than arbitrariness and the whim of rulers, that the state should exist
for the good of its members and not the reverse – if not in the principles
themselves. His conviction that the natural foundations of government
lay in the paternal authority of the family, for example, led him to reject

the principle of social contract as a basis or justification for political organization. Likewise, his radical historical and cultural relativism made him fundamentally unsympathetic to universalistic notions of absolute individual rights and like abstract ideals (Barnard 1965: 141–42). Rather, Herder drew inspiration from Rousseau's philosophy of the natural man, with its celebration of sentiment and emotion, its valorization of education on familial principles, its advocacy of popular sovereignty; from Justus Möser's vision of political life as emergent out of custom, tradition and local patriotism; from champions of the intellectual, artistic, and spiritual power of the German language, such as Christian Thomasius, F. G. Klopstock, and Johann Christian Gottsched (Barnard 1965: 18–29). As we have seen, he believed passionately that the true foundations of political community and political culture lay in the organic culture of a *Volk*, rooted in history, sustained by tradition, and manifested in language and poetry.

For our purposes, it is especially important to emphasize that in Herder's view, this authentic political culture is discursively – that is, textually – constituted. His sustained and passionate celebration of vernacular languages and poetic traditions, his language ideology, vested authority in the metadiscursive practices that gave life to the language, poetry, and tradition of a people, to the living expression of their *Volksgeist*. In his vision, as we have attempted to establish, this spirit of a people resided in its most authentic form in that social formation he identified as a *Volk* – either a whole "uncultivated" society with a unified linguistic and cultural tradition or that segment of modern complex society that was least corrupted by modern over-refinement, that best sustained custom and tradition, that is, the peasants, artisans, and tradespeople of the farms, towns, and market-places. This was not, however, simply a matter of according recognition and value to a suppressed voice in the social chorus. In authorizing the metadiscursive practices that were constitutive of folk-poetic tradition, Herder was in fact contributing powerfully to the *creation* of the *Volk* as a social formation and of folk poetry as the essence of folk culture.

Conclusion: Herder *vis-à-vis* Locke

Following the intellectual trajectory we have traversed from Locke to Herder, we have arrived, in Herder's writings, at an ideological position that stands in many ways at the opposite pole from Locke's ideology with which we concluded Chapter 2. Whether considered in terms of their own core principles or in the larger scope of subsequent intellectual history, the language ideologies of Locke and Herder contrast markedly in certain fundamental respects. Compare Locke's antipathy towards traditional authority with Herder's valorization of tradition; Locke's abstract and universalizing scientific rationalism with Herder's concrete, relativizing aesthetic particularism; Locke's suppression of indexicality and intertextuality with Herder's celebration of these associational principles as constitutive of culture; Locke's distrust of emotion with Herder's celebration of feeling and passion; Locke's primary focus on the word with Herder's emphasis on the text; Locke's rejection of the value of poetry and rhetoric with Herder's exaltation of poetic expression and its affecting power. Ultimately, Locke anticipates the realization of a pure language, autonomous from nature and society, which may then serve for the scientific discovery of natural truth and the establishment of a rationally founded, stable society. Herder, by contrast, insists from the beginning on a conception of language as a nature–society hybrid, simultaneously natural *and* social, which serves in turn as the instrument of social purification, the foundation of a homogeneous national society that is at the same time a fulfillment of human nature. Such fundamental epistemological and axiological differences cannot help but lead in different intellectual and ideological directions and yield different visions of modernity.

In broader scope, the lines of influence that may be traced from Locke to Herder extend in divergent directions. Hans Aarsleff, who has called Locke "the most influential philosopher of modern times" (1994: 252), credits him with laying "the foundation of the modern study of language" (1982: 24). Though we would not want to take such all-star rankings too seriously, Aarsleff's own eminence as an intellectual historian of linguistics gives weight to his assessment. Locke's theory of language, as developed in Book 3 of the *Essay Concerning Human Understanding*, stands as a cornerstone of "scientific" conceptions of language that rest upon the conventionality of the linguistic sign, the cognitivist linking of the linguistic sign to ideas, the privileging of the referential and propositional functions of language in the service of rational, philosophically rigorous thought and expression as against everyday "civil" discourse, and the suppression of indexicality (including prominently intertextuality) as inimical to pure reference (see, e.g., Aarsleff 1982, 1984; Guyer 1994; Yolton 1993: 115–20). These ideas do indeed occupy a wide space in modern linguistics; one index of their dominance is that the sociopolitical aspects of Locke's ideology of language do not figure in intellectual histories of linguistics, Aarselff's included, though as we have endeavored to show, they are radically bound up with his overall language ideology.

For Herder, the reverse is true. Jakob Grimm, as early as 1851, used Herder as a foil against which to mark the break between older, unscientific conceptions of language and modern scientific linguistics. Even as sympathetic a reader as Sapir (1908) dismisses most of Herder's theory of language, valuing only the suggestiveness of his ideas concerning the nexus of form and feeling, ideas which have not figured prominently in subsequent linguistic theory. Rather, it is precisely for the sociopolitical aspects of his work on language that Herder is acknowledged: the populist celebration of vernacular language and poetry, the relativist insistence on the distinctiveness of national languages, their indexical grounding in time and place, their linkage to the worldview and ways of thinking and feeling of a people, and their essential role in maintaining national identity and cohesion (see, e.g., Barnard 1969; Berlin 1976; Robins 1990). Herder is accorded a far more influential role in the development of disciplines outside linguistics, principally anthropology (in its Americanist guise) and folklore (see, e.g., Bendix 1997; Broce 1981; Cocchiara 1981; Kamenetsky 1973; Murray 1985; Wilson 1973). Here, it is the literary, philological, and expressive dimensions of his thought that are of principal significance: the idea that a people's culture is encoded in its traditional, vernacular artistic texts, and that these intertextually constituted traditions are the principal mechanisms of cultural continuity.

We must make clear that in playing up the contrasts between the Lockeian and Herderian views we do not at all mean to posit two fully separate, mutually incompatible intellectual traditions or to align Locke and Herder exclusively with separate disciplines. Already in Humboldt, one finds strong resonances both with Locke (e.g., on the semiotic linkage of the linguistic sign with ideas (1988: 56–59)) and with Herder (e.g., on language and poetry as the expression of the spirit of a people (1988: 42–46, 60)), and mixed strains may be found in varying degrees in much subsequent work.

With all due acknowledgment of the contrasts and convergences, however, it is useful in concluding this first section of our book to take direct account of certain key areas of correspondence between their respective language ideologies and the implications of those commonalities for subsequent language ideologies and metadiscursive practices. We focus especially on the structures of inequality that we have found to occupy a significant place in the language ideologies of Locke and Herder and that are foundational, we would argue, to the metadiscursive construction of modernity.

For Locke, we recall, the referential precision and consistency that is essential to rational philosophical discourse is an inherent property of language. Nevertheless, the achievement of a fully realized language of reason demands reflexive effort on the part of its speakers, who must attend constantly and rigorously to the cultivation of a pure, plain language. In Locke's view, every person is endowed from birth with the faculties and powers necessary to such reflexive awareness, but the ability to exercise those innate capacities to the fullest is limited by social factors such as occupation, class, and gender. Manual laborers, those of "low breeding," or women do not have access to the experience, education, company, leisure, or opportunities for practice that the reflexive cultivation of thought and language demand; they are effectively barred from those metadiscursive practices that might allow them to perfect their faculties and thus their language. For people in those stations of life, ordinary "civil" discourse will suffice, and under ordinary conditions, this will do no harm.

But Locke also saw in such uncultivated language the potential for social disorder and disruption, as people fall victim to the imperfections to which language and linguistic practice are susceptible: the distortion of reference and meaning that results from lexicosemantic ambiguity, poetic frivolity, dependency on the authoritative words of others, the rhetoric of ornament, self- or partisan interest, and disputation, all of which may yield confusion, untruth, wastefulness, and even outright conflict. The remedy, in Locke's view, is to extend rational discourse into the arena of public affairs. The plain, direct, disinterested language of reason, which allows us to know things as they are, will inevitably have a unifying effect, because truth is unitary and universal. Truly reasonable men will ultimately agree. Moreover, the language of this rational public discourse must be a purified, standardized, plain variety of the national language – for public affairs in England, English. Thus, in Locke's language ideology, the ideal metadiscursive order of the public sphere rests on a public discourse of one voice in one language. Locke is no proponent of vernacularization, however. The translinguistic semiotics at which he arrives, ultimately, is, if anything, hypercosmopolitan, beyond any natural language.

Herder, as we have established, advocates a very different metadiscursive order from that of Locke, placing highest value on the inherent poetic quality of language and on poetic expression grounded in *Besonnenheit*, the unitary reflexive capacity that comprehends feeling, reason, will, all the human faculties. Again, all people are endowed with *Besonnenheit* – it is the quality above all others that makes us human. The means and forms of expression, however – be they languages, genres, formal structures – are all variably shaped by differential experience, history, environmental factors, or cultural inheritance among the world's peoples. The most salient linguistic contrasts, in Herder's view, are those that differentiate national languages, which are at the same time the reservoirs and the means of giving expression to the distinctive spirit of a people, its *Volksgeist*. The process is one of mutual reinforcement: the highest and most potent expression gives voice to the *Volksgeist*, and in so doing contributes as well to its progressive cultivation.

The chief means of this cultural realization are the poetic traditions which encode, preserve, and transmit the most powerful and distinctive meanings and values of a people. Thus, the best speakers are poets, but all can participate in the cultivation of the folk spirit by learning and passing on the poetic traditions the poets have created and made memorable, affecting, and persuasive by giving them form. In the course of history, however, language and modes of expression are susceptible to potentially damaging influences – abstract and dispassionate philosophizing, artifice, the mediation of writing and print which distance people from the sensuous experience of affecting performance, cosmopolitanism – which rob the nation of its vitality. In Herder's own day, he felt, the vital traditions of the German people were fragmenting, sustained only in distressed remnants by the peasants, artisans, market traders – *das Volk der Bürger* – who still sang the songs and told the tales that had been abandoned by the cosmopolitan nobility, the over-refined philosophers, and the rabble. Significantly, however, the very reflexive capacities of *Besonnenheit* that are so essential to human existence appear no longer to operate in this context as Herder depicts it: those among whom the folk traditions are still to be found are nevertheless unable to treat their own means of expression analytically, to reflect upon their language and poetry, or to stem their decline. The capacity for linguistic reflexivity is reserved to the intellectuals of *das Volk der Gelehrsamkeit*, who must intervene in the process if folk culture is to be revitalized. The male intellectuals, we might add, for women, too, are unsuited for the intellectual task. It is these intellectual mediators, then, who are charged with metadiscursive responsibility for the purity and cultivation of the nation's poetic legacy. Poised between the natural folk and the over-refined intellectuals, those intellectuals who are attuned to the folk spirit are best equipped to manage the recontextualization of folk poetry from the singing of its naive traditional custodians and to recast it as the consciously cultivated vernacular touchstone of national culture.

As with Locke, Herder's language ideology also involved the extension of the metadiscursive practices he valued most highly into the public arena. The poetic traditions and their constituent expressive forms that give voice to the national spirit represent the authoritative basis for the cultural cohesion necessary to the establishment and maintenance of a viable polity. The desired goal of unification rests upon discursive unity, provided by the authority of tradition and a unified adherence to the national spirit. And here too, linguistic homogeneity is a necessary condition: "One people, one fatherland, one language" (SW 18: 347). In Herder's vision, a viable polity can only be founded on a national language resistant to the penetration of foreign tongues. Once again, a sphere of public discourse characterized by one voice in one language. For Locke, reaching this condition involves a rupture, the fundamental rupture of modernity itself, defined by a rejection of traditional transmission, while for Herder, the process is continuous, a developmental realization of the nature of language and tradition. The point we would emphasize, how-ever, is that whether we follow the path of Locke or of Herder, we arrive at convergent positions. We conclude, then, with two sets of implications to be drawn from these convergences, one scholarly, one more broadly political.

Beyond the metadiscursive regimentation of linguistic and folkloris-tic scholarship, we want also to adduce a further political implication of Locke's and Herder's language ideologies, having to to with the nature and discursive organization of the public sphere. Locke has an established place in the Habermasian conception of the rational public sphere that has oriented much recent discussion (Habermas 1989), as in the broader historiography of modern democracy as a political ideology. As a number of critics have observed, the image of open participation in a public dis-course that spans society has always coexisted with, if not facilitated, the exclusion of particular groups, issues, and forms of discourse (Calhoun 1992; Hansen 1993; Landes 1988; Negt and Kluge 1993). We believe that our discussion of Locke suggests that tension between an ideally open public sphere and practices of exclusion and marginalization did not simply arise from some sort of gap between "theory" and "practice" or "ideology" and "action." By way of providing a theoretical basis for assertions of the social and political necessity of rational, disinterested, and dispassionate discourse, Locke theorized the exclusion of most of the population from this discursive realm and urged the institutionalization of metadiscursive practices that would naturalize and sustain the use of public discourse in preserving social inequality.

By contrast with Locke, Herder does not figure in scholarly consider-ations of the public sphere within the Habermasian frame of reference, notwithstanding his lifelong interest in the political public.[6] Certainly, the conformation of the public sphere that Herder offers us is very dif-ferent from that of Locke; it is a public sphere of poetic performance in which the *vox populi* gives voice to the authoritative traditions in which political community is grounded and political values are proclaimed. It does not offer a charter so much for the political ideology of modern state democracy as for cultural nationalism in which language and folklore are

---

[6] The political public is the subject of one of Herder's earliest published works. "Do we still have the Public and the Fatherland of yore?" first published in 1765 (SW 1: 13–28/ Herder 1992: 53–64), as well as of the essay (SW 24: 271–72) published posthumously in 1803.

key symbols of cultural identity and persistence. Indeed, this romantic nationalism is taken as Herder's chief contribution to modern political ideology. But while Herder is justifiably celebrated as the populist champion of the common people, the *Volk* that he championed was a construct that excluded some social sectors (the rabble, for instance, or women). Moreover, we have suggested that this populism is tempered by a politics of culture that demands intervention from above in the metadiscursive management of the public sphere. The structure of inequality that is masked in most historical appreciations of Herder, as in articulations of romantic nationalist ideologies influenced by his own, is readily apparent in one of the last of his writings, published posthumously in 1803: " 'Vox populi, vox dei' it once was said; and although this praise must not be extended beyond the limits of what the folk can articulate, it does at least point out that in those things that concern the folk their sense of truth demands respect" (SW 24: 271–72). The limits of what the folk can articulate establish the interventionist baseline in the arena of public affairs for those players who are not so limited.

In addition to legitimating structures of inequality in the public sphere, the language ideologies of Locke and Herder converge in denying the legitimacy of multiple voices and multiple languages in public discourse. Their respective visions of political community and national interest have in common a principled insistence on linguistic and discursive standardization and regimes of purification: social and political cohesion demand one language, one metadiscursive order, one voice. This ideology of a monoglot and monologic standard has provided a charter not only for homogenizing national policies of language standardization and the regulation of public discourse, but for theoretical frameworks that normalize and often essentialize one society–one culture–one language conceptions of the relationships among language, culture, and society.

It is not our purpose here to offer an exposé of Locke's and Herder's ideological feet of clay, any more than it is to worship at them. Our goal, rather, is to increase our reflexive understanding of the historical foundations of modern ideologies of language and their role in the construction of modernity more generally. Locke and Herder ultimately point towards two very different modernities, produced by two very different ideologies of language. Locke's Enlightenment vision involves a decisive break with the past and a rigorous process of purification, of stripping language of its connections to both nature and society and rooting out all dimensions of tradition and traditional transmission. At the same time Locke renders language and knowledge maximally cosmopolitan by assimilating them to a translinguistic semiotics that is above all natural languages, vernacular or cosmopolitan. Herder's vision, by contrast, makes language modern by revitalizing its connection with the past and its vernacular attunement to the collective spirit, condemning a rationally founded purification and cosmopolitanism as the touchstones of a sterile modernity that impoverishes human existence. Herder champions instead a hybrid modernity, one that is at the same time distanced from the past and continuous with it, dependent for its vitality on the mediating force of a vernacular textual tradition, albeit a tradition that has been masculinized, bourgeoisified, and otherwise transformed by the intervention of intellectuals. Both visions, however, lend themselves equally well to the construction of social inequality by positing differences in the distribution and value of modes of consciousness and reflexivity and regulating access to the public sphere and other institutional arenas on the basis of the resultant discursive capacities. The languages, discursive forms, and practices of Others continue to play a significant role in this gate-keeping process down to the present day.

Beginning shortly after the turn of the nineteenth century, however, there were significant realignments of the contrastive visions we have traced from Locke to Herder. The burgeoning of nationalist movements and nation-state formation, the explosive expansion of agrarian and industrial capitalism in apparent fulfillment of eighteenth-century ideologies of progress, and the concurrent shifts in the tenor of imperially driven colonialism jointly stimulated the extensive empirical documentation and study of the discourse of Others as a means of calibrating the relationship of past to present to future. The recording, inscription, and publication of the textual corpora yielded by this effort compelled attention to metadiscursive problems of a new order. As scholars turned their attention more directly to problems of text-making and presentation, they became increasingly aware of the dialogic tensions attendant upon the juxtaposition of old forms of discourse, manifested in oral texts framed as "traditional" and literary, and the emergent discursive regimens of the intellectual disciplines, conceived as modern and scholarly – often as scientific – with which they felt a need to align themselves. The contrast between the language ideologies and visions of modernity we have identified with Locke and Herder, then, were played out in this arena. In the following chapters, we trace the further inflections of these contrastive visions in the text-making practices of scholars widely acknowledged as founders of a range of adjacent disciplines that center on the discourse of Others, principally folklore and cultural anthropology.

6 Scientizing textual production in the service of the nation: the Brothers Grimm and Germanic philology

Herder shook the linguistic foundations of the modernist project laid out by Locke. Herder sought to undermine the purifying practices that Locke had used to construct language as an autonomous domain, to sever its links to society and tradition. For Herder, not only was language intrinsically social, but linguistic differences and commonalities provided the prime means of defining families, communities, regions, and nations. While a purified language formed, for Locke, an obligatory passage point along the road to modernity, Herder saw modernity as a threat to language, potentially depriving it of social, political, and affective force. While Locke saw tradition, which he deemed to be extraneous to language, as a key source of social servitude, error, epistemological uncertainty, and, ultimately, conflict, Herder regarded it as the source of social order and political strength. At the same time that Locke's program for language was based on a universalistic rationality, Herder sought to reprovincialize language, asking it to give up cosmopolitan claims to universality, to transcend indexical claims to identities, communities, places, and times.

Even in the heyday of romantic nationalism, however, Locke's linguistic modernity did not simply go away. Herder thus presented modern subjects with something of a dilemma. As for Locke, language provided him with a key means of defining modernity. And language ideologies and practices played a crucial role in the very different modernity that Herder sought to construct, one that peopled territories with national citizens and the globe with nation-states, as Benedict Anderson (1991) suggests. So two divergent and influential models of language and modernity were available to writers and politicians in Europe. Both perspectives modeled social order and provided discursive blueprints for producing it.

The Brothers Grimm, Jacob (1785–1862) and Wilhelm (1786–1859), clearly stood on Herder's shoulders, embracing his nationalist project and advancing his lead in providing it with a linguistic and textual base. Their published collections, including the *Kinder- und Hausmärchen* (hereafter *KHM*) – perhaps the most famous "folk" texts of all time – extended

Herder's attempts to revitalize German literature by inserting *Volksdich-tung* collected from the marginal and disappearing *Volk* into its center. Nevertheless, their efforts to scientize and professionalize the study of language and literature evoked Locke's efforts to purify the relationship between language and society. By bringing these distinct ideologies of language and metadiscursive practices into a complex tension and fashioning texts as tools for creating powerful hybrids, they secured an influential place for the study of language and vernacular literature within schemes for imagining and naturalizing social inequality, both within and between "nations." Shortly after Kant proclaimed a rationalist and universalistic cosmopolitanism, the Grimms pioneered a cosmopolitan practice that assimilated provincialism and nationalism as its discursive foundation. Beyond the lasting influence of the particular hybridizing schemes that they championed, the Grimms' work provides a key site for seeing how contradictions between language ideologies and textual practices can help sustain new schemes for structuring time, space, and society. Their writings reveal with special clarity how Europeans could deprovincialize their own idealized self-representations, not by asserting their universality but by declaring their very provinciality.

Romanticism, scientism, and textual authority

Jacob Grimm announced this synthetic program in his *On the Origin of Language* (1984 [1851]), which was prompted by Friedrich Schelling's call to reopen the question addressed by Herder's own *Essay on the Origin of Language* (1966 [1787]). In opening his essay, Grimm immediately claims the mantle of science for the study of language, and he announces the centrality of purification to this effort. Commenting on the development of linguistic research in the eighty years since Herder's prize essay, Jacob asserts that "All language studies are nowadays more advantageously placed and equipped than at that time. Indeed they have grown, it can be said, only in our century to the status of a true science" (1984 [1851]: 1). The linguistic work of classical philology, according to Jacob, had labored in the service of grasping the spirit of enduring Greek and Latin literary "monuments" without direct attention to "the relationship of the languages to one another" or to "the inner fabric of language in itself," its "inner structure," or "historical changes" (1984 [1851]: 1). Jacob insists that in linguistics, as in the study of natural phenomena in general, the development of true science rests on a shift of concern from practical goals to unrestricted and disinterested investigation of phenomena in their own terms. This is what he saw as having taken place in the study of language in the first half of the nineteenth century. To be a scientist of language, a researcher must adopt a Lockean posture of disinterestedness. Jacob aligned the study of tradition with the *Naturwis-senschaften* in opposition to the *Geisteswissenschaften* (Sampson 1980: 17), thus distancing himself from Herder's more humanistic and philological conception. While the *Geisteswissenschaften* treated the interpretation of texts more as an end in itself, the approach championed by Jacob Grimm accorded texts the status of means towards broader analytic and histori- cal ends. The study of language must be purified of its relationship – and particularly its subordination – to other modes of inquiry and varieties of scholarly authority. The task of purification had thus taken on by the mid-nineteenth century the task of carving out of autonomous realms of specialized expertise.

Claiming a distinct form of scientific authority entailed constructing a distinct object of inquiry. If linguistics was to be parallel to natural sci- entific inquiry, then that object must be construed as natural, as existing apart from society. Following in Locke's footsteps, Grimm nonetheless changed the beat, constructing language as an architectonic, one that re- volves around phonological and grammatical as well as semantic content. Unlike Herder, for whom grammar was a later development on a lexical foundation, grammar became key – the "inner fabric" or "inner struc- ture" of language was the central object of study. In telling the origin story – that is, of scholarly perceptions of language as an autonomous sphere – Grimm points to the power of the quintessential Orientalist trope: "The perfection and powerful law of Sanskrit, although already opening a path to one of the oldest and richest poetries, really offered an invitation to become acquainted with it for its own sake" (1984 [1851]: 2). By characterizing the devotion to this "inner structure" as discovered, not invented, Grimm naturalizes the reimagination of language. But a thorny problem remained – how to sever language from society in Lockean fash- ion without losing its value for Herderian nationalist projects, to which the Grimms remained committed.

Rather than attempting to separate language from the social by fiat, Grimm links it initially to an evolutionist perspective on society. At the heart of Jacob's understanding of the origin of language is the key premise that language is first and foremost an instrument of thought and that thought is the essential faculty that makes us human. The origin and development of language, then, are centrally tied to the capacities of lan- guage as a vehicle of thought. "Man is not only called thus because he thinks, but is also man because he thinks, and he speaks because he thinks. This very close relationship between his ability to think and to speak, designates and guarantees to us the reason and origin of his language" (1984 [1851]: 12). Grimm's contemporary, Wilhelm von Humboldt (1988 [1836]) similarly stressed the language–speech–thought connec- tion. Based on this conception of the origin and function of language, then, Jacob sees the subsequent evolution of language as a process in which language and thought develop in tandem, with language change being shaped by the progressive development of logical and abstract thought – reason, in this sense.

Positing this equation did not lead, however, to a surrender of the autonomy of language or the authority of the linguist. Grimm takes up the task of reconstructing language by asking, rhetorically, "Do not the species of language resemble the species of the plants, of animals, indeed of men themselves in almost endless varieties of their changing form?" (1984 [1851]: 4). The nature of the inquiry is the same: "For that is just the true sign of science that it casts its net toward many-sided phenomena and snatches at, puts in place, and submits every perceptible property of things to the most tenacious test, no matter what finally comes of it" (1984 [1851]: 2). Autonomy is not surrendered to the natural sciences, however, as the "inner structure" of language is certainly different from the ordering principles that were being developed for plants and animals. Each language is isolated as a separate universe of inquiry, thereby constructing languages as bounded entities – surely an imagining of language that would be useful for emergent nationalist projects. Explaining the properties of each language became the essential scholarly task. Grimm construed explanation, developing his metaphysics of language, by asserting that "The peculiarity of every individual language is therefore dependent upon the place and time in which those using it are born and bred. Place and time are the cause of all alterations in human language" (1984 [1851]: 6). Scientizing language thus involves the development of temporalizing and spatializing practices specifically designed for charting linguistic difference based upon its relative distance from modern European languages. The prize competition provided Jacob Grimm, who played a much more important role than his brother in reshaping ideologies of language and practices of linguistic analysis, with the opportunity to present a global linguistic cartography.

Grimm's temporalizing schema was fundamentally modernist, involving discontinuities that defined bounded linguistic types. These breaks were defined vis-à-vis a Herderian dichotomy that pits the sensuous nature of language and its "form-perfection," "formational completeness" (1984 [1851]: 15) against the progressive development of logical and abstract thought – reason. These counter-tendencies constitute a continuum, with all known languages falling between the extremes:

Both directions are in no way sharply opposed to each other, and all languages are manifested in various similar, but unmatched steps. The form diminution had already begun even, e.g., in Gothic and in Latin. A preceding older and richer

form can be established for one language as well as for the other. . . . Expressed
generally and in other words a peak reached in formational completion of older
language can not at all be established historically. Just as little has the intellectual
refinement opposed to it even today reached a conclusion. It will not be such for
an incalculably long time yet. (1984 [1851]: 15)

Having delineated this developmental continuum, Grimm goes on to
characterize the state of language at three points: "the oldest language,"
"the middle language," and "the modern." As regards the oldest language, "Its appearance is simple, artless, full of life. . . . All words are
short, monosyllabic, almost all formed with short vowels and simple
consonants. . . . All concepts result from a sensory outlook" – echoes of
Herder again – "which itself was already a thought from which light
and new thoughts arise on all sides. . . ." Nevertheless, "Its thoughts have
nothing lasting, enduring. Therefore this earliest language founds yet no
monuments of the spirit" – no great literature – "and fades away like the
happy life of those oldest men without trace in history" (1984 [1851]: 20).
Here we have a second temporalizing principle, one that pertains to the
ability of a language to generate the types of linguistic forms that will enable it to achieve a larger space in the broader, evolutionary temporalizing
framework. The second principle neatly erases the violence of colonialism and imperialism – if languages and literatures disappear from history,
they have only themselves to blame. Genocide and the suppression of
languages and cultures would seem to have no role in shaping historical
trajectories.

In the middle language, "Instead of having dominating special concepts
along with the diminution of sensuous power of language and unbounded
series of words, beneficent aggregations and pauses result. These let the
essential stand out from the accidental, the predominating from the subordinate. The words have become longer and polysyllabic. . . . The whole
language is indeed still sensuously rich, but more powerful in thought. In
all that this entails, the flexibility of inflection assures a rapidly spread-
ing supply of animated and regulated expressions" (1984 [1851]: 21).
In characterizing the modern languages, Grimm resorts heavily to reification, attributing agency and will to language in the realization of its
developmental progress. "Now since, however, the whole nature of man
and consequently his language are indeed understood to be in eternal,
irresistible ascent," he writes:

the law of this second period of language development could not suffice for-
ever, but had to yield to the striving for still greater freedom of thought. Even
the grace and power of completed form seems to place limitations on this freedom. . . . The spirit of language strove to be released from the restraint of such
truly overpowering form. . . . One may regret that the purity of the whole sound

system was weakened, almost put out of joint. But none will fail to recognize that the intermediate tones arising have brought about unexpected new aids which could be made use of with the utmost freedom. A mass of roots are obscured by such sound changes. Henceforth, they are continually maintained no longer in their sensory primal meaning but only for abstract ideas. (1984 [1851]: 21)

Thus we move from a simple but formally perfect language, rooted in sensuous thought, to a language that is lexically, grammatically, and phonologically more complex, full of formal irregularities but far better adapted to abstract ideas. The earliest stage is hypothetical, but we can reconstruct what it must have been like by projecting backwards from the laws of change discoverable by examination of the later forms.

Much has been written of late regarding the centrality of cartography to colonialism, imperialism, and modernity.[1] Supposedly objective and universal criteria enabled European powers to project their own self-representations as measures that could compare all corners of the world in terms of the degree to which supposedly bounded and autonomous nations diverged from an elite European model. By constructing bounded and distinct languages, each of which possessed an "inner unity" that could be identified and compared only by a linguistic scientist, a new global cartography could be proposed. The position of each "nation" could be specified in terms of the qualities of abstraction and rationality possessed by its language, as measured independently of other social forms. This cartography was particularly useful to colonial projects, however, in that linguistic structures both presuppose and enable particular ways of thinking. While a scholar might praise the sensuous power and formal completeness of a language, doing so also provides a rationale for judging its people to be capable of abstract, rational thought – and thus, perhaps, self-government. Wilhelm von Humboldt placed this cartographic task at the center of his scholarly agenda, studying in detail every language for which he could obtain documentation. The resulting volumes used the notion that the "inner need of man" to create language constitutes "a thing lying in its own nature, indispensable for the development of his mental powers and the attainment of a world-view" (1988 [1836]: 27) as a point of departure for comparing languages and nations. While von Humboldt cloaked these comparisons more in a rhetoric of aesthetic intuition (see Aarsleff 1988), the Grimms elevated them to the level of a distinct science. Here the Grimms built on the Herderian legacy, which already had deep roots in philological inquiry. Transforming Herder's organic logic into a formal method added scientific legitimacy and a guise of political detachment to the construction

---

[1] For a recent example, see Walter Mignolo (2000).

of bounded and discrete linguistic wholes that corresponded to distinct nations. The temporal logic that informed this organicism also invited scientific comparisons between the formal principles evident in different languages, thereby projecting these imagined linguistico-social communities onto a hierarchically organized global evolutionary scale whose axis ranged from sensuous formalism to abstract logic.

The thrust of the Grimms' repositioning of language involved a task of purification, of severing the language–society entanglements promulgated by Herder. The language–speech–thought connection simultaneously enabled Jacob to open the door to hybrid forms in which linguistic patterns could be linked to national cognitive predispositions and then placed in varying degrees of temporal and spatial remove. What paraded as a liberal celebration of the formal elegance of a literature and language could thus implicitly function as a rationale for the political subjugation of its producers and their descendants.

Textual mediations of science and society

Although Jacob's essay provides useful insights into his language ideology, quasi-philosophical reflections on the origin of language did not lie at the center of the Grimms' research agenda. In additional to historical and comparative studies, much of their time was devoted to the production of dictionaries and grammars in addition to the well-known collections of legends, epics, and tales. Ironically – although not surprisingly for readers of Latour (1993) – the texts that the Grimms used in purifying language and tradition as natural objects constituted crucial hybrid forms that established language–tradition–political connections, networks that still shape how national identities and forms of social inequality are constructed in "modern" nation-states.

The Grimms frequently use botanical analogies in constructing tradition as being akin to nature, as *Naturpoesie*: "For with legends [like trees] nature protects the organism with eternal, self-generating renewals. No single human hand is capable of feigning the fundament and workings of a [folk] poem. The individual who attempted to do so would be expending the same fruitless energy as if he were seeking to devise a new language" (1981 [1816]: 4). Since vernacular works are thus like organisms of a particular species, their evolution is shaped by properties of their own unique "inner unity," not broader natural or social factors. At the same time, however, *Naturpoesie* is rooted in social communities in particular ways, which Jacob spells out in an early letter to Achim von Arnim, written in 1811 and employing Herder's distinction between *Naturpoesie* and *Kunstpoesie*:

folk poesy stems from the soul of the entire community (*das Ganze*). What I call art poesy (*Kunstpoesie*) stems from the individual. That is why the new poetry names its poets; the old knows none to name. It was not made by one or two or three, but it is the sum of the entire community. . . . The old poesy is completely like the old language, simple and only rich in itself. . . . The new language has lost innocence and has become richer outwardly, but . . . it sometimes needs greater preparation in order to express a simple sentence. . . . Therefore, I see in art poesy or whatever you want to call it what I designate as preparation. . . . In the nature poesy there is something that emanates from itself. (quoted in Zipes 1988b: 210)

Here the work of purification and hybridization or mediation work hand in hand. *Naturpoesie* is not shaped by social forces, it "emanates from itself," but, unlike *Kunstpoesie*, it is directly tied to communities – traditional ones, that is.

Like Herder, the Grimms placed this poetic emanation in spatial and temporal terms. In Jacob's developmental schema, it is the middle phase that lends itself best to poetic expression. At this stage, "we see language most highly suited to meter and poetry. For these beauty, harmony, and exchange of form are essential, indispensable. The Indian and Greek poetry designate for us a peak reached at the right moment in immortal works later unattainable" (1984 [1851]: 21). *Naturpoesie* is thus placed at substantial spatial and temporal distance from contemporary Europe. For Herder, poetry was intrinsic to language from its moment of origin, even though languages at certain stages of development may be more or less well suited to the purpose. Language, for Grimm, "Arising immediately from human thinking, conforming to and keeping pace with it . . . has become the common property and heritage of all men. . . . Poetry, music and other arts are the property of favored people only. Language belongs to all of us" (1984 [1851]: 23). Recall that Locke's expulsion of poetics from the universal core of language provided him with a rationale declaring its marginality to inquiry and social life – and even calling for its suppression. This denial of universal status did not lead Grimm, however, to relegate poetics to a more peripheral position. Poetics was rather part of language and thus a natural artifact that could be subjected to scientific investigation and claimed as an object of expert authority. Because texts possessed this sort of specificity, they could represent particular social classes, nations, and historical periods. By coming to represent the nation in a community of nations, vernacular texts could become central tools for both nationalist and cosmopolitan projects.

A key step in repositioning poetics *vis-à-vis* science, society, and modernity involved privileging certain genres and metadiscursive practices. In linking poetry with language in its middle stage, Jacob is speaking of poetry in a marked sense, as verse. In other contexts, the Grimms use the term *Poesie* to comprehend verbal art forms more generally. But the Grimms were little interested in *Poesie* in general or verse in particular; by codifying more subtle distinctions between genres, the Grimms singled out dimensions of traditional genres – *Naturpoesie*, as research foci for a nationalist poetics – epic and other narrative forms represented the collective expression of the nation, while lyric poetry, private and personal, was peripheral to their concerns (Peppard 1971: 99). Epic was of special interest because, as stated by Jacob, "Of all types of poetry according to their natural tendency and development the epic is closest in time and importance to the origin of language" (1984 [1851]: 24; cf. Zipes 1988b: 211). Epics, along with the *Märchen* and legends that absorbed so much of the brothers' joint efforts, were privileged scientific objects, providing more transparent windows on linguistic patterns at the same time that they were the quintessential hybrids – textual forms that embodied the nation. Constructing this notion of origins and attaching it to particular forms provided key means of purifying tradition; although traditions might get corrupted – this is, mixed up with modern forms – at some later point, their "origins" were pure and autonomous.

Central to the Grimms' purifying practices was the time-worn construction of tradition as vanishing, as unable to sustain the onslaught of modernity. Any contemporary embodiment of vernacular poetics was thus corrupt and fragmentary, a product of its distance from the middle period of efflorescence and the victim of the destructive onslaught of modernity. In the preface to volume I of the first edition of the *KHM* (1987 [1812]), the Grimms suggest that "when we review the riches of German poetry from olden times and discover that nothing of it has been kept alive, even the memory of it is lost – folk songs and these innocent household tales are all that remain" (1987 [1812]: 204). Just as the work of collection defines the border between modernity and tradition, it is rendered precarious by the tremendous inequality evident in this violent encounter. The Grimms remark frequently and romantically about the effects of the violence of modernity: "Ever on the watch for everything that is really still *left* of this poetry" (1987 [1812]: 204, emphasis in the original), they feel an obligation to record all that they can find of tales that are descended from the earlier forms (1987 [1812]: 204). The *German Legends* (1981 [1816–18]) was motivated similarly: "That which our collection is still able to include proclaims clearly as merely emaciated and fragmentary remnants of what was once the mighty treasure hoard of German folk poetry" (1981 [1816]: 2). In terms of their imagined cartography, the Grimms move from the center of modernity, a scientific, elite, and urban space, in order to cross the boundary into what had been an autonomous, pre-existing traditional world. This emerging map also spatializes a German nation in terms of a metaphysics of traditional presence; such areas as Hesse were deemed to remain closer to their traditional roots. The Grimms' nostalgic rhetoric suggests that they could cross the epistemological and social gap in order to stand in solidarity alongside the folk, lamenting the cruel way the latter have been treated by modernity – without, needless to say, losing their status as modern subjects. If members of *das Volk* cross the line, however, there is no going back – they lose their legitimate place in tradition. The Grimms thus become complex subjects, capable of assimilating multiple viewpoints and occupying various points in the spatio-temporal or chronotopic cartography (see Bakhtin 1981). Members of *das Volk*, on the other, can inhabit only one spatio-temporal location; the Grimms construct them as single-dimension subjects.

Now it might stand to reason, as it were, that depicting traditional texts as fragmentary and evanescent would undermine the scholarly position of their advocates and decrease the value of these cultural artifacts for modern, nationalist projects. We believe, however, that this nostalgic rhetoric rather greatly *augmented* their value in textual markets. The Grimms preserved Herder's reversal of the moral valence of the tradition/modernity dichotomy. Since tradition embodied a masculine national virility that rendered a people creative, powerful, and cohesive at the same time that modernity undermined these qualities, the demise of tradition was not only lamentable but threatened the future of modern nations and projects of state-building. If a cultural formation that had been largely lost to society was only preserved in memory, those individuals who specialized in locating these representations, rendering them into writing texts, and providing road maps as to how they should be reinserted into modern social sectors had a vital role to play in restoring the health of the nation. The Grimms thus elevated themselves to expert status and constructed their mode of knowledge production as of key political and social and well as scientific importance by claiming authority over the conversion of memory into texts.

Textual ideologies and metadiscursive practices

But if, one might say, the German people constituted a textual nation, how could texts become a scarce resource and the object of individual claims to authority? Here the Grimms departed from the model that Herder set forth in the *Volkslieder* by locating collection and editing skills as a scientific specialty. A good example of their response to collecting efforts that they deemed to be more motivated by literary and aesthetic impulses than scientific ones is evident in differences with their friends

Clemens Brentano and Achim von Arnim (1805), with whom they collaborated in their first efforts at collecting folktales. Brentano in particular would take only hasty notes on the narratives he heard, and he was less than meticulous in later recording the details. The Grimms believed that published versions should be as complete as possible, that no material should be added, and that less aesthetically pleasing variants should not be eliminated.[2]

In motivating their own practice, the Grimms created a model of textual stability and fidelity, sometimes expressed as *Echtheit* or authenticity, in vernacular transmission. Jacob commented: "if these numerous written memorials have only left us sundry bones and joints, as it were, of our old mythology, its living breath still falls upon us from a vast number of Stories and Customs, handed down through lengthened periods from father to son. With what fidelity they propagate themselves, how exactly they seize and transmit to posterity the essential features of the fable" (1883 [1844]: xiii). Note the patriarchal engendering of tradition on a Herderian model, as contrasted with John Aubrey's feminization of it. Claiming *Naturpoesie* for modernity involves reproducing this textual mimesis in both collecting and editing. He continues: "But the folk-tale wants to be gleaned or plucked with a delicate hand. Grasp it rudely, it will curl up its leaves, and deny its dearest fragrance. There lies in it such a store of rich development and blossom, that, even when presented incomplete, it contents us in its native adornment, and would be deranged and damaged by any foreign addition" (1883 [1844]: xiii). It is, he argues, tradition itself that resists alteration: "Every nation seems instigated by nature to isolate itself, to keep itself untouched by foreign ingredients" (1883 [1844]: xxiv). The scientific practice thus mirrors the character of its natural object.

The Grimms claimed to have been guided by this ideology in compiling the *KHM*. The following statement appears in the preface to the first volume of the first edition: "We have tried to collect these tales in as pure a form as possible.... No details have been added or embellished or changed, for we would have been reluctant to expand stories already so rich by adding analogies and allusions; they cannot be invented" (1987 [1812]: 210). The brothers characterized their metadiscursive practices in somewhat different terms in the preface to the second edition, which appeared in 1819: "So far as the manner in which we collected is concerned, accuracy and truth were what counted for us above all. We did not add anything from our own resources, nor did we embellish any events and features of the story itself. Instead we tried to relate the content just as we had heard it; we hardly need emphasize that the phrasing and filling

---

[2] The history of this collaboration is discussed by such authors as Kamenetsky (1992: 39–41) and Michaelis-Jena (1970: 47–54).

in of details were mainly our work, but we did try to preserve every particularity that we noticed so that in this respect the collection would reflect the diversity of nature" (1987 [1819]: 220). Here "content" and "phrasing" are clearly distinguished and hierarchicalized, such that it becomes permissible to change the latter but not the former. The Grimms draw on evaluative and often quasi-moral terms to characterize the desired relationship between printed texts and sources – "accuracy," "truth," "embellish," and "preserve." Elsewhere in their writings the Grimms use expressions such as "purity," "fidelity," and "retention" in describing the way that written texts should relate to their purported oral sources, and disapprove of texts that are described as having been "embellished," "changed," "augmented," or "added."

Nevertheless, this textual ideology went hand-in-hand with metadiscursive practices that transformed the tales in a host of ways. The substantial literature on textual and stylistic dimensions of the *KHM* provides a useful basis from which to consider their metadiscursive practices.[3] The availability of an 1810 manuscript containing a number of texts (Rölleke 1975)[4] and the seven full editions of the *KHM* enable us to gain insight into the stylistic transformations that lie at the heart of the Grimms' metadiscursive practices.

One of the most important changes resulted in the addition of direct discourse (quoted speech). Take the passage from "Thumbling's Travels" in which the Thumbling meets the robbers in the woods.[5] The manuscript simply notes:

---

[3] In addition to the above cited works by Rölleke, see Berendsohn (1968), Hamann (1970), Schmidt (1973), and Schoof (1959).

[4] As Kamenetsky (1992: 41) notes, it would involve a leap of textual naiveté to assume that the 1810 manuscripts are direct transcriptions of orally collected tales. The Grimms initially collected *Märchen* as part of a joint publishing venture with Clemens Brentano, and the "Oelenberg Manuscript" contained tales sent to Brentano. Kamenetsky suggests that the manuscript versions were more "sketches" than fully detailed versions of the stories. Ward (personal communication 1993) notes that the Grimms' distaste for the poetic elaboration undertaken by Brentano and Achim von Arnim in *Des Knaben Wunderhorn* might have prompted them to worry that more exacting texts would only become fodder for similar literary elaboration. Nevertheless, Kamenetsky's claim that the 1810 manuscripts should not be used in textual studies seems unfounded. While the manuscripts should not be taken as *Ur*-texts that provided a basis for subsequent editions, they clearly represent one stage in a process of textual transformation that continued through the various editions. (The seventh and final edition of the complete collection provides a partial exception in this regard in that few changes were made from the texts published in the sixth.)

[5] The translations are provided by Ellis (1983: 87–88). We draw on Ellis in this regard in view of the fact that he presents translations of several tales as taken from successive editions. The textual analysis presented here is our own. For careful textual analysis of the *KHM*, such writers as Bottigheimer (1987) and Rölleke (1975, 1985a, 1985b, 1986a, 1988a) and the works cited in note 3 should also be consulted.

They give him the task of slipping into the treasury and throwing the money out of the window to them.

The same passage is framed in the first edition as inner speech:

And when they see the little tailor, they think, he can be very useful to us, talk to him, tell him he is a good fellow.

As is often the case, direct discourse (fully fledged quotation) emerges in the second edition:

When they saw the little tailor, they thought, a fool like that can be very useful to us. "Ho there, cried one, you tough fellow, do you want to go to the treasury with us?"

The process entails not only the addition of direct discourse but framing passages that are grammatically marked as direct discourse with quotation marks. The sense of verisimilitude is also enhanced by quoting a particular mode of address: "you tough fellow." The seventh and last edition encloses the inner speech with quotation marks and clearly distinguishes the second quotation from its quotative frame:

When they saw the little tailor, they thought, "a little fellow like that can crawl through the key-hole and serve as a picklock for us." "Ho there," cried one, "you giant Goliath, do you want to go with us to the treasury?"

The last example illustrates the use of direct discourse in building characters that represented familiar social types and served as carriers for moral interpretations. The quotations used spatializing and temporalizing practices in placing the realm of *das Volk* at greater distance from the middle-class, urban, modern milieu of the Grimms and their readers.

Second, the Grimms sometimes identified characters with personal names, even when these were absent from the 1810 manuscript. In some cases these personal names were not only inserted into the text but became the title by which a particular tale became known. Johannes-Waterspring and Casper-Waterspring, for example, are not named in the 1810 manuscript. Strikingly, the names "Hansel" and "Gretel" do not appear in the manuscript, where the narrative was titled "The Little Brother and the Little Sister." The names then appear in the opening sentence which sets the scene for the tale in the first edition.[6]

---

[6] In her attempt to defend the Grimms against their critics, Kamenetsky (1992) argues that changes introduced in subsequent editions involved a principled process of drawing on other variants. Such reasoning could be used in attempting to explain the introduction of names and other elements. In the note on this tale, however, the Grimms (1884: 356) state that "Hansel" is the name of a Thumbling in other tales. No mention of Gretel is made in the note. Thus, while "Hansel" is taken from a clearly distinct tale, no motivation is given for the introduction of "Gretel."

Third, Mieder (1986a, 1986b, 1988) and Rölleke (1988b) have detailed the way that the Grimms drew on their interest in and knowledge of proverbs in editing the tales. Wilhelm Grimm stated in the preface to the sixth edition, "I have constantly taken pains to introduce folk sayings and curious figures of speech, to which I am always listening attentively" (translated by Rölleke 1988a: 109). Interestingly, his wife Dortchen, who served as the source of a number of the tales, was also quite interested in proverbs. Not only did she use them in her speech, but she contributed to Karl Shimrock's proverb collection, *Die deutschen Sprichwörten* (1988 [1846]; see Kamenetsky 1992; Mieder 1986a: 122–24). Like quoted speech, proverbs also helped motivate characters and actions. A strange circularity is evident in the Grimms' use of proverbs in editing the *KHM*. On the one hand, they sometimes relied on proverbial expressions and sayings in determining whether particular narratives were "genuine" (Kamenetsky 1992: 164). On the other hand, the Grimms added proverbs to texts in order to increase their aura of traditionality and authenticity. The Grimms moved the *Märchen* in the direction of a "mixed" or "blended" genre (cf. Bakhtin 1986 [1979]) through the addition of proverbs.

Fourth, as the Grimms themselves acknowledge, many of the tales were constructed from fragments or from several shorter narratives: "Various stories that complemented each other and that could be conjoined without the need to delete conflicting passages have been published as a single story" (1987 [18919]: 220).[7] Once carefully synthesized into a single narrative, the complex intertextual relations between the various component were obscured.[8]

A fifth type of stylistic transformation involves the enhancement of what linguists refer to as cohesion, links between discrete parts of an utterance or text (see Halliday and Hasan 1976). Ellis (1983: 59–61) draws attention to the Grimms' addition of elements that provide explicit motives for actions. Such elements also embed theories of action and a sense of a premodern *Weltanschauung* into the narratives. Another effect of these changes is to weave elements of the story together more tightly, particularly when the relationship between successive episodes is unclear in previous renditions. Another change involves the creation of symmetrical repetitions of actions and episodes. Successive events that are described

---

[7] It is interesting to note that the Grimms asserted in the Preface to their collection of German legends that "joining several short ones together" would be inappropriate in that "all the tailoring and coloring" would be lost (1981 [1816]: 6).

[8] It should be borne in mind, however, that some of these relationships are indicated in the third volume of the *KHM*, which contains notes on the tales compiled by Wilhelm Grimm. It has been repeated in Rölleke's (1980) edition of the *KHM*. (See also Bolte and Polivka 1963.)

in contrastive ways in the 1810 manuscript and/or in early editions are rendered cohesive through the use of parallelism. The narrative cohesion of the tales was similarly greatly enhanced by the development of what has been called the linear quality of the tales. Actions which occur *tout de suite* in earlier versions were later broken up into component phases, particularly as multiples of three, and each element came to point teleologically to what is to occur next. Clearly, parallelism and repetition are common narrative devices, and it would be ludicrous to suggest that the Grimms invented them. What is significant is the way the Grimms used them in lengthening the texts and giving them the highly conventional, formulaic structure for which they are famous.

An interesting example of this sort of parallelistic elaboration is evident in the description of the sleep state of the castle in Sleeping Beauty. The 1810 manuscript simply describes the beginning of the one-hundred-year period in the following terms (the translations are taken from Ellis 1983: 146): "Because in the moment the king and his court had returned, everything in the castle began to sleep, even the flies on the walls." No description is provided in the passage in which the prince searches for Sleeping Beauty. The awakening scene is also succinct: "Everything awoke from its sleep." In the sixth edition, however, the initial sleep scene is described as follows:

And this sleep spread over the whole castle: the king and queen, who had just come home and had entered the hall, began to fall asleep, and the whole court with them. Then the horses in the stable slept, the dogs in the courtyard, the doves on the roof, the flies on the wall, even the fire which was flaming on the hearth became still and fell asleep, and the roast meat stopped sizzling, and the cook, who wanted to pull the hair of the cook's boy, because he had neglected to do something, let go of him and slept. And the wind died down, and in the trees in front of the castle not a small leaf moved any more. (1983: 152)

The spectacle that awaits the prince as he enters the castle closely echoes the preceding description, with the exception of some reversal in the order.

In the castle yard he saw the horses and dappled hunting dogs lying asleep, on the roof the doves sat and had their heads tucked under their wings. And as he entered the house, the flies slept on the wall, the cook in the kitchen held his hand as if he meant to grab the boy, and the maid sat in front of the black hen that was to be plucked. Then he went on, and saw in the hall the whole court lying asleep, and up by the throne lay the king and queen. (1983: 153)

Finally, the awakening scene replays the description a third time. Here the order is exactly the same as in the initial sleep scene, except that the maid's plucking of the hen is not mentioned in the initial scene:

The king awoke and the queen, and the whole court, and they looked at one another astonished. And the horses in the courtyard stood up and shook themselves: the hunting dogs jumped and wagged their tails: the doves on the roof took their head from under their wings, looked around and flew off into the fields: the flies on the walls crept forward: the fire in the kitchen rose up, flamed, and cooked the meat: the roast meat began to sizzle again: and the cook boxed the boy's ear so that he cried out: and the maid finished plucking the hen. (1983: 153)

This example suggests that the addition of these sorts of parallelism and enhancements of cohesion are not limited to the transition from the 1810 manuscript to the first edition; although some of the parallelistic development in this example is evident in the first edition, changes appear in the second through sixth editions.

These textual transformations have proved to be controversial. Like Linda Dégh (1979, 1988) and Christa Kamenetsky (1992), Donald Ward defends the Grimms. He notes that "whereas other writers of this era freely adapted folk materials and used them as vehicles for their own individual poetic genius, the Grimms remained absolutely true to the style and ethos of the tales, if not always true to the exact words" (1981: 369). Joseph Campbell similarly asserts that earlier collectors "felt free to manipulate folk materials" and anthologists "arranged, restored and tempered," while the Grimms "let the speech of the people break directly into print" (1944: 834–35). Alan Dundes (1985), on the other hand, characterizes the Grimms' metadiscursive practices as the fabrication of "fakelore." The rhetoric employed by that arch opponent of the Grimms, John M. Ellis (1983), is particularly instructive. Here the quasi-moral lexicon that is often used by the Grimms and their defenders is turned to the task of accusing the Grimms of "deliberate deception" as they "concealed" names of sources (1983: 26), creating "an *enormous* discrepancy" between the 1810 manuscript and the first edition (1983: 38–39; emphasis in original). Ellis further declares that the Grimms do not deserve credit for "truth and authenticity" (40), and asserts that they were "both lazier and much less scientifically conscientious" in their collection practices than they led others to believe (27). As a result, the Grimms inflicted "damage" on the tales (62), and, because their practices lacked "fidelity" (85), they were guilty of "fraud and forgery" (103). Ellis concludes that "The Grimms appear to have been guilty of a pervasive habit of tinkering idly and uninhibitedly with the language of the texts" (85).

What is most interesting to us is that the Grimms' defenders and critics alike share a common set of assumptions regarding the nature of metadiscursive practices and how they should be assessed, which we will refer to as *the image of intertextual fidelity*. According to this image, texts created through transcription, translation, and editing should bear a direct and intrinsic connection to their sources, such that the former are extensions or synecdoches of the latter. "Truth," "authenticity," "fidelity," and the like are measured in two ways. First, the point of origin is ideally an oral rendition by a member of the "folk," preferably an illiterate peasant. How close the sources of the *KHM* lie with respect to this imagined ideal is also controversial. Textual scholarship has shown that the Grimms clearly did not traverse all of the regions of modern-day Germany, taking down *Märchen* verbatim from illiterate peasants and painstakingly preserving the words of the "folk."[9] In discussing their collection of legends, the Grimms themselves lamented that "many would have been better and more precisely recorded from the mouths of the folk" (1981 [1816]: 11). The brothers collected oral versions in a relatively small number of geographic areas and mainly from members of several middle-class families with whom they were acquainted. While the Grimms characterized the tales as authentic German "folk" culture and as sources for reconstructing a common Germanic heritage, some of their informants were French-speaking Huguenots. Not only were many informants literate, but a good number of the tales they told were taken from published collections. Once the narrative has been collected, each step of removal from the source purportedly diminishes the "authenticity," "purity," and "truth" of the text. Both champions and critics of the Grimms share the brothers' powerful modernist assumptions about texts, that is, that there is a natural and authentic mode of transmission associated with traditional knowledge, that printed collections can mirror this process in some fashion, and that the authenticity and legitimacy of published narratives can be assessed in this way. Textual ideologies and metadiscursive practices thereby reproduce imaginations of tradition, modernity, the border that separates them, and how people and cultural forms can (or cannot) cross it.

Second, the quality of collections is to be assessed in terms of the degree to which obvious gaps between the two sets of texts are rendered *invisible*. Note that even admissions that some rupture between the two moments are inevitable naturalize the notion that they are automatically and intrinsically linked and suggests that mimesis can, at least ideally, achieve complete fidelity. Natural and intrinsic intertextual links thus become the unmarked or baseline type of intertextual relations, while the revelation of a gap is highly marked. This rhetoric legitimates the notion that "folk" renditions are fully accessible to scholars and, at least ideally, fully reproducible in printed texts. It also provides a powerful means of according textual authority in the form of "authenticity" to the scholarly

---

[9] See especially Crane (1917, 1918) and Rölleke (1975, 1985a, 1985b, 1986b,1988a).

production and reception of texts – only a specialist would know how vernacular knowledge is transmitted and thus be able to judge whether or not a text had been reproduced in an authentic and legitimate fashion.

That textual reproduction produces both links and gaps, as embodied in features that draw attention to continuities and those that create awareness of their separation in social, textual, historical, and other means. The brilliance of the Grimms' combination of textual ideology and metadiscursive practices is that it is the very interventions into the narratives that help create the illusion of fidelity! Latour (1987) argues that by inserting columns, tables, graphs, and other illustrations into their texts, scientists "stack" them in such a way as to create the illusion that the natural phenomenon they are analyzing is actually inserted into the text. Reported speech, names, and proverbs seem to insert the voices of *das Volk* into the pages of the *KHM*, creating an illusion of intertextual fidelity. Standardizing plot sequences, augmenting parallelism, and, to be sure, adding what we now feel to be the mark of the genre – the framing devices "There was once..." and "They lived happily up to their end" – made the texts feel like authentic reproductions of authentic fairytales. And well they should – the texts reproduced the features of a relatively homogeneous genre that the Grimms had themselves created. These additions made texts into powerful devices for purifying relations between tradition and modernity, enabling audiences readily to distinguish *Naturpoesie* from *Kunstpoesie*. They also rendered them some of the most effective hybrids around. Tradition could be "gleaned or plucked with a delicate hand" and then made to yield "its dearest fragrance" in libraries and bourgeois homes, key loci of modernity, without "being deranged and damaged." Fragments of language produced by expert knowledge systems could stand in for premodern worlds and at the same time help restore political and cultural vitality to an excessively modernized nation – in the interest of creating a centralized, democratic state.

History, "inner unity," and the authority of scholarly metadiscursive practices

In seeking to discredit the Grimms, John Ellis makes much of the apparent discrepancy between the Grimms' claim in the preface to the first edition to have attempted "to write down these tales as purely as possible" and, in the preface to the second edition, their "uneasy, defensive statement" (Ellis 1983: 16), which we quoted above.[10] What Ellis fails to realize is that the second preface actually stakes a much *more* powerful claim

---

[10] The Grimms state in the preface to the second edition that while "content" of the tales remains intact, "we hardly need emphasize that the phrasing and filling in of details were mainly our work."

to textual authority than is entailed in the notion of a direct, one-to-one correspondence between published texts and sources. While Ellis stresses the passage in the preface to the second edition in which Wilhelm Grimm ranks content over expression, crucial clues emerge in sentences which precede and follow the assertion regarding "expression" and "content." The Grimms stress the goal of the process of collecting and retelling the *Märchen*: "It must be noted that first of all we were concerned with loyalty and truth." The way that they construct their own role as scholars later in the passage is telling: "Anyone who has undertaken a similar venture will understand that collecting this material is by no means a carefree and careless business. On the contrary, only with time does one acquire the kind of attentiveness and tact required to sort out what is pure, simple, and yet intact from what is inauthentic" (1987 [1819]: 220). Paying closer attention to these concepts of "purity," "simplicity," and the like can shed a great deal of light not only on the Grimms' metadiscursive practices and the scholarly authority that these techniques purportedly conferred on texts and their creators but on the ideological underpinnings of romantic nationalism itself.

The Grimms located the collection, editing, and analysis of *Märchen* and other forms in a larger historical and comparative enterprise. Poetic forms like the *Märchen* and legends, though variable in surface expression, had deep continuities with antecedent genres, establishing a conception of folk forms as continuous through time, traditional in that sense; "never fixed and always changing from one region to another, from one teller to another, they still preserve a stable core," a core that "must be very old" (1987 [1812]: 208). They could thus lead to the discovery of the vital principle that underlies a language, revealing the unified, permanent core that is obscured by the complex, mutable, and heterogeneous outer forms (see Amsterdamska 1987). Wherein lies the key to unlocking the historical value of language and text? Tales and other texts provided access to a deeper level of intertextuality; discovering their "inner unity" furthered the task of abstracting general underlying patterns and tracing their distribution in time and space. The ideal of fidelity in intertextual mimesis thus went beyond "the phrasing and filling in of details," which they could legitimately modify, to revolve around the content and "every particularity that we noticed," to quote again from the preface to the second edition (1987 [1819]: 220). Since language and poetry decay through time, the scholar must, as the Grimms (1981 [1816]: 9) argued with regard to their collection of legends, "deliver these legends from their new costumes and" return them to their naked truth and innocence.[11] Jacob

---

[11] This quote is taken from a discussion in the foreword to the collection in which the Grimms are commenting on their rationale for including Swiss legends published by Wyss, "who wove the narratives skillfully into longer poems" (1981 [1816]: 9).

Grimm provided a particularly striking analogy in a letter to Achim von Arnim. Having criticized von Arnim for modifying the texts in a collection of folksongs, the Grimms were criticized by von Arnim in turn for modifying the tales they published. Ward (1981: 369) characterizes their response as follows: "Jacob defended their method by saying that, in order to get to the yolk of an egg, you have to break the shell, but if you do it with care, the yolk will remain intact."

Thus, by establishing intertextual links between historical and contemporary texts and hierarchical relations between what were construed as different components of texts, the latter can be restored to their "simple," "pure," "integral," and "complete" form. Just as researchers are obliged to reject the "outer form" of a text in favor of their own analysis of its provenance and "inner unity," they are free to entextualize their analysis in the "outer form" of published versions. The brothers suggest that the "truth," "authenticity," and "fidelity" of a published text are not to be assessed simply in keeping with its intertextual relationship to the surface features of a source text(s) but by virtue of its ability to represent the scholar's analysis of underlying features and historical relationships. Since no text could be adequately edited or analyzed apart from this broader field, only researchers familiar with the full range of vernacular genres and lexical and grammatical forms in German and proto-German (if not Indo-European languages in general) were qualified to undertake this work. The Grimms' statement in the preface to the second edition of the *KHM* thus suggests that they were attempting to extend, not to attenuate, their claim to textual authority. Specialists become obligatory passage points between tradition and modernity, and the scientifically informed process of entextualization becomes the vehicle for effecting that passage.

Recall Jacob's reiteration of Herder's emphasis on the distinction between *Naturpoesie* and *Kunstpoesie*. Since only the former provided reflections of the genius of the people, the scholar's ability to distinguish them – which is still seen as a key prerogative and obligation of many folklorists – enables him or her alone to determine which texts provide insight into traditional society and constitute suitable vehicles for inserting tradition into modernity. Only scholars, who could compare the versions told by various narrators, could identify the fundamental characteristics of this collective knowledge and re-entextualize it properly on the printed page. If the value of individual texts could be obtained by reading individual texts and appreciating their surface features, then the specialist would enjoy the status of an obligatory mediator over the reinsertion of tradition into modernity only up to the point that the text was published. Since a broader practice of reading was needed, specialists could claim a monopoly over the entire process.

Creating texts and symbolic capital for nationalist and cosmopolitan projects

Pierre Bourdieu's (1991) notion of symbolic capital can help us assess the importance of the Grimms' project. To be sure, using this term presents us with the risks associated with adopting the economistic and capitalist lexicon from which he derives his labels for communicative processes. We adopt the term in this context not in the faith that capitalism provides an apt language for discussing discursive processes universally but specifically because one of the effects of the Grimms' work was to take symbolic forms that had been less fully integrated into a capitalist economy and insert them solidly into a capital-dominated textual market, infusing them with value along the way. In doing so, they helped to transform symbolic forms that had been, in their view, tied to particular places and social identities and transform them in such a way that they could circulate in a free textual market. Nevertheless, we can read this process as extracting knowledge from a cultural commons and converting it into symbolic capital that could be controlled by particular classes and commodities, published texts, that could be bought and sold in a capitalist market.

The first moment in this process was the work of purification that was vested in making traditional knowledge into a scientific object. Recall that vernacular texts possess, in the Grimms' view, a double relationship to society. On the one hand, they are elements of language, organisms that respond to their own laws and exist apart from society. Before communities become modernized, however, texts remain closely identified with social identities and relations. We might accordingly assume that some intellectual property rights would accrue to people who live in the places with which particular texts are associated, possess the social features of age, class, and gender that render them appropriate storytellers, and are recognized as performers of particular narratives or other forms. Although the Grimms suggest that traditional knowledge is often concentrated in a particular area, it simply represents a national resource that has been lost in other regions. Residents thus simply possess a piece of what rightfully belongs to the nation – or, to use a more appropriate image – have access to a cultural commons – but do not possess any special rights to it. Moreover, *das Volk* is by definition disappearing and losing contact with traditional knowledge; its members seemed to bequeath to the Grimms the symbolic capital that they could no longer retain, a gift that the brothers seem to earn through their fieldwork, scholarly work with texts, and their advocacy for *das Volk*.

The folk could not inscribe the texts themselves or shape how they would be reinserted into modernity, because "they are fortunately not consciously aware of their own quiet poetry" (1981 [1816]: 4).[12] Believing that the vitality of oral traditions lay in a time in which critical consciousness was absent, Jacob Grimm argued that these forms conveyed "eternal truths" by virtue of the "childlike innocence," "simplicity," and "naïveté" with which they were transmitted. While contemporary poets write consciously, at least in part, the creative process that gave rise to oral tradition was unconscious of itself (see Kamenetsky 1992: 63–66; Marschall 1991: 268). When folk narrators seem to be exercising a degree of control over their own performances, it turns out that they are only manifesting their subservience to tradition, as in the case of Frau Viehmann, the Grimms' ideal informant and the prototype for generations of such idealized folk sources. The Grimms observe, "how keen she is to narrate correctly; when she retells something, she never changes its substance and corrects an error as soon as she notices it, even it if means interrupting herself. Devotion to tradition is far stronger among people who always adhere to the same way of life than we (who tend to want change) can understand" (1987 [1814]: 212). The folk lack the conscious understanding of tradition that is afforded by historical and comparative knowledge. Specialists alone can reposition traditional knowledge within a modern national space. The Grimms would not, of course, have claimed that they (or other specialists) owned the texts. They rather gained the right to determine how they would be placed into a textual economy in which anyone could gain access to them – by purchasing a commodity, a book, that generated revenue for its publishers and editors. Anyone, that is, who could read and could either purchase copies of their book or consult them in what were still predominantly private libraries. In other words, access to this free market was hardly free or universal.

If folk texts were to become symbolic capital, there had to be a market for them. This is, of course, precisely where Herder intervened, suggesting that good Germans should be more interested in German works than foreign ones. The Romantic movement reshaped the textual economy, attempting to overcome a modernist aversion to what were characterized as premodern texts. In particular, the Grimms' celebration of *Naturpoesie* over *Kunstpoesie* challenged established hierarchies in the textual market. In a letter of 1812 to von Arnim about the *KHM* that they were about to publish, Jacob defended himself and his brother against the charge that they were overly zealous promoters of traditional texts: "If we overestimate their influence, let people reduce our statements by a little. Enough will remain to make up for the injustice that these tales have suffered by

[12] The unconscious relation of folk poets to their work is contrasted with the way "whereby the language will reveal the words to [the literate poet] half consciously and half unconsciously" (1981 [1816]: 4).

being overlooked for so long" (quoted in Michaelis-Jena 1970: 51). In arguing for their importance, Jacob noted that their value extended beyond scholarly research: "These tales deserve better attention than they have received so far, not only because of their poetry which is of a peculiar charm, and bestows on those who have heard the tales in childhood a precious lesson and a happy memory throughout life, but also because they belong to our national literature" (quoted in Michaelis-Jena 1970: 51). In 1856, Wilhelm celebrated the success of their efforts to transform textual hierarchies:

> how unique was our collection when it first appeared, and what a rich harvest has sprung up since! At that time people smiled indulgently when we asserted that thoughts and intuitions were preserved in these stories, the origin of which was to be sought for in the darkness of antiquity. Now this is hardly ever denied. Tales of this kind are looked for with full recognition of their scientific value, and with a dread of altering any part of their contents, whereas formerly they were only regarded as worthless amusements of fancy which might be manipulated at will. (quoted in Michaelis-Jena 1970: 177–78)

The *KHM* were blockbusters to rival Hollywood (except in absolute sales) in launching modest efforts that surprisingly dominate the market for years (here centuries). But the Grimms did not frame their efforts as a novel venture in print capitalism – they insisted that the comparative and historical study of language and tradition was a scientific practice in service to nationalist projects.

A key problem was that Romantic literati, such as the Grimms' collaborator Brentano, wanted to elevate *Naturpoesie* to the status of literature, not science. The Grimms' insistence on intertextual fidelity, the use of folk speech and rejection of literary embellishment, and the insertion of prefaces, introductions, critical notes, and appendixes marked their texts as scholarly and scientific, not popular works.[13] Ironically, it was the *KHM*, which were hardest to elevate in literary hierarchies, that met with the greatest marketing success. Like good marketers, the Grimms placed indications of the value of the texts on the surface of the products themselves through the sorts of transformations that we detailed for the *KHM* – the authenticity of a particular text was marked by folk speech and proverbs and its membership in a folk genre signaled by opening and closing formulae and plot sequences. As industrial capitalism transformed Europe, the Grimms produced a large number of unique items that all fit a standardized narrative model. Their status as

---

[13] With the exception, of course, of smaller collections of the *KHM* that they prepared for popular consumption. Indeed, the nature of the prose and the scholarly apparatus produced criticism from von Arnim, Brentano, and other literati (see Michaelis-Jena 1970: 53).

symbolic capital was enhanced by making them easier to reproduce. The Grimms reserved the right to assess value in this market – that is, the ability to separate authentic texts from false or modified ones, determine which modes of entextualization should be accorded the greatest value, and use specialized spatializing and temporalizing practices in assessing the place of each text and genre. By constructing specialists as uniquely qualified to produce texts and assess their value, the Grimms attempted to create a monopoly. Note the role of purification here. Only if tradition could be constructed as an autonomous domain could particular modes of hybridization – of crossing the modern/traditional boundary and bringing the spoils of the venture back to those who occupy the modern side – be imbued with scientific, political, and economic value.

Just as a process of scientizing tradition enabled the Grimms to link texts explicitly to the vanishing folk, it permitted them to create implicit links to another imagined community – a national one. By severing the indexical links that connected tradition to localities, texts could come to define a national space. Once discovery of the "inner unity" of texts had stripped away the effects of modernity and mediated regional differences, lo and behold – it was revealed that a shared national voice had been there all along. The German nation was thus not a political construct but a real entity with deep historical roots. Modernity had not invented nationalism, only discovered it and mapped its features. By mapping a range of genres, dialects, customs, rituals, and beliefs and demonstrating scientifically that they formed a unified, dynamic system, the Grimms could create the image of a German nation that is equally complex, unified, and organic – that is, living. If "no single human hand is capable of feigning the fundament and workings of a [folk] poem" (1982 [1816]: 4), then the nation – as it is defined through traditional texts – is intrinsically democratic. The nature of language and tradition thus seems to be the democratic nation-state model that the Grimms supported in their political statements and activities. Seemingly more accessible textual elements could synecdochally establish the reality and evoke the presence of more temporally distant elements. Consuming narratives that were still told in some areas could enable readers to sense the value of more ancient texts: "The true value of these tales must really be set quite high; they put our ancient heroic poetry in a new light that could not have been produced in any other way" (1987 [1814]: 212; cf. 1981 [1816]: 2). Similarly, the cultural monuments of Germanic mythology, which were being musically enshrined by Richard Wagner, could similarly augment the value of humble *Märchen* and legends.

Benedict Anderson (1991) argued that nationalism involves two crucial moves: creating a new idea and then reifying it, making it seem as if
people just naturally all derived their identities from allegiance to a nation. He also suggested that nationalism is quintessentially new, involving
a break with older orders and embracing a new technological and economic order, print capitalism. Hobsbawm and Ranger (1981) suggest,
however, that the trick is to make the new nation seem old and historically
continuous – creating a traditional ritual economy was a powerful means
of creating nations and national subjects. If mapping tradition played a
crucial role in creating and naturalizing the nation, then the Grimms and
other specialists on language and traditional texts had a crucial role to play
in making the project possible. Anderson himself argued that nationalism was predicated on a textual economy. But in focusing on newspapers
and novels, ways of consuming a modern history of the nation as it was
unfolding, he seems to have overlooked another key part of this print
capitalist economy – the market for traditional texts. As consuming these
texts became a sign of being a national subject, the hybridization process that linked natural organisms – words, grammatical forms, rituals,
and texts – with social units extended not only explicitly to *das Volk* but
implicitly to the bourgeoisie as well.

In suggesting that "the nation is always conceived as a deep, horizontal
comradeship," Anderson (1991: 7) reifies the extent to which the imagination of nations and the operation of nation-states served to exclude and
subordinate some bodies that were found within national borders. The
act of reading the daily newspaper, which he envisions as a key practice
for experiencing national subjecthood, often excluded or marginalized
women, children, the poor, and people who have enjoyed less access to
education. The comradeship associated with producing and consuming
folk texts was not horizontal either in Germany during the first half of the
nineteenth century. Consumption of the *KHM* in particular was geared
towards forms of gender and age inequality associated with the rise of
bourgeois families. Scholars have documented the way that the Grimms
selected texts and edited their content in order to render them appropriate reading material for the nurseries of the emerging bourgeoisie.[14] As
Wilhelm Grimm himself notes in the preface to the second edition, "We
have carefully eliminated every phrase that is not appropriate for children" (1987 [1819]: 217). Some of the Grimms' critics complained that
particular tales were not appropriate for juvenile audiences, and some
items, such as a story about children playing "butcher" in which one

----

[14] See Ruth Bottigheimer (1987), Maria Tatar (1987), and Jack Zipes (1979, 1983, 1988a).

child kills another, were deleted from later editions (Michaelis-Jena 1970: 171). One might add that the *KHM* played at least a small role in *shaping* a romantic image of the child as embodying the same sort of naiveté associated with both the past and contemporary peasants. Recall Jacob's remark that reading traditional texts "bestows on those who have heard the tales in childhood a precious lesson and a happy memory throughout life" (quoted in Michaelis-Jena 1970: 51). Traditional texts thus bear value for constructing the idealized affective parameters of a bourgeois childhood as well as imparting instructions on how to become a responsible national subject. Sexuality and the abuse and neglect of children were largely weeded out of the collection, while tales were selected and edited in keeping with the desire to create clear social types that exemplified moral conduct. The consumption of such texts became a part of the gendered practices involved in social reproduction and consumption on a bourgeois model.

Textual production and consumption were part of an ongoing process of reconfiguring class relations. Dictionaries and grammars that helped to define a national language helped to stratify society by providing standard forms and distributing differential access to and means of evaluating the place of individuals and communities in schemes of social inequality. Not only was the consumption of traditional texts mediated by access to print capitalism and education, but the texts distanced the bourgeoisie from premodern subjects by positing an epistemological gulf between them that could only be crossed by producing and consuming texts – not by challenging modernity or its structures of inequality. The folk were infantilized and deprived of historical agency at the same time that the bourgeoisie was provided a travel guide on how to penetrate their world: "One must quietly lift the leaves and carefully bend back the bough so as not to disturb the folk, if one wishes to steal a furtive glance into the strange yet modest world of nature, nestled into itself, and smelling of fallen leaves, meadow grass, and fresh-fallen rain" (1981 [1816]: 11). This nostalgic politics of sentiment and the idea that the bourgeoisie could contribute to the nationalist cause by preserving the words of a dying folk depoliticized the effects of industrial capitalism in displacing rural residents and converting them into impoverished laborers. The Grimms, like other German Romantics, imagined *das Volk* less as a social class than as an idea, the embodiment of a premodern world in which people lived in harmony with nature and God and exhibited an innocent, childlike spirit (see Schoof 1959; Kamenetsky 1992), thereby drawing attention away from actually existing class antagonisms and their material basis. Following Herder's lead, the Grimms transferred the legacy of the dying folk not to the descendants of peasants who were being forced into squalid urban quarters in order to provide cheap labor for industrial capitalism but to members of the bourgeoisie who read their books. Entextualizing class by creating images of tradition helped to draw attention away from social inequality and the active, sometimes violent way that exploitation and new fragmentations of space, time, and community were being resisted in the first half of the nineteenth century.

We would reify nationalism ourselves if we failed to appreciate the way that the Grimms' project extended beyond the borders of the German nation that they helped imagine. Their understanding of traditional texts was shaped by comparative research that embraced a wide range of European languages and folk genres. Corresponding with scholars across Europe, the Grimms actively sought to create an international market for their work. They actively encouraged translation of the *KHM*, which have now appeared in more than seventy languages, and the tales were incorporated into storytelling repertoires in many countries. They conceived of the *KHM* as providing a model that specialists in other countries should emulate in collecting and publishing folktales and other genres. They appended a list of hundreds of collections that had appeared since they published the first edition of the *KHM* in 1812. The Grimms suggested that letters of acknowledgment and prefaces credited them with setting the example for their work. The effects of the tales on national imaginaries were enhanced by their widespread incorporation into literature, art, and popular culture (see Michaelis-Jena 1970: 169). They translated texts from other countries into German and provided prefaces or introductions for others, and they often exchanged text collections with foreign scholars.[15] The cosmopolitan character of the project was also evident in the Grimms' comparative and historical linguistics. Even as they worked on a wide range of European languages, they encouraged scholars to use similar techniques (see Wiley 1971, 1990). Thus, the Grimms' efforts to make the production of texts on language and tradition a crucial part of the German nationalist project did not inhibit them from creating a cosmopolitan enterprise, carving out a transnational market for their works, and providing themselves with an international profile. The stylistic homogenization of the *Märchen* served them here as well. Just as the *KHM* could embody a national prototype that they had largely created, the *Märchen* were readily comparable to narratives that were cut on the same mold. Small wonder that Russian scholar Vladimir Propp (1968) could provide a single structural formulae for the folk or magical tale!

---

[15] Michaelis-Jena (1970: 167–87) outlines the Grimms' correspondence and collaboration with other European scholars.

A number of scholars have now argued that nationalism and cosmopolitanism go hand in hand.[16] We have suggested that just as peoples need novels, newspapers, histories, languages, landmarks, monuments, and other features to construct the status of a nation as a modern entity that results from a rupture with the past, they also need folktales, epics, legends, and other folk texts to embody continuities with the traditional base that (in theory) preceded it. Producing and consuming traditional texts became a crucial part of the process of imagining the nation and making it seem to be real, a natural phenomenon with deep historical roots. Here lies a problem with both the notion of the nation-state as modern (Anderson (1991) and as needing to "invent" traditions in order to legitimate itself (see Handler and Linnekin 1984; Herzfeld 1982; Hobsbawm and Ranger 1981; Wilson 1976). If modernity fundamentally involved an invention (if you will) of tradition as well as the techniques of purification and hybridization that created complex and contradictory relations between them, then constructing the nation-state as modern necessarily entailed the projection of a traditional foundation. Tradition was thus not invented, it was there from the start – meaning that its construction is of the same genealogical level as the state. In this sense, the notion that the state invents tradition presupposes the modernist reification of the state. We can thus say that Anderson and Ranger are victims of modernist understandings of the state *and* tradition.

But let us return to our move beyond the Grimms' nationalism to their cosmopolitan project. Theirs was hardly the only model for cosmopolitanism that was available at the turn of nineteenth-century Germany. Kant's "Idea for a Universal History with a Cosmopolitan Purpose," published nearly thirty years before the first edition of the *KHM* appeared, constructed "rational cosmopolitans" as the logical end point of the unfolding of "the germs implanted by nature in our species" (1991 [1784]: 43). The universalist rationalism that marks this hypothetical state is gained, Kant tells us, by leaving behind a state of "uttermost barbarism," which was shaped by natural instinct and "self-seeking animal inclination" (1991 [1784: 46). It takes little imagination to see how this process, which he developed in his famous essay on "Perpetual Peace," elevates socially and historically specific European elite self-representations into a model for "citizens of a universal state of mankind" (1991 [1795]: 99).

But rationalism and universalism did not corner the market on cosmopolitan projects in nineteenth-century Germany. By critically reflecting on the Grimms' project we can see that Europeans were pursuing

---

[16] See for example Robbins (1998: 2).

a variety of different strategies for creating monopolies over social and cultural forms. The Grimms claim to be provincializing Europe, at least on a national plane, by getting their fellow citizens to dis-identify with models of universal rationality and develop a strong attachment to socially and historically specific mappings of the soul. It is by virtue of the cosmopolitan dimension of this project that an apparent disavowal of universalistic pretensions created provincial visions of difference that could be marketed on an international scale.

Henry Rowe Schoolcraft (1793–1864) is accorded by intellectual historians a status similar to that of the Grimms, his close contemporaries, as a founding ancestor of folklore and anthropology.[1] A. I. Hallowell has observed that "Historically viewed, Schoolcraft was a pioneer in the collection of the folklore of any non-literate people anywhere in the world" (1946: 137); Rosemary Zumwalt has called him "the first scholar of American Indian culture to collect and analyze a large body of Indian folklore" (1978: 44); and W. K. McNeil credits him with being "the man generally recognized as the father of American folklore and anthropology" (1992: 1). As with the Grimms, critics are divided or ambivalent concerning the scholarly validity of Schoolcraft's work. Some, like Stith Thompson, are strongly negative: "Ultimately, the scientific value of his work is marred by the manner in which he reshaped the stories to suit his own literary taste. Several of his tales, indeed, are distorted almost beyond recognition" (1929: xv; see also Thompson 1922). The vocabulary and rhetoric here are strikingly similar to some of the assessments of the Grimms cited in our earlier discussion. Others, like Zumwalt and William Clements, author of an illuminating study of Schoolcraft's textual practices, credit many of Schoolcraft's pronounced methodological principles, but fault him for his lack of adherence to those principles in practice (Zumwalt 1978: 49; Clements 1996: 117). Most significantly, in terms of the intellectual developments we have traced in the foregoing chapters, Schoolcraft's engagement with the words of Others called upon him to navigate the same field of forces linking literature, science, commerce, and national aggrandizement that shaped the Grimms' scholarly ideology and practice. Schoolcraft's work, accordingly, stands in illuminating contrast with that of his German contemporaries.

Schoolcraft's first encounter with Native American oral narrative occurred within weeks of his arrival at Sault Ste. Marie in early July of

[1] Concerning Schoolcraft's life and career, see Bieder (1986), Bremer (1987), Freeman (1959), Marsden (1976).

226

1822 as newly appointed Indian agent for the Michigan Territory, only recently claimed for the United States by Governor Lewis Cass. Eager from the beginning to learn about his charges, he was initially frustrated by having to rely on traders and interpreters who were disappointingly ignorant concerning the fine points of the native languages and incapable of managing his more subtle inquiries into the "secret beliefs and superstitions" of the Indians (Schoolcraft 1851a: 106). When he moved into the home of John Johnston and his family, however, a week and a half after arriving at his post, a new world was opened to him. Johnston was a highly successful and respected Indian trader, Irish-born but of long experience on the frontier, and married to an Ojibwe woman of high status and political influence. Their children, bridging both cultures, were accomplished individuals, one of whom became Schoolcraft's wife. We will deal with the Johnston family further below, but suffice it to say here that they provided a privileged vantage point for Schoolcraft on Ojibwe language and culture.

Schoolcraft's inquiries into Indian culture were guided by a questionnaire, *Inquiries Respecting the History, Traditions, Languages, Manners, Customs, Religion... of the Indians Living Within the United States* (1823) circulated by Governor Cass to gather information that might serve as a guide in official dealings with the Indians. As Governor of the Michigan Territory and as Secretary of War in Jackson's cabinet, Cass played a major role in the development of US Indian policy (see, e.g., Brown 1953; Prucha 1967; Woodford 1950), and Schoolcraft's own ideological and scholarly orientation towards the Indians, as described in the pages that follow, were in close accord with those of his patron. As newly appointed Indian agent, he was understandably eager to cooperate in Cass's project, lauding him for "the researches which you have directed, and continue to direct, to the history and condition of [the nation's] traduced native population" (1975 [1825]: iv).

Among the questions posed in Cass's *Inquiries* were the following: "Do they relate stories, or indulge in any work of the imagination?" and "Are they in the practice of telling stories?" (Schoolcraft 1991: 290–91). One of Cass's motivations in targeting storytelling was an intellectual fascination with history, both in shorter scope, with a focus on the particulars of American history, and in the broader sweep of human history. He was especially concerned with the prevailing lack of information concerning "the moral character and feelings of the Indian... their mental discipline... their peculiar opinions, mythological and religious, and... all that is most valuable to man in the history of man" (quoted in Smith 1856: 159), and appears to have considered that the potential insights to be gleaned from Indian storytelling might help to fill that gap.

Two weeks after entering the Johnston household, Schoolcraft recorded his exciting and energizing discovery of the existence of oral narratives among the Indians, revealed to him by his hosts:

Nothing has surprised me more in the conversations which I have had with persons acquainted with the Indian customs and character, than to find that the Chippewas amuse themselves with oral tales of a mythological or allegorical character. . . . The fact, indeed, of such a fund of fictitious legendary matter is quite a discovery, and speaks more for the intellect of the race than any trait I have heard. Who would have imagined that these wandering foresters should have possessed such a resource? (1851a: 109)

Especially significant, the existence of oral storytelling among the Indians was for Schoolcraft a breakthrough of recognition; it transformed his vision of who they were, though not, as we shall see, his judgment of their cultural inferiority:

That the Indians should possess this mental trait of indulging in lodge stories, impressed me as a novel characteristic, which nothing I had ever heard of the race had prepared me for. I had always heard the Indian spoken of as a revengeful, bloodthirsty man, who was steeled to endurance and delighted in deeds of cruelty. To find him a man capable of feelings and affections, with a heart open to the wants, and responsive to the ties of social life, was amazing. But the surprise reached its acme, when I found him whiling away a part of the tedium of his long winter evenings in relating tales and legends for the lodge circle. (1851a: 196)

The sense of importance surrounding his discovery of imaginative tales among the Indians never left Schoolcraft; he saw it as being at the same time the basis of a major contribution to knowledge that would enhance his scholarly reputation, a matter of interest to his patron, Governor Cass, who strongly encouraged his further inquiries, and a point of entry into Ojibwe culture more broadly. One of the significant implications of Schoolcraft's sense of discovery was that he felt a lack of models and precedents to guide his collection, understanding, and rendering of these materials for dissemination to a wider audience. He was eager to publicize his discovery, but how? What were these tales? What was their significance? Who would be interested? In effect, Schoolcraft felt that he had to start from the very beginning in gathering the narratives, understanding their nature, meaning, and significance, identifying and engaging a public,[2] and making his discovery available and comprehensible to this

---

[2] We take a public to be an audience (in the general sense of receivers and consumers of communicative forms) that is held to share some commonality of attitude and interest and that may be mobilized to collective social action (cf. Crow 1985). In this sense, insofar as Schoolcraft intended his publication of Indian tales to influence people's attitudes towards Indians in support of particular national Indian policies, he was attempting to shape a public as well as an audience and a market.

audience. All of these factors had a formative effect on his textual ideology and practice.

As regards Schoolcraft's understanding of the nature of Indian narratives, he conceived of them simultaneously and in varying degrees and combinations as literary forms and ethnological data.[3] Schoolcraft himself employed the term "literary" repeatedly in his writings in referring to his narrative materials (e.g., 1992 [1839] I: v; 1851a: 254, 631), but it is necessary in developing this point to specify what "literary" implied for Schoolcraft and his readers.[4] First of all, "literary" meant, in its most general sense, "to be read." Insofar as literacy and access to books were tied to particular social strata, serving as a touchstone of bourgeois attainment, "literary" also carried a dimension of moral meaning, as implying *polite* learning, marked by standards of taste, decorum, and belletristic refinement that needed to be cultivated in the process of literary production. This element will figure significantly at a later point in our consideration of Schoolcraft's textual practice. At the same time, in the period comprehended by Schoolcraft's career, "literary" was connected as well with a heightening awareness of authorship, of literary works as intellectual property, commodities oriented to a growing bookselling market. Still further, it is important to recognize the national resonances of literary production as the ideologies we have traced in the preceding chapters exercised a greater and greater shaping influence on Western cultural production more generally in the nineteenth century. These factors too will receive further attention later in the chapter.

Finally, during the first half of the nineteenth century, the term "literary" came increasingly to designate creative, imaginative, aesthetically shaped works, and this sense of the term also marks Schoolcraft's usage. For example, he remarks on the "poetic" quality of the Indian narratives (e.g., 1975 [1825]: 409; 1992 [1839] I: v), not a matter of verse, but of aesthetic properties, as the narratives are rendered as prose and distinguished from "measured songs or poetry" (1975 [1825]: 427). That he conceived of them more particularly as *narrative* literature is amply attested by his pervasive – if loose – employment of such generic labels as "tale," "legend," and "story," and his references to "narration" (1992 [1839] I: 17), "narrators" (1992 [1839] I: 17; 1851a: 216), and

---

[3] Schoolcraft also includes historical accounts based upon Indian testimony among the narratives he presents, but these are of a different order from the "imaginative" tales with which we are primarily concerned; the texts themselves are not framed as being of native provenience.

[4] We are grateful to Michael Silverstein for pointing out to us the need to elucidate the meanings that "literary" carried in Schoolcraft's writings. Our discussion draws centrally from Williams (1983: 183–88).

"narrated" (1848: 130) in describing their provenance. In addition to their poetic qualities, a further dimension of Schoolcraft's conception of the Indian narratives as literature in this more marked sense of the term is revealed by his repeated reference to their "imaginative" and "fanciful" qualities (1975 [1825]: 403, 409; 1992 [1839] I: 15, 17; 1848: 68; 1851a: 109, 678; 1853: 314), which is to say that they were, for the most part, "fictitious" (1992 [1839] I: v; 1851a: 109, 196; 1851b: 216; 1853: 313). It is this last cluster of meanings that warrants Schoolcraft's use of the compound term, "oral literature." An early entry in his journal, dated 27 September 1822, bears the heading "Oral Literature of the Indians" (1851a: 120). Whether this heading appeared in the original journal or was added for publication in 1851 we cannot know, but the term is also employed in his 1848 volume, *The Indian in His Wigwam, or Characteristics of the Red Race of America*. It is worth remarking that from the vantage-point of the first sense of "literary" offered above, that is, "to be read," "oral literature" is an oxymoron; it becomes intelligible to the extent that "literary" designates primarily poetic, imaginative, creative works. Indeed, the tension encapsulated in the term "oral literature" highlights some of the most salient problems Schoolcraft had to confront in formulating and implementing his textual practices.

At the same time that Schoolcraft conceived of the Indian tales as literature, he recognized them from the beginning of his inquiries as privileged sources of scientific insight into the Indians' culture. In his first publication of Indian narratives, the subject matter of the final chapter of *Travels in the Central Portions of the Mississippi Valley* (1975 [1825]; hereafter, *Travels*), Schoolcraft prefaces a narrative entitled "The Funeral Fire" with a statement that makes clear the close interrelationship between narrative and custom (or tradition):

For several nights after the interment of a person, a fire is placed upon the grave.... The following tale is related as showing the origin of this custom. It will at once be perceived that their traditions and fictions are intimately blended. It would be impossible to decide whether the custom existed prior to the tale, or the tale has been invented to suit the custom. We may suppose that their customs and imaginative tales have alternately acted as cause and effect. (1975 [1825]: 404)

A bit later on, he suggests of one class of tales that they "appear to be designed to enforce the observance of certain customs, and to instill into the minds of the children a knowledge of those rites that are supposed to be necessary to the formation of their character" (1975 [1825]: 412).

The realization that Indian belief and custom were accessible through their narratives was for Schoolcraft an exciting and significant breakthrough. His early attempts to obtain such ethnological information by more direct inquiry were notably unsuccessful, a problem he attributed variously to misapprehension, evasion, and "restlessness, suspicion, and mistrust of motive" on the part of the Indians and the inadequacies of his early interpreters (1851a: 106; 1856: xv). But when he turned his attention to the narratives, the veil of secrecy was lifted. Indeed, this rhetoric of revelation, of bringing secrets to light, pervades Schoolcraft's framing of his Indian tales throughout his career. "Hitherto," he writes, "Indian opinion, on abstract subjects, has been a sealed book" (1856: xv). In the tales, however, "the Indian mind unbends itself and reveals some of its less obvious traits" (1851b: 216). The narratives

furnish illustrations of Indian character and opinion on subjects which the ever-cautious and suspicious minds of the people have, heretofore, concealed. They reflect him as he is. The show us what he believes, hopes, fears, wishes, expects, worships, lives for, dies for. They are always true to the Indian manners and customs, opinions and theories. They never rise above them; they never sink below them. . . . Other sources of information depict his exterior habits and outer garb and deportment; but in these legends and myths, we perceive the interior man, and are made cognizant of the secret workings of his mind, and heart, and soul. (1856: vii; see also 1848: 68; 1851a: 196)

Ultimately, Schoolcraft believed that the "chief value" of the tales lies in "the insight they give into the dark cave of the Indian mind – its beliefs, dogmas, and opinions – its secret modes of turning over thought – its real philosophy," and he considered that his revelation of these aspects of Indian life constituted the basis for the lasting importance of his work (1851a: 655; see also 1851a: 585).

The dual conception of oral narratives as simultaneously literary forms and ethnological data is, of course, not original to Schoolcraft; it is rooted in the philological tradition we have traced through the preceding chapters. Where Schoolcraft's work signals a new departure, we would suggest, is in his struggle to reconcile these dual aspects of "oral literature" in rendering the texts for publication, as ethnology and literature were drawn apart into the increasingly divergent intellectual and discursive domains of science and art. Schoolcraft clearly sees the two pursuits in separate terms, though he was drawn to both. He made much of his affinity for natural history and prided himself on his "strong propensity" for scientific description and analysis. "The study of Natural History," he observes in his journal, "presents some of the most pleasing evidence of exactitude and order, in every department of creation," and he considered that "the same mode of exactitude" might extend to the study of Indian languages and cultures (1851: 66, 283–84). At the same time, he testifies often to the pleasure he took in literary pursuits as a "writer on the frontier, who fills up a kind of elegant leisure by composition" (1851: 282). The tension between the two domains ramifies throughout Schoolcraft's statements concerning his textual practices. The first of these is a revealing footnote from Schoolcraft's first major publication of Indian narratives, in the concluding chapter of his *Travels* (1975 [1825]: 409):

These tales have been taken from the oral relation of the Chippewas, at the Sault of St. Mary, the ancient seat of that nation. Written down at the moment, and consequently in haste, no opportunity for literary refinement was presented; and after the lapse of some time, we have not judged it expedient to make any material alterations in the language adopted, while our impressions were fresh. A literal adherence to the sense of the original, to the simplicity of the narration, and, in many instances, to the peculiar mode of expression of the Indians, is thus preserved, while the order of the incidents is throughout strictly the same. Our collections on this subject are extensive. We do not feel assured that the selections here given present a just specimen of their merits – particularly in relation to the poetical machinery or invention of the Indians.

In this passage, we may observe clearly the play of meanings that shaped Schoolcraft's understanding of the Indian tales as literary. Note, for example, the coupling of "literary" with "refinement," suggesting that taking down the tales in writing was not sufficient to render them fully literary, for which further refining work was necessary. Writing down the tales makes them available for reading, but literary refinement distances them from their original oral qualities of expression. Even unrefined, however, they remain literary insofar as they are the products of "the poetical machinery" and "invention" of the Indians. The passage testifies to the difficulty Schoolcraft experienced in reconciling these various dimensions of the tales' literariness. We are immediately struck in this passage by Schoolcraft's effort to minimize the intertextual gap between the texts he has presented and "the oral relation of the Chippewas." His emphasis here is on freshness, immediacy, directness, preservation, adherence to an original, while explicitly disclaiming the potential distancing effect of textual "alterations." This is clearly purifying rhetoric, an effort to render his editorial intervention transparent, to erase the hybridizing effects of his own labors in recording the Ojibwe oral texts and preparing them for publication in print and in English.

Now, while it is clear that Schoolcraft had ample opportunity to experience storytelling directly, it is equally clear that his narrative materials did not come to him in as unmediated a fashion as this passage might suggest. Certainly, Schoolcraft's own observations of Indian storytelling constitute one of the chief bases for the rhetoric of revelation and authenticity that marks his presentation of the Indian tales. For example, in contrasting the public and formal demeanor of Indians "before a mixed assemblage of white men" with their more relaxed manner in their own villages, "away from all public gaze," Schoolcraft writes, "Let us follow the man to this retreat, and see what are his domestic manners, habits, and opinions." He continues, "I have myself visited an Indian camp, in the far-off area of the NORTHWEST, in the dead of winter, under circumstances suited to allay his suspicions," and then goes on to describe a sociable occasion of storytelling (1851b: 184; see also 1851a: 109). It is such direct experiences that allowed Schoolcraft to discover and reveal the secrets of Indian life, including the grand discovery of their storytelling. "It requires observation of real life," he insists, "to be able to set a true estimate on things" (1851a: 138), an early appeal to the authority of fieldwork, with all its rigors and remoteness and claims to privileged access to the real stuff, couched in the rhetoric of scientific empiricism. And, of course, the magnification of his own role in the gathering of these significant materials was quite consistent with his lifelong concern for his scholarly reputation (see, e.g., 1851a: 639, 655, 672, 703).

While we do not have direct information concerning the circumstances under which three of the four tales presented in *Travels* were collected, we do know the source of one of the narratives, "Gitshee Gauzinee" (1975 [1825]: 410–12). This tale, recounting a dream-vision of an Ojibwe chief relating to burial practices, was part of the repertoire of John Johnston, Schoolcraft's father-in-law, to whom it was earlier told by Gitshee Gauzinee himself (McKenney 1959 [1827]: 370; for fuller discussion, see Bauman 1993). While Johnston was fluent in Ojibwe, he would undoubtedly have recounted the narrative to Schoolcraft in English, as Schoolcraft's command of Ojibwe – notwithstanding his extended efforts at comprehending Ojibwe grammar – was limited (Bieder 1986: 158). Nevertheless, the mediation of the story through Johnston to Schoolcraft is elided in Schoolcraft's methodological statement, which implies that he himself recorded the tale directly from "the oral relation of the Chippewas." We shall have more to say about dimensions of mediation in Schoolcraft's textual practices below.

To be sure, Schoolcraft does suggest the intertextual gaps that are opened by the twin processes of intersemiotic and interlingual translation, that is, the taking down of the oral narratives in writing and their translation from Ojibwe into English, in his references to the haste with which the texts were recorded and to his lack of assurance that they adequately represent "the poetical machinery or invention of the Indians." These problems are minimized, however, by the claim that "A literal adherence to the sense of the original, to the simplicity of the narration, and, in many instances, to the peculiar mode of expression of the Indians, is . . . preserved, while the order of the incidents is throughout strictly the

same." There is an implication here, as well, of a form – content differentiation, insofar as Schoolcraft's statement suggests that "poetical
machinery" fares less well in the translation process than "the sense of
the original" and "the order of the incidents," that is, the meaning and
the plot. This distinction assumed a still greater place in Schoolcraft's
subsequent discussions of his textual practices, correlated with the dual
nature of the narrative materials as literature and ethnological data.

The issues of intersemiotic and interlingual translation figure in a somewhat more problematic way in Schoolcraft's most important collection of
Indian narratives, *Algic Researches* (1992 [1839]), the two-volume work
on which his reputation as a student of folklore principally rests and
for which he is best known beyond folklore and anthropology because
of its role as the central source of Indian lore for Henry Wadsworth
Longfellow in his composition of *The Song of Hiawatha* (1992 [1855]).
Algic Researches contrasts markedly with *Travels* in its contextualization
of Indian narratives. Where *Travels* incorporated tales into the format of
a travel account, *Algic Researches* is fully and exclusively a collection of
tales. In an introductory section entitled "Preliminary Observations on
the Tales," the reader encounters Schoolcraft's claim that his investigations of Ojibwe culture led him to the discovery "that they possessed a
story-telling faculty, and I wrote down from their narration a number
of these fictitious tales" (1992 [1839]: 17–18). As with the statement in
Travels, this assertion suggests a lack of mediation, a directness of recording, that is belied by the historical record, for we know that Schoolcraft's Johnston kinsmen, including prominently his wife Jane as well as
his sister-in-law Charlotte and his brothers-in-law George and William,
all bilingual and literate, collected a significant number of the narratives
included in Schoolcraft's collection and conveyed them to him already in
writing and in English (Osborn and Osborn 1942: 586, 589; Schoolcraft
1962: xxiv–xxv, 170n.). Schoolcraft's own shaping of the narrative texts,
accordingly, was performed on already written English translations, pre-
shaped by the linguistic skills and literary sensibilities of his bicultural
and multilingual Johnston relatives.

Later in the volume, in a note immediately preceding the texts themselves, Schoolcraft acknowledges these and other individuals for their
assistance as interpreters and translators of the narratives, though not
for the actual recording of the tales. The terms of the acknowledgment
are significant: "These persons are well versed in the respective tongues
from which they have given translations; and being residents of the places
indicated, a reference to them for the authenticity of the materials is
thus brought within the means of all who desire it" (1992 [1839] I: 26).
Here, then, for the first time, is an *explicit* indication of mediation in the

text-making process, but the recognition of the intertextual gap opened by the need for translation of the tales into English is framed in terms designed to minimize its distancing effects. The linguistic competence of the translators and their residence in Indian country is a warrant both for the accuracy of their translations and for the authenticity of the materials, a claim akin to the fieldworker's appeal to the authority of direct contact with the source. And the acknowledgment invites interested readers to contact Schoolcraft's Johnston relatives for verification of the materials' genuineness.

In *The Indian in His Wigwam* (1848), which drew together the eight numbers of Schoolcraft's magazine, *Oneota* (originally published in 1844–45), Schoolcraft did acknowledge his brother-in-law, George Johnston, as the source from whom he received three narratives (1848: 111, 130, 175) and his wife, Jane, as the transcriber of another (1848: 127); in addition, he notes of a fifth narrative that it was preserved through the Johnston family (1848: 109). The tales credited to George are probably the ones Schoolcraft acknowledged in a letter to his brother-in-law in May of 1838; they are all attributed to Nabinoi (also Nabunway, Nabunwa, Nabanois), a noted Ojibwe storyteller from whom Schoolcraft had urged George to collect stories several months earlier (Osborn and Osborn 1942: 586). Schoolcraft apparently received these tales too late to include them in *Algic Researches* (cf. Schoolcraft 1851a: 585).

Schoolcraft's relationship with George is illuminated in an especially telling way by a letter he wrote in August of 1844, some time after he had left Michigan, in which he urges his brother-in-law to send him further items of Indian lore. "You are favorably situated," he suggests,

for collecting traditions & traits of the Red Race, and their character and history; and possessing as you do, a full knowledge of their language with more than the ordinary share of English literature & letters, you would be, almost inexcusable, not to employ your leisure moments, in putting on record all you can find, among them, worthy of it. It is a debt you owe to them, & to the country, and such labours, if well directed & well executed, will form your own best claim to remembrance. Life is, at best, but short, & he only lives well, who does something to benefit others. So far as you may transmit to me, any thing you may collect, in names, or lodge-tales, or picture writing, or any other branch, I can assure you, that you shall have final & full literary credit. (Osborn and Osborn 1942: 589)

In this revealing document, Schoolcraft clearly acknowledges the special contribution that George was uniquely qualified to make – had, in fact, already made – to his studies, positioned as he was between Indian and white cultures, as the son of an Ojibwe woman and an Irish father. Schoolcraft emphasizes George's responsibility to the Indians and to the country – each in its way a national responsibility – holding out as well the prospect that George will be well remembered for his efforts and promising him full credit for his contributions. But note that it is Schoolcraft himself who is the gate-keeper of such credit and who is the most immediate beneficiary of George's work. The slim and partial credit that Schoolcraft did in fact accord to his brother-in-law (see also 1853a: 302–4; 1853b: 419) only highlights the degree to which he consistently reserved central authority, credit, and control for himself for the gathering, presentation, and authenticity of the Indian lore he published under his own name.

The concern with authenticity bedeviled Schoolcraft throughout his career, but especially strongly in connection with *Algic Researches*, as witness a pair of entries in Schoolcraft's journal (published in 1851) concerning his textual practices in the preparation of *Algic Researches* for publication. These entries are worthy of quotation at length. The first is dated 26 January 1838:

Completed the revision of a body of Indian oral legends, collected during many years with labor. These oral tales show up the Indian in a new light. Their chief value consists in their exhibition of aboriginal opinions. But, if published, incredulity will start up critics to call their authenticity in question. . . . If there be any literary labor which has cost me more than usual pains, it is this. I have weeded out many vulgarisms. I have endeavored to restore the simplicity of the original style. In this I have not always fully succeeded, and it has been sometimes found necessary, to avoid incongruity, to break a legend in two, or cut it short off. (1851a: 585)

The second entry dates from 21 June 1839, after the publication of *Algic Researches*:

it is difficult for an editor to judge, from the mere face of the volumes, what an amount of auxiliary labor it has required to collect these legends from the Indian wigwams. They had to be gleaned and translated from time to time. . . . They required pruning and dressing, like wild vines in a garden. But they are, exclusively . . . wild vines, and not pumpings up of my own fancy. The attempts to lop off excrescences are not, perhaps, always happy. There might, perhaps, have been a fuller adherence to the original language and expressions; but if so, what a world of verbiage must have been retained. The Indians are prolix, and attach value to many minutiae in the relation which not only does not help forward the denouement, but is tedious and witless to the last degree. The gems of the legends – the essential points – the invention and thought-work are all preserved. Their chief value I have ever thought to consist in the in-sight they give into the dark cave of the Indian mind – its beliefs, dogmas, and opinions – its secret modes of turning over thought – its real philosophy; and it is for this trait that I believe posterity will sustain the book. (1851a: 655)

Both of these entries, especially the first, reveal clearly the depth of Schoolcraft's concern that his narratives be recognized as authentically

Indian, that they not be taken as "pumpings up of my own fancy."
Tellingly, however, his anxiety on the matter is acknowledged as the principal motivation for the intensity of the hybridizing editorial labors he
has invested in the revision of the texts. These labors are enumerated in
some detail: the weeding out of vulgarisms (i.e., sexual and scatological
elements), the restoration of the simplicity of the style, the breaking of
compound tales into two, the abbreviation of texts, the lopping off of
excrescences.

These operations open ever more widely the gap between form and
content. While literary refinement remains a salient concern, Schoolcraft
clearly and explicitly assigns primary importance to the cultural content
of the tales as he views them, the "beliefs, dogmas, and opinions" which
are given expression in the narratives – these ethnological data are what
must be preserved for posterity. By the standards of Schoolcraft's literary
aesthetic, the tales are flawed, and any effort to achieve "a fuller adherence
to the original language and expressions" or to other formal features of
native expression would only detract from their literary appeal for his
readers. Their chief flaw, in Schoolcraft's view, lay in verbal excess –
prolixity, excessive verbiage, proliferation of minutiae, excrescences – that
renders them "tedious and witless to the last degree" and offers nothing
to the realization of the essential plot, the denouement.

One formal convention of Ojibwa storytelling that seems to have been
especially infelicitous in Schoolcraft's view is form–content parallelism
(Woodbury 1987) as realized in successive encounters of the dramatis
personae, played out as direct discourse. In describing Ojibwe narrative
style in the introduction to *Algic Researches*, Schoolcraft observes that
"Great attention is paid, in the narratives, to repeating the conversations
and speeches, and imitating the very tone and gesture of the actors. This
is sometimes indulged in at the risk of tautology" (1992 [1839] I: 43).
Here is a section of the story of Gitshee Gauzinee, relating his encounters
with various personages in the land of the dead:

He met an aged man, who stopped him to complain of the burdens his friends
had imposed upon him to carry to the land of the dead, and this man concluded
his address by offering him his gun. Shortly after, he met a very old woman, who
offered him a kettle, and a little further on, a young man, who offered him an
axe. All these presents he accepted out of courtesy, for he had determined to go
back for his own gun, and therefore stood in little need of these presents. (1975
[1825]: 411)

In this rendering, the reported speech of the aged man is reduced to
indirect discourse, while the speech of the old woman and the young
man is attenuated still further, reporting only the illocutionary force of

their offers. But Schoolcraft could be even more severe in his pruning. In another version, the same episodes are rendered as follows:

> One man stopped me and complained of the great burdens he had to carry. He offered me his gun, which I however refused, having made up my mind to procure my own. Another offered me a kettle. (1992 [1839] II: 130)

This version reduces the interlocutors to two and the reported speech to a bare minimum. The full repetition of the conversations that would have been engaging to an Ojibwe audience would only be boring to white readers, in Schoolcraft's judgment.

To a degree, Schoolcraft saw the stylistic deficiencies of the Indian narratives as inherent in their language itself. He noted his apprehension, for example, "that the language generally has a strong tendency to repetition and redundancy of forms, and to clutter up, as it were, general ideas with particular meanings" (1851a: 141). The conception of "primitive" languages as exhibiting an abundance of particular categories but a deficiency of general ones was, by Schoolcraft's time, a commonplace of evolutionary understandings of language development (see Chapter 3 for its antecedents in eighteenth-century philology). In a further indictment of Ojibwe morphology, he observed that "The Indian certainly has a very pompous way of expressing a common thought. He sets about it with an array of prefix and suffix, and polysyllabic strength, as if he were about to crush a cob-house with a crowbar" (1851a: 151).[5] Schoolcraft is likely referring here to the tendency of Ojibwe narrators to favor highly specific and morphologically complex verbs in storytelling, considered a mark of good narrative language (Valentine 1995: 203–4). And again, in a sweeping dismissal of the communicative capacities of Indian languages, "One of the principal objections to be urged against the Indian languages, considered as media of communication, is their cumbrousness. There is certainly a great deal of verbiage and tautology about them" (1851a: 171). Small wonder, then, that he considered the style of the narratives to be in need of repair by the standards of polite literary taste.

To appeal to this polite taste and to foreground the literariness of those texts he intended to present as literature, Schoolcraft adopted a flowery and elevated register, marked by high emotion, sentimental observations of nature, stilted dialogue, archaic pronominal usage ("thou," "thee," "ye"), and heavily sentimentalized rhymed poetry to index the inclusion of songs in native narrative performances. Some examples:

---

[5] This is in striking contrast with Sapir's aesthetically appreciative suggestion that "Single Algonkin words are like tiny imagist poems" (1921: 228).

They found themselves in a beautiful plain, extending as far as the eye could reach, covered with flowers of a thousand different hues and fragrance. Here and there were clusters of tall, shady trees, separated by innumerable streams of the purest water, which would their courses under the cooling shades, and filled the plain with countless beautiful lakes, whose banks and bosom were covered with water-fowl. (1992 [1839] I: 63)

"Brothers," he said, "an accident has befallen me, but let not this prevent your going to a warmer climate. Winter is rapidly approaching, and you cannot remain here. It is better that I alone should die than for you all to suffer miserably on my account." "No! no!" they replied, with one voice, "we will not forsake you; we will share your sufferings; we will abandon our journey, and take care of you, as you did of us, before we were able to take care of ourselves. If the climate kills you, it shall kill us. Do you think we can so soon forget your brotherly care, which has surpassed a father's, and even a mother's kindness? Whether you live or die, we will live or die with you." (1992 [1839] I: 234)

And she continued plaintively singing her chant.
   Raccoon, raccoon, monster thin!
   You have murdered all my kin:
   Leave not one to pine alone
   On these shores so late our own.
   You have glutted not a few,
   Stealthy monster, eat us too –
   Let the work be finished soon,
     Aissibun amoon*
     *Raccoon, eat us

                                       (1992 [1839] II: 120)

At this moment Manabozha happened to pass by seeing how things were. "Tyau!" [= *tyaayaa* 'man's expression of mild displeasue or disdain' (Nichols and Nyhold 1995: 112)] said he to the Raccoon, "thou art a thief and an unmerciful dog. Get thee up into trees, lest I change thee into one of these same worm-fish. . . ." (1992 [1839] II: 121)

A comparison of the opening sentences of "Peta Kway; or, The Tempest: An Algic Tale," from *Algic Researches* and Mary Lamb's version of *The Tempest* from the *Tales from Shakespear* suggests one possible source of inspiration for Schoolcraft's literary style (cf. Zolla 1973: 150):

There once lived a woman called Monedo Kway on the sand mountains called "the Sleeping Bear" of Lake Michigan, who had a daughter as beautiful as she was modest and discreet. (Schoolcraft 1992 [1839] I: 129)

There was a certain island in the sea, the only inhabitants of which were an old man, whose name was Prospero, and his daughter Miranda, a very beautiful young lady. (Lamb and Lamb 1903 [1807] III: 3)

In other places, it evokes the classic ballads: "There lived a hunter in the north..." (Schoolcraft 1992 [1839] II: 61).

On the other hand, Schoolcraft had a corresponding set of textual means for highlighting the ethnological "authenticity" and scholarly validity of his texts. Some of these involved the manipulation of the same sets of elements that could be utilized to foreground literary refinement, tempering, reducing, or eliminating them to foreground ethnological content and expository clarity. Thus, Schoolcraft might employ a less ornate, more expository register, reduce direct discourse, or eliminate the poems from the texts. At the extreme, this would yield a brief, informationally focused précis of what might elsewhere be a more extended "literary" narrative. Compare the following parallel episodes from two versions of the story of Gitshee Gauzinee; Gitshee Gauzinee has just awakened from his trance:

He related the following story to his companions – That after his death he traveled on towards the pleasant country, which is the Indian heaven, but having no gun could get nothing to eat, & he at last determined to go back for his gun – (Schoolcraft 1962: 7)

He gave the following narration to his friends:
"After my death, my Jeebi [= *jiibay* 'spirit' (Rhodes 1985: 580)] traveled in the broad road of the dead toward the happy land, which is the Indian paradise. I passed on many days without meeting with anything of an extraordinary nature. Plains of large extent, and luxuriant herbage, began to pass before my eyes. I saw many beautiful groves, and heard the songs of innumerable birds. At length I began to suffer for the want of food. I reached the summit of an elevation. My eyes caught the glimpse of the city of the dead. But it appeared to be distant, and the intervening space, partly veiled in silvery mists, was spangled with glittering lakes and streams. At this spot I came in sight of numerous herds of stately deer, moose, and other animals, which walked near my path, and appeared to have lost their natural timidity. But having no gun I was unable to kill them. I thought of the request I had made to my friends, to put my gun in my grave, and resolved to go back and seek for it. (Schoolcraft 1992 [1839] II: 127)

Also related to the language of the texts, one device favored by Schoolcraft to enhance ethnological verisimilitude was the employment of native-language words, idioms, or phrases (cf. "Jeebi" above), frequently with an accompanying English gloss in the text or a footnote. For still more scholarly effect, these Ojibwe forms might be further accompanied by linguistic commentary explicating their morphology or etymology. To cite one further device in the service of rendering cultural content accessible, Schoolcraft resorted frequently to metanarrational commentary, noting a particular action, behavior, or other feature as customary, or explaining its function. Some such comments might be interpolated into

the texts or presented as framing matter before or after a given narrative for all audiences, but for more scholarly tone, they might be rendered as expository footnotes. Being especially concerned with moral
issues, Schoolcraft used a special set of metanarrational devices to key
a moral interpretation, including genre designations in subtitles, such as
"allegory" or "fable," and explicit moral exegeses appended to the text.

In light of these considerations, Schoolcraft's statement that he has
"endeavored to restore the simplicity of the original style" might appear
contradictory. It is not entirely clear what he means by the notion of
"original style," but the sentence that follows, about breaking a legend
in two or cutting it off, would suggest that Schoolcraft had in mind a
conception of tales as properly consisting of unitary plots which were
compromised by storytellers' occasional tendency in certain contexts to
chain or blend multiple narratives into a single extended narration. This
too had to be fixed for an "original" quality to be restored.

Schoolcraft's preoccupation with unitary, coherent plots is related to
his consistent objectification of narrative texts by setting off each narrative
on the page as a bounded entity, with a title such as "Gitshee Gauzinee"
(1975 [1825]: 410–12), "Trance" (1962: 7), and "Git-Chee-Gau-Zinee
or The Trance" (1992 [1839] II: 127). The variable title reflects Schoolcraft's dual conception of the tale as a piece of literature and an item of
ethnological data, either of which may be foregrounded. "Gitshee Gauzinee" focuses attention on the protagonist, as dramatis persona, while
"The Trance" identifies an element of ethnological interest.

Given how accustomed modern readers may be to these processes
and devices of textual objectification, it is instructive to recognize
that there were alternatives available to Schoolcraft. Colonel Thomas
L. McKenney, US Commissioner of Indian Affairs, published in 1827
an account of a storytelling event that took place at the home of John
and Susan Johnston and at which Schoolcraft was very likely present
(McKenney 1959 [1827]: 370–72). In the course of that event, John
Johnston recounted a compound narrative relating two experiences of
Gitshee Gauzinee, one of which was the trance narrative subsequently
broken out by Schoolcraft. McKenney's representation is framed as an
account of a sociable gathering in which the compound narrative is embedded as the direct and continuous discourse of Johnston, as one of
the participants. In this account, Johnston attributes the story to Gitshee
Gauzinee himself, as source: "The following story I got from *Gitche-
gausine*" (McKenney 1959 [1827]: 370, italics in the original). The explicit invocation of a link to a source is consistent with Ojibwe practice, one means by which a performer establishes the legitimacy of his
own narration (Valentine 1995: 178). McKenney's book was available to

Schoolcraft, yet Schoolcraft elected to detach his published texts from all such contextual anchorings.

Ultimately, while Schoolcraft was able to devise a range of metadiscursive practices for rendering his texts that allowed for a series of ad hoc, shifting, and contrastively framed solutions to the problem of presenting the Ojibwe narratives in print, he was never fully satisfied that he had successfully reconciled the discursive tension between science and literature. The problem is neatly summed up in Schoolcraft's lament that "The narratives themselves are often so incongruous, grotesque, and fragmentary, as to require some hand better than mine, to put them in shape. And yet, I feel that nearly all of their value, as indices of Indian imagination, must depend on preserving their original form" (1851: 514).

Our emphasis thus far on Schoolcraft's ambivalent assessment of Indian tales as literature (literarily flawed, but with a potential appeal to literary audiences) and his judgment that their chief value lay in their content as a key to the native mind must not be taken to imply that he considered the beliefs, values, opinions, or "thought-work" that he was at such pains to preserve to be of positive worth, for such was decidedly not the case. Indeed, his assessment of native thought was fully as negative, notwithstanding occasional sympathetic gestures towards the Indian as a feeling human being. His common evaluation of both style and thought are clear in the following passage from *Algic Researches*:

The style of narration, the cast of invention, and the theory of thinking, are imminently peculiar to a people who wander about in woods and plains, who encounter wild beasts, believe in demons, and are subject to the vicissitudes of the seasons. The tales refer themselves to a people who are polytheists; not believers in one God or Great spirit, but of thousands of spirits; a people who live in fear, who wander in want, and who die in misery. The machinery of spirits and necromancy, one of the most ancient and prevalent errors of the human race, supplies the framework of these fictitious creations. Language to carry out the conceptions might seem to be wanting, but here the narrator finds a ready resource in the use of metaphor, the doctrine of metamorphosis, and the personification of inanimate objects; for the latter of which, the grammar of the language has a peculiar adaptation. Deficiencies of the vocabulary are thus supplied, life and action are imparted to the whole material creation, and every purpose of description is answered. The belief of the narrators and listeners in every wild and improbable thing told, helps wonderfully, in the original, in joining the sequence of parts together. (1992 [1839]: 18–19; see also 1851a: 196; 1856: xix–xx)

Style, plot, and error are all of a piece, and the limited capacities of the Ojibwe language (reminiscent of those adduced by Blackwell, for example), coupled with the primitive irrationality of Indian thought are substantially to blame. There is an important point to be made here concerning the interrelationship between form and content. This passage makes clear that Schoolcraft did in fact perceive certain dimensions of connection between the two, especially in regard to the relation between personification, agency, and the grammatical marking of animacy (cf. Valentine 1995: 219). From Schoolcraft's vantage-point, then, grammatical form, narrative function, and cultural meaning are mutually implicated, at least to this extent.

Schoolcraft's negative judgment of Indian thought did not extend to a belief in innate mental inferiority (1848: 67). Rather, he held that "It was not want of mental capacity, so much as the non-existence of moral power, and of the doctrines of truth and virtue, that kept them back" (1848: 68; cf. 1962: 16). For "moral power" and "the doctrines of truth and virtue" here, read "Christian moral power" and "the Christian doctrines of truth and virtue," for Schoolcraft was a devout Christian, an energetic champion of missionary efforts, and a strong believer in the need for the Indians to accept Christianity in order to secure their future in this world and save their souls in the next: "We believe christianity [sic] & civilization, act, as one together, as cause or effect. One cannot exist without the other" (1962: 13). Here, then, is the key to Schoolcraft's preoccupation with offering texts that foreground cultural content at the expense, if necessary, of fidelity to native style. Opening up "the dark cave of the Indian mind" is a critical prerequisite to bringing the Indian to the light of Christian belief, an essential basis for the formulation of a national policy towards these inevitable losers in "the contest for supremacy" on the North American continent. In the process of devising such a policy, "it is the dictate of a humane and liberal spirit to improve every opportunity for acquiring fresh information, and eliciting new and authentic traits of their character and history" (1962: 111). The policy must be humane, for the narratives establish the Indians' essential humanity, but it must be a policy of reclamation nevertheless. The crucial point for our argument is the mutual consistency in Schoolcraft of textual practices and political ideology. The intertextual gaps between the oral form of native storytelling and Schoolcraft's published texts are intended to serve the minimization of intertextual gaps in content, all in the greater service of cultural and political domination.

Colonialism, commodification, and the production of a national literature

Schoolcraft had great hopes for *Algic Researches*. The two-volume collection of tales was offered as the first series of an extended project. The full title of the work is *Algic Researches, Comprising Inquiries concerning the*

Mental Characteristics of the North American Indians, First Series: Indian Tales and Legends. In an introduction to volume I, Schoolcraft announces his plan to publish additional works on Indian "hieroglyphics, music, and poetry; and the grammatical structure of the languages, their principles of combination, and the actual state of their vocabulary" (1992 [1839] I: 9), all in the service of illuminating the mental characteristics of the Indians. This raises a significant point with regard to dimensions of contextualization in *Algic Researches*, namely, Schoolcraft's orientation to a public. Indeed, his outline of his plan for the extended project of which the narrative collection was the first part, makes clear Schoolcraft's need to *identify* – even to *create* – a public for his work. "At what time the remaining portions will appear," he writes, "will depend upon the interest manifested by the public in the subject" (1992 [1839] I: 9). "Public," here, it is important to point out, means in effect *market*; *Algic Researches* makes the Indian narratives into a commodity.

One of the reasons that Schoolcraft did not go forward with the extended project of *Algic Researches* is his disappointment in the failure of the first series to achieve commercial success. Although the collection received critical praise, it failed to sell well enough to recoup production expenses. Schoolcraft's journal makes repeated reference to his frustrations concerning the commercial viability of his work and his disappointment at the lack of interest in his project on the part of publishers and booksellers (1851a: 631, 697, 703). After *Algic Researches*, Schoolcraft did not publish another collection of Indian tales until 1856, when he attempted to cash in on the popularity of Longfellow's *Hiawatha* by issuing a selection of tales from *Algic Researches* and other sources under the title *The Myth of Hiawatha* (of which more later).

In any event, as noted, the two volumes of Indian tales and legends are the only ones of the projected *Algic Researches* to appear. While the broader orientation towards mental characteristics certainly had a shaping influence on the collection of narratives, the narrative volumes orient the materials in a more literary direction. We may note, for example, the literary thrust of the dedication of the collection to Lieutenant Colonel Henry Whiting. Whiting was the author of long narrative poems on Indian subjects, including *Ontwa, The Son of the Forest* (composed in 1822) and *Sannillac* (composed in 1831), the latter containing notes by Schoolcraft. The opening of the dedication is as follows:

Sir,
The position taken by you in favor of the literary susceptibilities of the Indian character, and your tasteful and meritorious attempts in introducing their manners and customs, in the shape of poetic fiction, has directed my thoughts to you in submitting my collection of their oral fictions to the press. (1992 [1839] I: v)

And later in the dedication, Schoolcraft appeals to his "ties of literary sympathy" with Whiting (1992 [1839] I: vi). What is asserted here, then, is the susceptibility of the Indian tales to serve as resources for the development of an American national literature, a potential subsequently realized more notably and successfully by Longfellow in *The Song of Hiawatha* in 1855 (see also Dippie 1982: 16–17).

Matters of literary sensibility are writ large, of course, in considerations of Longfellow's recontextualization of the Indian tales provided by Schoolcraft. Longfellow's debt to Schoolcraft has been the subject of extensive scholarly treatment, and to recapitulate the matter here would lead us away from the focus of this chapter. Suffice it to say that the story of Gitche-gausiné, which we discussed earlier, finds a place in Canto XIX, The Ghosts, of *The Song of Hiawatha*:

Do not lay such heavy burdens
  In the graves of those you bury,
  Not such weight of furs and wampum,
  Not such weight of pots and kettles,
  For the spirits faint beneath them.
  Only give them food to carry,
  Only give them fire to light them.

(Longfellow 1992 (1855): 140)

Here, in Longfellow's "Indian Edda," as he called his poem (1992 [1839]: 161), Gitche-gausiné's account of his dream vision is set to the meter of the *Kalevala*, the Finnish national folk epic, in creating a multiply internationalizing blend of literary resources that proved enormously popular in the United States, Britain, and on the continent (Moyne 1963). Indeed, popular conceptions of Native American folklore have been shaped much more during the past century and a half by Longfellow's literary transmogrifications of Schoolcraft's published materials in *The Song of Hiawatha* than by *Algic Researches*. As Stith Thompson observed in his early folkloristic critique (which itself preserves the savage/civilized dichotomy that shaped Schoolcraft's social and political ideology):

To the world of letters the legend of Hiawatha connotes Longfellow, without whose popular treatment it would be as little known as the adventures of Coyote or Raven, or a dozen other culture heroes of the Red Men. . . . Longfellow's poem is the only form in which the American Indian legend has reached the great mass of civilized men. (1922: 128)

Schoolcraft himself saw Longfellow's poem clearly in national and international terms. In a letter acknowledging a copy of *The Song of Hiawatha* sent to him by the author, Schoolcraft wrote that "Its appearance from the American press constitutes, in my opinion, a period in our imaginative literature which cannot but be regarded as a progressive feature" (Schoolcraft 1991: 316). He goes on to say that "by exhibiting these fresh tableaux of Indian life you have laid the reading world under great obligations" (Schoolcraft 1991: 317). As mentioned earlier, Schoolcraft capitalized on the popularity of Longfellow's *The Song of Hiawatha* by publishing a collection tales under the title *The Myth of Hiawatha* (1856). This work he dedicated to Longfellow, lauding the poet in these terms:

you have demonstrated, by this pleasing series of pictures of Indian life, sentiment, and invention, that the theme of the native lore reveals one of the true sources of our literary independence. Greece and Rome, England and Italy, have so long furnished, if they have not exhausted, the field of poetic culture, that it is, at least, refreshing to find both in theme and metre, something new. (Schoolcraft 1856: iv)

In a statement strongly reminiscent of Blair's framing of Macpherson's Ossian, Schoolcraft proclaims "native lore" as a source of American national literary independence within the arena of international poetic culture. The new nation now has a new basis for a new literature, fit to stand with that of Greece and Rome, England and Italy, full of the vigor that has been exhausted in the old world.

It is instructive to observe in this light the way in which Schoolcraft establishes the availability of this literary resource for commercial and national exploitation. In a section of "Preliminary Observations on the Tales," Schoolcraft poses the question of why the discovery of "oral imaginative lore" among the Indians should not have been made until the first quarter of the nineteenth century (1992 [1839] I: 31). His answer is telling: relations between the Indians and Europeans up to that point were antagonistic, defined largely by engagements of violence that were not at all conducive to the discovery of the qualities of the Indian mind, least of all in regard to artistic sensibilities. It was only when the "contest for supremacy" (1992 [1839] I: 36) had been decided, and the Indians conquered, that their tales and legends became accessible to outsiders. The point was implicit in *Travels*, the dedication of which celebrates Governor Cass for "carrying the national flag over wastes and morasses unvisited before"; it is this territorial expansion that in turn allows for "the dominion of science" to be extended over the Mississippi Valley (1975 [1825]: iv) and for the observations of places, natural resources, and Indian culture – including "Some Observations and Translations Attesting the Existence of Imaginative Tales, and Oral Poetry Among the Chippewas" – that are presented in the book. Now, in *Algic Researches*, Schoolcraft makes explicit that Indian lore became a literary resource only in the aftermath of conquest. The parallels with Ossian are striking. Just as the claim to the poetic resources of Highland Scotland can be asserted most confidently and realized most successfully only after resistance is suppressed, just as the Highlanders can be symbolically transformed from savage to sublime only when they have been conclusively subjugated, just as the Gaelic culture and literature of the Highlands can serve as a resource for national aggrandizement only when it is conclusively relegated to a disappearing past, so too with the Native Americans. In both cases, the words of Others are the spoils of war.

Simultaneous with the nascent nationalism suggested in *Algic Researches*, there is an assimilation of the Indians to the internationalizing discourse of comparative philology (1992 [1839] I: 33) and comparative mythology. Schoolcraft's linguistic researches were increasingly informed by and oriented towards the developing science of philology, and even while he lamented his lack of ready access to scholarly resources at his isolated post on the frontier, he did his best to remain *au courant* with the work of philologists such as Schlegel and established collegial relations with scholars such as Duponceau and Gallatin. *Algic Researches* displays some of his efforts to locate his own work within that scholarly context. The very term "Algic" is Schoolcraft's label for what came to be called the Algonquian stock, and the collection of tales included narratives not only from the Ojibwe but from other related tribes as well. The Algic languages are distinguished from the Ostic (Iroquoian), toward "a general philological classification" (1992 [1839] I: 12–13). Schoolcraft does not venture in *Algic Researches* to correlate these linguistic stocks with mythological repertoires, tending rather to treat Indian mythology in more general terms, observing that "they appear to be of a homogeneous and vernacular origin. There are distinctive tribal traits, but the general features coincide" (1992 [1839] I: 40). He does, however, offer certain international comparisons, relating both to language and mythology, such as "Nor does there appear to be, in either language or religion, anything approximating either to the Scandinavian or to the Hindoo races. With a language of a strongly Semitic cast, they appear to have retained leading principles of syntax where the lexicography itself has changed" (1992 [1839] I: 25). Or, with regard to mythology, Schoolcraft identifies the Algonquian Manabozho as "the Indian Hercules, Samson, or Proteus" (1992 [1839] I: 53), and in so doing draws the Indian tales into world mythology.

The national and international resonances of Native American tales figure prominently as well in Schoolcraft's final collection of tales, derived largely from *Algic Researches*, but entitled *The Myth of Hiawatha*, in the hope of capitalizing on the popularity of Longfellow's *The Song of Hiawatha*, published in the preceding year and inspired in significant part by Schoolcraft's publications of Indian lore. Here, more than thirty years after Schoolcraft first brought his discovery of Indian tales before the public, we find a drawing together of all of the principal themes and concerns that framed his career-long engagement with Native American oral narrative. Schoolcraft states emphatically at the very beginning of the preface what he considers to be the essential significance of these narrative materials:

It is this: they are versions of oral relations from the lips of the Indians, and are transcripts of the thought and invention of the aboriginal mind. As such, they furnish illustrations of Indian character and opinions on subjects which the ever-cautious and suspicious minds of this people have, heretofore, concealed. (1856: vii)

We recognize, first of all, in these lines Schoolcraft's characteristic rhetoric of immediacy. The tales are drawn from the lips of the Indians, direct from the source, a warrant of their authenticity. They offer direct access to the aboriginal mind. A little later, Schoolcraft goes on to assert that "The very language of the man is employed, and his vocabulary is not enlarged by words and phrases foreign to it" (1856: viii), notwithstanding all the language-oriented repairs that Schoolcraft had emphasized in earlier statements. This aura of immediacy and authenticity provides a protective cover, in turn, for those processes of mediation by which the tales come before the reader. They are not, after all, the oral relations from the lips of the Indians, but *versions* of them, *transcripts* of the Indian mind – in English. But the acknowledgment of mediation can itself become a claim to authority and authenticity:

To make these collections . . . the leisure hours of many seasons, passed in an official capacity in the solitude of the wilderness far away from society, have been employed, with the study of the languages, and with the very best interpreters. They have been carefully translated, written, and rewritten, to obtain their true spirit and meaning, expunging passages, where it was necessary to avoid tediousness of narration, triviality of circumstance, tautologies, gross incongruities, and vulgarities; but adding no incident and drawing no conclusion, which the verbal narration did not imperatively require or sanction. (1856: viii–ix)

Schoolcraft has been there, out in the wilderness with the Indians in an official capacity; he has studied their language; he has had recourse to the very best interpreters. These assurances notwithstanding, the intertextual gaps we have noted in earlier passages are here widened still further. Note, for example, that this passage acknowledges a still greater degree of editorial intervention than the earlier statements of textual practice we have considered, in the writing and *re*writing of the texts and in the addition of incidents and conclusions, albeit ones that are required or sanctioned by the verbal narration. Significantly, the "true spirit and meaning" of the tales, "the thought and invention of the aboriginal mind," are not "preserved," as before, but *obtained*, brought out, and in part *created* by Schoolcraft's own editorial work in repairing the literary deficiencies of "tediousness of narration, triviality of circumstances, tautologies, gross incongruities, and vulgarities." Accuracy and clarity of content must be won back from literarily flawed narration, and Schoolcraft's rhetoric is aimed at getting the reader to acknowledge his authority to do so.

Now, although Schoolcraft foregrounds the ethnological significance of the Indian myths and legends as keys to the hitherto concealed secrets of the Indian mind, the literary nature of the texts is also clearly salient. Schoolcraft acknowledges that *The Myth of Hiawatha* was published to capitalize on the success of *The Song of Hiawatha* (1856: xxi), and the work, as we have noted, is dedicated to Longfellow. If Longfellow could use Schoolcraft's native tales as a resource for the creation of an American national literature within the context of world literature, Schoolcraft himself could hope to gain the appreciative literary audience for the original source materials and financial success for himself that *Algic Researches* had failed to attract, still to his evident chagrin (1856: x, xxi). *The Myth of Hiawatha*, then, was an opportunity to offer the tales to the public "in a revised, and, it is believed, a more terse, condensed, and acceptable form, both in a literary and a business garb" (1856: xi). The revisions occasioned by this joint consideration of literature and business involved the removal of the verse materials – poetic renditions of the songs and chants from the tales and other poetry inspired by "aboriginal ideas" – to the end of the volume, leaving the narrative prose unencumbered.

In the closing passages of the Introduction to *The Myth of Hiawatha*, Schoolcraft muses on the implications of his lifelong effort to cast light on the "mental traits" of the Indians through their tales. Here, at the end of his career, he returns once again to his conviction that the existence of storytelling among the Indians is a testament to their humanity. At the same time, however, the narratives reveal the fatal flaws in the Indians' character, the reasons that "they have not adopted our industry and Christianity, and stoutly resisted civilization, in all its phases" (1856: xxi–xxii). They reveal "that it is fear that makes him suspicious, and ignorance superstitious; that he is himself the dupe of an artful forest priesthood; and that his cruelty and sanguinary fury are the effects of false notions of fame, honor, and glory" (1856: xxii). Schoolcraft acknowledges that the Indians' encounters with the civilizing force of American expansion have been painful: "If one century has kicked the Indian in America harder than another, it is because the kicks of labor, art, and knowledge are always the hardest, and in precise proportion to the contiguity of the object" (1856: xxii). But he never doubts that such kicks are necessary, and he is fully prepared for the ultimate outcome he foresees: extinction. In the face of this eventuality, then, the tales that he has recorded will stand as memorials to the qualities "worthy of remembrance," virtues such as "stoicism" in the face of "hunger and want," "devotion," and "dignity," that may qualify – though not displace – the negative elements that mark the Indian for extinction:

> The man, it may be, shall pass away from the earth, but these tributes to the best feelings of the heart will remain, while these simple tales and legendary creations constitute a new point of character by which he should be judged. They are, at least, calculated to modify our views of the man, who is not always a savage, not always a fiend. (1856: xxiii–xxiv)

Thus, where the Grimms labored to construct the peasant classes as custodians of the German national patrimony of folk poetry while hardening the structures of inequality that licensed the bourgeois appropriation of their discourse in the interests of the emergent nation-state, Schoolcraft constructed a more extreme scenario for the Native American sources of the corpus of tales that he assembled. Having appropriated the Indian tales for the expanding United States by right of conquest, having seen them made over with notable success into resources for a nascent national literature, he was ready to have the people themselves "pass away from the earth," leaving the tales for a posterity not their own.

Conclusion

Notwithstanding his attempt to ride the coat-tails of Longfellow's literary success and his own undeniable interest in the belletristic possibilities of his Indian tales, it was Schoolcraft's lifelong conviction that the chief value of his collections lay in the "insight they give into the dark cave of the Indian mind." Quite consistently, from 1822 onward, he framed his tales in mentalistic terms, describing Indian storytelling as a "mental trait," and the tales themselves as repositories of "belief, dogmas, and opinion," illustrating the "workings of his [the Indian's] mind."

For Schoolcraft, stationed out on the fringes of European learning, Indian storytelling and the light it shed on the native mind were surprising discoveries, but in the larger context of the intellectual history we have traced in these pages, his turn to the words of Others as a vantage-point in the primitive mind was no new thing. Indeed, all of the intellectual currents we have considered thus far framed discursive forms at least in part in epistemological terms and used discursive contrasts as a basis for constructing the epochal juncture that separated the primitive or ancient past from the modern present.

There were, however, significant differences of perspective and focus in the conceptualization of these forms and contrasts, as between what we have identified as the antiquarian and the philological orientations. The antiquarian line of inquiry was primarily cognitive in its frame of reference, oriented towards distinguishing modes of thought and their shaping effect on social practice, that is towards belief and custom and their discursive expression and circulation. The philological enterprise, by contrast, was primarily hermeneutic, motivated by a concern with the interpretive accessibility or intelligibility of ancient literary texts. More-over, the antiquarian orientation, as we have endeavored to show, was aligned most closely with the epistemology of Baconian Natural His-tory and Enlightenment rationalism, while the philological orientation represented a later inflection of Renaissance humanism and the quest for literary models that grounded literary form and meaning in national character.

Clearly, the orientations we have distinguished as antiquarian and philological were not at all mutually exclusive or incompatible, as wit-ness, for example, the scientific philology that enabled Lowth's discov-ery of canonical parallelism, the combined antiquarian and philological defense that Blair mounted in support of the authenticity of Macpher-son's Ossian, or the twin appeals to science and literature that motivated the Grimms' ambitious project. Thus, Schoolcraft's dual conception of Ojibwe narratives as oral literature amenable to belletristic presentation and as ethnological data calling for scientific investigation had ample precedent.

For Schoolcraft's predecessors, the blending, in various measures, of scientific and literary orientations to ancient texts, conceived simultane-ously as expressions of mind and as works of literature, occasioned little apparent strain. At the same time that these earlier thinkers were at pains to construct a clear disjunction between the old and the modern eras and to specify the contrastive modes of discourse that marked the gap that separated the two historical periods, the historical schemas they produced did as much to mediate between epochs and to affirm the commensu-rability of cultural formations across those very gaps as they did to keep them distinct: the concept of the antiquity, the process of tradition, the perspective of cultural relativism. This is only to corroborate Latour's insistence that "the two sets of practices" – purification and mediation – "have always already been at work" throughout the "modern" era (1993: 11).

One of the many reasons that make Schoolcraft worthy of attention, by contrast, is that we can see in his lifelong engagement with Indian tales, and especially in his efforts to prepare them for presentation to a wider public, some of the ways in which the ties of mediation that sustained the work of his intellectual predecessors came under strain in the mid-nineteenth century. Schoolcraft's least difficult course in rendering his texts for publication, it appears, was to foreground the contents of the tales as ethnological data, expressions of the native mind. In this presentational – and representational – mode, he could bracket the problems of translation, both linguistic and poetic, and rely upon the unadorned expository prose of scientific report. The problem, though, was that his linguistic knowledge and literary sensibilities made such formal problems difficult to ignore. Recognizing the desirability of "adherence to the original language and expressions" and the importance of the interrelationships linking "The style of narration, the cast of invention, and the theory of thinking," Schoolcraft could not, ultimately, rest content with editorial practices that did not take these formal matters into account in relation to modes of thought. But to remain faithful to Ojibwe grammar and narrative poetics, he feared, would only bring other problems to the fore, yielding texts that would jar the literary expectations and violate the tastes of the broader literary public he hoped to attract.

This problem, of course, could be remedied by editorial intervention, reworking the texts to bring them into line with the literary standards of the day. The difficulty here, however, was that while literary audiences might not be concerned with the distancing effects such editorial mediation would create between the Ojibwe originals and the English renditions – after all, by the standards of the day, literature *demanded* cultivation and refinement – to intervene in this manner is to compromise the immediacy and transparency to the phenomena under observation that are essential to good science.

To be sure, there is ample evidence in Schoolcraft's writings of a relatively undisciplined intellect, and the magnum opus he produced at the end of his career, the six-volume *Historical and Statistical Information Regarding... the Indian Tribes of the United States* (1851–57), is a notorious hotchpotch of disorganized materials, uncritically assembled and confusingly presented. It would be a mistake, however, to write off Schoolcraft's inability to reconcile his scientific and literary agendas as a reflection of his own intellectual shortcomings or as driven by the practical exigencies of earning a living by his writing in the years following his dismissal as Indian Agent in 1841. Whatever roles these factors may have played in shaping Schoolcraft's textual practices, we would argue, the difficulty he experienced in rendering his tales indexes a point at which a broader split between literature and science, along the epistemological and discursive fault-line opened by Bacon and Locke, became too wide to span. Certainly, by the last decade of Schoolcraft's life and career, the split was irreversible. The hugely favorable critical and commercial reception of Longfellow's *Hiawatha*, following its publication in 1855, marked decisively the path of success for literary recontextualizations of Indian lore: romantic, sentimental, idealized renderings of Indian themes, simulations of a national mythology for the commercial press. At the same time, the foundations of an institutionalized and disciplined scientific anthropology, in which the study of languages and texts figured prominently, were inscribed in the emergent charter of the newly founded national museum, the Smithsonian Institution.

Indeed, Schoolcraft himself submitted in an address to the very first meeting of the Smithsonian Institution Board of Regents a "Plan for the Investigation of American Ethnology," filled with rhetorical appeals to the standards and methods of scientific inquiry – "exact observation and description," a viewing of "the facts under lights of induction and historical analysis" – and noteworthy for its use of the term "ethnography," presumably for the "duty of observation in the field" that he includes among the key methods of this fledgling science (1886 [1846]: 908, 909, , 913). Schoolcraft's plan, as we would expect, included attention to "oral tales and legends" and "mythology" as manifestations of "intellectual existence" (1886 [1846]: 911).

There was an element of self-interest in Schoolcraft's appeal, as always, insofar as he hoped to be employed by the Smithsonian to implement the plan he proposed. In this, he was unsuccessful, but the Smithsonian did incorporate "the new and interesting department of knowledge called ethnology" into its mission (Henry 1854 [1847]: 123; 1855: 11). The Secretary of the Institution, Joseph Henry, even identified it as "a sacred duty which this country owes to the civilized world to collect everything relative to the history, the manners and customs, their physical peculiarities, and, in short, all that may tend to illustrate the character and history of the original inhabitants of North America" (1858: 36). It is noteworthy that in charting the place of ethnology in the Smithsonian, Henry identified it as a field "in the cultivation of which lovers of literature and science are equally interested" (1854: 11), indicating that the two sets of interests had not fully diverged. But the institutionalization of the scientific study of the languages and literatures of Others in the Smithsonian provided a foundation from which the fuller divergence of the scientific from the belletristic interest in "oral literature" could be promoted. By the end of the nineteenth century, museums and academic departments were claiming authority over the production, circulation, and interpretation of authentic and authoritative texts. While experimentation with metadiscursive practices continued, it took place more and more in institutional contexts and under the control of specialists. We turn, in Chapter 8, to the most influential force at the turn of the century in creating a canon of Native American texts and using it to create an academic discipline that was also an important player in shaping conceptions of race and culture in the public sphere, Franz Boas.

The foundation of all future researches: Franz Boas's cosmopolitan charter for anthropology

Social life in *fin-de-siècle* America placed many social scientists and social thinkers in an intellectual and political bind. They believed, on the one hand, in the power of modernity to produce a more enlightened and rational world, one in which freedom and democracy dominated. On the other hand, however, they were deeply concerned with the effects of modernity and industrial capitalism on contemporary society (see Ross 1991). Industrialization was often seen as having disrupted close-knit communities and pressed workers into impoverished urban quarters. The Jim Crow era was reversing the gains made by African Americans during Reconstruction. Crass exploitation of workers, especially immigrants and African Americans, elicited concerns that went beyond a politics of moral sentiment – it raised the specter of class warfare and socialist revolution. Some social scientists came to the conclusion that it was necessary to think beyond the nation-state and actually existing structures of inequality, and cosmopolitan imaginaries were woven into the theoretical foundations laid by a number of influential figures.

One of the most important of these was Franz Boas, a German immigrant of Jewish descent. George Stocking (1968: 149) points to the roots of Boas's liberalism in the lasting impact of the ideals of the Revolution of 1848 on many German intellectuals. Personal, scientific, and political goals merged in the form of a quest for truth that would ideally free humanity from the shackles of dogma. The humanistic impulse to fight for equality of opportunity for all went hand in hand, Stocking notes, with a commitment to progress, the infusion of science and rationality into social life, and a commitment to act as "a member of humanity as a whole" rather than as a national subject (Stocking 1968: 149). As Julia Liss (1990) suggests, Boas found in New York an urban milieu in which cosmopolitanism was both a dominant social fact and a central element of individual and collective imaginations. Boas the public intellectual attempted to shape the nature of New York cosmopolitanism and to extend its impact on social and political life in the United States.

Boas the anthropologist sought to identify what he saw as the universal resistance that cosmopolitanism encounters. In claiming for anthropology the status of an obligatory passage point (see Latour 1988) between the natural provincialism of human communities and the rational cosmopolitanism that he deemed necessary for freedom, democracy, peace, and the full development of each individual, Boas sought to join the two projects – in a way that would thrust Boasian anthropology into the scholarly and public limelight.[1]

In the academic realm, he identified evolutionism as a faux-science that sought to confer academic authority on provincialism and racism. In championing the notion that cultural patterns acquired in childhood were uniquely capable of explaining difference, Boas fashioned culture into a weapon for defeating evolutionism and transforming public policy. Politically progressive for his time, Boas attempted to redefine modernity by creating a world that would be free from racism, xenophobia, imperialism, and colonialism. Serving as a spokesperson for democracy and social justice, Boas tried to cast anthropology as a key site for promoting them. Speaking as a public intellectual, Boas argued that "no amount of eugenic selection will overcome those social conditions that have raised a poverty- and disease-stricken proletariat – which will be reborn from even the best stock, so long as the social conditions persist that remorselessly push human beings into helpless and hopeless misery" (1962: 118). Pointing to the tremendous gap between rich and poor, Boas argued that a truly democratic society would have to undertake "a program of justice" for poor children that would include huge expenditures in clothing, housing, and food in order to overcome the physiological effects of poverty in thwarting education (1945: 184, 193). At the same time that he embraced many goals articulated by socialist movements, Boas worried about "conflicts between the inertia of conservative tradition and the radicalism which has no respect for the past but attempts to reconstruct the future on the basis of rational considerations intended to further its ideals" (1962: 136–7). Boas sought to use the concept of culture in placing anthropology as a key site for building a third way of charting the future, a regime of knowledge that could help circumvent racism, fascism, and international conflict.

---

[1] We would like to make it clear from the outset that we are arguing specifically about anthropology in the United States. The concept of culture has not been central to the development of, for example, British or French anthropology. Interestingly, a major difference might seem to lie in the central role of linguistic work in shaping foundational concepts of US but not British or French anthropologies. We use the term "American anthropology" to refer to what is taking place in the United States, with apologies to our Canadian and Latin American colleagues.

Boas did not, however, celebrate culture; indeed, it was, for him, largely negative, an obstacle to the achievement of a more rational and cosmopolitan world. We have argued in previous chapters that constructions of language and tradition – along with practices for purifying and hybridizing them – crucially shaped modernist projects. Boas's concept of culture was built, we suggest, on the way he constructed language and tradition and the problematic way he placed them in relationship to modernity. This chapter focuses on the complex juxtaposition of Lockean and Herderian conceptions of language and tradition in Boas's culture theory and his production of a scientific textuality for representing culture. Sorting out these issues is, we claim, crucial for imagining more fruitful positions not only on the status of Boas's contribution but on the politics of culture. We suggest here that some of the lingering problems with anthropological conceptions of culture, which have caused tremendous debate within the discipline and beyond in recent years, are tied to the problematic constructions of language and tradition he embedded in culture and this negative relationship between culture and cosmopolitanism.

Boas's view of language

Dell Hymes and George Stocking have argued that it was not his academic training but the encounter with Native Americans that interested Boas in linguistics. He met Heyman Steinthal, the influential follower of Alexander von Humboldt, during the course of his studies in Germany (see Stocking 1992: 64; Hymes 1983: 143–44). Boas told Roman Jakobson (1944: 188), however, that he regretted having failed to attend any of Steinthal's lectures. Boas did not study Indo-European comparative and historical linguistics, and he did not deem it to be an appropriate framework for analyzing Native American languages. Michael Silverstein (1979) suggests that Boas's rhetorical strategy in his discussions of language was largely negative, constructing language by way of demonstrating the failure of Indo-European categories as points of reference. He challenged a prime conceit of Euro-American elites in arguing that the grammatical subtleties of many "primitive languages" can make that epitome of linguistic precision and elegance, Latin, "seem crude." Adopting this form of negative critique – and, as we will see, his deep commitment to the production of ethnographic texts – wrote its categories and rhetorical strategies deeply into Boas's anthropological program.

Beyond providing the clearest challenge to evolutionary schemas, linguistics afforded Boas a means of mapping the core and the boundaries of a broader "ethnological" inquiry. He suggested that linguistics was

of "practical" significance for anthropology in providing a means of circumventing the distorting influence of lingua francas, translators, and the
mediation of "intelligent natives" who embed their theories of culture –
and their perceptions of what the scientist wants to hear – in the way they
cross cultural and linguistic borders. Boas also privileged the "theoretical"
contribution that linguistics can make to ethnology. Language occupied
a pivotal place in Boas's efforts to demonstrate both that human mental
processes were fundamentally the same everywhere and that individual
languages and cultures shaped thought in unique ways; it thus enabled
Boas to present a broad outline of human universals and specificities – a
model of culture.

By editing the *Handbook of American Indian Languages* (1911), Boas
attempted to shape how language would be perceived through an anthropological lens, what role it would play in the discipline, and how
researchers would study Native American languages and produce texts.
His famous Introduction laid out this theoretical charter. Boas pressed
a number of his students into contributing chapters and following the
blueprint he imposed – which called for the inclusion of phonetic, grammatical, and lexical analysis as well as text collections. Notably, Sapir's
(1922) more extensive grammar of Takelma was published only in the
second volume, which appeared eleven years later. Sapir's structural and
humanistic view of linguistics made him reluctant to accept Boas's more
atomistic approach to grammatical categories.[2]

A fascinating and productive tension shapes the influence of Boas's
view of language on the way he constructed culture. On the one hand,
a crucial element of his attack on racism was the notion that language,
culture, and race do not form a single package but rather that each element pursues a different historical trajectory. Here Boas took on Herder
directly. Recall that language constituted *das Volk* in two ways for Herder.
On the one hand, forming a nation entailed sharing a common language,
history, religion, literature, folklore, and customs; language was thus one
key element in a list of essential attributes. At the same time, however,
language bore a privileged relationship to *das Volk*: "'Has a nationality,' a
character in one of Herder's dramas asks, 'anything more precious than
the language of its fathers? In this language dwell its whole world of tradition, history, religion and principles of life, its whole heart and soul'"
(Herder, *SW* 17: 58, quoted in Ergang 1966: 149–50). As we shall see,
Boas's position on this second manner of characterizing language was
complex. But a central element of his culture theory involved rejection
of the first proposition. Early in the pages of the Introduction to the

---

[2] See Darnell (1990, 1998), Hymes (1983), and Stocking (1992).

Handbook, Boas tore the logical form of Herder's organic formula apart piece by piece. Suggesting that linguistic, biological, and cultural units had never coincided, he adduced examples of changes in language and culture without shifts in "physical type," permanence of language in the midst of changes of physical type, and changes of culture in the face of biological and linguistic stability. Boas thus adopted a position much more closely aligned with the one pioneered by Locke: language is a distinct and separate social and epistemological domain. He suggested that his goal is to obtain "a clear understanding of the relationship of the languages, no matter by whom they may be spoken" (1911: 15). Limiting the discussion to "articulate speech; that is, to communication by means of groups of sounds produced by the articulating organs" (1911: 15), Boas focused on phonetics, words, and grammatical categories and processes.

Nevertheless, it is precisely the initial separation of language and culture that enables Boas to use constructions of language in imagining culture. This question has often been oversimplified as "the linguistic analogy" or "the linguistic relativity hypothesis." What is at stake here is more than a simple analogy or some sort of simplistic idea that linguistic categories determined culture (a position that neither Boas nor his students adopted); rather constructions of language and linguistics shaped Boas's imaginings of culture in a range of crucial ways. It is, in short, the very act of purifying categories of language and culture as separate domains that enabled Boas to embed linguistic ideologies in the way he imagined culture. We will lay out eight dimensions of this hybridization process here, reserving a ninth facet for later discussion.

1. Languages and cultures do not develop along simple, unilinear evolutionary sequences. In seeking to undermine evolutionist arguments for the increasing sophistication of all human institutions in a linear progression from primitive to civilized, Boas argued that "It is perhaps easiest to make this clear by the example of language, which in many respects is one of the most important evidences of the history of human development" (1965: 160). Venturing forth with a broad generalization regarding linguistic change, Boas argued that language seems to reverse the evolutionists' historical cartography, moving, on the whole, from more complex to simpler forms. In a host of works, including his publications on art (1927, 1940a), Boas extended this argument to cultural forms. As we shall see, the rejection of evolutionism did not entail the conviction that no universal framework for comparison could be discerned; indeed, as Hill and Mannheim (1992) point out, accounts of Boasian "relativism" fail to appreciate that he saw cultural and linguistic particulars as systematically related to universals.

2. *All humans have language and culture, but all languages and cultures are unique.* For Boas, language and culture constitute what is uniquely and fundamentally human. He argues that animals also have patterned ways of relating to nature and to each other. What is distinctively human is variability – behavior is learned through the internalization of "local tradition" rather than determined by environmental conditions or instinct (1965: 152). Boas asserted that "Language is also a trait common to all mankind, and one that must have its roots in earliest times" (1965: 156). In the Introduction to the *Handbook* and elsewhere, Boas argued that each language is distinct on phonological, lexical, and grammatical grounds. Thus the scientific study of what is most characteristically human lies not in discovering biological, cultural, or linguistic universals alone but in the empirical study of variability. Linguistics provided a privileged model for locating and comparing difference, in that it seemed to be the most universal – all societies possessed the ability to communicate through language – and the most variable at the same time, given the range of linguistic diversity. The influence of Herder would seem to be evident here, in his promotion of the idea that everyone has a national tradition and that every national tradition is different.

3. *Membership in linguistic and cultural communities involves the sharing of modes of classification.* One of the most crucial and widely explored dimensions of the linguistic analogy pertains to Boas's emphasis on the centrality of categories in social life. He suggested that "our whole sense experience is classified according to linguistic principles and our thought is deeply influenced by the classification of our experience" (1962: 54). The centrality of classification for Boas follows from a fundamental divergence between experience and the means available to encode it linguistically: "Since the total range of personal experience which language serves to express is infinitely varied and its whole scope must be expressed by a limited number of word-stems, an extended classification of experiences must necessarily underlie all articulate speech" (1965: 189). Cultural categories channel social life and relations with the natural environment in particular customary or traditional ways. Boas moves in *The Mind of Primitive Man* from acoustic articulations to the way that lexical and grammatical units categorize unique sense impressions and emotional states (1965: 189). Arguing that "In various cultures these classifications may be founded on fundamentally distinct principles," he uses color perception, food categories, the terminology of consanguinity and affinity, his famous Eskimo words for water and snow, and ways of perceiving illness and nature as examples (1965: 190–92). Both Locke and Herder saw language as central to the creation and human communities; Boas believed himself

to have pinpointed the source of this community-building capacity in the categories that shape social experience.

4. The principle of selectivity in languages and cultures. A crucial dimension of Boas's attack on ethnocentrism involved the principle of selection. He argued that "If in a language the number of articulations were unlimited the necessary accuracy of movements needed for rapid speech and the quick recognition of sound complexes would probably never develop" (1965: 188). Languages must select a limited number of "movements of articulation" from the vast range of possibilities, and the possibilities for combining them must be restricted as well (1965: 189). The question is not just one of which elements are chosen – each phonetic element is patterned in ways that contrast substantially with how similar sounds are embedded in other languages (1911: 18–19). Each culture similarly represented a unique selection from the vast range of human possibilities and a particular type of "structure" that links them (1965: 149).[3]

5. The operation of categories is automatized and unconscious. Constant repetitions of this limited number of articulations "bring it about that these accurate adjustments become automatic," resulting in firm associations between articulations and their corresponding sounds (1965: 189), which are utilized "automatically and without reflection at any given moment" (1911: 25). This quality limits speakers' ability to represent their own language: "the use of language is automatic, so that before the development of a science of language the fundamental ideas never rise into consciousness" (1965: 192–93). Language was thus free from the "secondary explanations" – distortions of the historical basis of the development of categories through rationalization – that so plagued the study of culture. Herein lies an important basis for advancing what Stocking (1968) calls Boas's displacement of biological or racial determinism by cultural determinism; the very possibility of communication and social order was based on surrender to categories over which individuals lack both control and awareness.

In the case of cultural forms, the constant repetition of actions also increases their emotional hold. Violations of accepted behavior and the need to transmit customs to children, who often misbehave or question the basis of accepted norms, create a need for explanations. Boas thus argued that adults generate secondary explanations that spring from the context

---

[3] Note that this trope was replayed prominently in Ruth Benedict's *Patterns of Culture*. After stating the principle of selectivity in phonology, she suggested that "In culture too we must imagine a great arc" of possibilities; a culture would be "unintelligible" if it failed to make quite limited selections from among them (1934: 24).

in which cultural forms are lodged in society at that moment, thereby obscuring their historical basis. Language provided a privileged site in which to study categories and their operation in that cultural data contrastively tend to get mixed up with secondary explanations. As Stocking (1968: 232) notes, these notions of unconscious patterns and secondary explanations "implied a conception of man not as a *rational* so much as a *rationalizing* being."

6. *The constant danger of distortion in cross-cultural research.* Particularly in his famous article "On Alternating Sounds," Boas argued that fieldworkers are not exempt from the distortions that arise when one set of unconscious patterns is projected onto another. He began with experimental evidence that smacked of his earlier work in psychophysics, suggesting that "we learn to pronounce the sounds of our language by long usage" (1889: 48). Other sound patterns are thus misperceived through the process of fitting them into familiar patterns. After reporting his own experiments on perceptions of the length of lines, Boas presented the now familiar argument that color terms shape the perception of color; an individual whose language lacks a term for "green" will perceive some green samples as yellow, others as blue, "the limit of both divisions being doubtful" (1889: 50). Boas asserted, however, that cross-cultural research produces more authoritative examples than conventional psychology.

In a classic move, Boas takes on claims to the effect that "alternating sounds," perceived fluctuations in how particular sounds in Inuit and Native American languages are pronounced, provide "a sign of the primitiveness of the speech in which they are said to occur" (1889: 52). They constitute, he argued, evidence of bad science, not faulty languages. He suggested that "the nationality even of well-trained observers" shapes how they perceive the sounds of a non-Indo-European language, reducing them to phonological patterns with which they are familiar (1889: 51). Moreover, "the first studies of a language may form the strong bias for later researchers" (1889: 52), imbuing the misperception with scientific authority. Boas brilliantly critiqued evolutionism, demoting its central claim regarding the greater simplicity and mutability of "primitive" forms, their presumed status as defective copies of European institutions, into a predictable form of laic distortion. In doing so, he appropriated the scientific authority formerly enjoyed by evolutionists for his own emerging anthropological perspective. Phonetic misperception and the misreading of Native American grammatical categories provided a model for thinking about the way that "the bias of the European observer" (1935: v) could distort the recording and interpretation of cultural material as well.

7. Charting the vast spectrum of human possibility. Boas mapped the vast phonetic spectrum of human possibility on two axes, the location of articulation (where the airstream is obstructed in the mouth and throat) and the manner in which air is impeded. Boas captured the cartography of human possibility for consonants in a single chart (see figure 1, page 264), thereby representing it abstractly, visually, and scientifically. This universal, objective phonetic grid helped transcend nationalistic and scientific biases evident in evolutionary research by locating the Indo-European languages spoken by observers simply as different sets of points on the same grid.

Boas goes on to extend the model of difference he developed for phonetics to words and grammatical patterns. Because cultural phenomena are encoded grammatically, anthropologists could transcend the limits imposed by Euro-American categories by analyzing Native American languages. The closest grammatical equivalent to a universal phonetic grid for Boas lay in what he described as the universal encoding of time, space, and form as well as distinctions between speaker, person addressed, and person spoken. In extending the problem to cultural variability, some of Boas's most interesting examples are evident in his comparisons of stylistic and symbolic dimensions of plastic arts. In his discussion of expressive art, he suggests that "The contents of primitive narrative, poetry and song are as varied as the cultural interests of the singers" (1927: 325).

8. The need for a "purely analytic" method of description and analysis. Boas argued that previous students of Native American languages lacked a rigorous research methodology, and the *Handbook* offered a model for systematic fieldwork and analysis guided by scientific principles. Boas taught his students how texts should be written phonetically, and he argued for "a presentation of the essential traits of the grammar as they would naturally develop if an Eskimo, without any knowledge of any other language, should present the essential notions of his own grammar" (quoted in Stocking 1992: 81). In this "purely analytic" technique, the unconscious categories of language thus became not only the central research object but the central methodological tool as well, thereby avoiding the distorting effects of Indo-European categories.

The goal in exploring customs was similarly to identify the categories that shaped not only how people behaved but how they perceived their actions. Hymes (1983: 28) points out that these categories served not only as tools for discovery and analysis but as "neat qualitative pigeon-holes for ordering ethnological data," both on the page and on the museum shelf (Boas 1974). If texts are based on Native American categories, their organization should iconically capture not only cultural patterns but

	Stops.			Spirants.		Nasals.		Trill.	
	Sonant.	Surd.	Fortis.	Sonant.	Surd.	Sonant.	Surd.	Sonant.	Surd.
Bilabial	b	p	p!	v	f	m	m̥		
Labio-dental				v	f				
Linguo-labial	d	t	t!	ç	¢	n	n̥		
Linguo-dental	d	t	t!	ç	¢	n	n̥		
Dental				j	c				
Lingual—									
Apical	d	t	t!	z	s	n	n̥	r	r̥
Cerebral									
Dorsal—									
Medial	g	k	k!	γ	x̣	ñ	ñ̥	r	ṛ
Velar	g	q	q!	γ̣	x	ṇ̃	ṇ̥̃	ṛ	R
Lateral	ʟ	L	L!	i	ɬ				
Glottal	ε								
Nasal	N								

Semi-vowels y, w: Breath, ʿh. Hiatus'.

Figure 1 Franz Boas's Table of Consonants. From his *Introduction to the Handbook of American Indian Languages* 1911, page 23 (enlarged).

people's implicit understandings of them just as linguistic analyses should reflect native speakers' "essential notions" of their grammar. Conducting research in a "purely analytic" fashion thus enabled anthropologists to bracket their special awareness of the universal framework and the biasing effects of the categories they learned as children and render their texts and analyses authoritative.

In sum, Boas constructed language and culture as separate domains calling for distinct methods, only to hybridize his construction of culture by deeply embedding language ideologies within it. Herein lies a central contradiction in Boas's epistemology. Languages and cultures are historically shaped and constantly changing. Nevertheless, rather than emerging as heterogeneous dimensions of social practices that themselves become objects of scrutiny and contention, languages are constructed as arrangements of sounds, words, and grammatical forms that are neatly stuck in each child's head in a place that is inaccessible to the conscious mind. As Hymes (1983: 25) suggests, this model of language leaves little room for interactive and social dimensions. Early in life, each individual learns one language, and, Boas told us, it is virtually impossible to fully assimilate a second one later in life.

This conservative view of languages and cultures as entities that come one-to-a-customer failed to come to terms with the possibility of living in a linguistically and culturally complex society that provides individuals and communities with multiple allegiances. It is remarkable that Boas's ethnographic success could depend for more than three decades on the multilingual and multicultural abilities of George Hunt, who was raised with overlapping English-Canadian, Tlingit, and Kwakwaka'wakw memberships, without creating a theoretical space for such diversity (see below). It is similarly remarkable that a German immigrant of Jewish ancestry did not recognize travel as fostering critical comparisons of culture and a blurring of borders between them.[4] Boas wrote that the existence of multiple perspectives helped children to think critically and reflexively about their own culture, but he saw the assimilation of immigrants and the disappearance of Native Americans as the natural course of American society. Boas keenly recognized that national languages and their use in legitimizing nationalist projects are recent inventions (1962: 91–2), but he could not see that his own notion of languages and their speakers was similarly constructed and that it erased other perspectives.

Linguistic anthropologists and other practitioners have radically questioned the assumptions that form the conceptual and methodological

---

[4] See James Clifford for a model of culture based on travel, in which "Practices of displacement might seem *constitutive* of cultural meanings rather than their simple transfer or extension" (1997: 3; emphasis in original).

foundations of the "linguistic analogy." Language has come to be seen less as an object that exists prior to and independently of efforts to study it than as an ideological field that shapes academic, social, and political projects. In a number of publications, Michael Silverstein (1979, 1981, 1985) pointed to the language ideologies that shape how people – including linguists – think about and use language. When the frame of reference shifts from the contents of linguistic and cultural models to their ideological production, the idea that anthropologists can discern common linguistic and cultural patterns that are "universally human" fits neatly into what Chakrabarty (2000) calls the "deprovincialization" of Europe, the projection of a particular set of elite categories as valid for all peoples and times. The notion of a universal linguistic framework, as defined by phonetic, lexical, and grammatical commonalities, is based on the idea that language can be neatly separated from that which is non-linguistic, supposedly including culture and society (see Hill and Mannheim 1992). Hymes's (1974) "ethnography of speaking" and Silverstein's "metapragmatics" (1976) point to the ideological work that needs to be done to reduce vast arrays of sign types and ideological representations to the Lockean vision of language as sets of referentially defined signs, that is, stable pairings of forms and referents. Hymes (1980: 55) has suggested that "It is only in our own century, through the decisive work of Boas, Sapir, and other anthropologically oriented linguists . . . that every form of human speech has gained the 'right,' as it were, to contribute on equal footing to the general theory of human language." But, although Boas may have incorporated Native American *content*, he deprovincialized a familiar Euro-American ideology of language.

Recent work in linguistic anthropology and other areas similarly challenges the assumptions that shored up Boas's notion of a "purely analytic" approach to individual languages and cultures. Practitioners have detailed the importance of Herderian assumptions regarding the shaping of each individual and collective identity through a single linguistic and cultural system in creating nation-states and colonial societies and other projects for producing and managing social inequality.[5] Beyond challenging the notion that multilingualism is unusual or pathological, they have explored the contemporary uses of Herderian ideologies in public policies and everyday practices that subordinate or exclude people with multiple linguistic and cultural identifications.[6] Similarly, the ideologies and power relations that underlie the idea that other people's linguistic

---

[5] See Blommaert (1999); Errington (1998); Fabian (1986); Herzfeld (1982, 1987); Irvine and Gal (2000); Mannheim (1991); Urla (1993).

[6] For examples, see Adams and Brink (1990); Hill (1998); Mendoza-Denton (1999); Morgan (1994); Urciuoli (1996); Woolard (1989); Zentella (1997).

and cultural worlds can be penetrated, ordered, and rendered transparent for scholarly audiences has been scrutinized. Briggs (1986, 2002b) and Cicourel (1982) point to the power that interviews afford researchers for constructing discourse in ways that maximize their insertability in academic publications. Nevertheless, these critiques have not succeeded in rooting out the reified models of language that are still woven into the way culture is imagined.

Tradition, anthropology, and the modern subject

Constructions of tradition also played a central role in Boas's development of the notion of culture and the methodology he proposed for documenting and analyzing it. Indeed, as Stocking (1968: 227) astutely observes, it was Boas's equation of tradition and culture that shifted the latter term from its humanistic sense as manifestations of increasing artistic and intellectual sophistication to the central feature of social life for everyone. At the same time that he drew on Herder in characterizing tradition as a basic source of beliefs, practices, and social relations, Boas inherited from Aubrey and Locke the notion that tradition limits progress towards enlightenment and rationality. He accordingly constructed culture as a force that limits individual freedom through the pervasive influence of "the fetters of tradition" (1965: 201). Boas's hybrid construction of tradition and the complex way that he wove it into his model of culture thus deserve careful scrutiny if we are to unravel how this notion both defined and limited Boas's broader modernist and cosmopolitan project.

As was the case with Boas's linguistics, Indo-European scholarship shaped his approach to the study of tradition, even as he rejected many of its basic tenets.[7] For Boas, philology offered both a model of the kinds of data necessary to the study of other cultures and a standard of scholarly adequacy appropriate to such study (1906). He thus accorded the highest priority to the production of linguistically rigorous corpora of native-language texts as the essential basis for cultural study. Not only would such texts constitute the materials to sustain current research, but they would be the chief legacy that anthropologists might provide to future scholars. In pushing anthropologists to learn Native American languages, Boas drew a direct parallel to the deep and rigorous knowledge of languages that informed philological study of classical civilizations: "It

---

[7] The philological cast of Americanist ethnology was established well before Boas. The work of Henry Rowe Schoolcraft had a formative influence (see Chapter 7), and the program established by John Wesley Powell for the Bureau of American Ethnology institutionalized a centrally philological orientation (see Powell 1883; see also Fine 1984; Hinsley 1981; Murray 1983). On Boas and Herder, see Broce (1981) and Bunzl (1996).

would seem to me that the classical archeologist or the classical philologist must always have an indulgent smile when he hears of serious anthropological studies carried on by investigators, who have neither the time, the inclination, nor the training to familiarize themselves with the language of the people whom they study" (1906: 642). Boas suggested by way of analogy that no one would be accepted as a classicist or an historian of the middle ages unless he or she could read the languages of the texts. Here Boas's project of professionalizing American anthropology and placing it alongside more established disciplines in the academic arena is apparent.

The remedy lay in the pursuit of an essentially philological program: "In regard to our American Indians we are in the position that practically no such literary material is available for study, and it appears to me as one of the essential things that we have to do, to make such material accessible. . . . As we require a new point of view now, so future times will require new points of view and for these the texts, and sample texts, must be made available" (7/24/1905, quoted in Stocking 1974b: 122–23). The pride of place that Boas assigned to texts taken down in Native American languages as a point of entry into the thought of other cultures placed him in a clear line of intellectual descent from Herder. As we suggested in Chapter 5, Herder argued that the *Volksgeist* of a nation is crucially embodied in traditional texts. George Stocking comments on the deeply Herderian cast of Boas's view of "primitive literature": "The mythology of each tribe embraced its 'whole concept of the world', its 'individuality' – one might almost say, its 'genius'" (1968: 224).

Boas was also heir to the methodological legacy of Indo-European philology in the emphasis he placed on close distributional and comparative study in the service of culture history (see Hymes 1970: 256–57). Still, as commentators such as Roman Jakobson (1944), Dell Hymes (1961, 1970), and George Stocking (1974a) have emphasized, Boas's work posed a challenge to key tenets of traditional historical philology in its rejection of universalistic evolutionary schemas in favor of close historical analysis. Folklore enabled Boas to attack evolutionism by rejecting degenerative bias of traditional philological approaches and countering E. B. Tylor's view that each folk element is a survival from a previous social form, one that was rational in its origins but became increasingly irrational (see Stocking 1968: 225). For Boas, folklore was deeply embedded in culture, and it was irrational all the way down.

Primitive literature, the rubric under which Boas analyzed narrative and poetics, provided him with a crucial basis for examining the relationship between tradition and creativity (1925b: 329; 1927: 1). Arguing that "The inherent relation between literary type and culture appears also clearly in narrative," Boas noted that various features of narrative content "give us a picture" of "the mode of life and the chief interests of the people" (1927: 329). Representations of "cultural setting" contained in narratives, particularly those focusing on human society, thus provide excellent tools for ethnographic documentation. In an essay included in what has come to be seen as his classic collection of texts, Boas asserted that "I give a description of the mode of life, customs, and ideas of the Tsimshian, so far as these are expressed in the myths" (1916: 393). Here he makes a strong claim for the accuracy of these custom–narrative connections:

> It is obvious that in the tales of a people those incidents of the everyday life that are of importance to them will appear either incidentally or as the basis of a plot. Most of the references to the mode of life of the people will be an accurate reflection of their habits. The development of the plot of the story, furthermore, will, on the whole, exhibit clearly what is considered right and what wrong.... Material of this kind does not represent a systematic description of the ethnology of the people, but it has the merit of bringing out those points which are of interest to the people themselves. They present in a way an autobiography of the tribe. (1916: 393)

In reflecting back on this study in 1935, Boas strengthened the claim still further: "The underlying thought of this attempt was that the tales probably contain all that is interesting to the narrators and that in this way a picture of their way of thinking and feeling will appear that renders their ideas as free from the bias of the European observer as is possible" (1935a: v).[8]

According to Boas, stories shape both collective and individual experience. He argued that works of art in general take on heightened affective and cognitive significance "because they recall past experiences or because they act as symbols" (1927: 12). Art thus played a crucial role in individual and collective memory and affective economies in that "The form and its meaning combine to elevate the mind above the indifferent emotional state of everyday life" (1927: 12). In the case of narratives, the relationship between experience and artistic representation is rich and complex, and it operated in both directions. Boas stated that "The local culture determines what kind of experiences have a poetic value and the intensity with which they act" (1927: 327). While Boas certainly emphasized the manner in which cultural patterns shape narratives, he also points, in *The Mind of Primitive Man*, to the way that myths and tales shape everyday thought and perception in "primitive" groups (1965: 221–23).

---

[8] Boas warned nevertheless that not all aspects of culture are portrayed in folktales (1940b: 475–76). In particular, some elements that may seem striking to "the foreign observer" but "self-evident to the Indian" were absent (1935a: v).

Boas's view of folklore was thus extremely positive – when it was viewed as a source of data for anthropological research. Its status as a force that shapes social life, including that of civilized nations, was quite another thing. For Boas, the question of tradition's effects on thinking and action is closely tied to the question of consciousness, and herein lies an important difference between his treatment of the form and content of narratives and his discussions of linguistic categories. As we saw earlier, Boas privileges the study of language precisely because linguistic patterns are not susceptible to conscious thought. Folklore, on the other hand, springs from these distorted attempts to reflect consciously on unconscious processes; by attempting to explain custom, these secondary explanations serve to legitimate cultural forms and processes. Tradition is thus to be studied not as a window into history or cultural process but as a means of documenting the social effects of secondary explanations.

Boas deems narratives to be a form of "primitive art," and they accordingly fall under the aegis of his general theory of aesthetics (see Boas 1927; Jonaitis 1995). For art in general, the creative process is almost entirely unconscious: "The mental processes of artistic production do not take place in the full light of consciousness. The highest type of artistic production is there, and its creator does not know whence it comes" (Boas 1927: 155). The conscious accessibility of narratives seems to emerge primarily when they are appreciated as objectified texts – Native Americans can make aesthetic judgments among multiple versions. Thus the product but not the process can rise into consciousness.

Wherein lie the sources of creativity? In the case of plastic arts, Boas paints for us the picture of a virtuoso who has mastered materials and techniques and who creates new patterns for the sake of their novelty and the enjoyment of new rhythms. Creativity is thus associated with mastery of technical processes, the bodily practices involved in the manipulation of materials, and the general character of sensory experience. Although the attention that Boas draws to the literal embodiment of art is fascinating, the body that Boas envisions is not a mindful body – corporeal mediation seems to preclude conscious reflection. Boas's aesthetics runs counter to Kant's in terms of the emphasis that he places on the historical and cultural determination of aesthetic judgment, but Boas is Kantian in locating artistic creativity beyond consciousness and cognition, apart from survival, necessity, and everyday life, and in opposition to collective experience. Boas's theory of art is, ironically, closer to the contemporary field of neuroaesthetics than to cultural anthropology.

Suggesting the creation of stories results from "the play of imagination with the events of human life," Boas goes on to argue that "the incidents of tales and myths . . . are not directly taken from every-day experience; that they are rather contradictory to it" (1940c: 405). Boas asserted that narratives provide an emotional rather than cognitive hold on "the events of human life," such that daily experiences are imaginatively transformed through wish fulfillment and "the materialization of the objects of fear" in the course of their narrativization. Boas's statement here may seem to contradict the assertions we cited earlier regarding the way that narratives "give us a picture" of "the mode of life and the chief interests of the people." Careful examination of these statements suggests that when Boas refers to the relationship between narratives and "habits" (1916: 393), "their way of thinking and feeling" (1935a: v), or "the mode of life, customs, and ideas" (1916: 393) he has in mind generalized, shared cultural patterns. When Boas speaks of the way narratives distort or transform "the events of human life," on the other hand, he is referring to specific, concrete historical events; in this case, Native American self-consciousness does not "exhibit clearly" or provide "an accurate reflection" of everyday life.

The relationship between narrative representations and events is doubly displaced once the narratives enter into circulation. While the conscious ascription of meaning is largely absent in the creative process, narratives become objects of consciousness as they are told, appreciated, and retold. The result is that secondary explanations are added on to them, elements that are "quite foreign" to the narratives themselves or "the actual historical happenings" (1927: 336, 129); the interpretation that is grafted on to a narrative rather reflects "the cultural interests of the people telling it" (1927: 336) or "a stylistic pattern controlling the imagination of the people" (1927: 336–37). Texts thus provided a window into primitive life, but refracted through a distorting glass that primitives could not accurately interpret; only anthropologists can read them authoritatively.

This leads us to a ninth point of contact between Boas's constructions of language and culture. As Stocking (1992: 91) suggests, Boas viewed linguistics largely as the study of written texts. The major problem that students of Native American groups had to face in linguistics – as in historical study – was the lack of a corpus of texts. Teaching Native Americans to write texts in their own language provided anthropologists with a means of generating a textual corpus to rival that of the classicists and imbuing it with authenticity and authority – in Derrida's (1974) terms, with a metaphysics of presence. Imagining the study of culture as a textual process similarly enabled Boas to fulfill anthropology's central promise and to face its principal dilemma. He argued that "Historical analysis will furnish the data referring to the growth of ideas among different people; and comparisons of the processes of their growth will give us knowledge of the laws which govern the evolution and selection of ideas" (1898: 127). On the other hand, he admitted that "in the domain of ethnology, where for most parts of the world, no historical facts are available except those that may be revealed by archaeological study," one must rely on "indirect methods" (1920: 314, 315). The systematic comparison of narratives and their distribution associated with "the modern investigation of American mythology" is cited as one of two examples of how this dearth of "historical facts" can be overcome (1920: 315). Boas thus advanced Schoolcraft's project of turning the production of Native American texts into a material grounding for both scientific and humanistic pursuits in the United States – at the same time that he attempted to eliminate nationalism as a basis for authorizing the endeavor.

But it was not their content alone that prompted Boas to afford texts such a crucial role in anthropology. A return to Shapin and Schaffer's (1985) analysis of the role of Robert Boyle's air pump in shaping science and society during the seventeenth century, mentioned in Chapter 1, might help to make sense of Boas's fixation with texts. Rather than tying scientific authority to grand deductive systems, Boyle located its nexus in the artificial context of actions performed in a transparent glass container located at the top of an apparatus capable of producing a vacuum. The production of scientific facts was tied to what took place in the container, the concurrence of credible witnesses to these events, and their abstraction and decontextualization as general principles that could explain how nature worked everywhere and anytime. The air pump thus placed those who controlled it in the position of an obligatory passage point (Latour 1988) for the production of scientific knowledge, and it enabled them to make huge leaps of scale between the particular contexts that they dominated and the world at large.

This analogy is as interesting for where it fails as for where it succeeds. The fieldwork encounter became for anthropology what the air pump was for seventeenth-century mechanical philosophy – a means of displacing grand deductive schemes (particularly those of the evolutionists) in favor of a mode of producing facts through observation. Fieldwork became a complex set of practices that had to be mastered through professional training; like owning an air pump, controlling access to this pedagogical process enabled Boas and those he trained to regulate the obligatory passage points that provided access to cultural knowledge. The analogy begins to break down, however, in that the air pump was designed to produce *public* knowledge, to open scientific work to scrutiny by groups of observers. Fieldwork placed the locus of observation far away from the center. Since people's perceptions of their own cultural patterns are shaped by secondary explanations, Boas does not deem "natives" to be credible witnesses.

Convincing skeptical colleagues that these unusual encounters between strangers produce substantive, reliable information still seems to be a never-ending task. Herein lies, we think, the solution to a question that seems to have puzzled many readers of Boas – why did he spend so much time collecting texts and why did he see them as so central to anthropological research? Texts could turn a unique, private encounter into something that was public and permanent, and it could transform the sorts of encounters that had been the purview of missionaries, colonial civil servants, and other amateurs into the key site in which scientists defined themselves and the knowledge they produced – as anthropology. Linguistics lent an aura of science and credibility to these interactions. The phonetic table ensured that fieldworkers would record accurately exactly what was said. Fieldwork produced observations of facts, not speculations about historical or psychological origins. Their publication, which constituted a major component of the Boasian program, transformed the texts into stable, publicly accessible observations that could be subjected to scrutiny, analysis, and comparison, like the collective observations on what took place in the glass container.

Texts collected and written down in the language of the informant constituted "the foundation of all future researches" (Boas 7/24/05, quoted in Stocking 1974: 123). They provided the raw data that had, in theory, been generated apart from any theoretical commitments and thus could provide the basis for new theoretical developments. Boas rhetorically engages "the distant observer" who may gain the impression that American anthropologists are simply lost "in a mass of detailed investigations" by asserting that "the ultimate problems of a philosophic history of human civilization...are as near to our hearts as they are to those of other scholars" (1920: 314). Just as textual scholarship afforded Boas a historical vantage-point on culture, it provided a model of how masses of details could be studied systematically, scientifically, and comparatively and eventually yield broad generalizations regarding issues of cultural constraint and creativity. Texts could help transform the perception of anthropology from "a collection of curious facts, telling us about the peculiar appearance of exotic people and describing their strange customs and beliefs" into a "science of man" that "illuminates the social processes of our own times" (1962: 11). By turning unique encounters between particular individuals into both reflections of a culture and a basis for comparison and the discernment of universals, these texts helped anthropologists solve epistemological problems of scale as well as the problems involved in converting discourse from the periphery into metropolitan knowledge.

The collaborative production of Native American texts

What, then, were these prized texts? How did they come into being, and how did they come to provide windows into cultural patterns? Recent work by Judith Berman and Ira Jacknis on the long-term collaboration between Franz Boas and George Hunt has contributed greatly to our ability to address these issues.[9] It is accordingly possible to examine in some detail how the Kwakw*aka*'wakw ("Kwakiutl") texts published by Boas and Hunt were produced, edited, and published.

When Boas began collecting narratives on the northwest coast, tape recorders were not available; Boas used the phonograph to record songs but not narratives. Therefore, prior to initiating his collaboration with George Hunt, Henry W. Tate, and others, Boas relied on dictation. Boas commented on the awkwardness of the dictation process: "The slowness of dictation that is necessary for recording texts makes it difficult for the narrator to employ that freedom of dictation that belongs to the well-told tale, and consequently an unnatural simplicity of syntax prevails in most of the dictated texts" (1917: 1). Such texts might therefore not be transparent reflections of traditional narratives in view of the technical difficulties and the need to teach narrators how to produce texts for dictation. Boas spent less than thirty months conducting fieldwork on the northwest coast (see Goldman 1975; Rohner 1969), and dictation alone thus could not produce the massive corpus of texts that he published. Rather, as Berman (1996: 224) suggests, Boas trained as many Native Americans and persons of mixed ancestry as he could find who were versed in an indigenous language and possessed sufficient literacy skills. In this fashion, textual production could continue unabated once Boas returned to New York. Boas's collaboration with George Hunt is by far the most extensive; Hunt worked with Boas for nearly forty years, producing one of the most extensive and detailed ethnographic records in existence. The Boas–Hunt collaboration thus provides us with an unusual opportunity to assess the practices that shaped the production of these texts.[10]

---

[9] See Berman 1991, 1992, 1994, 1996; Jacknis 1980, 1989, 1991, 1992, 1996.

[10] For studies of this collaboration, see Cannizzo (1983), Codere (1966), Cole (1985), Jacknis (1980, 1989, 1991, 1992), Maud (1982), and Rohner (1966, 1969). Berman's (1991, 1992, 1994, 1996) recent work is particularly pertinent in that it details the production of the Kwagul texts.

George Hunt was the son of a high-ranking Tlingit woman and an Englishman who worked for the Hudson Bay Company. Hunt was raised in Fort Rupert, a stockaded outpost and Hudson Bay Company station that brought together not only Kwakwaka'wakw but also English, Scots, Irish, French-Canadian, Métis, Iroquois, Hawaiian, Tlingit, Tsimshian, and Haida; it must have been a locus of cultural hybridity as much as hegemony. Hunt was perceived as a "foreign Indian" by the Kwakwaka'wakw, and he never considered himself to be Kwakwaka'wakw; he often referred to his wife's relatives as "these Kwaguls" (Berman 1991: 27). At the same time, Hunt's noble descent brought him high status, particularly after he married a high-ranking Kwakwaka'wakw woman (see Berman 1996: 228). Hunt's rank afforded him exposure to forms of knowledge and discourse owned by elite lineages, and it granted him a strong social position by virtue of the high-ranking lines' dominance of trade and indigenous–white relations.

Traditionalization and authentication guided Boas's and Hunt's efforts to secure both artifacts and texts. With regard to texts, Boas was particularly interested in what he considered to be traditional speech. This quest for the archaic and authentic related to form as well as content; Boas summarized his agenda as an attempt "to rescue the vanishing forms of speech" (Boas to Leonhard Schultz Jena, 10/10/1928). Hunt was certainly on the same page in this respect. Hunt did not take down material by dictation, but rather listened to the rendition and then went home and reconstructed – and thus re-entextualized – the discourse (see Berman 1991: 34; Cannizzo 1983; Jacknis 1991: 205, 222); after he had written the text in its entirety in Kwakw'ala, he added English interlineations (Berman 1991: 233–34). As he rephrased the materials in the written version, Hunt wrote in what Berman (1996: 234) refers to as "an authentic Kwakwaka'wakw speech style formerly used in the myth recitations," even when his consultants are likely to have used less archaic styles. Hunt attempted to locate and document speech styles that he deemed to be particularly traditional and authentic; regarding some of his texts on cooking, Hunt wrote Boas: "Thes will show you the oldest way of speaking" (Hunt to Boas, 3/29/1910). Hunt authorizes his texts vis-à-vis those obtained by others as being uniquely traditional and authentic. He bragged to Boas that consultants working with other "white men" gave them "patch up story," amalgamating various narratives into one, whereas "you got all the old way of the tsietsieko in your book" (Hunt to Boas, 5/7/1916).

Their correspondence suggests, however, that these texts resulted from the traditionalization of materials collected in keeping with Boas's scholarly agenda – Boas asked Hunt to produce texts in Kwakw'ala with

English interlineal translations "in answer to my requests and to specific questions" (1930: x). The correspondence complemented periods of face-to-face collaboration in providing a continuing forum for discussing which texts were to be produced, at what rate of speed, and how they should be crafted. At the same time that Boas asked Hunt to collect anything and everything, thereby providing Hunt with a degree of freedom in shaping the textual agenda, Boas exercised a great deal of control over the production process by continually laying out long-range research interests; as Berman (1996: 236) notes, Boas adumbrated topics as much as five years in advance. His foci changed over the years from technology and foodways to ethnozoology and ethnobotany to social organization and finally to "the way the Indians think and feel" (Boas to Hunt, 9/29/1920, quoted in Berman 1991: 43). Boas expected his collaborator to use his "requests and specific... questions" systematically as a guide to the entextualization of "Kwakiutl" culture: "I hope you are reading over my letters, and that you will try to answer one after another all the different questions. It would be best if you scratched them out one after another after they have been answered, then we shall know just where we are" (Boas to Hunt, 1/23/1918).

Boas sent Hunt copies of some of the volumes of texts that he had published, including those documenting other Native American groups. Hunt acknowledged receipt of an early volume in the following terms: "I have Received a Book also that you sent me with some of the Eskimo tales and songs in it which I thank you Very much for it. for it show me How to Put my letters to gather" (Hunt to Boas, 12/1/1897). Perusing such a volume would seem to provide a number of important models for narrative structures, rhetorical parameters, and stylistic features, as Hunt's thank you note suggests – beyond simply suggesting that culturally and geographically bounded Native American communities could be represented through published texts. It would seem difficult to believe that Boas did not anticipate that this sort of *implicit* metadiscursive modeling would take place. Boas also trained Henry W. Tate to record myths in Tsimshian.[11] Boas notes that he criticized Tate's initial work on the question of intertextual relations: "A few of the tales also bear evidence of the fact that Mr. Tate had read part of the collection of tales from the Kwakiutl published by myself in conjunction with Mr. George Hunt. A few others indicate his familiarity with my collection of tales from Nass River. At the time when I received these tales, I called his attention at once to the necessity of keeping strictly to the form in which the traditions are

[11] See Maud (1985, 2000) for very critical studies of the Tate–Boas collaboration.

told by the Tsimshian" (Boas 1916: 31). The way Boas chided Tate suggests, however, that when such intertextuality becomes recognizable in the form and/or content of the texts, "the form in which traditions are told by the Tsimshian" (or "the Kwakiutl") would be compromised and the texts would no longer seem as if they spring directly from oral tradition to written text.

Boas expressed continuing ambivalence regarding Hunt's texts. Many of his comments focus on questions of phonetic accuracy. On the positive side, Boas credited Hunt, as we noted above, with "constant improvement in his method of writing" (Boas and Hunt 1902b: 3). Nevertheless, Boas noted as late as 1925 that Hunt is "not absolutely reliable" in his phonetic writing (1925: v). Berman (1991: 30) suggests that Hunt was well aware of Boas's reservations. In the face of Boas's lingering doubts about his work, Hunt used a number of means of attempting to assert the authority of his texts. When Boas asked him for ethnographic descriptions, Hunt often provided a story that explained its origin. Hunt similarly tried to increase Boas's – and presumably the reader's – faith in his authority by emphasizing his participation in the enactment of tradition. Hunt deemed the provenance of his texts important, and he often reported in detail how he obtained a given body of information (Berman 1996: 233). In short, Hunt drew on a range of practices that sought to traditionalize the texts and artifacts he collected by linking them to antecedent forms, practices, and discourses (see Hymes 1975; Bauman 1993). But at other times he distanced himself from tradition by registering skepticism and placing himself in relationship to events as observer, interviewer, or local expert.

Some of the ways in which Hunt sought to enhance the value that Boas would place in his texts – and to augment his authority as a collector and writer – were tied to his awareness of the place of a work within the larger textual economy. Hunt asserts "of my 'Pexala' or Doctor songs" that "this is the first I gave away of the kind" (Hunt to Boas, 5/7/1916). He notes with regard to a series of women's wailing songs that "I will try to get them, for it is the only true story a women can tell. . . . And another thing the women at swasela. told me that she would not tell any one about her family Histoie. it is only the kindness I have towards her son. made her tell it to me. and I think that you will like it. for I know that you have never got this kind of wailing befor this" (Hunt to Boas, 10/7/1916). Hunt boasts that the wailing song is not only the best of its kind but a first for science. Hunt's economy was strongly shaped by his assessment of white researchers' preferences of which texts had been collected and published; he was, obviously, particularly attuned to Boas's textual value system, and his letters often contain predictions that his employer would particularly like a text or corpus or his hopes that his work would meet with favor.[12]

Hunt attempted to construct his authority vis-à-vis that of Boas. Hunt often framed texts through use of Kwakw'ala third-person-near-second-person demonstrative forms as communications addressed to Boas: "this thing that is near to you" (quoted in Berman 1991: 42). A sense of how deeply the two men's textual authority was intertwined, of the social and political-economic inequality that characterized their relationship, and of the esteem and affection with which Hunt regarded Boas are apparent in the former's acknowledgment of Boas's intention to place the text collection in the Columbia University Library in Hunt's name: "Now my Dear Dr. F Boas if you think it is best to put my name on the book as you say it will please me. But you know that I could not have get these stories without your great help to me, there for I say my work is only one third of it. to your two third. yet I think you very much for putting my humble name up for truly your the only help I got" (Hunt to Boas, 5/7/1916).

In spite of his reservations, Boas sought to legitimate Hunt's authority as a writer. The voice that Boas sought to authorize, however, was not that of George Hunt *qua* individual, not in terms of the particular features of his complex, hybrid social position. Rather, Boas downplayed Hunt's background, including his multiracial ancestry in characterizing Hunt as speaking "Kwakiutl as his native language" (1910: v). Which, we might ask? Boas similarly recontextualized Hunt's reflections on social life in Kwakw*a*ka'wakw communities as "Kwakiutl texts" and "Kwakiutl ethnology."[13] Boas accordingly mystified the contextual footing of the texts to such an extent that his characterizations, according to Berman, sometimes come close to being fabrications (1996: 228–30). When Hunt is an actor in the texts, Boas sometimes hides clues to his identity, particularly in the English translations. Hunt's first-person account of his shamanistic initiation is published in Kwakw'ala and English (Boas 1930 I, 1–40). The authorship of the texts is mentioned only in the preface to the Kwakw'ala edition (Berman 1991: 39); moreover, Boas does not state that Hunt is the initiate as well. In the widely known description of the 1894 winter dances (Boas 1897, 1966: 179–241), the central role played by Hunt and his relatives is obscured by the use of non-English names (Berman 1991: 39; Suttles 1991: 133). Similarly, Boas describes

---

[12] Hunt wrote to Boas, for example, on 3/9/1896, "It takes lots of stadying to Put it Down Right and I hope you like them now?"

[13] It should be noted, however, that Boas related some texts to "houses," "families," and "clans" rather than simply to "Kwakiutl culture" as a whole.

Hunt's marriage as an example of Kwakwaka'wakw marriage rites. Not only does he fail to identify Hunt, but Boas states that the "young man had no relatives" (1966: 57). Berman (1991: 40) suggests that this statement is flatly untrue; Hunt's relatives were certainly present, but they were of Tlingit, English, and mixed ancestry.

Acknowledging the multiethnic character of the marriage would have complicated the capacity of this example to represent "Kwakiutl culture," thus revealing both Hunt's complex and multifaceted mediation as well as the multicultural and multilingual dynamism of what Boas frames as "Kwakiutl culture." Foregrounding the cultural and historical complexity of the texts and the circumstances surrounding their production would have challenged the way that Boas was constructing their authority – as a voice that could speak for "Kwakiutl customs" in their entirety. Boas similarly extirpated the presence of English in the original texts, even though many of the narrators were bilingual or had at least some command of English (Berman 1991: 50). Hunt's responses in English to Boas's "requests and . . . specific questions" were likewise not included in the published versions (Berman 1991: 41). By giving the impression that members of Kwakwaka'wakw communities spoke no English, Boas greatly increased the monologicality and monoglossia of the texts and removed another sort of important evidence with respect to their rootedness in colonial contexts.

Beyond questions of revising texts and translations, the way that Boas located Hunt's texts within the published collections erased important dimensions of their entextualization and how Hunt attempted to authorize them. Although Hunt was vitally interested in contextualizing the texts vis-à-vis the way he had obtained the information (as personal experience, observation, or through elicitation from particular individuals), Boas does not seem to have been interested in these aspects of Hunt's metadiscursive practices, and he deleted this material from the published texts. Even though Hunt wrote the texts in his own voice, Boas often headed texts with the name of Hunt's source – giving the impression of a much less mediated route of transmission (Berman 1996: 234). While Boas thought it important to publish contrastive accounts of the "same" narrative or cultural practice that he obtained from different individuals, he did not point out instances in which Hunt had synthesized several individuals' versions in a single text.

Re-elicitation and cross-checking afforded Boas a formative role in the process of inscribing the texts, since he thereby reserved the right to assess when there was "a discrepancy of opinion" between consultants (Boas and Hunt 1902b: 3), between the texts he collected and those provided by Hunt, and between different versions produced by Hunt himself. Having transferred a great deal of the process of writing texts to Hunt, Boas reasserted his authority over the metadiscursive practices that produce final texts and translations for publication. We certainly do not want to deny credit where credit is due – while many anthropologists have published texts written by their collaborators without so much as acknowledging their authorship, Boas often conveyed Hunt's and Tate's participation on the title page. Authorship was not, however, extended to Hunt's first and second wives – even though he acknowledges their extensive and vital collaboration in his letters to Boas.[14] But sharing authorship did not lead to sharing control over metadiscursive practices. Boas's retention of control over the processes that produced the texts and translations is signaled by his sole authorship of the prefaces.

Although the caveats that Boas articulated in the prefaces to text collections may have limited the authority of the texts on specific points, they form part of a rhetoric that actually asserted their accuracy, authenticity, and authority. For example, Boas follows his comments on the fragility of Chinook material and on the way that some Kathlamet crept into Charles Cultee's Chinook with the assertion that "from a close study of the material I conclude that it is on the whole pure and trustworthy" (1894: 5). After lamenting that Cultee was his "only source" on both Kathlamet and Chinook, Boas concluded on the basis of "internal evidence" and the similarities in two versions of two stories elicited some three and a half years apart "that the language of the texts is fairly good and represents the dialect in a comparatively pure state" (1901: 5). We recounted above Boas's criticisms of Henry Tate's textual production; later in the preface to that collection, Boas suggested that the way that the narratives are told "to white people or to the younger generation" was distinct from how they were told "to the older generation, that followed the old way of living," particularly in the inclusion of explanatory material in the former setting. Nevertheless, Boas concluded that "On the whole, however, my impression is that only a slight amount of descriptive material has been introduced in this way" (1916: 393). These caveats give one the impression that Boas's metadiscursive practices provide reliable means of spotting such textual flaws when they occur; we can thus accept that the authority of the texts is limited only in the ways that he has specified

---

[14] After the death of his first wife, T'lalilhi'lakw (or, in English, Lucy), Hunt wrote Boas on 6/18/1908 that "This is about the Hardest thing I ever got. that is to lose my Dear loving wife. who was a great Help to Both you and me in the work I have to Do for you." He added in a letter written three months later that "I am trying to Do the work for you. and I find that it is Hard without the Help I use to get from my Dear wife for some times I would forget some thing in my writing these she would tell me. But now I got to get some one to tell me. and I have to Pay for It. so it come Hard for me" (Hunt to Boas, 9/18/1908).

and that they are, on the whole, trustworthy. In other words, the caveats that Boas mentions constitute marked figures that stand out against the background of texts that directly and transparently represent "the mind of the American native."[15] While readers may retain some of Boas's doubts about specific features of the his collaborators' work, we are invited to place our trust in Boas's textual authority.

Drawing on Berman and other sensitive readers of the corpus, we have argued that the texts are fascinating hybrid forms that provide valuable insights into a complex and power-laden relationship between two men who were locked in very different positions in a colonial situation. But this is not how Boas presented them. He wanted Native American texts to provide anthropology with the sort of literary corpus enjoyed by classicists and to turn those elusive fieldwork encounters into the sorts of public, accessible, and objective observations required of scientific research. Their potential for accomplishing these aims was contingent, however, on their possession of what Cicourel (1982) refers to as ecological validity; in other words, these rather artificial research contexts must bear a demonstrable relationship to "the mode of life and the chief interests of the people" – to what happens when anthropologists are not around. In order to imbue them with scientific value, Boas stripped off many of the features that tied texts to the contexts of their production and the social and political-economic relationship in which they were embedded. They were simultaneously traditionalized and scientized by Hunt's and Boas's agendas and the editing practices of the latter.

Boas wanted texts to turn fieldwork into anthropology's air pump, into an obligatory passage point for gaining insight into culture. The texts were ventriloquists that could enable the model of culture that he had created to speak. According them this role involved shaping the texts from start to finish – from the time Boas trained Hunt in phonetic transcription and provided him requests and specific questions until the publication of the collection – as literary objects that could sustain this illusion. Again, we are not suggesting that the texts are not valuable or that Boas was unethical. The point is that making the texts function in this manner entailed systematically decontextualizing them from specific contexts of production and reception in order to make them represent the unfolding of a collective unconscious that seemed to be purely traditional. Native

---

[15] Some important exceptions are worthy of comment. Boas does not follow his comments on the "disappearance" of "the whole culture of the Bella Bella" and the lack of informants with an assertion of the authority of the texts (1928a: ix). Boas comments in the preface to *The Religion of the Kwakiutl Indians* on the "imperfections" in Hunt's texts and the way that the predominance of material "from one single informant . . . leaves us in doubt whether we are dealing with individual or with tribal style" (1930: xi).

American texts thus helped define modernity in a purely negative fashion. Boas's textual practices constructed anthropology as a science of culture rather than of the colonial encounter, an historical mode of inquiry that rested on a principled effort to construct modernity in opposition to a pre-contact, romanticized past, thereby excluding the anthropologist and the constructed nature of anthropology's social and textual objects from its purview.

Language, tradition, and the anthropological gaze

Native Americans' rights to shape textual representations of themselves were thus limited in both theory and practice. Boas suggested that the manner in which stories were created and diffused and the distorting influence of secondary explanations rendered Native Americans incapable of accurately characterizing the way narratives relate to "the events of human life." Even such collaborators as Hunt could exercise little control over the production and reception process, including decisions as to which texts would be circulated to which audiences and how their authenticity and significance would be judged; most of the metadiscursive elements that Hunt inserted in his attempts to shape the reception of his texts were stripped off by Boas. Even though his textual practices reflected pervasive racial inequalities (and Boas was hardly alone in this regard), the point here is not that he was practicing textual discrimination. The more significant issue here is that Native Americans were not alone – culture itself rendered its bearers unable to grasp the patterns that shape their beliefs and actions. We all become, to use Arjun Appadurai's (1988) phrase, incarcerated by culture – except for anthropologists. Thus, for Boas, the notion of culture itself motivated a transfer of authority over the politics of difference to anthropologists. The construction of language and culture as separate spheres and the hybridizing "analogies" that linked them provided a key rationale for justifying this powerful and problematic assertion. We would like to map three rhetorical moves that Boas made in order to reach this position.

First, human beings lack a universal perspective that would enable them to understand critically the forces that shape their behavior and consider possible alternatives to their own cultural norms. The selectivity principle (listed above as #4) deprived people of awareness of linguistic and cultural elements not incorporated into their own systems, and the principle of automaticity and unconsciousness (#5) led them to conflate unique patterns with what is "universally human," thereby preventing non-anthropologists from grasping their failure to perceive this broader spectrum.

Second, Boas posited that people lack awareness of even that part of the arc of human possibilities that constitutes their language and culture. Linguistic and cultural patterns are acquired in childhood by imitation and then internalized through repetition; afterwards, "our behavior in later years is determined by what we learn as infants and children" (1962: 56). The principle of shared categories (#3) suggests that group membership fundamentally involves this sort of unquestioned, unreasoned sharing of culture. Because our relationship to cultural patterns is primarily emotional, attempts at conscious introspection simply produce secondary reasoning. Language played a dual rhetorical role here. On the one hand, linguistic patterns provided a means of demonstrating that native consultants do not need conscious awareness in order to provide anthropologists with scientific data – indeed, such attempts at conscious analysis only get in the way. On the other hand, since "habitual speech causes conformity of our actions and thought" (1962: 149), exploring these linguistic labels can enable anthropologists to replay the process in reverse, thereby discovering the nature and historical genesis of cultural categories.

In both his scientific writings and those aimed at more general audiences, Boas pointed to the political dangers latent in this process of cultural distortion. He argued in the *Mind of Primitive Man* (1965) that unconscious categories join disparate entities so powerfully that we fail to perceive their heterogeneity or the arbitrariness of the connection; this process is "one of the fundamental causes of error and the diversity of opinion" (1911: 70). The secondary reasoning invoked in explaining and justifying (erroneously) the nature and application of categories has even more pernicious effects:

These tendencies are also the basis of the success of fanatics and of skillfully directed propaganda. The fanatic who plays on the emotions of the masses and supports his teachings by fictitious reasons, and the unscrupulous demagogue who arouses slumbering hatreds and designedly invents reasons that give to the gullible mass a plausible excuse to yield to the excited passions make use of the desire of man to give a rational excuse for actions that are fundamentally based on unconscious emotion. (1965: 210)

The 1938 edition cited Hitler as a prime example. In short, the frequent attempts by non-anthropologists to reflect on their own culture are not only empirically misguided but politically dangerous.

Third, if people cannot grasp the broad range of human possibilities or their own linguistic and cultural systems, they are certainly not capable of grasping the relationship between the two. Just as speakers of a language cannot locate their phonetic elements on a cross-linguistic grid or specify how they contrast with other systems, bearers of a culture are unable to see how their categories relate to other possibilities. Because people take their own cultural patterns for universals, their attempts to look beyond their own cultural borders become value-laden judgments of good and bad or colonialist projections of one set of categories onto another society. Boas thus, in essence, deemed racism and xenophobia to be natural products of people's misrecognition of the nature of their cultural categories and their inability to see how they relate to what is "universally human." In *Race and Democratic Society* (1945) and *Anthropology and Modern Life* (1962), Boas argued that racism, colonialism, imperialism, and classism provide evidence of the political stakes for people's inability to identify the full spectrum of cultural expressions, to discern the nature of the categories they use, and to be able to relate the two. Boas's theoretical move thus dehistoricizes and depoliticizes imperialism by reducing it to general effects of a universal process of reifying unconscious categories when applied to cross-linguistic and cultural encounters. Balibar (1991) argues that this sort of reasoning provides neo-racists with a cultural logic that naturalizes racism. Although he seems to suggest that this trope constitutes a neo-racist distortion of anthropological constructions, we would argue that it follows from Boas's own culture theory.

Boas's reference to "the gullible mass" suggests that these processes of distortion and their political effects are differentially distributed. "Primitives" are the most gullible, because "their" traditional ideas are based on "crude, automatically developed categories" that are derived from experience. Boas provided two examples: "A sudden explosion will associate itself in his mind, perhaps, with tales which he has heard in regard to the mythical history of the world, and consequently will be accompanied by superstitious fear. The new, unknown epidemic may be explained by the belief in demons that persecute mankind" (1965: 200). Note that Boas located folklore and mythology, whose study he so strongly advocated and effectively institutionalized, as modernity's opposite, a source of conclusions that led entire populations to react irrationally. On the other hand, speaking for the civilized world, Boas suggested that "we have succeeded by reasoning to develop from the crude, automatically developed categories a better system of the whole field of knowledge, a step which the primitives have not made" (1965: 198). While primitives' categories are derived from "the crude experience of generations," modern knowledge springs from "centuries of experimentation" (1965: 199–200) and "the abstract thought of philosophers" (1965: 198). The "advance of civilization" has enabled "us" "to gain a clearer and clearer insight into the hypothetical basis of our reasoning" through increasing elimination of "the traditional element." Paul Radin, it should be noted, was later to turn this argument on its head in *Primitive Man as Philosopher* (1957 [1927]).[16] Boas similarly asserted that "primitives" do not abstract and generalize – their speech and thought focus on the concrete, on their immediate environments, rather than on philosophical speculation; primitive languages accordingly lack abstract categories (Boas 1911).

It would be wrong to suggest, however, that Boas saw "modern" thought as having been thoroughly transformed by science and rationality. In a classist rhetoric, Boas distinguishes the "lay public," "average man," and the "popular mind" from the educated. "The less educated" have benefited less from the eradication of "traditional elements" (1965: 201). Indeed, the "primitive" versus "civilized" opposition is projected into the midst of "modern society": Boas points to the "excessive" gap in "cultural status" between "the poor rural population of many parts of Europe and America and even more so of the lowest strata of the proletariat" as opposed to "the active minds representative of modern culture" (1965: 180). It is precisely the failure of "linguistic classifications" to "rise into consciousness" that links "primitive" and "uneducated" people (1965: 190). "The average man … first acts, and then justifies or explains his acts by such secondary considerations as are current among us" (1965: 214). For this reason, Boas suggested that just as "the educated classes" had to develop a nationalist spirit among "the masses" (1945: 118), it is "the educated groups of all nations" that must teach others how to overcome cultural provincialism and develop a cosmopolitan perspective (1945: 149). Abstract, rationally based thought that transcends concrete local contexts is, of course, the definition of the modern subject; Boas therefore confirms a two-centuries-old relegation of "primitives" and the working class to the premodern world, thereby helping to sustain the legitimacy of modern schemes for creating and naturalizing social inequality that he himself criticized. Nevertheless, even civilized individuals who try to free themselves from "the fetters of tradition" are still "controlled by custom" to a great extent within "the field of habitual activities" (1965: 201, 224, 225).

In a number of passages, however, Boas begins to turn the relationship between traditionality, rationality, and consciousness of class on its head. He argues that in societies with rigid class segregation, elites are guided by class self-interest and unquestioned traditions transmitted from past generations. The "masses," on the other hand, have had little chance to develop an emotional contact with tradition because of irregular attendance or little interest in school (1962: 197). He concluded: "For this reason I should always be more inclined to accept, in regard to fundamental

---

[16] We owe this observation to Regna Darnell.

human problems, the judgment of the masses rather than the judgment of the intellectuals, which is much more certain to be warped by unconscious control of traditional ideas" (1962: 199). Expert knowledge similarly came in for criticism; scientists, like the nobility, artists, and clergymen, can be bound by traditional modes of thought and their embodiment in catchphrases that "motivate people to action without thought" (1945: 183). Boas is quick to contain the effects of this reversal, however, suggesting that science can render intellectuals less dogmatic. In any case, he said, these remarks pertain only to "fundamental concepts of right and wrong," and he suggested that the masses lack the experience and knowledge to discern "the right way of attaining the realization of their ideals" (1945: 139).

We are, in short, doomed to be provincials, individuals who are so incapable of imagining cultural worlds beyond our own narrow circumstances that we take our patterns to be universal and condemn anything that does not seem to conform to them. Until liberated from culture, it is precisely our attempts to build a cosmopolitan perspective – based upon ethnocentric principles – that leads to evolutionism in science and imperialism in politics. If culture necessarily involves incarceration, there is one class of players that is uniquely qualified to break out of jail – anthropologists. Only they can open up the way for a truly cosmopolitan cosmopolitanism. For each of the three spheres that render people subject to tradition, Boas proposed a theoretical and methodological basis for developing the reasoned and critical perspective that he deemed necessary for production of free, enlightened, and cosmopolitan citizens.

First, identifying the broader framework of human possibilities constituted a major goal of anthropological endeavor. Boas argued that "a critical examination of what is generally valid for all humanity and what is specifically valid for different cultural types comes to be a matter of great concern to students of society" (1940e: 261). Learning which attitudes are "universally human" prepares anthropologists for determining which "specific forms" they take in each society (1940e: 262). Anthropological training pushes students to overcome the universal tendency "to consider the behavior in which we are bred as natural for all mankind" (1962: 206).

Second, a "purely analytic" approach to the study of particular languages and cultures enabled anthropologists to circumvent the natural tendency to project one's own categories onto others. Boas argued that "The scientific study of generalized social forms requires, therefore, that the investigator free himself from all valuations based on our culture. An objective, strictly scientific inquiry can be made only if we succeed in entering into each culture on its own basis" (1962: 204–5). Culture becomes an object of knowledge for anthropologists and their means of developing epistemological and political freedom at the same time that it constitutes the principal obstacle to objective knowledge, rationality, and freedom from traditional dogma for all others. To be sure, even the adoption of a "purely analytic" approach does not fully shield anthropologists from the principle of distortion (#6 above), but it does provide them with unique access to objective knowledge of particular cultures, thereby complementing their unique access to the domain of "the common property of mankind." This ability to penetrate alien cultural worlds apparently knows no limits, for it can include everything from art to kinship to religion to cooking.

Having established unique access to universal and culturally specific domains, anthropologists enjoy privileged access to the sphere of cross-cultural comparison. By virtue of its ability to compare a range of types of formal patterns using relatively abstract principles, linguistics can take unique elements and patterns and make them seem precisely comparable to other unique phenomena. Native American lexical and grammatical features could be compared to Greek, Sanskrit, and English, just as the social position of "chiefs of Polynesian Islands, kings of Africa, medicine men of many countries" (1962: 192) could be compared to the New York elites with whom Boas interacted.

Having discredited the cross-cultural forays of laypersons, evolutionists, and others as projections of one set of categories and values onto others, Boas could assert that anthropologists are uniquely qualified to compare systems and generalize about linguistic and cultural difference. Objective and analytic study prepares anthropologists to place a particular culture *vis-à-vis* others and in relationship to a universal framework on the basis of a "mind relatively uninfluenced by the emotions elicited by the automatically regulated behavior in which he participates as a member of our society" (1962: 207). Classicists, Orientalists, philologists, and historians lack a sufficiently broad basis of comparison to achieve this perspective, because what is needed is "the objective study of types of culture that have developed on historically independent lines or that have grown to be fundamentally distinct" (1962: 207). Differences between "Europeans and their descendants" are slight, because a common basis in Greek and Roman culture suggests that "the essential cultural background is the same for all of these" (1962: 206). Anthropologists may invite psychologists, sociologists, and other colleagues into the comparative enterprise of determining what is "universally human," but it will be on anthropological terms and using anthropological data.

To borrow a term from Bruno Latour (1988), Boas attempted to fashion anthropology into an obligatory passage point for academic and popular debates regarding the politics of difference and human nature.

Admitting that anthropologists could not predict what was going to happen or engage in experimentation (1962: 215), Boas did not try to make anthropology into an "exact" or "experimental" science. On a number of occasions, he similarly expressed doubt that cultural phenomena could be reduced to laws or "to a formula which may be applied to every case, explaining its past and predicting its future" (1940f: 257). Rather than limiting the scope of anthropological authority, however, this move expanded it. If anthropological expertise was reduced to a formula, it could be easily decontextualized and used by other specialists or laypersons, persons who had not been transformed by anthropological training and fieldwork. The authority to guide societies through the quagmires of culture ultimately lay with anthropologists rather than with the products of their research.

Boas suggested in a number of popular works that the unique ability of the anthropologist to reach "a standpoint that enables him to view our own civilization critically, and to enter into a comparative study of value" (1962: 207) is needed to counter racism and war, and to secure democracy from majoritarian and state censorship. Rather than providing laws or formulas, the anthropologist's duty is "to watch and judge day by day what we are doing, to understand what is happening in the light of what we have learned and to shape our steps accordingly" (1962: 245). Cosmopolitanism was a process, not a product. Since any culture would necessarily devolve into provincialism, no matter how cosmopolitan it had become, the anthropologist's gaze and voice would remain central, no matter how enlightened people might become. Boas stated in the Introduction to *Race and Democratic Society* that "a new duty arises. No longer can we keep the search for truth a privilege of the scientist. We must see to it that the hard task of subordinating the love of traditional lore to clear thinking be shared with us by the larger and larger masses of our people" (1945: 1–2). Teaching the masses was clearly a primary mission of the anthropological museum (Boas 1907). He further argued that "the task of weaning the people from a complacent yielding to prejudice" (1945: 2) involves a process of resocialization in which unquestioned emotional attachment to tradition is replaced during childhood by a critical weighing of cultural alternatives. Anthropologists thus need to guide what takes place in homes and schools as well as in domestic and foreign policy decisions, providing knowledge that can move societies beyond racism, xenophobia, and war.

Boas uses his model of culture in deconstructing competing claims to a cosmopolitan vision associated with aristocratic elites (such as he encountered in New York), evolutionists, missionaries, and US and European colonialists and in asserting that the only true cosmopolitan vision can emerge from the adoption of an anthropological practice of cultural criticism. And Boas's intervention into the competition between these actually existing cosmopolitanisms was mediated by ethnographic text. By producing texts scientifically through the use of codified discursive practices, anthropologists distinguished their representations from the texts produced by and the epistemological claims of travelers, missionaries, colonial administrators, and other amateurs – and from the analyses offered by anthropologists who relied on such data, including British, French, and German colleagues. Boas's work and that of his students, such as Ruth Benedict and Margaret Mead, had a role in shaping which cosmopolitanisms would get connected to modernity in the twentieth century.

On the cultural limits to anthropological cosmopolitanism

Just as anthropology held the key to a new modernity, the sort of anthropology that Boas proclaimed was predicated on a new set of modernist premises. This transformation could only take place, he argued, if the dominant equation between modernity and nationalism was severed or at least subordinated to a cosmopolitan definition of modernity. Long before Benedict Anderson published *Imagined Communities* (1991), Boas argued that "nationality" was an abstraction. He traced the history of nationalist conceptions in several European countries, suggesting that the idea of nationalism lacked connection to the lived experience of most segments of society; it had to be taught to the "most strongly localized groups, as in the peasantry" (1945: 117), particularly through educational institutions. He also suggested that nationalism was still unevenly spread in the populations of his day, such that the notion had little hold on the lives of many. Boas's analytic separation of language, culture, and race and his deconstruction of supposedly natural and primordial links between language and nation helped him show that the construction of neat Herderian packages containing a common language, history, territory, people, race, and religion distorted history and misrecognized social processes. Nationality only becomes a driving force, Boas sagely notes, when there are states (1962: 95); the big problem comes when states harness nationalism in keeping with their own interests, bending individuals to state ideologies and promoting imperialism, colonialism, and war by elevating national beliefs and practices to the status of moral universals.

Boas's solution followed the path laid out by Kant in his essay on "Perpetual Peace" (1991), and the way in which he articulated it was surprisingly Kantian. Examining how "the narrow-minded local interests of cities and other small political units" had been overcome in the formation of nation-states, Boas suggested that "The federation of nations is the next necessary step in the evolution of mankind" (1962: 97) and that "the whole history of mankind points in the direction of a *human* ideal as opposed to a *national* ideal" (1962: 100; emphasis in original). In this federation, nations would resolve disputes as citizens do within them, by judicial means. Boas's view of the cosmopolitan future was similarly predicated on individuals developing a critical relationship to their own thinking and becoming more rational. Both Kant's and Boas's formulations were deeply spatialized; as Chakrabarty (1992, 2000) argues, spatializing culture and consciousness replicates the logic of modernity and its practices for reproducing inequality. Boas's cosmopolitanism was friendly to capitalism; he repeatedly equated tariffs and trade barriers with the way that closed primitive groups privilege the welfare of their members over those of strangers (1945: 130, 151). He similarly saw commerce, like art and science, as fostering "ties that bind together mankind regardless of nationality" (1945: 114). Boas denounced imperialism and colonialism, but he did so on cultural and political grounds; opposing them did not lead Boas to question the logic of capital. However, Boas's conception of the federation was shaped by a concern with social justice, and he argued that great inequities between nations must be legislatively resolved in order to "permit justice to the needs of each nation" (1945: 150) and uphold the principle that "no nation has the right to impose its individuality upon another" (1945: 112).

Boas, like Kant, conceded that the historical period in which he wrote was not yet ready to embrace a broadly human ideal and its embodiment in a federation of nations. In seeking to identify the roots of the problem, Boas returned to his characterization of primitive society in building two sorts of arguments. He used an origin myth in illustrating the first. "In the early days of mankind," hunters and gatherers roamed over a thinly settled earth in culturally homogeneous and highly collective hordes (1962: 68). Beyond the range of these territorialized groups lay other hordes that were linguistically and culturally distinct. Sharing no community of interest, the members of one horde placed the interests of their members above those of other groups, and "man considered it an act of high merit to kill the stranger" (1962: 69). While the narrative structure evokes Rousseau, Boas's picture of early human communities takes on a negative cast. This insular and xenophobic nature does not disappear with the advent of civilization, because "the nation is also a segregated class, a closed society" (1962: 194). Erroneously elevating one set of national ideals to the status of "the true ideals of mankind" and imposing them on others was thus a extension of this "primitive" pattern. Colonialism, imperialism, and the deprovincialization of European and US culture was, according to this reading, not an historical or cultural product but the unfolding of a universal tendency.

A second obstacle to the emergence of cosmopolitanism or at least a more benign nationalism lies in the traditional character of culture. If anthropology's special domain is culture, it is remarkable that Boas constructed it in largely negative terms. It was, as we saw, the linguistic ideology built into Boas's model of culture that led him to see culture as based on emotional attachments to unconscious patterns that we assimilate uncritically from previous generations, that is, tradition. Naturalizing these patterns as universal and morally superior, we project them on to others and react aggressively when members of other cultures do not meet our expectations. Tolerance, justice, and a cosmopolitan politics require exactly the opposite: "True freedom means that we ourselves should be able to rise above the fetters that the past imposes upon us; that we should understand what actions that we perform are simply due to habit and to the emotional value that habitual actions acquire, and how much is due to true rational thought" (1945: 179).

As Robbins (1998) and Mignolo (2000) suggest, even when nationalism and cosmopolitanism are opposed to one another, they enter into complex, mutually defining relationships. Boas was not urging the elimination of nationality or pressing for a global cultural homogeneity. He argued that national cultural differences are needed to help people become aware of their own culture and its traditional basis. At the same time that Boas sought to mute what he saw as a dangerous nationalism evident in the first half of the twentieth century, his goal seems to have been to place it in a new relationship to cosmopolitanism – thereby transforming nationalism's nature and effects. Boas credited his own education, both at home at school, as having inoculated him against "one-sided nationalism." But people seldom developed a conscious sense of their status as cultural beings or the ability to discern which of "those cherished ideas with which we operate are traditional phrases without any kind of rational significance, ... to raise them into consciousness and to make them the subject of examination" (Boas 1945: 179). Boasian anthropologists, on the other hand, were able systematically and consciously to grasp their own cultural patterns, thereby gaining the ability to examine them rationally, choose among them, and eliminate irrational elements – even if they were not immune to survivals of cultural provincialism. With the emergence of this unique anthropological consciousness, Boas suggested, "a new duty arises. ... We must see to it that the hard task of subordinating the love of traditional lore to clear thinking be shared with us by the larger and larger masses of our people. We must do our share in trying to spread the art, and to engender the habit of clear thinking" (1945: 1).

Tradition is what makes culture culture, that is, renders it compelling, affectively powerful, shared, and unconscious. And it is precisely the traditional element that the anthropologist must help erase. Anthropology, both as disciplinary knowledge and public practice, is thus founded on a fundamental contradiction. Without culture, American anthropology would lose its symbolic capital – its efforts to achieve status as an obligatory passage point in discussions of difference would fail. Yet culture, at least before it becomes a body of rationalized knowledge placed within a global series of such knowledges, is the obstacle to overcoming racism, colonialism, injustice, and war, that is, to cosmopolitan knowledge and practice. Anthropologists must indict a phenomenon that only they can represent authoritatively, and they stake their claim to authority on the broader public and political stage by promising to help rationalize the very cultural (traditional, unconscious) patterns of which they are supposed to be the visionaries and spokespersons. Fully realizing Boas's utopian vision of cultural enlightenment would eventually put anthropologists out of a job once the processes of traditional cultural assimilation gave way to educational systems that permitted each child to examine rationally the premises with which she or he was confronted and kept the state or the elders from controlling which principles each chose to accept. Thanks to anthropologists, culture as we know it – traditional and incarcerating – would cease to exist.

To add to the irony, the project of analyzing culture rested on a pre- or extra-cultural domain that was not constructed or deconstructable. Boas wrote that "It is, therefore, one of the fundamental aims of scientific anthropology to learn which traits of behavior, if any, are organically determined and are, therefore the common property of mankind, and which are due to the culture in which we live" (1962: 206). Language and culture seem ultimately to respond to external organic requirements. His phonetic model suggested that the spectrum of possible sounds is determined by the physiology of the vocal apparatus, and the universal classification of sound is based on its landscape (lips, tongue, teeth, alveolar ridge, etc.) and the range of its movements. Boas also used the example of walking in linking these two domains. That humans walk on their feet is organically determined, but how people in a particular community walk is cultural (1962: 138). He generalized: "In all these cases the *faculty* of developing a certain motor habit is organically determined. The particular *form* of movement is automatic, acquired by constant, habitual use" (1962: 139; emphasis in original). Awareness of this universal grounding for human experiences is open only to members of "educated groups" in modern society, and it is not susceptible to deconstruction. Boas thus imposed a fundamental limit to American anthropology's deconstructive moves as a price for asserting its own authority and scientific status. If Boas had started with religion or mythology rather than linguistics, finding this universal basis – and particularly its physiological underpinnings – might have been more of a challenge. At the same time that anthropology's authority and our collective cosmopolitan future rode on the ubiquity and inescapability of culture, the ability to perceive and represent culture rested on a foundation that lay beyond it.

In order to stake a claim to authority over culture, anthropologists must deny that very authority to all others, all the while admitting that the people who are duped by culture are the sources of the anthropologist's knowledge. The only way that non-anthropologists can claim to speak rationally for culture, and thus become part of the cosmopolitan project, is to speak like anthropologists. Boas thus replicates precisely the rhetorical move that he identified as the essence of cultural naturalism and, derivatively, of all forms of intolerance, the deprovincialization of one's own perspective as universal truth. Claiming anthropological authority on the basis of culture thus fosters precisely the sort of inequality that Boas decried. If subaltern subjects cannot develop awareness of the historical genesis of either "civilized" or "primitive" categories, their critical insights cannot be used in developing anthropological challenges to colonialism. Similarly, the doors of Columbia and other universities were rather more easily accessible to "the educated groups" than to "the masses"; access to anthropological enlightenment was accordingly shaped by race and class-based gate-keeping mechanisms. This conception of culture thus opened the door to modern modes of producing power and knowledge at the same time that it sought to defeat them.

Conclusion

Now, some hundred years from the heady days in which Boas was first articulating these positions, it might be fairly asked how they speak to attempts by anthropologists and others to grapple with the politics of culture. We suggest not only that similar imaginings of language and tradition still inform constructions of culture but that the basic rhetorical functions that Boas assigned to them continue to shape debates about culture.

From the 1970s to the present, it would seem that many anthropologists have sought to deflate the value of their disciplinary capital. The epistemological and political underpinnings of the culture concept have figured importantly in the decentering impact of poststructuralist, postmodern, postcolonial, feminist, Marxist, and other perspectives on anthropology. Johannes Fabian (1983) argues that anthropological constructions of culture and cultural relativity have helped foster a "denial of coevalness" that has legitimated colonialism and imperialism by locating other cultures outside the temporal sphere of modernity. The ambivalence of James Clifford's (1988: 10) often quoted admission that "culture is a deeply compromised idea I cannot yet do without" expresses a process of critical scrutiny that has, for many anthropologists, repositioned notions of culture as research objects rather than as tools of discovery, analysis, and exposition (see also Clifford and Marcus 1986; Marcus and Fischer 1986).

Some anthropologists have declared that "culture" is dead or dying – or that it should "be quietly laid to rest" (Kahn 1989: 17). Lila Abu-Lughod suggests that use of the term "culture" necessarily places in operation processes of separating selves and others that continue to elevate Western elites and subordinate subaltern subjects; she argues that it is thus necessary to develop "strategies for writing *against* culture" (1991: 138; emphasis in original). Michel-Rolph Trouillot (1991) notes that critiques of anthropological concepts of culture have, no less than invocations of cultural reasoning, sustained the value of "the savage slot" in Western society by maintaining the illusion of anthropology's epistemological autonomy from the symbolic and material processes that created the West.

Threats to the usefulness of culture as anthropology's symbolic capital have certainly not emanated from within the discipline alone. Both Claude Lévi-Strauss (1966) and Clifford Geertz (1973) were so successful in promoting their differing models of culture that their formulations were appropriated by literary critics, historians, sociologists, political scientists, and others. Anthropologists lost their monopoly on ethnography and cultural analysis as a "cultural turn" – which paralleled a "linguistic turn" – gained proponents in a range of disciplines (see Bonnell and Hunt 1999). Even as notions of "multiculturalism" essentialized and homogenized notions of culture taken from anthropological reasoning (see Segal and Handler 1995), anthropologists have seldom been afforded central roles in shaping multicultural projects.

Practitioners in cultural and literary studies, postcolonial studies, ethnic and women's studies, American studies, and other fields have often claimed the authority to define culture in ways that they see as countering the perceived complicity of anthropological constructions in consolidating hegemony. In their introduction to a collection entitled *The Politics of Culture in the Shadow of Capital*, for example, Lisa Lowe and David Lloyd (1997: 23) argue for "a conception of culture as emerging in economic and political processes of modernization" rather than Orientalist and anthropological notions that characterize "premodern cultures" as simple and undifferentiated, aestheticize culture, and extract it from economic and political forces. If culture "constitutes a site in which the reproduction of contemporary capitalist social relations may be continually contested" (1997: 26), anthropology becomes, for many scholars, a synonym for locations in which hegemonic notions of culture and attempts to reproduce inequality themselves get reproduced.

Recently, anthropologists have aggressively defended anthropological constructions of culture. In adumbrating the broad range of ways that the concept has been critiqued, Robert Brightman (1995) argues that critics commit the very sin that they ascribe to "culture" – *it* gets constructed as homogeneous, bounded, and stable in the process. He gives the impression that the end result has been more a renaming game than an epistemological transformation. Herbert Lewis (1998) goes further, suggesting that culture's critics are guilty of "the misrepresentation of anthropology" and the distortion of its history. Marshall Sahlins (1999) accuses postmodernists (largely unnamed) of having invented the notion that Boas and his students saw cultures as bound, stable, and self-contained. Brightman, Lewis, and Sahlins point to work by the Boasians that presents culture as a dynamic and historical entity, internally differentiated, and often contested by its "bearers."

Some anthropologists demand that we end the story here, assailing those who dare to critically assess Boas's *oeuvre* as attempting to denigrate the reputation of American anthropology's most distinguished ancestor. Herbert Lewis (2001: 448) claims that our assessment (Briggs and Bauman 1999) of the Boas–Hunt texts is "harsh" and that we regard the corpus as "truly harmful." Our argument, which we have recapitulated here, seems to us not to condemn the texts but to attempt to relocate their value away from models of ventriloquism and towards revelations of the complexity of the cultural encounters that produced them. We have tried to use these texts just as Boas suggested: "As we require a new point of view now, so future times will require new points of view and for these the texts, and sample texts, must be made available" (7/24/1905, quoted in Stocking 1974b: 122–23).

It seems worthwhile to point out that the main thrust of Boas's work was a penetratingly critical – one might even say "harsh" – reassessment of extant anthropological approaches. Given his clear and consistent commitment to academic freedom and the spirit of critical inquiry, attempts to silence criticism violate the very spirit of Boas's academic and popular contributions. Indeed, Boas believed that intellectual freedom and democracy required each generation to reflect critically on what they had been bequeathed: "[I]t is our task not only to free ourselves of traditional prejudice, but also to search in the heritage of the past for what is useful and right, and to endeavor to free the mind of future generations so that they may not cling to our mistakes, but may be ready to correct them" (1962: 200–1). Therefore, suggesting ways that Boas's linguistic and cultural modeling dulled the effectiveness of his critical tools and proposing avenues for recasting these principles seems to us to be truer to the Boasian spirit than defensive celebrations of Boasian clairvoyance.

Moreover, these attempts to shield anthropological concepts of culture from criticism fail to come to grips with two sorts of issues. First, they do not take into account the degree to which Boasian notions of culture have become social facts that shape contemporary social and political processes. Many institutions of the nation-state have turned to cultural reasoning as a means of overcoming crises of legitimacy and resources associated with globalization and taking advantage of new opportunities for surveillance and regulation spawned by rising social inequality. Briggs with Mantini-Briggs (2003), Steven Epstein (1996), and Paul Farmer (1992, 1999) point to the use of cultural arguments in rationalizing the "reemergence" of such "old" infectious diseases as tuberculosis, malaria, dengue, and cholera and the "emergence" of HIV/AIDS. Kristin Koptiuch (1991) argues that cultural images of the residents of US inner cities assist in squashing protest, imposing new regimes of segregation, and legitimizing high rates of incarceration for racialized minorities. Jacqueline Bhabha (1996) observes that the US Immigration and Naturalization Service uses cultural arguments to construct a double standard: while human rights discourses may be used in condemning gender-based discrimination and female genital mutilation as barbaric, denials of refugee protection to individuals seeking to escape them are justified through a language of cultural relativism as a need to be sensitive to the norms of the home country. Research suggests that cultural reasoning is often invoked in judicial settings, and it can rhetorically transform denials of the legal rights of people of color into the criminalization of racialized individuals and the racialization of crime (see Briggs and Mantini-Briggs 2000; Roberts 1997; Volpp 2000). Here is the flipside of the "savage slot" problem that Trouillot (1991) articulated; culture is not only embedded in the political economy of Western hegemony but has helped structure it. Culture is now a social fact that shapes contemporary social life. Anthropologists would be naive to think that since they made it, they have the power to decide how – or if – it will be used.

Second, Sahlins (1999) and other critics of culture's critics are right in arguing that Boas and his students did not simply portray culture as bounded, stable, self-contained, and homogeneous. But Boas did suggest that the primordial foundation of social life is the socialization of each individual vis-à-vis one language and one culture. The idea that individuals are unable, with few exceptions, to understand or to deal sympathetically with people socialized in other cultures does construct culture as rather cohesive and bounded. Although Boas described specific cultures as heterogeneous, shifting, and porous, his characterizations of cross-cultural encounters presented a rather less complex view of culture. But the basic problem here is not whether culture is bounded, homogeneous, and stable – Boas didn't think so, and neither do most contemporary anthropologists. What is at stake here are questions of cultural determinacy and authority, who it incarcerates, who can see it clearly and resist its distorting influence, and who gets to represent it. Culture, for Boas, operates unconsciously; when its bearers attempt to grasp or represent it, they produce distortions. Some of these, like folklore, may be of academic interest. But, Boas told us, most are not, and anthropologists must learn to set native representations aside and come up with their own. The question is not that Boas was wrong about culture. It is rather that he told anthropologists that they are the only ones who are right.

In doing so, Boas retraced a number of crucial Lockean moves. He distinguished, on the one hand, a premodern mode of understanding (which nonetheless persisted in his day), an unconscious reification of culture and its unfolding as intolerance and, on the other, a modern, scientific subject position that was only fully realized in the anthropologist. It was, once again, a new form of knowledge that would lead to modernization of the world, here embodied in a cosmopolitan utopia. And the locus was the same – individuals who succeeded in freeing themselves from emotional attachment to the "fetters of tradition" by the power of rational thought. He stood with Aubrey in characterizing tradition as the essence of the premodern world and as the chief obstacle to rationality and science. He followed Herder and especially the Grimms in creating corpora of texts that directly embodied tradition and in placing it at the center of efforts to redefine modernity. Contra the Grimms, however, these texts were used to build a cosmopolitanism that confronted, rather than naturalized, nationalism.

We should never lose track of the fact that Boas's project was progressive; his anthropology's fundamental task was to challenge racism, "intolerant nationalism," and other forms of inequality. Boas should be lauded for sounding a brave internationalist voice that challenged privileges of race, nation, and class. His courage in standing up to censorship in the academy and beyond and in pushing a pacifist agenda during World War I is remarkable. As many anthropologists seek to become public intellectuals and give anthropology a much stronger voice in policy and media debates, we still have a lot to learn from Boas. As many progressive academics are attempting to foster a critical cosmopolitan stance, Boas's attempt to fashion anthropology as a cosmopolitan discipline deserves broader appreciation. The difficulty is that the fundamental modernist move of claiming consciousness and rationality for oneself and one's followers and denying it to others was embedded deeply within the concept of culture that lay at the heart of this project. Boas used constructions of language and tradition centrally in characterizing anthropology as the epitome of modern knowledge. And it was precisely the politics of inequality embedded in the notion of culture that limited its value as a means of challenging inequality and charting a cosmopolitan project.

9   Conclusion

We began this book by aligning ourselves with Dipesh Chakrabarty's (1992, 2000) and Partha Chatterjee's (1993) project of "provincializing 'Europe'," of exploring how categories and relations tied to particular places and times came to be elevated to the status of universals and then used in representing – and dominating – the rest of the world. Our goal has been to open up a new range of insights regarding how Europe got deprovincialized. We have tried to show that constructions of language (meaning both ideologies of language and metadiscursive regimes) and tradition played a central role in creating the modernist project.

When language becomes the focus for telling the story of modernity we can see clearly that what got deprovincialized was not a set of actually existing social forms, European or otherwise. Locke did not take European views of language or modes of speaking and writing and elevate them to the status of universals. He rather targeted the ways of thinking about language espoused by such advocates of modernity as Bacon and his fellow members of the Royal Society, received discursive practices (associated with the Scholastics), and ways of speaking he attributed to the poor, merchants, and women as the central *obstacle* to modernity. Locke labeled a broad range of ways that language could be used – expressively, poetically, rhetorically, reflectively, persuasively – as the enemies of conceptual and political order. A reductionist, atomistic, and individualistic construal of language then became a model not just of communication but of thought, rationality, and sociability. This new discursive model could then be constituted as the obligatory passage point for representations that claimed the status of abstract, decontextualized, and disinterested knowledge – that is, as truth.

We then built on Bruno Latour's (1993) cartography of modernity in extending our analysis of how this transformation of linguistic ideologies and practices made deprovincialization work. Locke's (1959 [1690]: IV. xxi. 5) positioning of language as one of the three "great provinces of the intellectual world" that are "wholly separate and distinct" is crucial. Separating language from both nature/science and society/politics, Locke could place practices for purifying language of any explicit connections with either society or nature at the center of his vision of modern linguistic and textual practices. At this point, deprovincialization really got off the ground. If language forms and practices were inextricably connected to social groups and sites – and particularly to the marketplace, as Bacon believed – then no voice could be divorced from its social location and situated interests. But if language constituted an autonomous domain, then individuals could (in theory) strip words of any indexical connections to provincialities. Propositions expressed in this purified language could masquerade as being deprovincialized and public. Locke and his followers could thereby create a user's manual for constructing modern subjects and making truth claims that seemed to speak for humanity, truth, and nature rather than for themselves or any socially and spatially locatable community. Deprovincialization was in large measure a linguistic illusion, one made possible by an ideological invention of language.

Language thus became a key site for establishing a local/global or provincial/cosmopolitan dichotomy. Since all utterances, written or spoken, provide measures of purification, deccontextualization, precision, and rationality, all individuals could be subjected to constant surveillance with respect to the degree to which they embodied the model of the modern subject. Ideological purity and practices of purification ironically provided a powerful basis for creating sociolinguistic hybrids. Locke the educational theorist provided regimes for teaching individuals how to use speech in such a way that they would seem autonomous, rational, disinterested, and knowledgeable. As the speech forms it produced were disseminated, language standardization created speech forms and practices that seemed to provide icons of privileged social categories; hybrids that linked purified speech forms to enlightened social classes provided a generalized currency that its bearers could readily muster in proffering signs of their own class standing. Locke placed education at the heart of the hybridizing process by virtue of its role in producing hybrid forms and in creating a broad range of forms of sociolinguistic subordination – structuring social relations by providing various types of access to education and instituting gate-keeping mechanisms. Recall that women, even members of the landed aristocracy, needed only to learn by "Roate, Custom, and Memory" in a "plain Natural way," imitating "those that are allow'd to speak properly," while elite men were to be taught grammatical rules and to have the skills to become linguistic models (1989 [1693]: 221, 224). Scientific-linguistic hybrids emerged as the discursive practices associated with mechanical philosophy came to provide a model of linguistic, social, and political order. As gentlemen learned discursive practices that enabled them to distance themselves from their own disinterested words and to make their speech seem to stand apart from the social and interpersonal arenas in which it was produced and received, the epistemologies needed to create the modern project and its deprovincialized façade intensified their hold.

To be sure, Locke's practices of purification were not uncontested; he did not succeed in expunging other varieties of both purifying and hybridizing practices. A century later, Herder reconfigured the project of modernity once again by recuperating some of the constructions of language that Locke attempted to erase and placing them in a new social and political mold. This type of hybridizing – especially imagining a social category, the folk, and mapping its linguistic embodiments – became a practice that gained substantial visibility and moral ascendancy in the late eighteenth and nineteenth centuries. Tradition continued to be constructed as an autonomous domain that preceded – and thus defined – modernity, even as it gained a positive valence. But once the Grimms reified these sociolinguistic forms and scientized their study, purification – the production of a German national language and its dictionary, grammar, legends, *Märchen*, and so forth – became the dominant practice, even if it was justified in part through ideologies of hybridization.

While our narrative ends with Franz Boas's elaborate means of purifying and hybridizing language in relationship to modernity, rationality, and the cosmopolitan, this is hardly the end of the story. Constructing language and tradition and placing them in relationship to nature/science and society/politics continues to play a key role in producing and naturalizing new modernist projects, new sets of legislators, and new forms of social inequality. Which is not to say that the "new" does not often bear a remarkable resemblance to what has come before, often centuries earlier.

Indeed, it would be difficult to imagine a time that the power of this process was more apparent than the end of the twentieth century and the beginning of the twenty-first. It is the very success of purifying and hybridizing practices that enabled language to become a key neo-conservative tool in debates regarding race and immigration in the United States during the past two decades. Proponents of a constitutional amendment declaring English as the official language of the United States, such as semanticist and senator S. I. Hayakawa, argue that a perceived threat to the predominance of English constitutes a real menace to democracy and political order. Hayakawa served as co-founder of US English, an organization that lobbied for national and state measures to declare English as the official language of the United States and to restrict rights to public uses of other languages, such as in bilingual ballots or bilingual education programs. He argued that it is English that "keeps us in communication with each other to create a unique and vibrant culture" (1992: 98). Racial conflicts between blacks and whites do not pose a threat to the body politic, he suggests, because "they quarrel with each other in one language," but efforts by Latino leaders to promote bilingual education and bilingual ballots could undermine the fabric of American society. Senator Walter Huddleston, who also introduced an Official English amendment into Congress, similarly argued that a common language, English, "has allowed us to discuss our differences, to argue about our problems, and to compromise on solutions. It has allowed us to develop a stable and cohesive society that is the envy of many fractured ones" (1992: 114).

James Crawford (1992a, 1992b) has documented the connections between US English and efforts to depict Latinos as posing a threat to the economic and political rights of non-Latino US citizens waged by organizations with eugenic and xenophobic agendas. As Kathryn Woolard (1989) has shown, even liberal whites and Latinos who would reject any explicit anti-Latino measure voted in favor of state and local official English propositions. How could language policies become key battlegrounds for efforts to scapegoat immigrants, especially Latino immigrants, for the effects of economic globalization without being generally viewed as racist? On the one hand, purification practices cast language as a referential, bounded, stable, and homogeneous code whose job it is to permit the exchange of information and the achievement of mutual comprehension. The echo of Locke's voice looms large here in the notion that the lack of a fixed, stable code makes it impossible for people to think clearly or understand one another, thereby precluding the achievement of consensus and rationality in political processes and raising the specter of civil war. As Woolard (1989) suggests, pro-Official English rhetorics suggested that individuals can only become autonomous, informed, and rational voters when they master this common linguistic system; bilingualism and bilingual ballots can thus be depicted as encouraging political bossism, block voting, and the participation of unqualified and uninformed voters. On the other hand, Herder's legacy lies at the heart of the one-nation-equals-one-language argument, the notion that a common language is the social glue that binds a nation together, engenders a unique and shared culture, and is also requisite to a viable democratic state. A common language is construed as a common heritage, unconsciously transmitted through time; creating language policy at the polls can thus be construed as an effort to prevent "special interests" (especially Latino leaders) or federal bureaucrats from undermining a natural process through government intervention. While some voters are more swayed by the power of purification, the idea that everyone must be provided access to an autonomous code that is needed for communication and political equality, others are attracted by underlying hybridizing logics that equate Spanish with Latinos and stereotype them as anti-democratic, excessively fertile, and an economic and political threat. But when opponents call attention to linguistic-racial hybrids in Official English rhetoric, purifying practices can be invoked to suggest that proposals have nothing to do with politics – they simply attempt to provide immigrants with enhanced opportunities to master a linguistic code and thus to become modern, American subjects. It is not the working of a single, dominant language ideology but a shifting and dynamic juxtaposition of contradictory but widely accepted practices of purification and hybridization that has proven to be very powerful – particularly because opponents also engage in these practices.

The hegemonic functions served by this dynamic mix of purifying and hybridizing practices became a lead story for the national media in the United States in late 1996 and early 1997. On 18 December 1996, Oakland's Board of Education unanimously adopted a resolution that drew on "numerous validated scholarly studies [that] demonstrate that African-American students as a part of their culture and history as African people possess and utilize a language described in various scholarly approaches as 'Ebonics.'" The Resolution officially recognized Ebonics, established programs for familiarizing teachers with its principles, and legitimized using Ebonics in the classroom "to facilitate their acquisition and mastery of English language skills" (reprinted in Perry and Delpit 1998: 143, 145). In the discord that ensued, the harmonizing of voices that are usually antagonistic was remarkable. Jesse Jackson appeared on NBC News's *Meet the Press* with William J. Bennett (Secretary of Education under Reagan), Mario M. Cuomo (former New York governor), and Senator Joseph I. Lieberman (Democrat of Connecticut), a mix of individuals who are identified with progressive, liberal, and conservative politics. Jackson declared the resolution to be foolish and insulting, "an unacceptable surrender, borderlining on disgrace," and his fellow panelists certainly did not rise to defend the Resolution (Lewis 1996).[1] In criticizing the Resolution, the Clinton Administration echoed a finding by Ronald Reagan's Department of Education that black English is not a separate language (Bennett 1996). How could one policy statement by a local school board create such strange bedfellows and stimulate such passion?

To be sure, the Official English campaign and related efforts by neoconservatives to depict English as being under siege – just as it was, thanks to the globalization of economies and media, consolidating its position as

---

[1] After meeting with members of the Board of Education, Jackson later supported their efforts to find new ways of helping African-American students and argued that the media had distorted the Resolution (Anonymous 1996).

Figure 2 "Lord, I miss English", a *Non Sequitur* cartoon by Wiley Miller. Distributed by Universal Press Syndicate. Reprinted with permission. All rights reserved.

the global language – and as a victim of liberals' attempts to undermine core American values created a situation in which any language policy debate could be turned into a moral panic. But Theresa Perry's (1998) question – why did African-Americans critically evaluate the way that the O. J. Simpson trial and its aftermath demonized African-American males as violent, impulsive, and abusive but not subject media accounts of the Oakland Ebonics case to equally rigorous scrutiny? – suggests that the specifics of the latter case warrant discussion. A cartoon that appeared in the *Arizona Daily Star* after the Resolution crisis is revealing (see figure 2). The artist depicts a world in which the Ebonics Resolution has not only been adopted but has led to obligatory teacher retraining in such areas as "Womenonics," "Caucasionics," "Asianonics," and "Menonics." These terms attack imagined sociolinguistic hybrids created by identity politics, imagining women, men, Caucasians, and Asians as declaring that they constitute communities whose autonomy is marked by a separate language. The last term, "Psychobabble," is intriguing. We might surmise that its presence suggests distrust of expert authority on questions, such as language, that seem to be common sense. The principal figure in the cartoon seems to voice the announced neo-conservative fear that protecting the linguistic rights of marginalized populations would eventually result in the demise of English; in this linguistic imaginary of the future, English is already dead.

The debate over Ebonics pointed to the existence of a dominant if dynamic economy of language purification and hybridization practices in the United States. Linguists and their kin are expected to be purists, to define and describe autonomous languages in technical ways that render invisible their social and political embeddedness. Moreover, they should be purifying *English*, maintaining the illusion that it constitutes a single language system with a homogeneous core (Standard English) that linguistically unifies all speakers and defends boundaries against other languages (such as Spanish). Dialects provide a space in which hybridization is permitted – that is, when they are viewed as varieties or dialects of a common language that are used in private contexts by persons who employ Standard English in public contexts. The Oakland Resolution, particularly in its media projections, violated this dominant economy of purification and hybridization in several ways. First, experts attempted to purify a hybrid form by declaring it to be a language. Purification apparently becomes politically subversive when applied within domains of "the English language." Second, the Resolution attempted to use purification to challenge the relationship between "black slang" or "street language" and the standard on linguistic grounds. It thus potentially exposed the implicit racialization of perceived language varieties. While Standard English is rationalized in Lockean terms as providing greater precision and rationality than stigmatized varieties and as uniting all speakers of American English, African American English seems to embody display, emotion, and difference. The original Resolution mustered linguistic authority to argue, as scholars such as Labov (1972a) had for decades, that African American English is as rule-governed as the standard and is as effective a communicative tool. The debate thus helped expose the assumption that middle-class whites naturally speak Standard English while African Americans naturally speak a distinct and substandard variety, and it drew attention to the role of this sociolinguistic hybrid in creating a white public space (see Hill 1998). Third, the Resolution placed sociolinguistic hybrids in a public sphere, that of educational policy; in schools, as in other public sphere contexts, the dominance of Standard English should go unchallenged.

The emergence of such strange bedfellows suggests to us once again that dominant economies of purifying and hybridizing practices play key roles in structuring social and political relations. Actors who seem to disagree on just about everything often tacitly hold very similar allegiances to these practices. Efforts to challenge racial and other structures of inequality will be sapped of their interpretive and political efficacy from the outset if they fail to challenge the ideological and metadiscursive underpinnings of established practices for purifying and hybridizing language.

Tradition, which has been reportedly on the verge of dying for more than three centuries, similarly continues to provide useful means of producing and legitimizing new modernist projects, sets of legislators, and schemes of social inequality. Interestingly, Zygmunt Bauman, an eminent critic of modernity, persists in relying on an uncritical foundational concept of tradition even as he provides an account of the social construction of modernity through differences in power and knowledge:

What strikes us most in the picture of the communal world is that the available means of production of security (and indeed, the fundamental conditions of human cohabitation), however effective they might have been in the traditional setting, reacted badly to an extension of their social space. By their very nature, they could only be operated in a relatively small group, on a relatively confined territory. They were also geared to a relatively stable setting, where points of reference, the other partners in the solid network of solidary relations, stay fixed over a protracted stretch of time. (1987: 39)

This representation of "the traditional setting" bears all the features of the modernist discourses from which it was taken. Tradition is taken as a bounded, real, stable object that can be defined with respect to relations and representations that are shared, relatively homogeneous, and tied to a restricted geographic space. In defining the social space of the traditional, Bauman evokes the image of face-to-face social interaction. He suggests that demographic pressures, along with political-economic and technological changes, brought this world to an end in the seventeenth century (1987: 40).

In characterizing modernity as "post-traditional," Anthony Giddens similarly argues that tradition, being "the glue that holds premodern social orders together" (1994: 62), constrains collective memory, requires rituals, revolves around "a formulaic notion of truth" that is pervasive in "oral cultures," is regulated by individuals whose authority is conferred by status rather than competence, and is authorized through its "moral and emotional content" (1994: 63). Tradition is resolutely local (and thus provides an excellent foil for imagining globalization). Tradition is so pervasive, he argues, that members of premodern societies are not even

aware that it exists or of the way that it shapes social relations and constitutes truth. Tradition, being all that modernity is not, must necessarily
disappear once modernity is firmly in place. As Giddens (1994: 91) puts
it succinctly, "Modernity destroys tradition." Their coexistence, that is,
a process in which modernity is eradicating tradition but has not yet succeeded in completing erasing it, marks "earlier phases of modern social
development." But with the emergence of high modernity or "reflexive
modernization" (see Beck 1994), the localized sites in which tradition
is sustained undergo "evacuation" in the wake of "growing time-space
distanciation" (Giddens 1994: 93). Beck (1994) tells us that "reflexivity"
involves self-confrontation, abstraction, the questioning of "the fundamental assumptions of the convention social order," and a shift to the
individual as the locus of politics and epistemology.

New social theories are often founded rhetorically on very old notions. Even as we become increasingly critical of all terms that stem from
the root "modern," the category of the traditional still seems – even to
critical and left-leaning social scientists – to be stable and transparent,
to be excused from the need for deconstruction. This is, of course, the
founding modern move – positing a category of tradition, making it seem
autonomous, and then creating new hybrids that contain tradition by
virtue of being defined in opposition to it. Here contemporary students
of modernity, globalization, reflexive modernity, and the like rehearse
classic modern moves. We hope that the cases we traced in previous
chapters show that any claim to deconstruct or get beyond modernity
that invokes these sorts of constructions of tradition is bound to fail
in that it infiltrates a founding modernist move into its own rhetorical,
epistemological, and political foundations. Paul Heelas (1996) suggests
that we can talk about a process of "detraditionalization" rather than
two discrete objects (tradition and modernity), and he notes that some
theorists think of forms of coexistence between detraditionalization and
retraditionalization. Nevertheless, a more nuanced opposition continues
to inform notions of (post)modernity, and the logic of temporality continues to structure imaginations of difference and social inequality. As
Chakrabarty (2000) forcefully reminds us, this sort of temporalization,
including the projection of notions of coexisting discrepant temporalities,
is modernity in a nutshell. Johannes Fabian (1983) noted long ago that
the "denial of coevalness" that structures colonial schemes of Otherness
is foundational to the project of modernity.

It is not simply high theorists, however, who seek to preserve the tradi-
tion/modernity opposition and use it to legitimize structures of authority.
Consider, for example, the ongoing efforts of United Nations agencies
for the "protection" and "safeguarding" of folklore. A cornerstone of

this effort is the *Model Provisions for National Laws on the Protection of Expressions of Folklore Against Illicit Exploitation and Other Prejudicial Actions* (1985), put forward by the World Intellectual Property Organization (WIPO). The framing of this document incorporates a classic othering device of modernity, the distinction between "industrialized" and "developing" countries, noting, in a metadiscursive inflection, that "Particularly in developing countries, folklore is a living, functional tradition, rather than a mere souvenir of the past" (1985: 3). But folklore, defined in good Herderian terms as "productions consisting of characteristic elements of the traditional artistic heritage developed and maintained by a community... or by individuals reflecting the traditional artistic expectations of such a community" (1985: 9), is under threat by "distorted" and "improper exploitation" (1985: 3). As in Herder's day, the supposedly unconscious or unreflexive nature of traditional knowledge justified the creation of specialists and specialized regimes: "In countries – where the traditional artistic heritage of a community is basically considered as a part of the cultural heritage of the nation, or where the communities concerned are not prepared to adequately administer the use of their expressions of folklore themselves, 'competent authorities' may be designated, to give the necessary authorizations in form of decisions under public law" (1985: 20).

Likewise, the UNESCO *Recommendations on the Safeguarding of Traditional Culture and Folklore* (1989), is motivated in significant part by recognition of "the extreme fragility of the traditional forms of folklore, particularly those aspects relating to oral tradition and the risk that they might be lost" (1989: 3), "eroded by the impact of the industrialized culture purveyed by the mass media" (1989: 5). How, then, are these fragile oral traditions, nested protectively in communities, to be safeguarded against the juggernaut of industrialized culture? The solution: more intervention by experts, enabled by Member States: encouragement of scientific, universalizing, rationalized tasks and tools (national inventories, global registers, coordinated classification systems, standard typologies, harmonized collecting and archiving methods), establishment of an institutional infrastructure for such expert tasks (national archives, documentation centers, libraries, museums, seminars, congresses), and support for the specialists who do the safeguarding work (training courses, full-time jobs for folklorists).

Here again, in these international documents produced at the *fin de millénaire*, is the vigorous reinstantiation of the "power/knowledge syndrome" that we have traced from Locke to Boas and that Zygmunt Bauman (1987: 2–3) identifies as "a most conspicuous attribute of modernity," namely, the intellectual as "legislator," authorized on the basis of claims to superior knowledge to make authoritative statements about the "maintenance and perfection of the social order" in the service of state power. Ironically, three centuries after the first framing of this distinctively modern syndrome in terms of discursive gaps between the past and the present, it still seems necessary to construct the demise of the premodern and to legitimate the ascendency of the modern in terms of the same dying gasps of "tradition" that Aubrey heard three hundred years ago. The venue may change from the Royal Society for the Improving of Natural Knowledge, chartered by the British king, to the UNESCO Committee of Governmental Experts on the Safeguarding of Folklore, an international body; the technologies of communication that put traditional discourse under threat may change from print to the televisual mass media; but metadiscursively speaking, *plus ça change, plus c'est la même chose.*

Disrupting modernity

If time-worn strategies for purifying language vis-à-vis nature/science and society/politics and for reinscribing the opposition between tradition and modernity – and for creating hybrids that link these terms in shifting ways – continue to be a facet of our (post)modern world, how can becoming aware of the historical dynamics of this process aid us in negotiating a politics of the present? Many writers have suggested that challenging schemes for the production and naturalization of social inequality centrally involves exposing the modernist epistemologies and practices they presuppose. Chatterjee and Chakrabarty similarly argue that understanding how Europe got deprovincialized is a necessary prerequisite to reprovincializing new universalist schemas, stripping them of their claims to speak for humanity apart from the historical, social, and power formations in which they are embedded. We have suggested that contemporary critical projects themselves bolster key foundations of the modernity they claim to challenge by engaging in the same purification and hybridization practices regarding language and tradition. We thus hope to have provided a new set of resources for scholarly attempts to disrupt the production of modernist projects and new strategies for exposing and resisting the structures of inequality they seek to legitimate. We have argued that claims to possess special techniques for creating conscious awareness of forms and processes that other subjects experience in an unexamined, unconscious, or distorted fashion bolster academic claims to the status of legislators.

Over the closing decades of the twentieth century, a number of scholarly challenges have been posed to received techniques for purifying and hybridizing language. Derrida (1967) criticized the way that such influential linguists as Saussure and Jakobson reified language; he thereby brought to light assumptions regarding the arbitrariness of the sign and the artificial character of writing *versus* the primordial status of speaking, and he traced the way that particular imaginings were transformed into cartographies of linguistic reality. Foucault (1970) provided an archaeology that details the history of efforts to construct language as an autonomous domain, starting with Cervantes's *Don Quixote*. Building on their insights, we have attempted to discern the broader project of purification that brought language, as a modern object of knowledge, into being. At the same time, we have attempted to show that even during single historical periods, practices of purification coexisted with hybridizing techniques. We have thus attempted to show that the power of language did not emerge due to the success of unified and pervasive regimes of purification but through their coexistence with techniques, sometimes explicit (as in the case of Herder) and often hidden (as for Locke), for creating sociolinguistic hybrids. Austin (1962) explored everyday hybridization of speech by pointing to the ways that language does things and that this performative quality is embedded in conventions and institutions. The work of Bakhtin (1981) and Vološinov (1973) are particularly valuable in discerning these hybridizing practices and how they operate within even the most austere regimes of purification. Their work seems to offer a challenge even to the concept of hybridization itself, the notion of connecting entities that had been previously purified, by showing how social categories are discursively constructed as they become attached to voices, words, and genres, just as speech forms emerge in relationship to social categories and relations. Our goal has not been to focus on purification and hybridization *per se*, but rather to suggest how these practices and the domain of language that they constructed made the very project of modernity possible. We have tried to show that rendering language invisible – or rendering it as a vital and acknowledged part of organic Herderian wholes – has played a key role in imagining and naturalizing new schemes of social inequality since the seventeenth century.

These more philosophical and literary approaches have often been viewed as antithetical to work that emerged in some relation to linguistics, be it sociolinguistics, linguistic anthropology, or some other hybrid form. But long ago, Sapir showed how grammatical patterns can be used in constructing women – and in subordinating them (1949). Labov (1966, 1972b) demonstrated that minute phonological and syntactic variations can carry a great deal of social information, even if he stopped short of showing how discourse helps constitute the categories of race, ethnicity, gender, and class that he examined and failed to challenge purified definitions of language. Hymes's (1974) ethnography of communication explicitly challenged the most purified view of language that had emerged, Chomsky's (1965) transformational grammar, by showing how deeply and how variably social knowledge was embedded in linguistic forms and communicative patterns. Jakobson (1957) and Silverstein (1976, 1979) have helped to challenge a major tenet of most purification practices by rejecting the reduction of language to decontextualized referential units; their work reveals the importance of the indexical connections that embed linguistic structure and meaning in social life. Silverstein (1979, 1981, 1985) has pointed to the language ideologies that shape how people – including linguists – think about and use language, and a number of collections have outlined the power of language ideologies in generating and legitimizing schemes of governmentality and structuring everyday life (see Kroskrity 2000; Schieffelin, Woolard, and Kroskrity 1998). In Europe, Critical Discourse Analysis reveals the linguistic strategies that are currently deployed in racializing and racist projects (see Bloomaert and Bulcaen 2000; Fairclough 1992; van Dijk 1993; Wodak and Reisigl 1999).

To be sure, such approaches have sometimes advanced the work of purification through the use of specialized terms and modes of analysis that preserve the authority of linguistic legislators. But the common construal of this work by practitioners in cultural and literary studies, cultural anthropology, philosophy, and other fields as a positivist and formalist enterprise that cannot inform larger theoretical and political questions erases its contribution to challenging practices of purification and revealing sociolinguistic hybrids that sustain projects of inequality. But rejecting linguistic analysis out of hand as mere formalism and positivism or, on the other hand, claiming to possess special tools that reveal the structures that non-linguists cannot discern, both serve to sustain modernist projects by leaving one of its cornerstones – the notion of an autonomous domain of language – intact. Both of these (broadly defined) research traditions have provided crucial resources for challenging modernist practices of purification and hybridity yet neither is sufficient in and of itself to enable the formulation of an effective critical stance.

Recently, scholars have pointed to the importance of practices of the imagination, whether they be aimed at imagining racial projects (Omi and Winant 1994), historical narratives (White 1978), or commodities and symbolic forms that circulate globally (Appadurai 1996). We have, of course, pointed consistently to the imaginings of language and tradition that provide the political technologies on which practices of the imagination can be produced and legitimized. But we have also argued consistently that tracking ideological dimensions is not enough. Beyond the tremendous differences that separated Locke's and Herder's respective ways of imagining language and tradition – and thus the dissimilar sets of purifying and hybridizing practices they promoted – they are much more similar with respect to the metadiscursive regimes that they promoted. In both cases, they accorded a type of consciousness to elites that they denied to subalterns, and they promoted particular types of literacy practices, imbued them with value, and provided access to aristocratic and bourgeois men respectively. Here we have tried to move beyond Foucault and Derrida by analyzing the role of formative texts – some still famous and others nearly forgotten – in terms of the way that they created metadiscursive regimes, shaped who would control them, channeled practices of the imagination, and established limits to what could be imagined and whose imaginings would be deemed authentic (the Other's) and whose would be authoritative (the elite's).

We have tried to point to the pivotal importance of *decontextualization*: what counts as a legitimate way of extracting discourse from persons, communities, nations, contexts, genres, etc. (all of these being social constructs) and recontextualizing it in others. As Bakhtin (1981) pointed out, this process creates relations of intertextuality, connections between the various discourses that are brought into dialogue in this process. We have argued that one of the most important ways that metadiscursive regimes are organized is in terms of purifying and hybridizing texts. Locke, for example, claimed that only texts that stood on their own discursive feet, without seeming to rely explicitly on any other person, text, or time, could make a claim to the truth. Although he thus promoted exclusive reliance on textual purification at the explicit level, his texts built their authority in part by dialogically engaging other texts – generally in order to denigrate them (as in his attack on Filmer in the first *Treatise*). Herder, the Grimms, Schoolcraft, and Boas, on the other hand, all pioneered techniques of textual hybridization in which written texts came to mirror as transparently and authentically as possible a set of primordial oral, traditional texts that they purported to recontextualize and the communities that collectively uttered them. To different degrees, they erased overt traces of textual gaps, indications of ways that their discourses were simultaneously claiming forms of elite authority that separated them from the supposedly unconscious, unreflective nature of their discursive precedents. We have argued that the devil is in the details, that it is necessary to look at the specifics of how these practitioners made texts and how they exhorted others to do so. These textual models helped to concretize metadiscursive regimes and thus to authorize particular practices of imagination, marginalize or eliminate others, and distribute control over this process in very unequal ways. And we have tried to show systematically how these interventions shaped modernity, science, and politics. In particular, ways of imagining language and tradition and shaping practices for representing them are always tied to schemes of social inequality, modes of imagining and controlling Others, and efforts to naturalize inequality.

We hope to have contributed significantly to grasping how Euro-American social forms and practices were deprovincialized or universalized by demonstrating how particular metadiscursive regimes were rendered powerful, became naturalized, and were projected as the universal bases of knowledge, truth, culture, nation, rationality, science, politics, and modernity – as unmarked, historically transcendent, and natural foundations of social life. One of the most fruitful aspects of Derrida's (1974) work is his constant deconstruction of the hierarchical logic of supposedly symmetrical binary oppositions, in which one term claims to transcend and encompass its opposite. Derrida thereby draws our attention to a central modernist strategy – claiming social, historical, and metadiscursive transcendence over peoples and discourses that lie at some social, geographic, and/or historical distance. Locke, for instance, did not simply contrast the linguistic epistemologies and practices he advocated to the projected understandings of women, the poor, merchants, cooks, lovers, the residents of Asia and America, and the Scholastics, but claimed to reveal the true nature of language; the models he constructed perfectly reflected this nature, while other practices entered the picture as avenues to the "cheat and abuse" of words, distortions and subversions of linguistic universals. This transcendental illusion cut the explicit links that bound Locke's doctrine to its social and historical location and cast it as a universal schema; the same move is apparent in his political theory. This strategy consisted of a sort of magical projection. It placed his epistemology outside of the historical and social setting in which it emerged and fashioned it into a powerful historical tool for unifying and reifying the heterogeneous ideologies and practices associated with the people and positions that Locke embraced and opposing these to a reified construction of those embraced by Others – who happened to represent nearly all of English society and most of the rest of the world.

Chatterjee (1993: 33) argues that colonial history is of critical theoretical and political importance not as a means of "seeing exceptions to universal history but how the supposed exceptions were part of the production of this universality, which is equally true of populations that have theoretically been turned into a body of citizens with equal rights." This question is of great importance for challenging the right of dominant ideologies, institutions, classes, and nation-states to subordinate and pathologize both internal Others as well as the numerically dominant "Third World"; identifying and challenging the ideologies and practices that underlie this process helps to strengthen the links that have been formed between a range of subaltern struggles. We hope to have contributed to this project in two principal ways.

First, an impressive body of literature has scrutinized the way that the creation of categories of Others played a key role in European expansion (see for example Greenblatt 1991; Hall 1996; Pratt 1992; Taussig 1987, 1993; Todorov 1984). We have tried to show that the construction of premodern or anti-modern groups played a key role in creating and legitimating modern discourses and social formations *from the start*, even in cases in which writers focused primarily on the transformation of Europe itself; moreover, imagining Others never seems to have lost its value as a means of producing and validating modern social forms. *Contra* Latour, the "Great Divide" opened up between moderns and premoderns is not "external," as opposed to the "Internal Great Divide" between nature/science and society/politics, nor is the former merely "a simple exportation" of the latter (1993). By the same token, imagining language and promoting metadiscursive regimes played a key role in practices for creating Others and naturalizing schemes of social inequality. Our discussion of purification and hybridization points to two fundamental techniques for imagining Others and establishing the bases for such categorical distinctions as natural and real. By making language seem faceless, decontextualized, abstract, and socially and historically disembodied, practices of purification could imagine Others by virtue of their projection failure to speak and write this language of the modern subject. Particular discursive failures thus implicitly identified classes of subaltern subjects. The Herderian–Grimmsian alternative was to imagine specific discursive practices and then attach them directly and explicitly to particular social categories. In both cases, textual gaps between speaking and writing practices then provided modes of turning social categories into real people, making them speak words that articulated their own subaltern status, and granting elites the power to ventriloquize their words in public arenas, or, in Spivak's (1981) terms, to make the subaltern speak and to speak for the subaltern. We hope to have illuminated why this process is so powerful and how it formed a key component of modernist projects from the start.

We have argued that modernist metadiscursive practices produce intertextual links and gaps, recontextualizing heterogeneous discursive forms in ways that create powerful senses of presence and absence, and then project them as social markers on mouths, bodies, and texts. Just as tradition always seems to be on the verge of disappearing, individuals, classes, or nations are accorded the mantle of the modern by virtue of their devotion, like Max Weber's (1930) Protestants in their anxious quest for salvation, to a range of practices that few can fully and consistently embody. Rather than anachronistically placing the proponents of dominant metadiscursive practices into the camp of the winners, we have tried to show how metadiscursive forms and practices associated with pre- or anti-modernity mingled intimately with markedly modern forms, even within single texts. Boyle's fascination with alchemy should not be erased in the interests of simplifying histories of scientific progress.

The reformist spirit of early English modernism can thus be characterized most fruitfully not as an historical exception but as an indicator of the mode of operation of modernist metadiscursive practices; since no one may exhibit the full range of social markers, each individual, class, gender, race, and nation can be ranked by virtue of the precise degree to which their words, texts, and actions are regimented by these practices. Chakrabarty (1992: 21) suggests that "Nowhere is this irony – the undemocratic foundations of 'democracy' – more visible than in the history of modern medicine, public health, and personal hygiene." This apt phrase, "the undemocratic foundations of 'democracy'," would seem to describe, however, at least as well the metadiscursive practices that shaped modernity.

Since modernist metadiscursive practices are ideologically linked to human nature, rationality, the nature of language, political and social relations, and other dimensions of social life, they can be projected as modes of social definition and surveillance that are applicable to all persons and all times. At the same time, since the degree to which modern metadiscursive practices are deemed to be embodied by particular individuals and communities reflects the social and political-economic constraints that mediate access to the distribution of social markers (educational institutions, professions, texts, technologies, and the like), who is able to embody the universal and to what degree can be carefully and subtly controlled. We feel that Chapters 2–4 provide a strong counterstatement to the widespread belief that the universalist and relativist strands of Enlightenment thought rendered it antithetical to formulations that explicitly legitimated social inequality, including racism – thereby characterizing slavery, for example, as a contradiction or exception. Rather, we have stressed the way that the ideologies and practices we analyzed from the Enlightenment and the Romantic Nationalist periods provided contrastive if equally effective modes of rationalizing social inequality and rendering it a cornerstone of modernity.

Second, we have tried to show that representations of the "exceptions" to modern ideologies and practices do not simply pit subaltern classes, race, or nations against a unified European provincialism. *Contra* Foucault and Habermas, we have not sought to reveal the presence of unified, all-pervasive epistemes, disciplinary technologies, or communicative structures. A clue is once again provided by Locke's inclusion of the "schoole-men" who practice the "art of disputation" along with merchants, lovers, cooks, tailors, women, the poor, "the day labourer in a country village" (1971 [1881]: 10), and the residents of Asia and the Americas among the cast of characters that he construes as modernity's Others. Boas's ideologies of history, art, and narrative and his metadiscursive practices similarly established the authority of anthropology to record and represent Native Americans as against the claims not only of Native Americans themselves but of journalists, missionaries, literati, and academics in other emergent or established disciplines. Elevating one set of practices as modern involved marginalizing challenges presented by other elite European males as well as by subaltern communities, even if crucial differences are evident in the strategies used in countering different challenges and particularly in the contrastive social and political effects that ensued when dominance was achieved. Discursive violence, if one wishes to use the expression, is not to be confused with genocide, slavery, or imperialism.

It is tempting to try to answer the important question of how this discussion can help us create research and political programs that try to avoid reproducing these structures of modernity and inequality. To do so, of course, might help ensure the textual success of our project by providing a set of formulae that can be easily recontextualized in future contexts, thereby advancing our own academic visibility. We have chosen not to do so. It seems clear that two white middle-class North American men are not in a position to dictate what would constitute an enlightened position on language and tradition for all readers of this book. Moreover, we would simply advance the process of declaring the failure of past approaches and attempting to launch a new reform movement, one that would consolidate our role as the new legislators of the moment. Nor is it enough to simply declare the death of purification, to argue that language is always already social and political, outlaw purification practices, and loudly proclaim another hybridizing bandwagon. The many ways that Herder's legacy has been used, including the uses of tradition to legitimize racist politics (by the Third Reich, for example) or the celebrations of national languages and literatures that run cover for efforts to extirpate minority languages and literatures, suggest that hybridizing practices are not automatically progressive and that a valid role for purification should not be ruled out. We would like, however, to offer some suggestions towards staking out more productive positions in dealing with these issues.

First, examining assumptions about language (including communication, discourse, text, literacy, etc.) and tradition (including premodernity, Otherness, etc.) must become a crucial part of the work of critically

assessing and challenging modernist projects. When language and tradition are deemed not to be of sufficient importance to warrant attention,
received practices of purification and hybridization – and the problematic
assumptions that lie behind them – go unchallenged. As we have argued,
this hiatus places important limits on the degree to which any study or
social, culture, and political project can challenge structures of inequality.

Second, scrutinizing ideologies of language and tradition is not sufficient. Using the term "language ideologies" should not lead us to internalize purification practices, that is, to think that once we analytically
isolate ideologies whose representational schemes revolve around notions of language, linguistics, orality, literacy, text, and conversation
from ideologies whose referents do not accord prominence to these notions, we have opened the door to human liberation. Similarly, studying
"traditional" or "premodern" people, practices, places, and so forth in
isolation from the "modern" entities they help constitute only reproduces
the status quo, as many critics of anthropology have argued in recent
decades.

Third, never let constructions of language and tradition masquerade as
cartographies of the real. These notions follow the path traced by Hayden
White (1978) for historical narratives – what is first imagined is then
transformed into the real, thereby covering up practices of imagination
and naturalization alike. The same cautions that James Clifford (1988)
provides for cultural constructions, never forgetting that they are partial,
fragmented, constructed, contested, and interested, applies just as clearly
to constructions of language and tradition.

Fourth, always ask whose models of language and tradition get purified
and hybridized. This step is necessary if we hope to challenge supposedly universal categories and process and prevent new deprovincializing
schemes from succeeding. Excluding people from purified categories of
modern, linguistically sophisticated subjects produces and naturalizes social inequality just as surely as placing individuals and populations in subordinated and stigmatized hybrid categories. Insofar as purification practices work, these relations become increasingly difficult to track, and both
dominant and subaltern positions become more and more internalized.

Fifth, analyze who gets to decide how language and tradition are constructed, how they relate to modernity, science, nature, politics, and society, which purification and hybridization practices will be visible and
which invisible, which legitimate and which denigrated, and who gets to
assess how individuals and populations get fixed by this process. Power
does not just accrue to those who claim it as the self-anointed embodiments of precision, rationality, truth, and the like. Some anthropologists
and linguists, for example, who assert that they do not fit in any normal

cultural or linguistic boxes (by virtue of possessing special forms of consciousness) claim power by virtual of their supposedly exclusive ability to see the boxes and determine how they get made. In short, it is crucial to track agency at every step of the way.

Finally, get down in the trenches without losing sight (to sustain a problematic metaphor) of the battlefield as a whole. We have argued consistently that it is crucial to study ideological constructions of language and tradition and the discursive practices of purification and hybridization that sustain them; once reified as properties of the real world, they become social facts that become visible, audible, and tangible aspects of social formations, spatial arrangements, public policies, etc. But we have also suggested that such study alone is not enough. Constructions of language do not overdetermine metadiscursive practices, and the dialectical relationship between the two includes important contradictions. Likewise, metadiscursive regimes vary considerably between sites they seek to regulate (educational, medical, judicial, and academic institutions, public assistance agencies, political debates, etc.), even when they presuppose relatively similar ideological constructions of language. The value of work inspired by Foucault notwithstanding, broad generalizations about linguistic epistemes end up reifying modern modes of reproducing inequality if they do not engage with the intricacies and the intimacies of metadiscursive regimes. Both the broad view and the detailed examination of practices of purification and hybridization are needed to provide tools for resisting structures of inequality and attempting to build less oppressive futures. Our book has been largely devoted to linking these two perspectives in the study of hegemonic texts, and we have accordingly left to the side examination of the enactment of metadiscursive regimes in everyday life. But we hope to have provided an analytic and historical account of why this project is so important to a politics of the present and we hope to have laid out ways of imagining how it might be carried out.

Epilogue: imagining postmodern futures

We opened our book with a quotation from Chakrabarty's project of provincializing Europe in order to locate our own political and epistemological work. We return to the text as we bring ours to a close, because it seems to suggest how deeply the issues we have raised are woven into modernity, including attempts to deconstruct or move beyond it. Chakrabarty finds the potential for a critical corrective to the hegemony of European historicism in the experience of the contemporary Bengali poet, Arunkumar Sarkar. In identifying the wellspring of his poetic vocation, Sarkar recalls the poetic ambience of his childhood:

Ever since I was a child, I was attracted to [the] sound [of language], and it was this attraction that gave rise to the desire to write poetry. My mother used to recite different kinds of poems, my father Sanskrit verses of praise [to deities], and my grandmother the hundred and eight names of [the god] Krishna. I did not understand their meanings, but I felt absorbed in the sounds. (quoted in Chakrabarty 2000: 251)

Keying on Sarkar's attunement to his parents' and grandmother's recitations, Chakrabarty goes on to explicate the temporalities implicit in Sarkar's recollection:

Arun Sarkar's statement nicely captures the nondecisionist aspects of his relationship to both the past and the future within which the "now" of his "writing poetry" moves. The "having been" of his mother's recitation of poetry, his father's of Sanskrit verses, and his grandmother's of the names of the Hindu god Krishna is (re)collected here in a movement of existence whose direction is futural. The futural direction of the movement is indicated by the phrase "the desire to write poetry." It is within this futurity that Arun Sarkar's poetry writing happens. (Chakrabarty 2000: 251–52)

What Sarkar is foregrounding in his recollection from childhood, and what Chakrabarty finds so suggestive, is the experiential and social and expressive resonance that derives from the assimilation of discourse to other discourse, the ways in which utterances are aligned to the already-said and anticipate the to-be-said in the discursive realization of social – here kinship – relations through time. In deriving his own writing of poetry from his mother's and father's and grandmother's recitations, themselves iterations of poetic texts from the past and of their own prior recitations (note the habitual aspect of "used to recite"), Sarkar is engaging in what we might identify as an elementary act of traditionalization. Here, tradition is a discursive accomplishment, a symbolic, interpretive construction creating discursive links to the past, rather than an intrinsic quality of pastness inherent in a perduring textual object. Note, too, that form matters in this act of traditionalization: it is the sonic texture of his parents' and grandmother's performances, impressed upon him from childhood, that provides the basis on which Sarkar can align his poetry to theirs. His father's and grandmother's recitations, though, bore a far closer intertextual relation to poetic antecedents than Sarkar's own compositions; the Sanskrit verses of praise and the one hundred and eight names of Krishna stand in a long line of recitational iterations that were held close to the textual mark, as we know, by metadiscursive ideologies that demand faithful replication in each recitation (Parthasarathy 1998: 240). That is to say that Sarkar realizes the futurity contained in his parents' recitations in a way markedly different from his father's realization of the futurity anticipated by the antecedent recitation of the source from whom he learned the Sanskrit praises. Sarkar's father closely replicates whole texts; Sarkar carries over sound patterns.

When Sarkar's reminiscence is opened out in these terms, we begin to hear resonances between his experience and his location in webs of discourse and the language ideologies and metadiscursive practices we have elucidated in the foregoing chapters. Chakrabarty and Sarkar might take us back to Herder, for example, who urged his readers to be attuned to an intertextually constituted tradition in which poetic form potentiates reiteration and textual fidelity, and in which poetic precedent anticipates further artistic production. Herder – and Sarkar's father and grandmother – valorize a metadiscursive regime of textual fidelity, close alignment of the now-said to the already-said; Sarkar himself stretches the intertextual gap by aligning his poetry to the sound patterns of the texts he heard as a child, but does not replicate the texts themselves; while Locke, at the other end of the spectrum, would maximize the intertextual distance between current and antecedent discourse in his determination to do away with traditional authority. That is to say that in significant part, all of the language ideologies and metadiscursive regimes we have examined – and we include Sarkar's here – are about the differential calibration of interrelationships that link current to past and future discourse, the values that are attached to them, and the practices by which they are accomplished.

Now, Chakrabarty makes a point of contrasting "the plurality of futures that already 'are'" in Arunkumar Sarkar's "desire to write poetry" from "the future that 'will be'" in what he identifies as "the politically modern position" (2000: 251). This future that will be is the anticipated future of modernity's master narrative, the full realization of the universal modernity by all who have not *yet* achieved modernity, stuck in the historicist backwaters of a premodern or underdeveloped or non-literate state. As Chakrabarty presents them – Sarkar too, one expects – the temporalities and intertextualities of this Bengali case are unencumbered by the weighty baggage of the European ideologies we have examined: no epochal gap separating antiquity from modernity; no forms of Othering that sustain the creation and promulgation of oppositional, Great Divide structures of social inequality; no essentialization and nationalization of language and culture, founded on homogenizing constructions, policies, and practices that neutralize or silence difference; no rhetorics of cultural etiolation and distress or of authenticity; no authorization of intellectuals as legislatiors; no universalizing telos of modernity. But is this in fact the case? Pretending to no expertise whatsoever in the language, culture, literature, or history of Bengal, we do not know (though we can surmise at least that the Sanskrit praises recited by Sarkar's father are the legacy of a Sanskrit cosmopolitanism that was at one time vast in its reach).

But that is just the point. If we truly want to provincialize Europe, a perspective via Bengali poetics and the experience of Arunkumar Sarkar is a good place from which to begin, but the indexical reach of parental and grandparental recitations and the temporalities created by acts of traditionalization in Bengali terms are only a beginning. We would want to know how the relationships among discourses are ideologized: where and by whom and under what circumstances they are articulated, what linguistic and discursive features they foreground or background in the calibration of intertextual links and gaps, what interests they serve, what alternative ideologies they challenge, and so on. And we would want to look closely – with careful attention to form and to form–function– meaning interrelationships – at the metadiscursive practices by which the calibrations of intertextual links and gaps are accomplished. What, precisely, is the relationship between Sarkar's father's recitations and antecedent ones? And between Sarkar's poetry and the recitations of his parents and grandmother? Is Chakrabarty's identification of Sarkar as a "*modern* Bengali poet" (Chakrabarty 2000: 251; emphasis added) merely a recognition of his contemporaneity? Or is it related somehow to his creation of a marked intertextual gap between his poetic compositions and his parents' and grandmother's recitations, by contrast with their close adherence to ready-made texts and performance conventions, a contrast akin to the discursive junctures identified by all of the figures we have considered as marking the advent of modernity? Finding answers to these questions demands that we look closely at the texts and the textual practices by which they are made and by which they are aligned to other texts, past and future. Again, form matters. If it matters to Sarkar – and to Blackwell or the Grimms or Boas – it should matter to those of us who want to comprehend their ideologies and their practices and to elucidate their implications for the politics of culture. That is the program that has guided this book, and that is what we commend to our readers, both as a vantage-point on history and on the discursive accomplishment of social life and as a critical and reflexive vantage-point on our own scholarly practice.

References

Aarsleff, Hans. 1982. *From Locke to Saussure: Essays on the Study of Language and Intellectual History*. Minneapolis: University of Minnesota Press.

— 1988. Introduction. In Wilhelm von Humboldt, *On Language: The Diversity of Human Language-Structure and Its Influence on the Mental Development of Mankind*. Peter Health, trans. Cambridge: Cambridge University Press.

— 1994. Locke's Influence. In *The Cambridge Companion to Locke*. Vere Chappell, ed., pp. 252–89. Cambridge: Cambridge University Press.

Abu-Lughod, Lila. 1991. Writing against Culture. In *Recapturing Anthropology: Working in the Present*. Richard G. Fox, ed., pp. 137–62. Santa Fe, NM: School of American Research Press.

Adams, Karen L., and Daniel T. Brink, eds. 1990. *Perspectives on Official English: The Campaign for English as the Official Language of the USA*. Berlin: Mouton de Gruyter.

Amsterdamska, Olga. 1987. *Schools of Thought: The Development of Linguistics from Bopp to Saussure*. Dordrecht: D. Reidel.

Anderson, Benedict 1991 [1983]. *Imagined Communities: Reflections on the Origin and Spread of Nationalism*. Revised edition. London: Verso.

Anonymous. 1996. Media Distort Black English Policy, Jackson Says. *New York Times* 31 December 1996.

Appadurai, Arjun. 1988. Putting Hierarchy in Its Place. *Cultural Anthropology* 3 (1): 36–49.

— 1996. *Modernity at Large: Cultural Dimensions of Globalization*. Minneapolis: University of Minnesota Press.

Aristotle. 1949. *The Organon*. Cambridge, MA: Harvard University Press.

Aubrey, John. 1862. *Wiltshire: The Topographical Collections of John Aubrey, F.R.S, A.D. 1659–70*. John Edward Jackson, ed. Devizes: Wiltshire Archaeological and Natural History Society.

— 1898. *"Brief Lives," Chiefly of Contemporaries*. 2 vols. Andrew Clark, ed. Oxford: Clarendon Press.

— 1949. *Aubrey's Brief Lives*. Oliver Lawson Dick, ed. Harmondsworth: Penguin.

— 1969 [1847]. *Aubrey's Natural History of Wiltshire*. K. G. Ponting, ed. New York: Augustus M. Kelley.

— 1972a. *Three Prose Works*. John Buchanan-Brown, ed. Carbondale: Southern Illinois Press.

— 1972b. *Aubrey on Education*. J. E. Stephens, ed. London and Boston: Routledge & Kegan Paul.

2000. *Brief Lives*. J. Buchanan Brown, ed. New York: Penguin Putnam.

Austin, John L. 1962. *How To Do Things with Words*. Cambridge, MA: Harvard University Press.

Bacon, Francis. 1860a. The Great Instauration. In *The Works of Francis Bacon*. James Spedding, Robert Leslie Ellis, and Douglas Denon Heath, eds. Vol. IV. New York: Garrett Press.

1860b. Novum Organum. In *The Works of Francis Bacon*. James Spedding, Robert Leslie Ellis, and Douglas Denon Heath, eds. Vol. IV. New York: Garrett Press.

1860c. Of the Dignity and Advancement of Learning. In *The Works of Francis Bacon*. James Spedding, Robert Leslie Ellis, and Douglas Denon Heath, eds. Vol. IV. New York: Garrett Press.

1860d. Preparative Towards a Natural and Experimental History. In *The Works of Francis Bacon*. James Spedding, Robert Leslie Ellis, and Douglas Denon Heath, eds. Vol. IV. New York: Garrett Press.

1860e. *De augmentis scientarium*. In *The Works of Francis Bacon*. James Spedding, Robert Leslie Ellis, and Douglas Denon Heath, eds. Vol. IV. New York: Garrett Press.

1968 [1857–74]. *The Works of Francis Bacon*. James Spedding, Robert Leslie Ellis, and Douglas Denon Heath, eds. 14 vols. New York: Garrett Press.

Bakhtin, M. M. 1981. *The Dialogic Imagination: Four Essays*. Caryl Emerson and Michael Holquist, trans. Michael Holquist, ed. Austin: University of Texas Press.

1986 [1979]. The Problem of Speech Genres. In *Speech Genres and Other Late Essays*. Caryl Emerson and Michael Holquist, eds., pp. 60–102. Austin: University of Texas Press.

Balibar, Etienne. 1991. Is There a "Neo-Racism"? In Etienne Balibar and Immanuel Wallerstein, *Race, Nation, Class: Ambiguous Identities*, pp. 17–28. London: Verso.

Barilli, Renato. 1989. *Rhetoric*. Guiliana Menozzi, trans. Minneapolis: University of Minnesota Press.

Barnard, F. M. 1965. *Herder's Social and Political Thought*. Oxford: Clarendon Press.

1969. *Herder on Social and Political Culture*. Cambridge: Cambridge University Press.

Bauman, Richard. 1992. Contextualization, Tradition, and the Dialogue of Genres: Icelandic Legends of the Kraftaskáld. In *Rethinking Context: Language as an Interactive Phenomenon*. Alessandro Duranti and Charles Goodwin, eds., pp. 125–45. Cambridge: Cambridge University Press.

1993. The Nationalization and Internationalization of Folklore: The Case of Schoolcraft's "Gitshee Gauzinee." *Western Folklore* 52: 247–69.

1995. Representing Native American Oral Narrative: The Textual Practices of Henry Rowe Schoolcraft. *Pragmatics* 5 (2): 167–83.

2001. Tradition, Anthropology of. In *International Encyclopedia of the Social and Behavioral Sciences*. Neil J. Smelser and Paul B. Baltes, eds., pp. 15819–24. London: Elsevier.

324   References

Bauman, Richard. and Charles L. Briggs. 1990. Poetics and Performance as Critical Perspectives on Language and Social Life. *Annual Review of Anthropology* 19: 59–88.

Bauman, Zygmunt. 1987. *Legislators and Interpreters: On Modernity, Postmodernity and Intellectuals*. Ithaca: Cornell University Press.

    1991. *Modernity and Ambivalence*. Cambridge: Polity.

Beck, Ulrich. 1994. The Reinvention of Politics: Towards a Theory of Reflexive Modernization. In *Reflexive Modernization: Politics, Tradition and Aesthetics in the Modern Social Order*. Ulrich Beck, Anthony Giddens, and Scott Lash, eds., pp. 1–55. Palo Alto, CA: Stanford University Press.

Bendix, Regina. 1997. *In Search of Authenticity: The Formation of Folklore Studies*. Madison: University of Wisconsin Press.

Benedict, Ruth. 1934. *Patterns of Culture*. Boston: Houghton Mifflin.

Bennet, James. 1996. Administration Rejects Black English as a Second Language. *New York Times* 25 December 1996.

Berlin, Isaiah. 1976. *Vico and Herder*. New York: Vintage.

Berendsohn, Walter. 1968 [1921]. *Grundformer volkstümlicher Erzählerkunst in den Kinder- und Hausmärcher der Brüder Grimm*. Hamburg: W. Gente. Reprinted, Wiesbaden: Martin Sändig.

Berman, Judith. 1991. The Seals' Sleeping Cave: The Interpretation of Boas' Kwakw'ala Texts. Unpublished Ph.D. dissertation, University of Pennsylvania.

    1992. Oolachan-Woman's Robe: Fish, Blankets, Masks, and Meaning in Boas's Kwakw'ala Texts. In *On the Translation of Native American Literatures*. Brian Swan, ed., pp. 125–62. Washington: Smithsonian Institution Press.

    1994. George Hunt and the Kwak'wala Texts. *Anthropological Linguistics* 36 (4): 483–514.

    1996. "The Culture as It Appears to the Indian Himself": Boas, George Hunt, and the Methods of Ethnography. In *Volksgeist as Method and Ethic: Essays on Boasian Ethnography and the German Anthropological Tradition*. George W. Stocking, Jr., ed., pp. 215–56. Madison: University of Wisconsin Press.

Bhabha, Jacqueline. 1996. Embodied Rights: Gender Persecution, State Sovereignty, and Refugees. *Public Culture* 9: 3–32.

Bieder, Robert E. 1986. *Science Encounters the American Indian, 1820–1880*. Norman: University of Oklahoma Press.

Birkerts, Sven. 1994. *The Gutenberg Elegies: The Fate of Reading in an Electronic Age*. Boston: Faber and Faber.

Blair, Hugh. 1970 [1765]. *A Critical Dissertation on the Poems of Ossian, Son of Fingal*. New York: Garland Publishing.

    1970 [1785]. *Lectures on Rhetoric and Belles-Lettres*. 3 vols. New York: Garland Publishing.

    1996 [1760]. Preface. In *The Poems of Ossian and Related Works*. Howard Gaskill, ed., pp. 5–6. Edinburgh: Edinburgh University Press.

Blackall, Eric. 1978. *The Emergence of German as a Literary Language, 1700–1775*. Ithaca: Cornell University Press.

Blackwell, Thomas. 1970 [1735]. *An Enquiry Into the Life and Writings of Homer*. New York: Garland.

1976 [1748]. *Letters Concerning Mythology*. New York: Garland.

Blommaert, Jan, and Chris Bulcaen. 2000. Critical Discourse Analysis. *Annual Review of Anthropology* 29: 447–66.

Boas, Franz. 1889. On Alternating Sounds. *American Anthropologist* 2: 47–53.

1894. Chinook Texts. *Bureau of Ethnology, Bulletin No. 20*. Washington: Government Printing Office.

1896. The Indians of British Columbia. *Journal of the American Geographical Society of New York* 28: 229–43.

1897. *The Secret Societies and Social Organization of the Kwakiutl. Report of the US National Museum*. Washington: Government Printing Office.

1898. *The Mythology of the Bella Coola Indians. The Jesup North Pacific Expedition, Anthropology, Memoirs of the American Museum of Natural History*, Vol. II.

1901. Kathlamet Texts. *Bureau of American Ethnology, Bulletin No. 26*. Washington: Government Printing Office.

1902. Tsimshian Texts. *Bureau of American Ethnology, Bulletin No. 27*. Washington: Government Printing Office.

1906. Some Philological Aspects of Anthropological Research. *Science* (n.s.) 23 (591): 641–45.

1907. Some Principles of Museum Administration. *Science* 25: 921–33.

1909. *The Kwakiutl of Vancouver Island. Publications of the Jesup North Pacific Expedition, Memoirs of the American Museum of Natural History*, Vol. VIII, Pt. II. New York: Stechert.

1910. *Kwakiutl Tales. Columbia University Contributions to Anthropology*, Vol. II. New York: Columbia University Press and Leyden: E. J. Brill.

1911. Introduction. In *Handbook of American Indian Languages*. Franz Boas, ed., pp. 5–83. Washington: Government Printing Office.

1916, Tsimshian Mythology. In *Thirty-First Annual Report of the Bureau of American Ethnology*, pp. 29–1037.

1917. Introductory. *International Journal of American Linguistics* 1 (1): 1–8.

1918. Kutenai Tales. *Bureau of American Ethnology, Bulletin No. 59*. Washington: Government Printing Office.

1920. The Methods of Ethnology. *American Anthropologist* 22 (4): 311–21.

1921. Ethnology of the Kwakiutl. In *Thirty-Fifth Annual Report of the Bureau of American Ethnology, 1913–1914*, Part 1, pp. 41–794. Washington: Government Printing Office.

1925a. Contributions to the Ethnology of the Kwakiutl. *Columbia University Contributions to Anthropology*, Vol. III. New York: Columbia University Press.

1925b. Stylistic Aspects of Primitive Literature. *Journal of American Folklore* 38: 329–39.

1927. *Primitive Art*. Oslo: H. Aschehoug.

1928a. *Bella Bella Texts. Columbia University Contributions to Anthropology*, Vol. V. New York: Columbia University Press.

1928b. Keresan Texts. *Publications of the American Ethnological Society*, Vol. III, Parts I and II. New York: American Ethnological Society.

1930. *The Religion of the Kwakiutl Indians, Part I: Texts*. New York: Columbia University Press.

1935a. *Kwakiutl Culture as Reflected in Mythology*. New York: American Folk-Lore Society.

1935b. Kwakiutl Tales: New Series. Part I: Translations. *Columbia University Contributions to Anthropology*, Vol. XXVI. New York: Columbia University Press.

1938. Mythology and Folklore. In *General Anthropology*. Franz Boas, ed., pp. 609–26. Boston: D. C. Heath.

1940a [1908]. Decorative Designs of Alaskan Needlecases: A Study in the History of Conventional Designs, Based on Materials in the U.S. National Museum. In *Race, Language and Culture*, pp. 564–92. New York: Free Press.

1940b [1914]. Mythology and Folk-Tales of the North American Indians. In *Race, Language and Culture*, pp. 451–90. New York: Free Press.

1940c [1916]. The Development of Folk-Tales and Myths. In *Race, Language and Culture*, pp. 397–406. New York: Free Press.

1940d [1917]. Introduction to *International Journal of American Linguistics*. In *Race, Language and Culture*, pp. 199–210. New York: Free Press.

1940e [1930]. Some Problems of Methodology in the Social Sciences. In *Race, Language and Culture*, pp. 260–69. New York: Free Press.

1940f [1932]. The Aims of Anthropological Research. In *Race, Language and Culture*, pp. 243–59. New York: Free Press.

1943. Recent Anthropology II. *Science* 98: 334–37.

1945. *Race and Democratic Society*. New York: J. J. Augustin.

1962 [1928]. *Anthropology and Modern Life*. New York: W. W. Norton.

1965 [1911]. *The Mind of Primitive Man*. New York: Free Press.

1966. *Kwakiutl Ethnography*. Helen Codere, ed. Chicago: University of Chicago Press.

1974 [1905]. The Educational Functions of Anthropological Museums. In Stocking 1974b, pp. 297–300.

Boas, Franz, and George Hunt. 1902a. *Kwakiutl Texts I. Publications of The Jesup North Pacific Expedition, Anthropology*, Vol. IV, *Memoirs of the American Museum of Natural History*, Vol. V.

1902b. *Kwakiutl Texts II. The Jesup North Pacific Expedition, Memoir of the American Museum of Natural History*, Vol. III. Leiden: E. J. Brill.

1905. *Kwakiutl Texts III. The Jesup North Pacific Expedition, Memoir of the American Museum of Natural History*. Leiden: E. J. Brill.

Böker, Uwe. 1991. The Marketing of Macpherson: The International Book Trade and the First Phase of German Ossian Reception. In *Ossian Revisited*. Hugh Gaskill, ed., pp. 73–93. Edinburgh: Edinburgh University Press.

Bolte, Johannes, and Georg Polivka. 1963 [1913–32]. *Anmerkungen zu den Kinder- und Hausmärchen der Brüder Grimm*. 5 vols. Leipzig: Dieterich. Reprinted, Hildesheim: Georg Olms.

Bonnell, Victoria E., and Lynn Hunt, eds. 1999. *Beyond the Cultural Turn: New Directions in the Study of Society and Culture*. Berkeley: University of California Press.

Bottigheimer, Ruth. 1987. *Grimms' Bad Girls and Bold Boys: The Moral and Social Vision of the Tales*. New Haven: Yale University Press.

Bourdieu, Pierre. 1991. *Language and Symbolic Power*. Gino Taymond and Matthew Adamson, trans. Cambridge, Mass.: Harvard University Press.

Bourne, Henry. 1977 [1725]. *Antiquitates Vulgares or the Antiquities of the Common People*. New York: Arno Press.

Brand, John. 1777. *Observations on Popular Antiquities*. Newcastle upon Tyne.

Braunschwig, Henri. 1974. *Enlightenment and Romanticism in Eighteenth-century Prussia*. Chicago: University of Chicago Press.

Bremer, Richard G. 1987. *Indian Agent and Wilderness Scholar: The Life of Henry Rowe Schoolcraft*. Mt. Pleasant: Clark Historical Library, Central Michigan University.

Briggs, Charles L. 1986. *Learning How to Ask: A Sociolinguistic Appraisal of the Role of the Interview in Social Science Research*. Cambridge: Cambridge University Press.

1993. Metadiscursive Practices and Scholarly Authority in Folkloristics. *Journal of American Folklore* 106: 387–434.

1997. Sequentiality and Temporalization in the Narrative Construction of a South American Cholera Epidemic. *Journal of Narrative and Life History* 7 (1–4): 177–83.

2002. Interviewing, Power/Knowledge, and Social Inequality. In *Handbook of Interview Research: Context and Method*. Jaber F. Gubrium and James A. Holstein, eds., pp. 911–22. Thousand Oaks, CA: Sage.

Briggs, Charles L., and Richard Bauman. 1992. Genre, Intertextuality, and Social Power. *Journal of Linguistic Anthropology* 2: 131–72.

1999. "The Foundation of All Future Researches": Franz Boas, George Hunt, and the Textual Construction of Modernity. *American Quarterly* 51 (3): 479–528.

Briggs, Charles L. and Clara Mantini Briggs. 2003. *Stories in the Time of Cholera: Racial Profiling in a Medical Nightmare*. Berkeley: University of California Press.

Brightman, Robert. 1995. Forget Culture: Replacement, Transcendence, Relexification. *Cultural Anthropology* 10 (4): 509–46.

Britton, John. 1845. *Memoir of John Aubrey, F.R.S.* London: J. B. Nichols & Son.

Broce, Gerald. 1981. Discontent and Cultural Relativism: Herder and Boasian Anthropology. *Annals of Scholarship* 2: 1–13.

Brown, Elizabeth G. 1953. Lewis Cass and the American Indian. *Michigan History* 37 (3): 286–98.

Bryson, Gladys. 1945. *Man and Society: The Scottish Inquiry of the Eighteenth Century*. New York: Augustus M. Kelley.

Buchanan-Brown, John 1972. Introduction. In Aubrey 1972, pp. xvii–xxxix.

Bunzl, Matti. 1996. Franz Boas and the Humboldtian Tradition: From Volksgeist and Nationalcharakter to an Anthropological Conception of Culture. In *Volksgeist as Method and Ethic: Essays on Boasian Ethnography and the German Anthropological Tradition*. George W. Stocking, Jr., ed., pp. 17–78. Madison: University of Wisconsin Press.

Bysveen, Josef. 1982. Epic Tradition and Innovation in James Macpherson's Fingal. *Acta Universitatis Upsaliensis, Studia Anglistica Upsaliensia 44*. Uppsala: Uppsala University.

Caffentzis, Constantine George. 1989. *Clipped Coins, Abused Words, and Civil Government: John Locke's Philosophy of Money.* Brooklyn, NY: Autonomedia.

Calhoun, Craig ed. 1992. *Habermas and the Public Sphere.* Cambridge, MA: MIT Press.

Campbell, Joseph. 1944. Folkloristic Commentary. In *The Complete Grimms' Fairy Tales.* James Stern, ed., Margaret Hunt, trans. New York: Pantheon.

Cannizzo, Jeanne. 1983. George Hunt and the Invention of Kwakiutl Culture. *Canadian Review of Sociology and Anthropology* 20 (1): 44–58.

Carroll, John B. ed. 1956. *Language, Thought, and Reality: Selected Writings of Benjamin Lee Whorf.* Cambridge, MA: MIT Press.

Centre for Contemporary Cultural Studies. 1982. *The Empire Strikes Back: Race and Racism in 70s Britain.* London: Hutchinson in association with the Center for Contemporary Cultural Studies, University of Birmingham.

Chakrabarty, Dipesh. 1989. *Rethinking Working-class History: Bengal, 1890–1940.* Princeton, NJ: Princeton University Press.

1992. Postcoloniality and the Artifice of History: Who Speaks for Indian Pasts? *Representations* 37: 1–26.

2000. *Deprovincializing Europe.* Princeton, NJ: Princeton University Press.

Chartier, Roger. 1994. *The Order of Books: Readers, Authors, and Libraries in Europe Between the Fourteenth and Eighteenth Centuries.* Lydia G. Cochrane, trans. Stanford: Stanford University Press.

Chatterjee, Partha. 1993. *The Nation and its Fragments: Colonial and Postcolonial Histories.* Princeton, NJ: Princeton University Press.

Chomsky, Noam. 1965. *Aspects of the Theory of Syntax.* Cambridge, MA: MIT Press.

Cicourel, Aaron V. 1982. Interviews, Surveys, and the Problem of Ecological Validity. *American Sociologist* 17: 11–20.

Clark, Robert J., Jr. 1969. *Herder: His Life and Thought.* Berkeley and Los Angeles: University of California Press.

Clements, William M. 1990. Schoolcraft as Textmaker. *Journal of American Folklore* 103: 177–92.

Clifford, James. 1988. *The Predicament of Culture: Twentieth-century Ethnography, Literature, and Art.* Cambridge, MA: Harvard University Press.

1997. *Routes: Travel and Translation in the Late Twentieth Century.* Cambridge, MA: Harvard University Press.

Clifford, James, and George E. Marcus eds. 1986. *Writing Culture: The Poetics and Politics of Ethnography.* Berkeley: University of California Press.

Cocchiara, Giuseppe. 1981 [1952]. *The History of Folklore in Europe.* Philadelphia: ISHI.

Codere, Helen. 1966. Introduction. In *Franz Boas, Kwakiutl Ethnography.* Helen Codere, ed., pp. xi–xxxii. Chicago: University of Chicago Press.

Cole, Douglas. 1985. *Captured Heritage: The Scramble for Northwest Coast Artifacts.* Seattle: University of Washington Press.

1991. The History of the Kwakiutl Potlatch. In *Chiefly Feasts: The Enduring Kwakiutl Potlatch.* Aldona Jonaitis, ed., pp. 135–68. New York: American Museum of Natural History and Seattle: University of Washington Press.

Collins, Randall. 1998. *The Sociology of Philosophies: A Global Theory of Intellectual Change*. Cambridge, MA: Harvard University Press.

Constantine, David. 1984. *Early Greek Travellers and the Hellenic Ideal*. Cambridge: Cambridge University Press.

Cooper, Thompson. 1963 [1917]. John Brand. In *Dictionary of National Biography*. Vol. II. Leslie Stephen and Sidney Lee, eds., pp. 1121–22. Oxford: Oxford University Press.

Courtney, William P. 1963 [1917]. Robert Wood. In *Dictionary of National Biography*. Vol. XXI. Leslie Stephen and Sidney Lee, eds., pp. 844–46. Oxford: Oxford University Press.

Crane, T. F. 1917. The External History of the Kinder- und Hausmarchen of the Brothers Grimm. *Modern Philology* 14: 577–610 and 15: 65–77, 353–83 (1918).

Crenshaw, Kimberle. 1989. Demarginalizing the Intersection of Race and Sex: A Black Feminist Critique of Antidiscrimination Doctrine, Feminist Theory and Antiracist Politics. *The University of Chicago Legal Forum* 139.

——— 1991. Mapping the Margins: Intersectionality, Identity Politics, and Violence against Women of Color. *Stanford Law Review* 43: 1241–99.

Cranston, Maurice. 1957. *John Locke: A Biography*. London: Longmans, Green.

Crawford, James. 1992a. *Hold Your Tongue: Bilingualism and the Politics of "English Only."* Reading, MA: Addison-Wesley.

——— ed. 1992b. *Language Loyalties: A Source Book on the Official English Controversy*. Chicago: University of Chicago Press.

Cripps, R. S. 1953. Two British Interpreters of the Old Testament. *Bulletin of the John Rylands Library* 35: 385–404.

Crow, Thomas. 1985. *Painters and Public Life in Eighteenth-Century Paris*. New Haven: Yale University Press.

Daiches, David. 1964. *The Paradox of Scottish Culture*. London: Oxford University Press.

——— 1986. The Scottish Enlightenment. In *A Hotbed of Genius: The Scottish Enlightenment, 1730–1790*. David Daiches, Peter Jones, and Jean Jones, eds., pp. 1–41. Edinburgh: Edinburgh University Press.

Darnell, Regna. 1990. Franz Boas, Edward Sapir, and the Americanist Text Tradition. *Historiographia Linguistics* 17 (1/2): 129–44.

——— 1992. The Boasian Text Tradition and the History of Anthropology. *Culture* 12 (1): 39–48.

——— 1998. *And Along Came Boas: Continuity and Revolution in Americanist Anthropology*. Amsterdam: John Benjamins.

——— 2001. *Invisible Genealogies: A History of Americanist Anthropology*. Lincoln: University of Nebraska Press.

Dégh, Linda. 1979. Grimm's Household Tales and Its Place in the Household: The Social Relevance of a Controversial Classic. *Western Folklore* 38: 83–103.

——— 1988. What Did the Grimm Brothers Give to and Take from the Folk? In *The Brothers Grimm and Folktale*. James M. McGlathery, et al. eds., pp. 66–90. Urbana: University of Illinois Press.

Derrida, Jacques. 1967. *Writing and Difference*. Alan Bass, trans. Chicago: University of Chicago Press.

1974 [1967] *Of Grammatology*. Gayatri Chakravorty Spivak, ed. Baltimore: Johns Hopkins University Press.

1988. *Limited, Inc.* Evanston, IL: Northwestern University Press.

Dick, Oliver Lawson. 1949. The Life and Times of John Aubrey. In Aubrey (1949): 17–161.

Dippie, Brian W. 1982. *The Vanishing American*. Lawrence: University Press of Kansas.

Dorson, Richard M. 1968. *The British Folklorists*. Chicago: University of Chicago Press.

Dundes, Alan. 1969. The Devolutionary Premise in Folklore Theory. *Journal of the Folklore Institute* 6: 5–19.

1985. Nationalistic Inferiority Complexes and the Fabrication of Fakelore: A Reconsideration of Ossian, the Kinder- und Hausmärchen, the Kalevala, and Paul Bunyan. *Journal of Folklore Research* 22: 5–18.

Dunn, John. 1969. *The Political Thought of John Locke*. Cambridge: Cambridge University Press.

1984. *Locke*. Oxford: Oxford University Press.

Dwyer, John. 1991. The Melancholy Savage: Text and Context in the Poems of Ossian. In *Ossian Revisited*. Howard Gaskill, ed., pp. 164–206. Edinburgh: Edinburgh University Press.

Eisenstein, Elizabeth L. 1979. *The Printing Press as an Agent of Change: Communications and Cultural Transformations in Early Modern Europe*. Two volumes. Cambridge: Cambridge University Press.

Eisner, Robert. 1991. *Travelers to an Antique Land: The History and Literature of Travel to Greece*. Ann Arbor: University of Michigan Press.

Ellis, John M. 1983. *One Fairy Story Too Many: The Brothers Grimm and Their Tales*. Chicago: University of Chicago Press.

Emeneau, Murray. 1943. Franz Boas as a Linguist. In *Franz Boas, 1858–1942*. A. L. Kroeber, et al. eds., pp. 35–38. Memoir 61, American Anthropological Association.

Epstein, Steven. 1996. *Impure Science: AIDS, Activism, and the Politics of Knowledge*. Berkeley: University of California.

Ergang, Robert. 1966 [1931]. *Herder and the Foundations of German Nationalism*. New York: Octagon Books.

Evans, Joan. 1956. *A History of the Society of Antiquaries*. Oxford: Oxford University Press for the Society of Antiquaries.

Fabian, Johannes. 1983. *Time and the Other: How Anthropology Makes Its Object*. New York: Columbia University Press.

Fairclough, Norman. 1992. *Discourse and Social Change*. Cambridge: Polity.

Farley, Frank E. 1903. *Scandinavian Influences in the English Romantic Movement*. Boston: Ginn and Company.

Farmer, Paul. 1992. *AIDS and Accusation: Haiti and the Geography of Blame*. Berkeley: University of California Press.

1999. *Infections and Inequalities: The Modern Plagues*. Berkeley: University of California Press.

Feldman, Burton, and Robert D. Richardson eds. 1972. *The Rise of Modern Mythology, 1680–1860*. Bloomington: Indiana University Press.

Fine, Elizabeth C. 1984. *The Folklore Text: From Performance to Print*. Blooming-
ton: Indiana University Press.
Fitzgerald, Robert P. 1966. The Style of Ossian. *Studies in Romanticism* 6: 22–33.
Foerster, Donald M. 1947. *Homer in English Criticism: The Historical Approach in
the Eighteenth Century*. New Haven: Yale University Press.
    1950. Scottish Primitivism and the Historical Approach. *Philological Quarterly*
    29: 306–23.
Formigari, Lia. 1988. *Language and Experience in 17th-century British Philosophy*.
Amersterdam: John Benjamins.
    1993. *Signs, Science and Politics: Philosophies of Language in Europe 1700–1830*.
    William Dodd, trans. Amsterdam: John Benjamins.
Foucault, Michel. 1970 [1966]. *The Order of Things: An Archaeology of the Human
Sciences*. New York: Vintage.
    1991. *The Foucault Effect: Studies in Governmentality*. Graham Burchell, Colin
    Gordon, and Peter Miller, eds. Chicago: University of Chicago Press.
Freeman, John F. 1959. Henry Rowe Schoolcraft. Ph.D. dissertation, History of
American Civilization, Harvard University.
Fugate, Joe K. 1966. *The Psychological Basis of Herder's Aesthetics*. The Hague:
Mouton.
Gaier, Ulrich. 1990. "Volk" und "Volker." In *Volkslieder, Übertragungen, Dich-
tungen*, by Johann Gottfried Herder. [=Johann Gottfried Herder, Werke,
vol. 3], pp. 865–78. Frankfurt-am-Main: Deutscher Klassiker Verlag.
Gaskill, Hugh. 1996. Herder, Ossian, and the Celtic. In *Celticism*. Terence Brown,
ed., pp. 257–71. Amsterdam: Rodopi.
Geertz, Clifford. 1973. *The Interpretation of Cultures: Selected Essays*. New York:
Basic Books.
Giddens, Anthony. 1994. Living in a Post-Traditional Society. In *Reflexive
Modernization: Politics, Tradition and Aesthetics in the Modern Social Order*,
by Ulrich Beck, Anthony Giddens, and Scott Lash, pp. 56–109. Palo Alto,
CA: Stanford University Press.
Gillies, Alexander. 1933. *Herder und Ossian*. Berlin: Junker und Dunnhaupt.
Gillingham, S. E. 1994. *The Poems and Psalms of the Hebrew Bible*. Oxford: Oxford
University Press.
Goody, John Rankin. 1977. *The Domestication of the Savage Mind*. Cambridge:
Cambridge University Press.
Greenblatt, Stephen Jay. 1991. *Marvellous Possessions: The Wonder of the New
World*. Chicago: University of Chicago Press.
Grimm, Jacob. 1819. *Deutsche Grammatik*. Vol. I. Göttingen: Dieterichs.
    1883 [1844]. *Teutonic Mythology*. James Steven Stallybrass, trans. Vol. III.
    London: George Bell and Sons.
    1984 [1851]. *On the Origin of Language*. Raymond A. Wiley, trans. Leiden:
    E. Brill.
Grimm, Jacob, and Wilhelm Grimm. 1884. *Grimm's Household Tales*. Margaret
Hunt, trans. 2 vols. London: George Bell and Sons.
    1981 [1816]. Foreword. In *The German Legends of the Brothers Grimm*. Donald
    Ward, ed. and trans. Vol. I, pp. 1–11. Philadelphia: Institute for the Study
    of Human Issues.

1981 [1816–18]. *The German Legends of the Brothers Grimm.* Donald Ward, ed. and trans. 2 vols. Philadelphia: Institute for the Study of Human Issues.

1986. *Kinder- und Hausmärchen: Gesammelt durch die Brüder Grimm. Vergrößerter Nachdruck der zweibändigen Erstausgabe von 1812 und 1815 nach dem Handexemplar des Brüder Grimm-Museums Kassel mit sämtlichen handschriftlichen Korrekuren und Nachträgen der Brüder Grimm sowie einem Ergänzungsheft, Transkriptionen und Kommentaren.* Heinz Rölleke, ed. with Ulrike Marquardt. 3 vols. Göttingen: Vandenhoeck and Ruprecht.

1987 [1819]. Preface to the second edition of *Die Kinder- und Hausmärchen.* In *The Hard Facts of the Grimms' Fairy Tales*, Maria Tatar, ed., pp. 215–22. Princeton: Princeton University Press.

Grimm, Wilhelm. 1856 [1850]. Literatur. In *Kinder- und Hausmärchen.* Jacob and Wilhelm Grimm. Vol. III, pp. 213–415. Göttingen: Dieterich'schen Buchhandlung.

Grobman, Neil. 1974. Eighteenth-Century Scottish Precursors of Folklore Research. Ph.D. dissertation in Folklore and Folklife, University of Pennsylvania.

Groom, Nick. 1996. Celts, Goths, and the Nature of the Literary Source. In *Tradition in Transition: Women Writers, Marginal Texts, and the Eighteenth-Century Canon.* Alvaro Ribeiro and James G. Basker, eds., pp. 275–96. Oxford: Clarendon Press.

Gruner, Rolf. 1977. *Theory and Power: On the Character of Modern Sciences.* Amsterdam: B. R. Gruner.

Guyer, Paul. 1994. Locke's Philosophy of Language. In *The Cambridge Companion to Locke.* Vere Chappell, ed., pp. 115–45. Cambridge: Cambridge University Press.

Habermas, Jürgen. 1987. *The Philosophical Discourse of Modernity.* Cambridge, MA: MIT Press.

1989 [1962]. *The Structural Transformtion of the Public Sphere: An Inquiry Into a Category of Bourgeois Society.* Thomas Burger and Frederick Lawrence, trans. Cambridge, MA: MIT Press.

Hall, A. Rupert. 1963. *From Galileo to Newton, 1630–1720.* New York: Harper and Row.

Hall, Stuart. 1996. The West and the Rest: Discourse and Power. In *Modernity: An Introduction to Modern Societies.* Stuart Hall, David Held, Don Hubert, and Kenneth Thompson, eds., pp. 184–227. Cambridge, MA: Blackwell.

Hall, Stuart, et al. 1996. Introduction. In *Modernity: An Introduction to Modern Societies.* Stuart Hall, David Held, Don Hubert, and Kenneth Thompson, eds. Cambridge, MA: Blackwell.

Halliday, M. A. K., and Ruqaiya Hasan. 1976. *Cohesion in English.* London: Longman.

Hallowell, A. Irving. 1946. Concordance of Ojibwa Narratives in the Published Works of Henry R. Schoolcraft. *Journal of American Folklore* 59: 136–53.

Hamann, Hermann. 1970 [1906]. *Die literarischen Vorlagen der Kinder- und Hausmärchen und ihre Bearbeitung durch die Brüder Grimm.* Berlin: Mayer and Müller. Reprinted, New York: Johnson Reprint.

Handler, Richard, and Jocelyn Linnekin. 1984. Tradition, Genuine or Spurious. *Journal of American Folklore* 97: 273–90.

Hansen, Miriam. 1993. Foreword. In *Public Sphere and Experience: Toward an Analysis of the Bourgeois and Proletarian Public Sphere*. Oskar Negt and Alexander Kluge, eds., pp. ix–xli. Minneapolis: University of Minnesota Press.

Harbsmeier, Michael. 1989. World Histories before Domestication: The Writing of Universal Histories, Histories of Mankind, and World Histories in Late Eighteenth-Century Germany. *Culture and History* 5: 93–131.

Harshbarger, Scott. 1995. Robert Lowth's Sacred Hebrew Poetry and the Oral Dimension of Romantic Rhetoric. In *Rhetorical Traditions and British Romantic Literature*, pp. 199–214. Bloomington: Indiana University Press.

Havelock, Eric A. 1963. *Preface to Plato*. Oxford: Blackwell.

   1982. *The Literate Revolution in Greece and its Cultural Consequences*. Princeton, NJ: Princeton University Press.

   1986. *The Muse Learns to Write: Reflections on Orality and Literacy from Antiquity to the Present*. New Haven, CT: Yale University Press.

Hayakawa, S. I. 1992 [1985]. The Case for Official English. In *Language Loyalties: A Source Book on the Official English Controversy*. James Crawford, ed., pp. 94–100. Chicago: University of Chicago Press.

Haywood, Ian. 1986. *The Making of History: A Study of the Literary Forgeries of James Macpherson and Thomas Chatterton in Relation to Eighteenth-Century Ideas of History and Fiction*. London and Toronto: Associated University Presses.

Heelas, Paul. 1996. Introduction: Detraditionalization and its Rivals. In *Detraditionalization: Critical Reflections on Authority and Identity at a Time of Uncertainty*. Paul Heelas, Scott Lash, and Paul Morris, eds., pp. 1–20. Cambridge, MA: Blackwell.

Hecht, Hans. 1933. *T. Percy, R. Wood und J. D. Michaelis: Ein Beitrag zur Literaturgeschichte der Genieperiode*. Stuttgart: W. Kohlhammer Verlag.

Heim, Michael. 1999. *Electric Language: A Philosophical Study of Word Processing*. 2nd ed. New Haven: Yale University Press.

Henry, Joseph. 1854 [1847]. Report of the Secretary [for 1847]. *Eighth Annual Report of the Board of Regents of the Smithsonian Institution*, pp. 119–39. Washington, DC: Government Printing Office.

   1855. Report of the Secretary. *Ninth Annual Report of the Board of Regents of the Smithsonian Institution*, pp. 7–30. Washington, DC: Government Printing Office.

   1858. Report of the Secretary. *Twelfth Annual Report of the Board of Regents of the Smithsonian Institution*, pp. 12–37. Washington, DC: Government Printing Office.

Hepworth, Brian. 1978. *Robert Lowth*. Boston: Twayne.

Herder, Johann Gottfried. 1833 [1782]. *The Spirit of Hebrew Poetry*. James Marsh, trans. 2 vols. Burlington, VT: Edward Smith.

   1966 [1787]. *Essay on the Origin of Language. On the Origin of Language: Jean Jacques Rousseau, Essay on the Origin of Languages and Johann Gottfried Herder, Essay on the Origin of language*. John H. Moran and Alexander Gode, trans. Chicago: University of Chicago Press.

1967 [1877–1913]. *Sämtliche Werke*. Bernhard Suphan, ed. 33 vols. Hildesheim: Georg Olms Verlagsbuchhandlung.

1968 [1784–91]. *Reflections on the Philosophy of the History of Mankind*. Chicago: University of Chicago Press.

1969. *Herder on Social and Political Culture*. F. M. Barnard, ed. Cambridge: Cambridge University Press.

1985. *Schriften zum Alten Testament*. Rudolf Smend, ed. *Werke in Zehn Bänden*. Gunter Arnold, et al., eds. Vol. II, pp. 11–23. Frankfurt am Main: Deutscher Klassiker Verlag.

1992. *Selected Early Works, 1764–1767*. Ernest A. Menze and Karl Menges, eds., Ernest A. Menze with Michael Palma, trans. University Park: Pennsylvania State University Press.

1993. *Against Pure Reason: Writings on Religion, Language, and History*. Marcia Bunge, ed. and trans. Minneapolis: Fortress Press.

1997. *On World History: An Anthology*. Hans Adler and Ernest A. Menzes, with Michael Palma, eds. Armonk, NY: M. E. Sharpe.

Herzfeld, Michael. 1982. *Ours Once More: Folklore, Ideology, and the Making of Modern Greece*. Austin: University of Texas Press.

1987. *Anthropology Through the Looking-glass: Critical Ethnography in the Margins of Europe*. Cambridge: Cambridge University Press.

Hill, Jane. 1998. Language, Race, and White Public Space. *American Anthropologist* 100 (3): 680–9.

Hill, Jane, and Bruce Mannheim. 1992. Language and World View. *Annual Review of Anthropology* 21: 381–406.

Hinsley, Curtis M., Jr. 1981. *Savages and Scientists: The Smithsonian Institution and the Development of American Anthropology, 1846–1910*. Washington, DC: Smithsonian Institution Press.

Hobbes, Thomas. 1968 [1651]. *The Leviathan*. C. B. MacPherson, ed. Harmondsworth, Middlesex: Penguin.

Hobsbawm, Eric, and Terence Ranger, eds. 1983. *The Invention of Tradition*. Cambridge: Cambridge University Press.

Höpfl, H. M. 1978. From Savage to Scotsman: Conjectural History in the Scottish Enlightenment. *Journal of British Studies* 17: 19–40.

Hrushovski, Benjamin. 1971. Prosody, Hebrew. *Encyclopedia Judaica* 7: 1200–2. New York.

Hubatsch, Walther. 1975. *Frederick the Great of Prussia: Absolutism and Administration*. London: Thames and Hudson.

Huddleston, Walter. 1992 [1983]. The Misdirected Policy of Bilingualism. In *Language Loyalties: A Source Book on the Official English Controversy*. James Crawford, ed., pp. 114–18. Chicago: University of Chicago Press.

Hudson, Nicholas. 1996. "Oral Tradition": The Evolution of an Eighteenth-century Concept. In *Tradition in Transition: Women Writers, Marginal Texts, and the Eighteenth-Century Canon*. Alvaro Ribeiro and James G. Basker, eds., pp. 161–76. Oxford: Clarendon Press.

Humboldt, Wilhelm von. 1988 [1836]. *On Language: The Diversity of Human Language-Structure and Its Influence on the Mental Development of Mankind*. Peter Health, trans. Cambridge: Cambridge University Press.

Hume, David. 1932. *Letters of David Hume*. 2 vols. J. Y. T. Grieg, ed. Oxford: Oxford University Press.

Hume, David. 1964. On the Authenticity of Ossian's Poems. In *Essays, Moral, Political, and Literary*. T. H. Green and T. H. Grose, eds., Vol. II, pp. 415–24.

Hunter, Michael. 1975. *John Aubrey and the World of Learning*. London: Duckworth.

1982. *The Royal Society and its Fellows 1660–1700: The Morphology of an Early Scientific Institution*. Chalfont St. Giles, Bucks, England: British Society for the History of Science.

Hymes, Dell H. 1961. Review of the Anthropology of Franz Boas. Walter Goldschmidt, ed. *Journal of American Folklore* 74: 87–90.

1970. Linguistic Method in Ethnography, In *Method and Theory in Linguistics*. Paul L. Garvin, ed., pp. 249–311. The Hague: Mouton.

1974. *Foundations in Sociolinguistics: An Ethnographic Approach*. Philadelphia: University of Pennsylvania Press.

1975. Folklore's Nature and the Sun's Myth. *Journal of American Folklore* 88: 346–69.

1980. *Language in Education: Ethnographic Essays*. Washington, DC: Center for Applied Linguistics.

1983. *Essays in the History of Linguistic Anthropology*. Amsterdam: John Benjamins.

Irvine, Judith T., and Susan Gal. 2000. Language Ideology and Linguistic Differentiation. In *Regimes of Language: Ideologies, Polities, and Identities*. Paul V. Kroskrity, ed., pp. 35–83. Santa Fe, NM: School of American Research.

Jacknis, Ira. 1980. Franz Boas and Photography. *Studies in Visual Communication* 10: 2–60.

1989. The Storage Box of Tradition: Museums, Anthropologists, and Kwakiutl Art, 1881–1981. Ph.D. dissertation, Department of Anthropology, University of Chicago.

1991. George Hunt, Collector of Indian Specimens. In *Chiefly Feasts: The Enduring Kwakiutl Potlatch*. Aldona Jonaitis, ed., pp. 177–224. New York: American Museum of Natural History and Seattle: University of Washington Press.

1992. George Hunt, Kwakiutl Photographer. In *Anthropology and Photography: 1860–1920*. Elizabeth Edwards, ed., pp. 143–51. New Haven: Yale University Press.

1996. The Ethnographic Object and the Object of Ethnology in the Early Career of Franz Boas. In *Volksgeist as Method and Ethic: Essays on Boasian Ethnography and the German Anthropological Tradition*. George W. Stocking, Jr., ed., pp. 185–214. Madison: University of Wisconsin Press.

Jacobs, Melville. 1959a. Boas' View of Grammatical Meaning." In *The Anthropology of Franz Boas: Essays on the Centenary of His Birth*. Walter Goldschmidt, ed., pp. 139–45. San Francisco: Howard Chandler.

Jakobson, Roman. 1944 Franz Boas' Approach to Language. *International Journal of American Linguistics* 10 (4): 188–95.

1957. *Shifters, Verbal Categories, and the Russian Verb*. Cambridge, MA: Harvard University Russian Language Project.

1960. Closing Statement: Linguistics and Poetics. In *Style in Language*. Thomas A. Sebeok, ed., pp. 350–77. Cambridge, MA: MIT Press.

Jameson, Frederic. 1972. *The Prison-house of Language*. Princeton: Princeton University Press.

Jardine, Lisa. 1974. *Francis Bacon: Discovery and the Art of Discourse*. Cambridge: Cambridge University Press.

Jaszi, Peter. 1991. Toward a Theory of Copyright: The Metamorphoses of "Authorship." *Duke Law Journal* 3: 455–502.

Jiriczek, Otto L. 1935. Zur Bibliographie und Textgeschichte von Hugh Blair's Critical Dissertation on the Poems of Ossian. *Englishche Studien* 70: 181–89.

Johns, Adrian. 1998. *The Nature of the Book: Print and Knowledge in the Making*. Chicago: University of Chicago Press.

Jonaitis, Aldona, ed. 1995. *A Wealth of Thought: Franz Boas on Native American Art*. Seattle: University of Washington Press.

Kahn, Joel. 1989. Culture: Demise or Resurrection? *Critique of Anthropology* 9 (2): 5–25.

Kamenetsky, Christa. 1973. The German Folklore Revival in the Eighteenth Century: Herder's Theory of Naturpoesie. *Journal of Popular Culture* 6: 836–48.

1992. *The Brothers Grimm and Their Critics*. Athens: Ohio University Press.

Kant, Immanuel. 1991 [1795]. Perpetual Peace: A Philosophical Sketch. In *Kant: Political Writings*. Hans Reiss, ed. H. B. Nisbet, trans., pp. 93–130. Cambridge: Cambridge University Press.

1991 [1784]. Idea for a Universal History with a Cosmopolitan Purpose. In *Kant: Political Writings*. Hans Reiss, ed., H. B. Nisbet, trans., pp. 41–53. Cambridge: Cambridge University Press.

Keller, Evelyn Fox. 1985. *Reflections on Gender and Science*. New Haven, CT: Yale University Press.

Kernan, Alvin. 1987. *Printing Technology, Letters and Samuel Johnson*. Princeton: Princeton University Press.

Kite, Jon Bruce. 1993. *A Study of the Works and Reputation of John Aubrey (1626–1697), with Emphasis on His Brief Lives*. Lewiston: The Edwin Mellen Press.

Klein, Lawrence E. 1994. *Shaftesbury and the Culture of Politeness: Moral Discourse and Cultural Politics in Early Eighteenth-Century England*. Cambridge: Cambridge University Press.

Koerner, Konrad. 1990. Jacob Grimm's Position in the Development of Linguistics as a Science. In *The Grimm Brothers and the Germanic Past*. Elmer H. Antonsen, ed. with James W. Marchand and Ladislav Zgusta, pp. 7–23. Amsterdam: John Benjamins.

Kopff, E. C. 1996. Society of Dilettanti. In *An Encyclopedia of the History of Classical Archaeology*. Nancy Thomson de Grummond, ed., Vol. II, pp. 1037–38. Westport, CT: Greenwood Press.

Koptiuch, Kristin. 1991. Third-Worlding at Home. *Social Text* 9: 87–99.

Kozol, Jonathan. 1991. *Savage Inequalities: Children in America's Schools*. New York: Crown.

Kroskrity, Paul, ed. 2000. *Regimes of Language: Ideologies, Polities, and Identities*. Santa Fe: SAR Press.

Kugel, James L. 1981. *The Idea of Biblical Poetry*. New Haven: Yale University Press.

Labov, William. 1966. *The Social Stratification of English in New York City*. Washington, DC: Center for Applied Linguistics.

1972a. *Language in the Inner City*. Philadelphia: University of Pennsylvania Press.

1972b. *Sociolinguistic Patterns*. Philadelphia: University of Pennsylvania Press.

Landes, Joan. 1988. *Women and the Public Sphere in the Age of the French Revolution*. Ithaca, NY: Cornell University Press.

Laslett, Peter. 1960. Introduction. In *Two Treatises of Government by John Locke*. Peter Laslett, ed., pp. 15–135. Cambridge: Cambridge University Press.

Latour, Bruno. 1987. *Science in Action*. Cambridge, MA: Harvard University Press.

1988 [1984]. *The Pasteurization of France*. Alan Sheridan and John Law, trans. Cambridge, MA: Harvard University Press.

1993 [1991]. *We Have Never Been Modern*. Cathererine Porter, trans. Cambridge, MA: Harvard University Press.

Latour, Bruno, and Steve Woolgar. 1979. *Laboratory Life: The Construction of Scientific Facts*. Beverly Hills, CA: Sage.

Leersson, Joep. 1998. Ossianic Liminality: Between Native Tradition and Pre-romantic Taste. In *From Gaelic to Romantic: Ossianic Translations*. Fiona Stafford and Howard Gaskill, eds., pp. 1–16. Amsterdam: Rodopi.

Lehmann, W. C. 1930. *Adam Ferguson and the Beginnings of Modern Sociology*. New York: Columbia University Press.

Levine, Joseph M. 1991. *The Battle of the Books: History and Literature in the Augusan Age*. Ithaca: Cornell University Press.

Lévi-Strauss, Claude. 1966. *The Savage Mind*. Chicago: University of Chicago Press.

Lewis, Herbert S. 1998. The Misrepresentation of Anthropology and its Consequences. *American Anthropologist* 100 (3): 716–31.

2001. The Passion of Franz Boas. *American Anthropologist* 103 (2): 447–67.

Lewis, Neil A. 1996. Black English Is Not a Second Language, Jackson Says. *New York Times* 23 December 1996.

Liss, Julia Elizabeth. 1990. The Cosmopolitan Imagination: Franz Boas and the Development of American Anthropology. Unpublished Ph.D. dissertation, University of California, Berkeley.

Locke, John. 1714 [1689]. Letter on Toleration. In *The Works of John Locke*. Vol. II, pp. 229–56. London: John Churchill.

1714 [1691]. Some Considerations of the Consequences of the Lowering of Interest, and Raising the Value of Money. In *The Works of John Locke*. Vol. II, pp. 1–55. London: John Churchill.

1714 [1695]a. Further Considerations Concerning Raising the Value of Money. In *The Works of John Locke*. Vol. II, pp. 63–98. London: John Churchill.

1714 [1695]b. The Reasonableness of Christianity, as Delivered in the Scriptures. In *The Works of John Locke*. Vol. II, pp. 471–541. London: John Churchill.

1714 [1697]. A Second Vindication of the Reasonableness of Christianity, &c. In *The Works of John Locke*. Vol. II, pp. 555–671. London: John Churchill.

1954. *Essays on the Law of Nature*. Oxford: Clarendon Press.

1959 [1690]. *An Essay Concerning Human Understanding*. 2 vols. New York: Dover.

1960 [1690]. *Two Treatises of Government*. New York: New American Library.

1966. *Of the Conduct of the Understanding*. Francis W. Garforth, ed. New York: Teachers College Press.

1989 [1693]. *Some Thoughts Concerning Education*. Oxford: Clarendon Press.

Longfellow, Henry Wadsworth. 1992 [1855]. *The Song of Hiawatha*. Rutland: Charles E. Tuttle Co.

Lord, Albert Bates. 1960. *The Singer of Tales*. Cambridge, MA: Harvard University Press.

Lowe, Lisa, and David Lloyd. 1997. Introduction. In *The Politics of Culture in the Shadow of Capital*. Durham, NC: Duke University Press.

Lowth, Robert. 1969 [1787]. *Lectures on the Sacred Poetry of the Hebrews*. 2 vols. Hildesheim: Georg Olms Verlag.

1979 [1762]. *Short Introduction to English Grammar*. New York: Scholars' Facsimiles and Reprints.

1995 [1778]. *Isaiah: A New Translation*. London: Routledge/Thoemmes Press.

MacCraith, Mícheál. 1996. The "Forging" of Ossian. In *Celticism*. Terence Brown, ed., pp. 125–41. Amsterdam: Rodopi.

MacPherson, C. B. 1962. *The Political Theory of Possessive Individualism: Hobbes to Locke*. Oxford: Oxford University Press.

Macpherson, James. 1996. *The Poems of Ossian and Related Works*. Howard Gaskill, ed. Edinburgh: Edinburgh University Press.

Mannheim, Bruce. 1991. *The Language of the Inka since the European Invasion*. Austin: University of Texas Press.

Marcus, George E., and Michael M. J. Fischer. 1986. *Anthropology as Cultural Critique: An Experimental Moment in the Human Sciences*. Chicago: University of Chicago Press.

Marschall, May Horning. 1991. Oral Traditions, Written Collections: Johann Gottfried Herder and the Brothers Grimm. Unpublished Ph.D. dissertation, Johns Hopkins University.

Marsden, Michael T. 1976. Henry Rowe Schoolcraft: A Reappraisal. *The Old Northwest* 2: 153–82.

Maud, Ralph. 1982. *A Guide to B.C. Indian Myth and Legend: A Short History of Myth-Collecting and a Survey of Published Texts*. Vancouver, BC: Talonbooks.

1985. The Henry Tate-Franz Boas Collaboration on Tsimshian Mythology. *American Ethnologist* 16: 156–62.

2000. *Transmission Difficulties: Franz Boas and Tsimshian Mythology*. Burnaby, BC: Talonbooks.

McKean, Thomas A. 2001. The Fieldwork Legacy of James Macpherson. *Journal of American Folklore* 114 (454): 447–63.

McKenney, Thomas L. 1959 [1827]. *Sketches of a Tour to the Lakes*. Baltimore: Fielding Lucas. Repr. ed. Minneapolis: Ross & Haines.

McNeil, W. K. 1992. New Introduction. In *Schoolcraft* 1992 [1839]: 1–18.

Meek, Donald E. 1991. The Gaelic Ballads of Scotland, Creativity and Adaptation. In *Ossian Revisited*. Howard Gaskill, ed., pp. 19–48. Edinburgh: Edinburgh University Press.

Meek, Ronald L. 1976. *Social Science and the Ignoble Savage*. Cambridge: Cambridge University Press.

Mehta, Uday Singh. 1992. *The Anxiety of Freedom: Imagination and Individuality in Locke's Political Thought*. Ithaca, NY: Cornell University Press.

Mendoza-Denton, Norma. 1999. Sociolinguistics and Linguistic Anthropology of US Latinos. *Annual Review of Anthropology* 28: 375–95.

Merchant, Carolyn. 1980. *The Death of Nature*. San Francisco: Harper & Row.

Michaelis-Jena, Ruth. 1970. *The Brothers Grimm*. London: Routledge and Kegan Paul.

Mieder, Wolfgang. 1986a. *"Findet, so werdet ihr suchen!": Die Brüder Grimm und das Sprichwort*. Berne: Peter Lang.

1986b. Wilhelm Grimm's Proverbial Additions in the Fairy Tales. *Proverbium* 3: 59–83.

1988. "Ever Eager to Incorporate Folk Proverbs": Wilhelm Grimm's Proverbial Additions in the Fairy Tales. In *The Brothers Grimm and the Folktale*. James M. McGlathery, ed. with Larry W. Danielson, Ruth E. Lorbe, and Selma K. Richardson, pp. 112–32. Urbana: University of Illinois Press.

Mignolo, Walter. 2000. The Many Faces of Cosmo-Polis: Border Thinking and Critical Cosmpolitanism. *Public Culture* 12 (3): 721–48.

Morgan, Marcyliena. 1994. Theories and Politics in African American English. *Annual Review of Anthropology* 23: 325–45.

Morton, Michael. 1989. *Herder and the Poetics of Thought*. University Park: Pennsylvania State University Press.

Mossner, Ernest C. 1970 [1954]. *The Life of David Hume*. Oxford: Clarendon Press.

Moyne, Ernest J. 1963. *Hiawatha and Kalevala*. FFC 192. Helsinki: Suomalainen Tiedeakatemia.

Murray, Stephen O. 1983. *Group Formation in Social Science*. Carbondale, IL and Edmonton, Alberta, Canada: Linguistic Research.

1985. A Pre-Boasian Sapir? *Historiographia Linguistica* 12: 267–69.

Negt, Oskar and Alexander Kluge. 1993. *The Public Sphere and Experience*. Peter Labanyi, Jamie Daniel, and Assenka Oksiloff, trans. Mineapolis: University of Minnesota Press.

Nichols, John D. and Earl Nyholm. 1995. *A Concise Dictionary of Minnesota Ojibwe*. Minneapolis: University of Minnesota Press.

Olender, Maurice. 1992. *The Languages of Paradise: Race, Religion, and Philology in the Nineteenth Century*. Arthur Goldhammer, trans. Cambridge, MA: Harvard University Press.

Omi, Michael and Howard Winant. 1994. *Racial Formation in the United States: From the 1960s to the 1990s*. New York: Routledge.

Ong, Walter J. 1967. *The Presence of the Word: Some Prolegmoena for Cultural and Religious History*. Mineapolis: University of Minnesota Press.

1982. *Orality and Literacy: The Technologizing of the Word*. London: Methuen.

Osborn, Chase and Stellanova Osborn. 1942. *Schoolcraft → Longfellow → Hiawatha*. Lancaster: Jaques Cattell Press.

Parmentier, Richard J. 1985. Sign's Place *in medias res*: Peirce's Concept of Semiotic Mediation. In *Semiotic Mediation: Sociocultural and Psychological Perspectives*. Elizabeth Mertz and Richard J. Parmentier, eds., pp. 23–48. Orlando, FL: Academic Press.

Parry, Graham. 1995. *The Trophies of Time: English Antiquarians of the Seventeenth Century*. Oxford: Oxford University Press.

Parry, Milman. 1971. *The Making of Homeric Verse: The Collected Papers of Milman Parry*. Adam Parry, ed. Oxford: Clarendon Press.

Parthasarathy, R. 1998. Indian Oral Traditions. In *Teaching Oral Traditions*. John Miles Foley, ed., pp. 239–49. New York: Modern Language Association.

Pateman, Carole. 1980. *The Disorder of Women: Democracy, Feminism and Political Theory*. Cambridge: Polity.

1988. *The Sexual Contract*. Stanford, CA: Stanford University Press.

Pearce, Roy Harvey. 1945. The Eighteenth-Century Scottish Primitivists: Some Reconsiderations. *Journal of English Literary History* 12: 203–20.

Peirce, Charles Sanders. 1932. *Collected Papers of Charles Sanders Peirce*. Vol. II, *Elements of Logic*. C. Hartshorne and P. Weiss, eds. Cambridge, MA: Harvard University Press.

Peppard, Murray B. 1971. *Paths Through the Forest: A Biography of the Brothers Grimm*. New York: Holt, Rinehart and Winston.

Perry, Theresa, and Lisa Delpit, eds. 1998. *The Real Ebonics Debate: Power, Language, and the Education of African-American Children*. Boston: Beacon.

Phillipson, Nicholas. 1981. The Scottish Englightenment. In *The Enlightenment in National Context*. Roy Porter and Mikul's Teich, eds., pp. 19–40. Cambridge: Cambridge University Press.

Pollock, Sheldon, 1998a. Indian in the Vernacular Millennium: Literary Culture and Polity, 1000–1500. *Daedalus* 127 (3): 41–74.

1998b. The Cosmopolitcan Vernacular. *Journal of Asian Studies* 57 (1): 6–37.

2000. Cosmopolitan and Vernacular in History. *Public Culture* 12 (3): 591–625.

Poovey, Mary. 1998. *A History of the Modern Fact: Problems of Knowledge in the Sciences of Wealth and Society*. Chicago: University of Chicago Press.

Porter, James. 2001. "Bring Me the Head of James Macpherson": The Execution of Ossian and the Wellsprings of Folkloristic Discourse. *Journal of American Folklore* 114 (454): 396–435.

Porter, Roy. 2000. *The Creation of the Modern World: The British Enlightenment*. New York: W. W. Norton.

Powell, John Wesley. 1883. Report of the Director. *Second Annual Report of the Bureau of [American] Ethnology, 1880–1881*. Washington, DC: Government Printing Office.

Pratt, Mary Louise. 1992. *Imperial Eyes: Travel Writing and Transculturaltion*. London: Routledge.

Prickett, Stephen. 1986. *Words and the Word: Language, Poetics and Biblical Inter-pretation.* Cambridge: Cambridge University Press.

Propp, V. 1968. *Morphology of the Folktale.* Laurence Scott, trans., Louis A. Wagner, ed. Austin: University of Texas Press.

Prucha, Francis Paul. 1967. *Lewis Cass and American Indian Policy.* Detroit: Wayne State University Press.

Purver, Margery. 1967. *The Royal Society: Concept and Creation.* Cambridge, MA: MIT Press.

Radin, Paul. 1957 [1927]. *Primitive Man as Philosopher.* New York: Dover.

Raynor, David. 1991. Ossian and Hume. In *Ossian Revisited.* Howard Gaskill, ed., pp. 147–63. Edinburgh: Edinburgh University Press.

Rhodes, Richard A. 1985. *Eastern Ojibwa–Chippewa–Ottowa Dictionary.* Berlin: Mouton.

Rizza, Steve. 1991. A Bulky and Foolish Treatise? Hugh Blair's Critical Disser-tation Reconsidered. In *Ossian Revisited.* Howard Gaskill, ed., pp. 129–46. Edinburgh: Edinburgh University Press.

Roberts, Dorothy. 1997. *Killing the Black Body: Race, Reproduction, and the Mean-ing of Liberty.* New York: Vintage.

Robbins, Bruce. 1998. Introduction Part I: Actually Existing Cosmopolitanism. In *Cosmopolitics: Thinking and Feeling Beyond the Nation.* Peng Cheah and Bruce Robbins, eds., pp. 1–19. Minneapolis: University of Minnesota Press.

Robins, R. H. 1990. *A Short History of Linguistics.* 3rd ed. London: Longman.

Rohner, Ronald. 1966 Franz Boas: Ethnographer on the Northwest Coast. In *Pioneers of American Anthropology: The Uses of Biography.* June Helm, ed., pp. 149–212. Seattle: University of Washington Press.

ed. 1969. *The Ethnography of Franz Boas: Letters and Diaries of Franz Boas Written on the Northwest Coast from 1886 to 1931.* Chicago: University of Chicago Press.

Rölleke, Heinz, ed. 1975. *Die älteste Märchensammlung der Brüder Grimm: Synopse der handschriftlichen Urfassung von 1810 und der Erstdrucke von 1812.* Cologny: Fondation Martin Godmer.

1980. *Brüder Grimm. Kinder- und Hausmärchen.* 3 vols. Stuttgart: Reclam.

1985a. *Die Märchen der Brüden Grimm.* Munich: Artemis.

1985b. *"Wo das Wünschen noch geholfen hat": Gesammelte Aufsätze zu den 'Kinder- und Hausmärchen' de Brüder Grimm.* Bonn: Bouvier Verlag Herbert Grundmann.

1986a. *Jacob und Wilhelm Grimm: Vorträge und Ansprachen.* Göttingen: Vandenhoeck and Ruprecht.

1986b. The "Utterly Hessian" Fairy Tales by "Old Marie": The End of a Myth. In *Fairy Tales and Society: Illusion, Allusion, and Paradigm.* Ruth B. Bottigheimer, ed., pp. 287–300. Philadelphia: University of Pennsylvania Press.

1988a. New Results of Research on Grimms' Fairy Tales. In *The Brothers Grimm and the Folktale.* James M. McGlathery, ed. with Larry W. Danielson, Ruth E. Lorbe, and Selma K. Richardson, pp. 101–11. Urbana: University of Illinois Press.

1988b. *"Redensarten des Volks, auf die ich immer horche": Das Sprichwort in den Kinder- und Hausmärchen der Brüder Grimm.* Bern: Peter Lang.

Ross, Dorothy. 1991. *The Origins of American Social Science.* Cambridge: Cambridge University Press.

Rossi, Paolo. 1968. *Francis Bacon: From Magic to Science.* Chicago: University of Chicago Press.

Roston, Murray. 1965. *Poet and Prophet: The Bible and the Growth of Romanticism.* London: Faber and Faber.

Rubel, Margaret Mary. 1978. *Savage to Barbarian: Historical Attitudes in the Criticism of Homer and Ossian in Britain, 1760–1800.* Amsterdam: North Holland Publishing Co.

Sahlins, Marshall. 1999. Two or Three Things that I Know about Culture. *Journal of the Royal Anthropological Institute* 5: 399–421.

Said, Edward. 1978. *Orientalism.* New York: Pantheon.

Sampson, Geoffrey. 1980. *Schools of Linguistics.* Stanford, CA: Stanford University Press.

Sapir, Edward. 1908. Herder's "Ursprung der Sprache." *Modern Philology* 5: 109–42.

    1921. *Language.* New York: Harcourt, Brace & World.

    1922. The Takelma Language of Southwestern Oregon. In *Handbook of American Indian Languages,* Part 2. Franz Boas, ed., pp. 1–296. Bureau of American Ethnology, Smithsonian Institution, Bulletin 40. Washington: Government Printing Office.

    1949 [1929]. Male and Female Forms in Yana. In *Selected Writings of Edward Sapir in Language, Culture and Personality.* David G. Mandelbaum, ed., pp. 206–12. Berkeley: University of California Press.

Saussure, Ferdinand de. 1959 [1916]. *A Course in General Linguistics.* Wade Baskin, trans. New York: McGraw-Hill Book Company.

Schieffelin, Bambi B, Kathryn Woolard, and Paul V. Kroskrity, eds. 1998. *Language Ideologies: Practice and Theory.* Oxford: Oxford University Press.

Schiffman, Zachary S. 1992. *On the Threshold of Modernity: Relativism in the French Renaissance.* Baltimore: Johns Hopkins University Press.

Schmidt, Kurt. 1973 [1932]. *Die Entwicklung der Kinder- und Hausmärchen der Brüder Grimm seit der Urhandschrift.* Halle: Max Niemeyer. Reprinted, Walluf bei Wiesbaden: Martin Sändig.

Schmitz, Robert M. 1948. *Hugh Blair.* New York: King's Crown Press.

Schoof, Wilhelm. 1959. *Zur Entstehungsgeschichte der Grimmschen Märchen.* Hamburg: Ernst Hauswedell.

Schoolcraft, Henry Rowe. 1848. *The Indian in His Wigwam, or Characteristics of the Red Race of America.* New York: W. H. Graham.

    1851a. *Personal Memoirs of a Residence of Thirty Years with the Indian Tribes on the American Frontier.* Philadelphia: Lippincott, Grambo & Co.

    1851b. *The American Indians, Their History, Condition and Prospects.* Rochester: Wanzer, Foot & Co.

    1851–57. *Historical and Statistical Information, Respecting the History, Condition and Prospects of the Indian Tribes of the United States.* 6 vols. Philadelphia: Lippincott, Grambo.

    1853. *Information Respecting the History, Condition and Prospects of the Indian Tribes of the United States. Part I.* Philadelphia: Libbincott, Grambo & Co.

1856. *The Myth of Hiawatha and Other Oral Legends, Mythologic and Allegoric, of the North American Indians.* Philadelphia: J. B. Lippincott & Co.

1886 [1846]. *Plan for American Ethnological Investigation. Annual Report of the Board of Regents of the Smithsonian Institution. Part I.* Washington, DC: Government Printing Office.

1962. *The Literary Voyager or Muzzeniegun.* Philip P. Mason, ed. East Lansing: Michigan State University Press.

1975 [1825]. *Travels in the Central Portions of the Mississippi Valley.* New York: Collins and Hannay. Repr. ed. Millwood: Kraus Reprint Co.

1991. *Schoolcraft's Indian Legends.* Mentor L. Williams, ed. East Lansing: Michigan State University Press.

1992 [1839]. *Algic Researches, First Series: Tales and Legends.* 2 vols. New York: Harper & Bros. Repr. ed. in one vol., Baltimore: Clearfield Co.

Schütze, Martin. 1921. The Fundamental Ideas in Herder's Thought III. *Modern Philology* 19: 113–30.

Segal, Daniel, and Richard Handler. 1995. US Multiculturalism and the Concept of Culture. *Identities* 1 (4): 391–407.

Shapin, Steven. 1994. *A Social History of Truth: Civility and Science in Seventeenth-century England.* Chicago: University of Chicago Press.

Shapin, Steven, and Simon Schaffer. 1985. *Leviathan and the Air-pump: Hobbes, Boyle, and the Experimental Life.* Princeton, NJ: Princeton University Press.

Sher, Richard B. 1982. "Those Scotch Imposters and their Cabal": Ossian and the Scottish Enlightenment. In *Man and Nature/L'Homme et la Nature.* Roger L. Emerson, Gilles Girard, and Roseann Runte, eds., pp. 55–63. *Proceedings of the Canadian Society for Eighteenth-Century Studies*, Vol. I. London, Ont.: Faculty of Education of the University of Western Ontario for the Society.

1985. *Church and University in the Scottish Enlightenment: The Moderate Literati of Edinburgh.* Edinburgh: Edinburgh University Press.

Silverstein, Michael. 1976. Shifters, Linguistic Categories, and Cultural Description. In *Meaning in Anthropology.* Keith Basso and Henry Selby, eds., pp. 11–55. Albuquerque: University of New Mexico Press.

1979. Language Structure and Linguistic Ideology. In *The Elements: A Parasession on Linguistc Units and Levels.* Paul R. Clyne, William Hanks, and Carol L. Hofbauer eds., pp. 193–247. Chicago: Chicago Linguistic Society.

1981. *The Limits of Awareness.* Sociolinguistic Working Paper 84. Austin: Southwest Educational Development Laboratory.

1985. Language and the Culture of Gender: At the Intersection of Structure, Usage and Ideology. In *Semiotic Mediation: Sociocultural and Psychological Perspectives.* Elizabeth Mertz and Richard Parmentier, eds., pp. 219–59. Orlando: Academic Press.

1993. Metapragmatic Discourse and Metapragmatic Function. In *Reflexive Language: Reported Speech and Metapragmatics.* John A. Lucy, ed., pp. 33–58. Cambridge: Cambridge University Press.

1996. Monoglot "Standard" in America: Standardization and Metaphors of Linguistic Hegemony. In *The Matrix of Language.* Donald Brenneis and Ronald H. S. Macauley, eds., pp. 284–306. Boulder: Westview.

Silverstein, Michael and Greg Urban, eds. 1996. *Natural Histories of Discourse.* Chicago: University of Chicago Press.

Simrock, Karl. 1988 [1846]. *Deutschen Sprichwörter.* Grankfurt am Main: Brönner. Reprinted, with an introduction by Wolfgang Mieder, Stuttgart: Reclam.

Smith, Olivia. 1984. *The Politics of Language, 1791–1819.* Oxford: Clarendon Press.

Smith, W. L. G. 1856. *The Life and Times of Lewis Cass.* New York: Derby and Jackson.

Spivak, Gayatri Chakravorty. 1988. Can the Subaltern Speak? In *Marxism and the Interpretation of Culture.* Cary Nelson and Lawrence Grossberg, eds., pp. 271–313. Urbana: University of Illinois Press.

Sprat, Thomas. 1958 [1667]. *History of the Royal Society.* Jackson I. Cope and Harold Whitmore Jones, eds. St. Louis: Washington University Studies.

Stafford, Fiona. 1988. *The Sublime Savage: A Study of James Macpherson and the Poems of Ossian.* Edinburgh: Edinburgh University Press.

    1996a. Introduction: The Ossianic Poems of James Macpherson. In *The Poems of Ossian and Related Works.* Howard Gaskill, ed., pp. v–xxi. Edinburgh: Edinburgh University Press.

    1996b. Primitivism and the "Primitive" Poets: A Cultural Context for Macpherson's Ossian. In *Celticism.* Terence Brown, ed., pp. 79–96. Amsterdam: Rodopi.

Sternberg, Meier. 1985. *The Poetics of Biblical Narrative: Ideological Literature and the Drama of Reading.* Bloomington: Indiana University Press.

Stewart, Susan. 1991. *Crimes of Writing: Problems in the Containment of Representation.* New York: Oxford University Press.

Stillman, Robert E. 1995. *The New Philosophy and Universal Languages in Seventeenth-Century England: Bacon, Hobbes, and Wilkins.* Lewisburg: Bucknell University Press.

Stocking, George W., Jr. 1968. *Race, Culture, and Evolution: Essays in the History of Anthropology.* New York: Free Press.

    1974a. The Boas Plan for the Study of American Indian Languages. In *Studies in the History of Linguistics: Traditions and Paradigms.* Dell H. Hymes, ed., pp. 454–84. Bloomington: Indiana University Press.

    ed. 1974b. *The Shaping of American Anthropology, 1883–1911: A Franz Boas Reader.* New York: Basic Books.

    1992. *The Ethnographer's Magic and Other Essays in the History of Anthropology.* Madison: University of Wisconsin Press.

Stross, Brian. 1999. The Hybrid Metaphor: From Biology to Culture. *Journal of American Folklore* 112 (445): 254–67.

Sutton, Charles W. 1963 [1917]. Henry Bourne. In *Dictionary of National Biography.* Leslie Stephen and Sidney Lee, eds., Vol. II, p. 937. Oxford: Oxford University Press.

Tatar, Maria. 1987. *The Hard Facts of the Grimms' Fairy Tales.* Princeton, NJ: Princeton University Press.

Taussig, Michael. 1987. *Shamanism, Colonialism and the Wild Man: A Study in Terror and Healing.* Chicago: University of Chicago Press.

1993. *Mimesis and Alterity: A Particular History of the Senses.* New York: Routledge.

Taylor, Talbot J. 1990a. Liberalism in Lockean Linguistics. In *North American Contributions to the History of Linguistics.* Francis P. Dinneen and E. F. Konrad Koerner, eds., pp. 99–109. Amsterdam: John Benjamins.

1990b. Which is to be Master? The Institutionalization of Authority in the Science of Language. In *Ideologies of Language.* John E. Joseph and Talbot J. Taylor, eds., pp. 9–26. London: Routledge.

Thomson, Derick S. 1952. *The Gaelic Sources of Macpherson's "Ossian."* Aberdeen University Studies 130. Edinburgh: Oliver and Boyd.

1987. Macpherson's Ossian: Ballads to Epics. In *The Heroic Process: Form, Function, and Fantasy in Folk Epic.* Bo Almqvist, Seamas O'Cathain, and Padraig O'Healai, eds., pp. 243–64. Dublin: Glendale Press.

1998. James Macpherson: The Gaelic Dimension. In *From Gaelic to Romantic: Ossianic Translations.* Fiona Stafford and Howard Gaskill, eds., pp. 17–26. Amsterdam: Rodopi.

Thompson, Stith. 1922. The Indian Legend of Hiawatha. *Publications of the Modern Language Association* 30: 128–40.

1929. *Tales of the North American Indians.* Cambridge, MA: Harvard University Press.

Todorov, Tzvetan. 1984 [1982]. *The Conquest of America: The Question of the Other.* Richard Howard, trans. New York: Harper and Row.

Trevor-Roper, Hugh. 1983. The Invention of Tradition: The Highland Tradition of Scotland. In *The Invention of Tradition.* Eric Hobsbawm and Terence Ranger, eds., pp. 15–41. Cambridge: Cambridge University Press.

Trouillot, Michel-Rolph. 1991. Anthropology and the Savage Slot: The Poetics and Politics of Otherness. In *Recapturing Anthropology: Working in the Present.* Richard G. Fox, ed., pp. 17–44. Santa Fe, NM: School of American Research.

Tylden-Wright, David. 1991. *John Aubrey: A Life.* New York: Harper Collins.

United Nations Educational, Scientific and Cultural Organization. 1989. *Recommendations on the Safeguarding of Traditional Culture and Folklore.* Paris: UNESCO.

Urciuoli, Bonnie. 1996. *Exposing Prejudice: Puerto Rican Experiences of Language, Race, and Class.* Boulder, CO: Westview Press.

Urla, Jacqueline. 1993. Contesting Modernities: Language Standardization and the Production of an Ancient Modern Basque Culture. *Critique of Anthropology* 13 (2): 101–18.

Valentine, Lisa. 1995. *Making It Their Own: Seven Ojibwe Communicative Practices.* Toronto: University of Toronto Press.

Van Dijk, Teun. 1993. *Elite Discourse and Racism.* Newbury Park, CA: Sage.

van Dülmen, Richard. 1992. *The Society of the Enlightenment: The Rise of the Middle Class and Enlightenment Culture in Germany.* New York: St. Martin's Press.

Vološinov, V. N. 1973 [1930]. *Marxism and the Philosophy of Language.* Ladislav Metejka and I. R. Titunik, trans. New York: Seminar Press.

Volpp, Leti. 2000. Blaming Culture for Bad Behavior. *Yale Journal of Law and the Humanities* 12: 89–116.

Ward, Donald. 1981. Epilogue. In *The German Legends of the Brothers Grimm.* Vol. II. Donald Ward, ed., pp. 341–84. Philadelphia: Institute for the Study of Human Issues.

    1988. New Misconceptions about Old Folktales: The Brothers Grimm. In *The Brothers Grimm and the Folktale.* James M. McGlathery, ed. with Larry W. Danielson, Ruth E. Lorbe, and Selma K. Richardson, pp. 91–100. Urbana: University of Illinois Press.

Watson, Wilfred G. E. 1984. Classical Hebrew Poetry: A Guide to its Techniques. *Journal for the Study of the Old Testament Supplement Series* 26. Sheffield: JSOT Press.

Weber, Max. 1930. *The Protestant Ethic and the Spirit of Capitalism.* Talcott Parsons, trans. London: G. Allen and Unwin.

    1946. *From Max Weber: Essays in Sociology.* H. H. Gerth and C. Wright Mills, trans. and eds. New York: Oxford University Press.

Wellek, René. 1941. *The Rise of English Literary History.* Chapel Hill: University of North Carolina Press.

Westby-Gibson, John. 1963 [1917]. Thomas Blackwell. In *Dictionary of National Biography.* Leslie Stephen and Sidney Lee, eds. Vol. II, pp. 609–11. Oxford: Oxford University Press.

White, Hayden. 1978. *Tropics of Discourse: Essays in Cultural Criticism.* Baltimore: Johns Hopkins University Press.

Whitney, Charles. 1986. *Francis Bacon and Modernity.* New Haven, CT: Yale University Press.

Whitney, Lois. 1924. English Primitivist Theories of Epic Origins. *Modern Philology* 21: 337–78.

    1926. Thomas Blackwell: A Disciple of Shaftesbury. *Philological Quarterly* 5: 196–211.

Wiley, Raymond A., ed. and trans. 1971. *John Mitchell Kemble and Jakob Grimm: A Correspondence 1832–1852.* Leiden: E. J. Brill.

    1990. Grimm's Grammar Gains Ground in England, 1832–52. In *The Grimm Brothers and the Germanic Past.* Elmer H. Antonsen, ed., pp. 33–42. Amsterdam: John Benjamins.

Wilkins, John. 1668. *An Essay Towards a Real Character and a Philosophical Language.* London: S. Gellibrand.

Williams, Raymond. 1983. *Keywords.* Rev. ed. New York: Oxford University Press.

Wilson, William A. 1973. Herder, Folklore and Romantic Nationalism. *Journal of Popular Culture* 6: 819–35.

    1976. *Folklore and Nationalism in Modern Finland.* Bloomington: Indiana University Press.

Wodak, R, and M. Reisgl. 1999. Discourse and Racism: European Perspectives. *Annual Review of Anthropology* 28: 175–99.

Wood, Robert. 1971 [1753]. *The Ruins of Palmyra, Otherwise Tedmor, in the Desart.* Farnsborough: Gregg International Publishers.

    1971 [1757]. *The Ruins of Balbec.* Farnsborough: Gregg International Publishers.

    1971 [1775]. *An Essay on the Original Genius and Writings of Homer: With a Comparative View of the Ancient and Present State of the Troade.* New York: Garland.

Woodbury, Anthony C. 1987. Rhetorical Structure in a Central Alaskan Yupik Eskimo Traditional Narrative. In *Native American Discourse: Poetics and Rhetoric*. Joel Sherzer and Anthony C. Woodbury, eds., pp. 176–239. Cambridge: Cambridge University Press.

Woodford, Frank B. 1950. *Lewis Cass: The Last Jeffersonian*. New Brunswick: Rutgers University Press.

Woodmansee, Martha. 1984. The Genius and the Copyright: Economic and Legal Conditions of the Emergence of the "Author." *Eighteenth-Century Studies* 17 (4): 425–48.

Woodmansee, Martha, and Peter Jaszi, eds. 1994. *The Construction of Authorship: Textual Appropriation in Law and Literature*. Durham: Duke University Press.

Woolard, Kathryn A. 1989. Sentences in the Language Prison: The Rhetorical Structuring of an American Language Policy Debate. *American Ethnologist* 16 (2): 268–78.

———. 1998. Introduction: Language Ideology as a Field of Inquiry. In *Language Ideologies: Practice and Theory*. Bambi B. Schieffelin, Kathryn A. Woolard, and Paul V. Kroskrity, eds., pp. 3–47. Oxford: Oxford University Press.

Woolard, Kathryn A. and Bambi B. Schieffelin. 1994. Language Ideology. *Annual Review of Anthropology* 23: 55–82.

Woolhouse, Roger. 1997. Introduction. In *An Essay Concerning Human Understanding*. John Locke, pp. ix–xxiv. New York: Penguin Books.

World Intellectual Property Organization. 1985. *Model Provisions for National Laws on the Protection of Expressions of Folklore Against Illicit Exploitation and Other Prejudicial Actions*. Paris and Geneva: UNESCO and WIPO.

Yolton, John W. 1970. *Locke and the Compass of Human Understanding: A Selective Commentary on the "Essay."* Cambridge: Cambridge University Press.

———. 1993. *A Locke Dictionary*. Oxford: Blackwell.

Zammito, John H. 2002. *Kant, Herder, and the Birth of Anthropology*. Chicago: University of Chicago Press.

Zentella, Ana Celia. 1997. *Growing up Bilingual: Puerto Rican Children in New York*. Malden, MA: Blackwell.

Zipes, Jack. 1979. *Breaking the Magic Spell: Radical Theories of Folk and Fairy Tales*. London: Heinemann.

———. 1983. *Fairy Tales and the Art of Subversion: The Classic Genre for Children and the Process of Civilization*. New York: Wildman Press.

———. 1988a. *The Brothers Grimm: From Enchanted Forests to the Modern World*. New York: Routledge.

———. 1988b. Dreams of a Better Bourgeois Life: The Psychological Origins of the Grimms' Tales. In *The Brothers Grimm and the Folktale*. James McGlathery, ed., pp. 205–19. Urbana: University of Illinois Press.

Zolla, Elémire. 1973. *Writer and the Shaman: A Morphology of the American Indian*. Raymond Rosenthal, trans. New York: Harcourt Brace Jovanovich.

Zumwalt, Rosemary. 1978. Henry Rowe Schoolcraft, 1793–1864. *The Kroeber Anthropological Society Papers* 53/54 (Spring/Fall 1976): 44–57.

Index

folklore
  Boas, 270, 284–5
  protection, 307–8
  Schoolcraft, 226
Foucault, Michel, 8–9, 10–18, 32, 310,
  312, 315, 318
Frederick the Great, 187–8
Fugate, Joe, 173

Gaier, Ulrich, 183
Galileo, 62
Galland, Antoine, 93–4, 124
Gallatin, Albert, 247
Geertz, Clifford, 294
Germany, 164–5, 187–8
  Aufklärung, 188
Giddens, Anthony, 306–7
Goffman, Erving, 47
Goldberg, David, 67
Goldman, Irving, 274
Goody, Jack, 107
Gottsched, Johann Christoph, 165,
  189
grammars, 64, 199, 203, 222
  Eskimos, 263
  Takelma, 258
Greek, 52
Greek mythology, 90, 104–5
Greenblatt, Stephen J., 314
Grimm, Brothers, 301
  collecting activities, 206–8, 213
  generally, 197–8
  metadiscursive practices, 206–14
  authority, 214–16
  nationalism and cosmopolitanism,
    217–25
  poetry, 203
  romanticism, 198–203
  science and society, 203–6
  scientism, 198–203
  Sleeping Beauty, 211–12
  textual authenticity, 206–14
  tradition, 205–6, 217
Grimm, Dortchen, 210
Grimm, Jakob, 190, 215–16
  collecting texts, 207
  development continuum, 200–2
  middle language, 201–2, 204
  modern language, 202
  oldest language, 201
  On the Origin of Language, 198–203
  traditional forms, 218–19
Grimm, Wilhelm, 210, 215, 219, 221
Groom, Nick, 143
Gruner, Rolf, 62

Crawford, James, 302
Cultee, Charles, 280
Cuomo, Mario, 303

Daiches, David, 157
decontextualization, 312
deference, 47–8
Dégh, Linda, 212
Delpit, Lisa, 303
Derrida, Jacques, 24, 271, 309, 312,
  313
Dick, Oliver Lawson, 79
dictionaries, 64, 203, 222
Dippie, Brian, 245
Dorson, Richard, 72, 73, 84
Dundes, Alan, 212
Duponceau, Peter S., 247
Durkheim, Emile, 136

ebonics, 303–5
economics, Locke, 61–2
Edinburgh, 131
education, 43, 60, 79
Ellis, John, 210, 212, 214–15
English
  official US language, 301–3
  purification, 305
Enlightenment, 4, 109, 315
  Herder, 186–7
  Scotland, 131, 157, 158–9
epic
  Grimm Brothers, 205
  Homer. See Homer
  Ossian. See Ossian
  Serbo-Croatian, 161
Epstein, Steven, 296
equality. See social inequality
Ergang, Robert, 169–70, 258
ethnology, 253
Evans, Joan, 72
evolutionism, 256, 259, 262
exclusion. See otherness
experiments, 19–20, 22

Fabian, Johannes, 294, 307
Fairclough, Norman, 311
Farley, Frank, 141
Farmer, Paul, 296
Ferguson, Adam, 131, 154
Filmer, Robert, 53–4, 55, 312
Finland, 161
Fischer, Michael, 294
Fitzgerald, Robert, 129
Fliegelman, Jay, 103
folk tales. See Grimm, Brothers

Studies in the Social and Cultural Foundations of Language

The aim of this series is to develop theoretical perspectives on the social and cultural character of language by methodical and empirical emphasis on the occurrence of language in its communicative and interactional settings, on the socioculturally grounded "meanings" and "functions" of linguistic forms, and on the social scientific study of language use across cultures. It will thus explore the essentially ethnographic nature of linguistic date and language practices, whether synchronic or diachronic, whether normative or variational, whether spontaneously occurring or induced by an investigator. Works appearing in the series will make substantive and theoretical contributions to debates over the nature of language's embeddedness in social and cultural life, and over the role of language in sociocultural systems. The series will represent the concerns of scholars in the anthropology and sociology of language, sociolinguistics, and socioculturally informed psycholinguistics.

Editors
Judith T. Irvine
Bambi Schieffelin

Editorial Advisers
Marjorie Goodwin
Joel Kuipers
Don Kulick
John Lucy
Elinor Ochs
ˌ Michael Silverstein

Studies in the Social and Cultural Foundations of Language

Editors
JUDITH T. IRVINE
BAMBI SCHIEFFELIN

Printed in Great Britain
by Amazon

30854085R00214